Nation-States and the
Global Environment

Nation-States and the Global Environment

New Approaches to International Environmental History

EDITED BY

ERIKA MARIE BSUMEK, DAVID KINKELA, AND
MARK ATWOOD LAWRENCE

OXFORD
UNIVERSITY PRESS

OXFORD
UNIVERSITY PRESS

Oxford University Press is a department of the University of Oxford.
It furthers the University's objective of excellence in research, scholarship,
and education by publishing worldwide.

Oxford   New York
Auckland   Cape Town   Dar es Salaam   Hong Kong   Karachi
Kuala Lumpur   Madrid   Melbourne   Mexico City   Nairobi
New Delhi   Shanghai   Taipei   Toronto

With offices in
Argentina   Austria   Brazil   Chile   Czech Republic   France   Greece
Guatemala   Hungary   Italy   Japan   Poland   Portuga   Singapore
South Korea   Switzerland   Thailand   Turkey   Ukrainle   Vietnam

Oxford is a registered trademark of Oxford University Press
in the UK and certain other countries.

Published in the United States of America by
Oxford University Press
198 Madison Avenue, New York, NY 10016

Library of Congress Cataloging–in–Publication Data
Nation-states and the global environment: new approaches
to international environmental history / edited by
Erika Marie Bsumek, David Kinkela, and Mark Atwood Lawrence.
    pages; cm
ISBN 978-0-19-975535-6 (alk. paper) — ISBN 978-0-19-975536-3 (alk. paper)
1. Environmental policy—International cooperation.   2. Conservation
of natural resources—International cooperation.   I. Bsumek, Erika Marie.
GE170.N34 2013
333.7—dc23   2012038212

9 8 7 6 5 4 3 2 1
Printed in the United States of America
on acid-free paper

Contents

Contributors

Greg Bankoff is a professor of modern history at the University of Hull. He writes on environmental-social interactions with respect to natural hazards, resources, human-animal relations, and issues of social equity and labor. His most recent publication (coedited with Uwe Luebken and Jordan Sand) is *Flammable Cities: Urban Fire and the Making of the Modern World* (2012), and he is currently completing projects on flooding and forestry.

Emily Brownell is an assistant professor of African history at the University of Northern Colorado. Her work focuses on transnational environmental history and on urban environmental history in East Africa. She is currently working on a monograph tentatively titled "Going to the Ground: An Environmental History of Urban Crisis in Dar es Salaam, Tanzania."

Erika Marie Bsumek is an associate professor of history at the University of Texas at Austin. She is the author of *Indian-Made: Navajo Culture in the Marketplace, 1868–1940* (2008) and numerous articles and chapters on the history of Native Americans and the American West. She is currently working on an environmental history of the American West.

Mark Cioc is a professor of history at the University of California, Santa Cruz. His most recent books include *The Rhine: An Eco-Biography, 1815–2000* (2002) and *The Game of Conservation: International Treaties to Protect the World's Migratory Species* (2009). He served as editor of *Environmental History* from 2006 to 2010.

Benedict J. Colombi is an assistant professor in the American Indian Studies program, the School of Anthropology, and the School of Natural Resources and Environment at the University of Arizona. He is author of *Keystone Nations: Indigenous Peoples and Salmon across the Northern Pacific* (2012) as well as a number of articles and chapters on the anthropology of indigenous peoples, natural resource management, globalization and sustainability problems, and options for the future.

Gregory T. Cushman is an associate professor of international environmental history at the University of Kansas. He has published widely on environmental history in Latin America, the Caribbean, and the Pacific Basin and is author of *Guano & the Opening of the Pacific World: A Global Ecological History* (2012).

Janet M. Davis is an associate professor of American studies, history, and women's and gender studies at the University of Texas at Austin. She is author of *The Circus Age: Culture and Society under the American Big Top* (2002); editor of *Circus Queen and Tinker Bell: The Life of Tiny Kline* (2008), by Tiny Kline; and author of *The Gospel of Kindness: Animal Welfare and the Making of Modern America*, which will be published by Oxford University Press.

Kurk Dorsey is an associate professor of history at the University of New Hampshire. He is the author of *The Dawn of Conservation Diplomacy: U.S.-Canadian Wildlife Protection Treaties in the Progressive Era* (1998) and a forthcoming book on whaling in the twentieth century.

Carmel Finley is a lecturer in the Department of History at Oregon State University. She is the author of *All the Fish in the Sea: Maximum Sustained Yield and the Failure of Fisheries Management* (2011).

Seth Garfield is an associate professor at the University of Texas at Austin. He is the author of *Indigenous Struggle at the Heart of Brazil: State Policy, Frontier Expansion, and the Xavante Indians, 1937–1988* (2001). His current research examines the history of the Brazilian Amazon during World War II.

David Kinkela is an associate professor of history at the State University of New York Fredonia. He is author of *DDT and the American Century: Global Health, Environmental Politics, and the Pesticides That Changed the World* (2011).

Mark Atwood Lawrence is an associate professor of history at the University of Texas at Austin. He is the author of *Assuming the Burden: Europe and the American Commitment to War in Vietnam* (2005) and *The Vietnam War: A Concise International History* (2008) as well as numerous articles and chapters on the history of the Cold War.

J. R. McNeill is a professor of history and University Professor at Georgetown University. He is author of *Mosquito Empires: Ecology and War in the Greater Caribbean* (2010) and president of the American Society for Environmental History.

James E. McWilliams is a professor of history at Texas State University-San Marcos. He is the author of several books and articles about food and agriculture, including *American Pests: The Losing War on Insects from Colonial Times to DDT*.

David Zierler is a historian in the Office of the Historian at the Department of State, where he focuses on the Soviet intervention in Afghanistan. He is the author of *The Invention of Ecocide: Agent Orange, Vietnam, and the Scientists Who Changed the Way We Think about the Environment* (2011).

Preface

This book rests on two convictions—that global environmental problems deserve urgent attention and that historians can play a productive role in thinking about effective responses. In fundamental ways, after all, present-day problems are nothing new. For centuries, national governments as well as local authorities, international bodies, activist groups, and indigenous communities have sought to regulate features of the natural environment that refuse to recognize political boundaries. Through the case studies presented in this book, we hope to show that historians, too often wary of "presentism" and cautious about drawing out the implications of their work, have something of great importance to add to contemporary debates.

In pursuing this agenda, we have benefited enormously from the enthusiastic support of the Institute for Historical Studies at the University of Texas at Austin, which, since its founding in 2008, has grown into a leading center for innovative scholarship. Perhaps most important to the present volume, the Institute has placed a high value on discussions and research with the potential to cross the boundaries separating the academy from a wider readership. This book grew out of one of the Institute's first public events, a major conference entitled "The Nation-State and the Transnational Environment," which took place in Austin in April 2009.

Our thanks go first and foremost to Institute director Julie Hardwick, who deserves credit not just for our project but for making the entire IHS initiative a great success. We also owe heartfelt thanks to Courtney Meador, who performed organizational miracles before and during the conference and has helped in innumerable ways ever since. Erika and Mark benefited greatly from stints as internal IHS fellows in recent years, while Dave was part of the inaugural class of external fellows in 2008–2009.

Thanks go, too, to several scholars and friends whose participation in the 2009 conference helped make this a better book: Neel Baumgardner, Brett Bennett, Tzeporah Berman, Kathleen Brosnan, Joshua Busby, Frank de la Teja, William E. Doolittle, Jonathan Hunt, Kairn Klieman, John McKiernan-Gonzales, Martin V. Melosi, Judith Shapiro, and especially J. Robert Cox for providing a remarkable set of comments on all of the papers at the final session.

In the Department of History at UT-Austin, the indefatigable chair, Alan Tully, merits a special word of thanks for his leading role in creating the IHS and his enthusiasm for this book. Our gratitude goes as well to Laura Flack, who offered her usual blend of expertise and patience. Thanks, too, to the entire UT-Austin history faculty.

Since preliminary discussions of the project in 2008, Susan Ferber at Oxford University Press has been steadfast in her commitment to this book. She provided a critical reading of the manuscript in its early form, and she has been a tremendous source of support throughout the publication process. We cannot thank her enough. We would also like to thank the anonymous readers for their insightful comments and criticism. For their invaluable help in the closing stages of the project, we are grateful to Jeff Iorio and Eileen Austen.

Erika Bsumek thanks her colleagues at the University of Texas and elsewhere who spent time discussing this project over the years. David Kinkela would like to thank his colleagues at the State University of New York Fredonia for all their support. Mark Lawrence is grateful to International Security Studies at Yale University and the Political Science Department and Leadership Studies Program at Williams College, all of which generously supported him at various times during his work on this book.

Nation-States and the Global Environment

Introduction

Mark Atwood Lawrence, David Kinkela,
and Erika Marie Bsumek

The coincidence was striking when negotiators from around the world gathered at Cancún, Mexico, in late 2010 to make progress on an agreement to curb emissions of greenhouse gases. The last time the globe had experienced significant warming—about 120,000 years ago—the Cancún coastline had been deluged by a seven-foot rise in ocean levels over several decades.[1] Would governments, after years of inaction, embrace a binding deal to head off rising sea levels, extreme weather, disruptions of food production, and other potentially cataclysmic results of a warmer atmosphere? Predictably, the answer was no. Despite abundant evidence of impending disaster for many low-lying parts of the world, the representatives from 194 nations agreed to only minor, face-saving new provisions to encourage cooperation. The reasons for this disappointing result were the same ones that have bedeviled climate-change negotiations since they began under United Nations auspices in 1990: differences over strategies for combating emissions, disagreements over how large reductions should be, and, above all, divisions among the nations of the developed world, which have reaped the benefits of fossil-fuel-based industrialization for many years, and less-developed nations, which view restrictions as an unfair limitation on their economic growth.

Such disputes are merely outward manifestations of a more fundamental problem at the root of the climate-change talks. A meaningful solution to global warming, deforestation, species extinctions, and other major environmental problems will require global commitments to common policies. Yet nation-states, the basic building blocks of the international order, have great difficulty prioritizing the general good over their narrower interests. Global problems, in other words, require a kind of cooperation inconsistent with the jealously guarded sovereign prerogatives and economic concerns of individual nations. Activists and supranational institutions have clearly recognized the problem and consistently urged national governments to look beyond their own interests. "I have been urging them to speak and to act as global leaders; just go beyond their national boundaries," UN secretary general Ban Ki-moon asserted in 2009 before a major climate meeting in Copenhagen.[2] But such appeals have produced few results. As flows of pollution—not to mention people, money, goods, and information—have become increasingly global, national governments have failed to keep pace by establishing new cooperative regimes or ceding authority to supranational regulatory institutions. As journalist Fareed Zakaria succinctly summarized in 2008, "Formal political power remains firmly tethered to the nation-state, even as the nation-state has become less able to solve most…problems unilaterally."[3] The human future seems likely to depend on how the international community manages what has often been called the "global commons," but striking a new balance between global priorities and those of the nation-state will continue to be a key challenge for years to come.[4]

As this book demonstrates, the predicament is not nearly as new as some recent commentary on climate change and other global challenges suggests. In fact, understanding present-day dilemmas may be as much a matter for historians as for natural and social scientists, journalists, and futurologists. Nations have long confronted the need to manage features of the natural environment, whether disagreeable pollutants, fragile habitats, or desirable resources, which, acting with a kind of agency of their own, pay little or no heed to artificial geopolitical boundaries drawn and defended by humans. Nation-states have, for example, long sought agreements to manage migratory wildlife, just as they have negotiated conventions governing the release of toxic materials or the exploitation of rivers and other bodies of water. Similarly, nation-states have long attempted to exert influence over resources that lie beyond their borders, to impose their standards of proper environmental use on others, and to import expertise developed elsewhere to cope with domestic environmental problems. To be sure, the scale, urgency, and visibility of such endeavors have increased dramatically in recent times. But present-day efforts to find international solutions to transboundary environmental challenges unquestionably have historical precedents. As environmental historian William Cronon has eloquently observed, "Current environmental problems almost always have historical analogues from which we have much to learn if only we pay attention both to discontinuities *and* continuities that link past, present, and future."[5]

This collection aspires to draw attention to some of these analogues by exploring the complex interplay between nation-states and the global environment in the nineteenth and twentieth centuries. Uncovering these histories provides context, reference points, and perhaps even lessons that can inform ongoing debates about how to close the yawning gap between environmental problems and the political mechanisms that are available to address them. The authors of some chapters, especially in the first half of the book, are directly concerned with understanding the reasons for the successes and failures of past regulatory regimes. But the collection as a whole does not advance any single policy agenda or line of argument, and some chapters may even contradict each other in their implications. Indeed, the most important point to emerge may be the maddening complexity of the political, social, cultural, and technological issues at hand and the impossibility of simple solutions. Various chapters highlight an array of barriers to effective cooperation inherent in the nature of nation-states—their parochial range of vision, their tendencies to set short-term concerns above long-term interests, their desires for competitive advantage in a world mostly lacking in recognized legal norms, and their responsiveness to domestic rather than global constituencies.

The chapters also show, however, that nation-states are neither self-contained nor equal units when it comes to dealing with the global environment. Even as governments have tried to pursue national priorities, they have been challenged by activists, scientists, and other nonstate groups seeking in different ways to subvert, coopt, or constrain the ability of nation-states to make decisions about the environment. Such groups, explored in the second half of this collection, have long shaped—just as they do in the present era of globalization—the ability of nation-states to erect and defend meaningful boundaries and insist on strictly national priorities. This book, then, depicts nation-states as doubly challenged in their attempts to regulate natural processes and enforce those regulations. In some of the historical case studies offered in this volume, authors demonstrate different ways in which nation-states have channeled and represented their interests, even as they processed and "domesticated" pressures, sometimes from subnational groups but increasingly from transnational networks, to alter their environmental practices.

In pursuing this agenda, we aim to contribute to the fields of international history and environmental history, but we especially aim to push ahead the important work of combining these two fields. International/diplomatic history and environmental history have been extraordinarily dynamic fields of historical scholarship in recent years. Yet the work of building bridges between them and developing what might be called "international/diplomatic environmental history" has only just begun. This is not to say that no outstanding work in this genre has yet appeared. On the contrary, as we show in this introduction, a number of scholars, including several contributors to this collection, have published pioneering studies since the 1990s. Our goal in this book is to reinforce the point that environmental and international historians can learn a great deal from each other and build on earlier accomplishments by offering new case studies that might offer models for further work. Collectively, the chapters consider not just how nation-states have sought to control and regulate nature but also how cultural, ideological, and economic forces have shaped and constrained the options available to nation-states as they have struggled to master an ever-changing global environment.

One might reasonably argue that the latter forces are so powerful that the nation-state is now obsolete as a unit of analysis. Within the academy, many scholars have certainly questioned the utility of studying the history of nations, arguing that a focus on the nation-state tends to naturalize "imagined communities" and obscure broader transnational or global processes.[6] Meanwhile, journalists and policy analysts have repeatedly observed the ways in which globalization has eroded the once unquestioned authority of nation-states in policy arenas ranging from economics to culture.[7] For some indigenous groups, moreover, the term is contested on philosophical and ideological grounds. A book focusing on the nation-state—even using the term in its title—may therefore seem out of touch with important intellectual trends. Still, the concept of the nation-state is undeniably central to the existing world order, and its decline can be easily exaggerated. Over the past two hundred years, national governments have played a pivotal role in regulating, damaging, and sometimes protecting the environment, and they retain much of their power in the twenty-first century. We take up the question posed by the environmental historian Joachim Radkau in 2008: "If one recognizes that environmental protection cannot do without the state, what lessons does history offer us in this regard?"[8] The challenge is to examine the role of the nation-state alongside both local and supranational entities that increasingly make their influence felt in environmental matters and always have, to one degree or another.

While this book aims to sweep across the spectrum from the local to the transnational and address a broad range of environmental issues, it is less ambitious with respect to chronology and geography. Chronologically, the chapters cover only the nineteenth and twentieth centuries. This approach admittedly excludes periods deserving just as much attention, but it carries the benefit of analytical cohesion that flows from a focus solely on the industrial and postindustrial eras. The recent time span also enables contributors to draw relatively tight links between historical studies and the present, contributing to the goal of drawing out implications for the twenty-first century. Geographically, the following chapters deal in depth with only a few countries and regions, and the United States receives especially heavy attention, to the exclusion of other areas that merit just as much scrutiny. The United States has had an unusually global reach, but this disproportionate attention mostly reflects the fact that international and environmental historians have concentrated so much of their work on the trans-Atlantic arena. This imbalance, however, is not intended to let the United States stand in for other countries or to exclude other perspectives.

I

The field of international environmental history grows from various strands of historical inquiry rooted in questions about diplomacy, state formation, environmental politics, human impacts on ecology, the shifting cultural meanings associated with nature, and the flow of people, plants, animals, and diseases across the world. Existing scholarship in all these areas is both expansive and rich with insight, but it has not often addressed the central questions of this volume. In this section, the introduction maps out influential strands of such work, examining the ways in which diplomats and diplomatic historians have written about environmental issues and how environmental historians have explored transnational themes. Consideration is also given to the problems and questions scholars have identified as they have moved the field forward. While limits on space prohibit us from offering a comprehensive survey of diverse subfields, we seek to introduce key themes that have drawn scholarly interest as they relate to this book.

Some of the concerns of this collection have been addressed in previous studies about the formation of global environmental agreements. In 1981, for instance, political scientist Robert Boardman charted new terrain by examining how state and non-governmental organizations forged a series of international accords to protect endangered species. A decade later, Richard Elliot Benedict, a US Foreign Service officer, described diplomatic efforts to regulate the use of chlorofluorocarbons, one of the leading causes of ozone depletion. Lawrence Susskind's 1994 *Environmental Diplomacy* offered one of the earliest critiques of global environmental governance, explaining why international environmental agreements often failed to produce desired results. Susskind proposed a multistep policy solution that he dubbed "sequenced negotiations" as a way to solve complex environmental problems and preserve the sovereignty of individual nations. In his 1998 book *Global Environmental Diplomacy*, Mostafa K. Tolba, the executive director of the United Nations Environment Programme from 1976 to 1992, provided a critical account of his leadership on a number of international agreements, including the Montreal Protocol, the Basel Convention on Hazardous Wastes, and the Biodiversity Convention.[9] Political scientists and environmental policy makers have continued to produce important books in this field of study that examine the failure or difficulties in forging international environmental agreement among nation-states and illustrate the influence of non-government organizations in environmental policy making at national and international levels.[10]

Recent years have also seen a steady flow of new publications by historians in the field of environmental diplomacy. Mark Lytle did as much as anyone to jump-start the trend with his seminal 1996 article "An Environmental Approach to American Diplomatic History."[11] The subfield continued to gather momentum two years later with publication of Kurkpatrick Dorsey's *The Dawn of Conservation Diplomacy*.[12] Robert Darst and Marc Cioc have made additional contributions with their studies on, respectively, transboundary air pollution and protection of migratory animals.[13] In 2008, editors of the journal *Diplomatic History* published a series of short articles examining the intersection of international history and environmental history.[14]

The recent volume edited by J. R. McNeill and Corinna Unger, *Environmental Histories of the Cold War* (2010), furthers this research agenda, adding new insight to our understanding of Cold War historiography and environmental diplomacy.[15] In that volume, for example, Kai Hünemörder argues that the concept of "environmental crisis" created a framework in which diplomats on both side of the Cold War divide could work together in a new spirit of détente in the 1970s. Many of the contributors to *Environmental Histories of the Cold War* are environmental historians working in the field of diplomatic history, rather than diplomatic historians exploring environmental issues. It remains to be seen whether diplomatic historians will pick up on these important environmental themes.

To be sure, several scholars have successfully examined the geopolitical dimensions of certain natural resources that have proved both valuable and scarce. Authors such as Daniel Yergen, Michael Stoff, David Painter, and Kevin Phillips, for instance, have explored the global struggle for oil.[16] Others have examined conflicts over water, timber, fish, and rubber.[17] These authors have done much to advance the field and have set the stage for explorations of how nations have coped more generally with transnational environmental challenges that stemmed from resource extraction, management, and transportation. Given both the contemporary and historical crises associated with such issues, we consider this area to be especially ripe for further scholarly assessment.[18] The history of disease has also opened fresh analytical terrain, particularly in connection with national-security concerns.[19]

For their part, environmental historians have been much more interested in transnational and/or international themes than diplomatic historians have been interested in the environment. This greater attention surely results from the obvious ways in which the histories of land use, domesticated and wild animals, water, and disease lend themselves to approaches that cut across borders. Indeed, the emergence of environmental history in the early 1970s was fueled by strong interest in big questions and broad themes. Alfred Crosby's pathbreaking 1972 book *The Columbian Exchange* offered an early model of transborder history that explored the ecological consequences of human and nonhuman migration. The book established environmental history as a field that is both interdisciplinary (drawing on ecology, evolutionary biology, and historical geography, among other approaches) and global in the sense that it was not bounded by any one nation or region. Moreover, Crosby forced historians to reckon with a series of questions that remain relevant today. How has human activity shaped the environment? What constitutes "natural" patterns of change? How have humans valued or decried such changes?

Crosby laid out a research agenda that other scholars have taken up. The eminent environmental historian Donald Worster has been most vocal in challenging environmental historians to embrace transnational themes, arguing that national borders impose artificial barriers that limit the scope of historical analysis. His 1982 essay "World without Borders" made this argument especially forcefully. Worster questioned the importance of the nation-state as the focus of historical inquiry, emphasizing the movement of human, plant, and animal life as well as the movement of ideas about the natural world around the globe.[20]

Clearly, environmental historians were at the forefront of the transnational turn, and they have continued to push spatial and temporal boundaries. J. Donald Hughes's *An Environmental History of the World: Humankind's Changing Role in the Community of Life* (2002), J. R. and William McNeill's *The Human Web* (2003), and I. G. Simmons's *Global Environmental History* (2008), for instance, not only capture the intertwined histories of humans and nature across time and space but also emphasize the destructive capacity of people and societies, focusing on agricultural production, resource depletion, and capital accumulation. Such an approach has been replicated by a number of innovative European, Asian, South American, and North American scholars who continue to work on a global, rather than strictly national, scale.[21]

David Christian's *Maps of Time* aspires to go even further than world history will take him. Christian's notion of "Big History" transforms the idea of time and the concept of nature by looking at the past from the Big Bang and the beginning of the universe to the present. For Christian, the planetary limits of Earth dissolve as part of an intergalactic explanation of our collective history. While the expansiveness of Big History requires a conscious effort to keep track of the fact that borders are historically significant, the temporal dimensions and interdisciplinary nature of its approach offer intriguing possibilities for rethinking environmental history on a national, global, and even universal scale.

Environmental historians working on such expansive scales owe an intellectual debt to the French historian Fernand Braudel, one of the last influential scholars of the *Annales* school. In 1949, Braudel published his magisterial two-volume *The Mediterranean and Mediterranean World*, which was translated into English in 1973. Braudel challenged prevailing notions of empire, economic exchange, and nature. But it was his analysis of geographical, social, and individual time that pointed in new interpretive directions. For Braudel, the natural world moved on a completely different time scale from that of the human world.

Influenced by Braudel, the American historian Immanuel Wallerstein developed a "world-system" approach aimed at explaining historical processes over the *"longue durée."* Both Braudel and Wallerstein offered novel approaches to complex social, political, economic, and, to a larger extent, environmental processes that expanded our understandings of space and time. Despite being somewhat out of favor in a current climate that values all things transnational, these earlier works provide a model for scholars who wish to trace how specific environmental factors shaped human economic, social, and political processes. Applying Braudel's and Wallerstein's ideas to later centuries illuminates the nation-state's role in accelerating both destructive and constructive human capacities, creating political and environmental problems (and potential solutions) particular to the modern period. A reassessment of the themes of space and time might prove imperative for understanding the state of the global environment in the twenty-first century.

Indeed, while Braudel and others encouraged historians to think beyond the nation-state, American environmental historians have persisted in using the concept of the nation-state to frame their work. The field of environmental history has unquestionably become more international, with dynamic and illuminating studies on the environmental histories of South America, Africa, Asia, and Europe. Yet American environmental historians have generally framed their scholarship within politically imposed, rather than naturally delineated, borders. In 2001, Richard Grove, a specialist in the British Empire and South Asian environmental history, criticized American environmental historians for their "very narrow interpretation of the antecedents and scope of the subject."[22] Similarly, in 2003 J. R. McNeill remarked that US environmental historians "are exceptional...in their reluctance to confront American engage-ment with the rest of the world, even close neighbors."[23] Despite this criticism, an emerging literature situating American environmental history within an international context has emerged over the past decade. Innovative works by Richard Tucker, John Soluri, and Thomas Andrews, among others, suggest that such a move is underway.[24]

Scholars working on European environmental history have often tran-scended national boundaries to examine the ecological history of the continent. Since the 1970s, political scientists and environmental historians have written extensively on the political and environmental challenges and opportunities European nations face individually and collectively.[25] Many of these studies were born out of not only scholarly interest but also the political reality of Europe's interconnected environmental problems. Beginning in 1973, for example, the European Commission adopted the first Environmental Action Programmes, which stipulated that "the protection of the environment belongs to the essential tasks of the Community." Subsequent agreements sought "to reduce energy or material inputs and to close cycles, so that waste streams could be minimised" and promote an "integrative approach to environmental problem solving."[26] In 2012, the Commission is in the process of finalizing the seventh such agree-ment. These international accords recognized the ecological connections between European nations and the limits on the ability of any nation to solve environmental problems alone. European environmental history has emerged largely along parallel tracks, one emphasizing the continent's ecology and inte-grative history and the other framed by the political borders of nation-state.[27]

European environmental historians have also added to our understand-ing of the ecological impacts of colonialism and empire. Focused on global trade, environmental change, and power, this rich literature illuminates often-overlooked aspects of European colonialism, namely, the environmen-tal consequences of sugar and cotton production, the spice trade, and timber harvesting.[28]

Scholars of Latin America, Asia, and Africa have expanded on this lit-erature by similarly looking at the long-term ecological consequences of colo-nialism. James McCann's *Maize and Grace* (2005), for instance, examined how American maize reshaped African agriculture and food culture. Warren Dean's *With Broadax and Firebrand* (1995) examined the human exploita-tion of the Brazilian forest over time, while stressing why certain groups of people harvested timber at particular moments in time. For Dean, European colonialism was only part of a larger story on the destruction of the Brazilian forest, a process that unfortunately continues to this day. Other scholars have demonstrated that the legacy of European colonialism and global trade is a deep and lasting scar on environments throughout the world even as indigenous and colonized peoples themselves altered the environment for their own reasons.[29]

Recent research has shown that environmental degradation in much of the Global South was not simply a result of European colonialism but was also rooted in local economic and political practices. At the height of British rule in India, for example, local elites, in an effort to exert political authority and exploit local resources, undertook projects that at times were much more ecologically damaging than projects designed by the colonial rulers.[30] Various indigenous, local, and colonized communities have thus taken part in environmental transformation. Scholars of Chinese environmental history have also shown that environmental change and exploitation resulted not from European colonialism, capitalism, or global trade but from political and economic forces within China.[31] Indeed, scholars working in Asian, European, Latin American, and African environmental history have developed a vast literature rooted in the study of the migrations of ideas, people, plants, animals, and germs that impact local environments and communities.

Collaborators in this book have worked to integrate the elements that either defy or directly challenge the importance of the nation-state: insects, birds, whales, fish, trees, trash, and tornados care little about national borders or states. The humans who realize this—whether government officials, citizens, scientists, or non-governmental actors—and have sought to control nature put themselves in an odd position, attempting to negotiate between sovereign nationals and naturally independent forms of life or natural forces.

Yet the speed and breath of environmental change over the past century has radically changed the way observers might think about nations and nature. McNeill's *Something New Under the Sun* suggests that political and economic competition between nation-states has altered the environment in ways unimaginable before the twentieth century. Somewhat differently, Joachim Radkau's *Nature and Power* proclaims that in our current manifestation of globalization we have seen the "deepest rupture in the history of the environment," a process that has been the "most profound...turning point in global environmental history." In a recent essay, entitled, "More 'Trans-,' Less 'National,'" Matthew Frye Jacobson remarked that of "the one hundred largest economic units in the world, only forty-nine are countries, while the other fifty-one are *corporations.*"[32] It is clear that globalization has dramatically altered the political calculus on a number of fronts, including environmental governance, but it remains unclear how corporations will respond to environmental concerns that transcend any one nation. If the past is any guide, the future certainly does not look bright.

II

To better connect the fields of diplomatic history and environmental history, this book has been organized into two sections that group chapters by theme rather than geography or chronology. Part I, "Nature, Nation-States, and the Regulatory Dilemma," examines how nations sought to establish environmental regulations to cope with problems that seemed to require international collaboration. While covering divergent topics, the chapters cohere around two fundamental questions. What kinds of obstacles have nations faced as they tried to set up effective regulatory regimes to serve global interests as well as the interests of particular nations? And under what conditions have such efforts either failed or succeeded? Unsurprisingly, the chapters offer markedly different answers to these questions. Mostly, they illustrate the complexity of the problems that have confronted governments and the activist groups that worked with or against them in attempting to establish meaningful international cooperation.

In the first chapter, Mark Cioc explores the history of the Rhine Commission, one of the oldest continuous interstate institutions in Europe. Over time, Cioc notes, Rhine commissioners transformed the river into a waterway, a process that tamed the wildness of the river. In reconfiguring a natural system into an efficient transportation network, Cioc argues, the Rhine Commission engineered the river in a manner that left little room for fish or trees. For Cioc, however, the story of the commission is not only a cautionary tale of the ecological consequences of large-scale development schemes but also an illustration of the failure of international governance. Cioc sees the Rhine Commission as an organization that shifted political control over the river from the local to the international, effectively bypassing the nation-state. This international consortium of state actors "thought globally," thus rendering moot all local concerns about industrial pollution, watershed management, and conservation. Given the size and scope of the current environmental crisis, Cioc warns, international organizations like the Rhine Commission may not be the best means to protect nature.

The second chapter, Kurk Dorsey's analysis of the International Whaling Commission (IWC), provides an illuminating case study of both the problems that have inhibited effective cooperation and at least one important condition that might be necessary to overcome those obstacles. After the Second World War, Dorsey explains, the international community agreed that global regulations were necessary to preserve the whaling industry over the long term. However, many nations, jealous of their sovereignty, showed little desire to implement effective measures once the IWC had been established. Only in the 1970s, Dorsey demonstrates, did the situation change as the result of successful efforts by environmentalists to redefine whales as fascinating, sentient beings and thereby to recast whaling as a moral issue that resonated with the public. The result was dramatic: a worldwide ban on commercial whaling that remains in force in the twenty-first century. Still, Dorsey strikes an ambivalent note. If effective international regulation depended ultimately on the unusual "charisma" of whales, what are the chances of reaching agreements to protect unglamorous species or rallying public support for solutions to highly technical problems such as climate change?

Carmel Finley provides abundant evidence in the next chapter that Dorsey's concerns are well founded. Finley poses the question of why the international community has failed so dismally to protect a notably uncharismatic fish, the tuna. Her answers partly echo Dorsey's findings. As with whaling, the desire for sensible policy conflicted with the desire among major fishing nations to protect their sovereignty and to promote their domestic fishing industries. In the United States, a third factor also cut against equitable management of the global commons—determination dating from the early Cold War to preserve uninhibited access to the world's oceans for US naval ships. Finley differs from Dorsey in painting a gloomier picture of the relationship between policy makers and scientists. Whereas Dorsey suggests that national policy makers often brazenly ignored the best available science, Finley focuses on a case in which the United States manipulated flimsy science for self-serving purposes. The principle that fishing should be allowed up to a "maximum sustainable yield" possessed the veneer of scientific authority but actually rested on scant research. The United States, and later other major fishing nations, accepted the notion mostly, Finley suggests, because it provided a rationale for relatively unfettered access to fish stocks and to the high seas in which they swam. The implications for the future—that nations will cherry-pick science that supports their narrow goals and that entire international conventions might be rooted in such science—are disturbing indeed.

Shifting the focus from water to terra firma, Greg Bankoff examines the history of peace parks, a concept that he suggests has gained "a place of prominence" in international conflict resolution. Although Bankoff calls attention to the rapid growth of peace parks over the last two decades, he argues that this phenomenon is rooted in a longer history of conflict and resolution. Nature, Bankoff contends, has played an important role in defusing human conflict and mitigating border disputes. The chapter invites readers to think of peace parks as transnational spaces, environments laden with political, social, and cultural meaning for people moving through or living within or beyond the borders.

David Zierler analyzes the campaign waged by environmental scientists in the 1970s to convince governments around the world to ban the use of herbicidal weapons such as Agent Orange. Activist scientists began condemning the use of herbicides almost as soon as the United States deployed them in Vietnam in the early 1960s. It was not until a decade later, however, that they began to achieve a degree of success in their efforts to ban the practice. What changed was not the stridency of the scientists' warnings but the political climate in which they made their case. In Zierler's analysis, well-intentioned scientists achieved results as their message increasingly meshed with a broad mood of hostility to the Vietnam War and mounting concern for the global environment. Joining forces with sympathetic congressmen willing to concede sovereign prerogatives in the interest of avoiding environmental Armageddon, the scientists successfully pushed the US government to acknowledge that herbicides were a form of chemical weapon whose use was banned under the Geneva Protocol. The scientists then took their case to the United Nations, where many governments welcomed their appeal for a global prohibition on herbicidal warfare. The scientists' achievement in raising global consciousness—and in producing a real policy shift in the United States—thus provides a welcome example of environmental protection trumping national self-interest. Essential to this outcome, however, was the collaboration of political leaders predisposed to hear what the scientists had to say, a condition that has prevailed only on rare occasions.

David Kinkela examines a similar issue—the regulation of chemical pesticide DDT by the US government—in roughly the same period. Like Zierler, Kinkela notes the remarkable clout enjoyed by environmental scientists and the environmental movement more generally in the 1960s and 1970. Just as activist scientists succeeded in banning the use of herbicidal weapons, in 1972 they convinced US authorities to ban the use of DDT within US borders. That success marks just the starting point for Kinkela's analysis, which focuses on the knotty dilemma that confronted environmentalists in later years: whether a product banned for domestic use should also be banned for export and use around the world. The debate exposed an uncertainty that complicates efforts to establish common approaches to a range of transnational environmental challenges. Might practices deemed unacceptable in one nation be considered permissible in another, where different histories and divergent social and economic norms yield dissimilar calculations of the costs and benefits associated with regulation? How should a healthy respect for social, economic, and cultural differences among nations be reconciled with the urgency of international rule setting? Kinkela does not answer these questions so much as show how powerfully they asserted themselves in connection with one of the twentieth century's best-known pollutants.

Part II, "Nature, Nations, and Global Networks of Knowledge and Exchange," explores how individuals and groups acting outside national

governments—scientists, farmers, activists, indigenous groups, and trash traders, among others—have sought to promote agendas that in diverse ways challenged the sovereign prerogatives of states. Taken together, these chapters reveal
the complex interplay between national priorities and the circulation of ideas and
goods within and especially across national boundaries. The section explores in
part how and under what conditions such nonstate actors have succeeded or
failed to promote their agendas, but it is especially concerned with the consequences of those successes and failures and the implications for the future.
How past experiences shape expectations about interactions between a growing
global consciousness of environmental interconnectedness and the persistent
power of individual nations? The chapters reveal the possibilities and limits of
nonstate actors pushing the nation-state to effect environmental change.

In the first chapter of Part II, Greg Cushman examines the development
of hurricane science during the nineteenth century. Tracing the work of Jesuit
missionaries in the Caribbean and the Pacific, Cushman investigates the transnational networks of scientists and their relationship to imperial power. In
developing the world's first operational warning systems for tropical cyclones,
Jesuit scientists played an important role in understanding storms. They also
operated within and beyond imperial boundaries, reaffirming or at times con-
testing the political aspirations of the state. Jesuit scientists influenced how
various state actors understood the destructive capacity of the ocean worlds
that transcended any one nation. In this way, scientific networks developed
to understand hurricanes created a multidimensional transnational space,
shaped not only by the people who studied storms but also by the oceans that
created them.

James McWilliams shifts the focus from scientists to farmers, dem-
onstrating that nineteenth-century agriculturalists possessed a remarkably
sophisticated understanding of their environment. By tracing the efforts of scientifically minded American farmers who used insects to control pests from
the mid-nineteenth to the early twentieth centuries, McWilliams reveals how
these people worked with state-sponsored agencies such as the US Department
of Agriculture while also developing policies that shaped an agricultural system
that crossed national borders. McWilliams demonstrates that a globalization
of sorts thrived during the mid-to-late nineteenth century, which he calls the
"heyday of biological control." This process meant, ironically, that agriculture
on the cusp of industrialization was more globalized than it would be later in
the century when chemical insecticides came to dominate agriculture and isolationist tendencies became more common. Reversing common understanding of globalized farming in this way, McWilliams notes that the transition
from biological control to chemical insecticide blunted both biological diversity

and international flows of information and good will. In short, assertion of national control destroyed the freer flow of information that had underpinned notably constructive environmental practices.

Janet Davis, by contrast, suggests that transnational flows could have oppressive effects. Her chapter shows that Western desires to civilize Asian "savages" involved not just physical occupation but also the imposition of cultural agendas. Davis offers a provocative look at the links between animal conservation and political independence in the Philippines. American animal rights advocates and at least some of those in charge of the occupying forces viewed the two ideas as interconnected moral imperatives. Tracing the history of efforts by animal welfare advocates to export their beliefs, Davis demonstrates that such activists participated in colonizing and "civilizing" the Philippines by imposing their ideals on Filipino children as they attended primary school, and on their parents as they engaged in agricultural work and animal husbandry or participated in animal-centered forms of entertainment like cockfighting. Davis argues that such efforts had a dual purpose: to protect animals and to revise the "violent legacies of conquest with a symbolic program of uplift" that downplayed the aggressiveness of the American occupation in the eyes of Filipinos and other nations. Residents of the Philippines resisted and sought to retain control of their animals, just as they sought control over their own system of governance.

Benjamin Colombi shifts attention to the American Northwest and explains how indigenous nations have managed to hold out, to a degree, against the forces of nation-state consolidation and the global economy during an era when one of their key resources, salmon, developed a high market value and was exported far beyond the borders of their reserve. Colombi examines a culturally distinct population resisting both national and transnational forces through its engagement with the environment and its management of salmon. As the US government attempted to control the Nez Perce population by bringing salmon under its domain though state-sponsored dam building, the Nez Perce drew on their status as a sovereign "domestic dependent nation" to resist. Despite a dramatic remapping of their traditional homeland by national, transnational, and even global corporations, the Nez Perce fought to preserve their salmon-based culture. In turn, the preservation of this culture has reinforced Nez Perce sovereignty. Colombi asserts that the circulation of salmon and the importance the Nez Perce place upon the fish as an economic and cultural resource have helped the tribe engage in a form of "adaptive resistance" that has helped them preserve their culture, economy, and even their political independence.

Seth Garfield's chapter investigates how activists made the Amazon rainforest a symbol of the current global environmental crisis. Because of its biodiversity and status as the "lungs of the earth," the Amazon holds a special place in the minds of environmentalists, who universally believe that the Amazon requires protection against the powerful forces of capitalist accumulation. Protecting such a place, however, often encroaches on national prerogatives as well as the economic needs of people who live within the region, creating a set of political disagreements as diverse as they are contentious. Garfield examines how multiple actors, including nonhuman ones, have shaped and continue to shape the region from within and beyond the Amazon. As a transnational space, Garfield asserts, the Amazon continues to be reimagined by a set of transnational entities with conflicting views about nature, race, and state power, while those who live within it fight to protect their greatest assets.

Finally, Emily Brownell focuses on a very tangible, if unwanted, product: trash. Brownell's chapter examines the environmental, cultural, and economic value of waste discarded by Western nations that hope it will somehow "disappear" or be utilized or consumed once it leaves their borders. Brownell documents how that waste has historically circulated, gathering or losing value in the process. Concentrating on what happens when wealthier nations no longer have the space or will to store their own refuse, Brownell demonstrates how, by the late twentieth century, the West was doing more than just dumping food, clothing, and chemical waste on Africans. Wealthy countries were also reinforcing the notion of Africa as a "wasted continent." Brownell calls attention to the pathways by which discarded items made their way to different African nations, and she invites readers to consider how objects, people, nations, and their environments can be altered by such economic processes as consumption.

In tracking nation-state regulatory efforts and examining the challenge posed by nonstate actors to the power of nations, all the contributors to this collection force us think beyond borders by acknowledging that the modern world is, in geopolitical if not environmental terms, both indifferent to them and defined by them. By examining the ways in which nation-states have attempted to regulate, respond to, alter, or control the flow of animals, products, or ideologies, we hope this book demonstrates that historians of the international environmental experience have much to add in the quest to understand the present state of the transnational environment.

NOTES

1. Charles J. Hanley, "As World Warms, More Talks," Associated Press, in *Austin American-Statesman*, November 25, 2010, A17.

2. Quoted in Neil MacFarquhar, "You First, Nations Say, as 100 Leaders Prepare to Meet on Climate Change," *New York Times*, September 20, 2009, 6.

3. Fareed Zakaria, *The Post-American World* (New York: Norton, 2008), 31–2.

4. A number of political scientists, and economists have explored this term. See Susan J. Buck, *The Global Commons: An Introduction* (Washington DC: Island Press, 1998); John Volger, *The Global Commons: Environmental and Technological Governance,* 2nd ed. (New York: Wiley, 2000); and Michael Goldman, *Privatizing Nature: Political Struggles for the Global Commons* (London: Pluto Press, 1998).

5. William Cronon, forward in Kurkpatrick Dorsey, *The Dawn of Conservation Diplomacy: U.S.-Canadian Wildlife Protection Treaties in the Progressive Era* (Seattle: University of Washington Press, 1998), xi. Emphasis in original.

6. On "imagined communities," see Benedict Anderson, *Imagined Communities: Reflections on the Origins and Spread of Nationalism,* new ed. (New York: Verso, 2006). On the challenge to national history, see, for example, Thomas Bender, ed., *Rethinking American History in a Global Age* (Berkeley: University of California Press, 2002), and A. G. Hopkins, ed., *Global History: Interactions between the Universal and the Local* (New York: Palgrave, 2006).

7. For example, Thomas L. Friedman, *The World Is Flat: A Brief History of the Twenty-First Century* (New York: Farrar, Straus, and Giroux, 2005).

8. Joachim Radkau, *Nature and Power: A Global History of the Environment,* trans. Thomas Dunlap (Cambridge: Cambridge University Press, 2008), 306.

9. Robert Boardman, *International Organization and the Conservation of Nature* (Bloomington: Indiana University Press, 1981); Richard Elliot Benedict, *Ozone Diplomacy: New Directions in Safeguarding the Planet,* 2nd ed. (Cambridge, MA: Harvard University Press, 1998); Lawrence E. Susskind, *Environmental Diplomacy: Negotiating More Effective Global Agreements* (New York: Oxford University Press, 1994); and Mostafa K. Tolba, *Global Environmental Diplomacy: Negotiating Environmental Agreements for the World, 1973–1992* (Cambridge, MA: MIT Press, 2008).

10. See, for example, James Gustave Speth and Peter Haas, *Global Environmental Governance: Foundations of Contemporary Environmental Studies* (Washington, DC: Island Press, 2006); Ronnie D. Lipschutz, *Global Environmental Politics: Power, Perspectives, and Practice* (Washington, DC: CQ Press, 2006); Jacqueline Vaughn, *Environmental Politics: Domestic and Global Dimension,* 6th ed. (Belmont, CA: Wadsworth Publishing, 2011); and Hilary French, *Vanishing Borders: Protecting the Planet in the Age of Globalization* (Washington, DC: Worldwatch Institute, 2000).

11. Mark Lytle, "An Environmental Approach to American Diplomatic History," *Diplomatic History* 20 (1996): 279–300.

12. Dorsey, *Dawn of Conservation Diplomacy.*

13. Robert Darst, *Smokestack Diplomacy: Cooperation and Conflict in East-West Politics* (Cambridge, MA: MIT Press, 2001); and Marc Cioc, *The Game of Conservation: International Treaties to Protect the World's Migratory Animals* (Athens: Ohio University Press, 2009).

14. Kurpatrick Dorsey, "Dealing with the Dinosaur (and Its Swamp): Putting the Environment in Diplomatic History," *Diplomatic History* 29, no. 4 (September 2005): 573–87. See also Anna-Katherine Wöbse, "Oil on Troubled Waters? Environmental Diplomacy in the League of Nations"; Jacob Darwin Hamblin, "God and Devils in the Details: Marine Pollution, Radioactive Waste, and an Environmental Regime circa 1972"; Thomas Robertson, "'This is the American Earth': American Empire,

the Cold War, and American Environmentalism"; Lisa M. Brady, "Life in the DMZ: Turning a Diplomatic Failure into an Environmental Success"; and J. Brooks Flippen, "Richard Nixon, Russell Train, and the Birth of American Environmental Diplomacy," in "Forum: New Directions in Diplomatic and Environmental History," special issue, *Diplomatic History* 32, no. 4 (September 2008): 519–638. For an early attempt to explain Richard Nixon's environmental legacy see, John C. Whitaker, *Striking a Balance: Environment and Natural Resources Policy in the Nixon-Ford Years* (Washington DC: American Enterprise Institute for Public Policy Research, 1976).

15. J. R. McNeill and Corinna R. Unger, *Environmental Histories of the Cold War* (New York: Cambridge University Press, 2010), especially chapters by Kristine C. Harper and Ronald E. Doel and Kai Hünemörder.

16. Daniel Yergen, *The Prize: The Epic Quest for Oil, Money, and Power* (New York: Free Press, 1993); Michael B. Stoff, *Oil, War, and American Security: The Search for a National Policy on Foreign Oil* (New Haven, CT: Yale University Press, 1980); Kevin Phillips, *American Theocracy: The Peril and Politics of Radical Religion, Oil, and Borrowed Money in the Twenty-First Century* (New York: Viking, 2006). See also David Painter, *Oil and the American Century: The Political Economy of US Foreign Oil Policy, 1941–1954* (Baltimore, MD: Johns Hopkins University Press, 1986); Francisco Parra, *Oil Politics: A Modern History of Petroleum* (London: I. B. Taurus, 2004); and Myrna I. Santiago's *The Ecology of Oil: Environment, Labor, and the Mexican Revolution, 1900–1938* (New York: Cambridge University Press, 2009).

17. Steven Solomon, *Water: The Epic Struggle for Wealth, Power, and Civilization* (New York: Harper, 2010); Peter Dauvergne, *Shadows in the Forest: Japan and the Politics of Timber in Southeast Asia* (Cambridge, MA: MIT Press, 1997); Warren Dean, *With Broadax and Firebrand: The Destruction of the Brazilian Atlantic Forest* (Berkeley: University of California Press, 1995); Micah S. Muscolino, *Fishing Wars and Environmental Change in Late Imperial and Modern China* (Cambridge, MA: Harvard University Press, 2009); and Mark R. Finlay, *Growing American Rubber: Strategic Plants and the Politics of National Security* (New Brunswick, NJ: Rutgers University Press, 2009).

18. For example, William Houston, *Water: The Final Resource* (Petersfield, United Kingdom: Harriman House, 2004); Fred Pearce, *When the Rivers Run Dry: Water—the Defining Crisis of the Twenty-First Century* (Boston: Beacon, 2007); Marq de Villers, *Water: The Fate of Our Most Precious Resource* (New York: Mariner Books, 2001); and Maude Barlow, *Blue Covenant: The Global Water Crisis and the Coming Battle for the Right to Water* (New York: New Press, 2009).

19. The list of books examining the history of disease is long and cannot be properly examined here. Recent works include James L. A. Webb Jr. *Humanity's Burden: A Global History of Malaria* (Cambridge, MA: Cambridge University Press, 2008); J. R. McNeill, *Mosquito Empires: Ecology and War in the Greater Caribbean, 1640–1914* (New York: Cambridge University Press, 2010); Sonia Shah, *The Fever: How Malaria Has Ruled Humankind for 500,000 Years* (New York: Farrar, Straus and Giroux, 2010); Nicholas B. King, "The Influence of Anxiety: September 11th, Bioterrorism, and American Public Health," *Journal of the History of Medicine and the Allied Sciences* 58, no.4 (2003): 433–41; and King, "Security, Disease, Commerce: Ideologies of

Post-Colonial Global Health," *Social Studies of Science* 32, no. 5/6 (2002): 763–89. Also
see Andrew T. Price-Smith, *The Health of Nations: Infectious Disease, Environmental
Change, and Their Effects on National Security and Development* (Cambridge, MA: MIT
Press, 2001), and Price-Smith, *Contagion and Chaos: Disease, Ecology, and National
Security in the Era of Globalization* (Cambridge, MA: MIT Press, 2009). While not
specifically related to national security, J. N. Hays's *The Burdens of Disease: Epidemics
and Human Response in Western History*, rev. ed. (New Brunswick, NJ: Rutgers
University Press, 2010) provides a useful analysis of the impact and understanding of
disease.

20. Donald Worster, "World without Borders: The Internationalizing of
Environmental History," *Environmental Review* 6, no. 2 (fall 1982): 8. Worster's
essay also appeared in Kendall Bailes, ed., *Environmental History: Critical Issues and
Comparative Perspective* (Lanham, MD: University Press of America, 1985).

21. Also see Donald Hughes, *An Environmental History of the World: Humankind's
Changing Role in the Community of Life* (2009); William Beinart and Lotte Hughes,
Environment and Empire (New York: Oxford University Press, 2007); Ramachandra
Guha, *Environmentalism: A Global History* (New York: Longman, 2000); Clive
Ponting, *A New Green History of the World: The Environment and the Collapse of Great
Civilizations*, rev. ed. (New York: Penguin, 2007); and Anthony Penna, *The Human
Footprint: A Global Environmental History* (Malden, MA: Wiley-Blackwell, 2009).

22. Richard Grove, "Environmental History," in *New Perspectives on Historical
Writing*, ed. Peter Burke (University Park: Penn State University Press, 2001), 263.
Richard White made a similar critique in "The Nationalizing of Nature," *Journal of
American History* (December 1999): 976–86.

23. J. R. McNeill, "Observations on the Nature and Culture of Environmental
History," *History and Theory* 42, no. 4 (December 2003): 5–43.

24. Also see Alfred W. Crosby, *Children of the Sun: A History of Humanity's
Unappeasable Appetite for Energy* (New York: W. W. Norton, 2009); David Igler,
"Diseased Goods: Global Exchanges in the Eastern Pacific Basin, 1770–1850,"
American Historical Review 109 (June 2004): 693–719; Richard Tucker, *Insatiable
Appetite: The United States and the Ecological Degradation of the Tropical World*
(Berkeley: University of California Press, 2000); Londa Schiebinger, *Plants and
Empire: Colonial Bioprospecting in the Atlantic World* (Cambridge, MA: Harvard
University Press, 2007); John Soluri, *Banana Cultures: Agriculture, Consumption, and
Environmental Change in Honduras and the United States* (Austin: University of Texas
Press, 2006); and Thomas G. Andrews, *Killing for Coal: America's Deadliest Labor War*
(Cambridge, MA: Harvard University Press, 2008). Also useful is "Transnational
Environments: Rethinking the Political Economy of Nature in a Global Age," special
issue, *Radical History Review* (spring 2010), ed. David Kinkela and Neil Maher.

25. On the policy side, see Andrew Jordan, ed. *Environmental Policy in the EU:
Actors, Institutions and Processes*, 2nd ed. (London: Routledge, 2005), Andrew Jordan,
Environment Policy in Europe: The Europeanization of National Environmental Policy
(London: Routledge, 2005), Philipp M. Hildebrand, "The European community's
environmental policy, 1957 to '1992': From incidental measures to an international
regime?" *Environmental Politics* 1, no. 4 (1992): 13–44; Mikael Skou Andersen and

Duncan Liefferink, eds., *European Environmental Policy: The Pioneers* (Manchester, United Kingdom: Manchester University Press, 1997); and Mark Blacksell and Allan M. Williams, eds., *The European Challenge: Geography and Development in the European Community* (Oxford: Oxford University Press, 1994); Peter Brimblecombe and Christian Pfister, eds., *The Silent Countdown: Essays in European Environmental History* (Berlin: Springer-Verlag, 1993). Also see, Mark Cioc, Björn-Ola Linnér, and Matthew Osborn, "Environmental History Writing in Northern Europe," *Environmental History* 5, no. 3 (2000): 396–406; and Michael Bess, Mark Cioc, and James Sievert, "Environmental History Writing in Southern Europe," *Environmental History* 5, no. 4 (2000): 545–56.

26. Christian Hey, "EU Environmental Policies: A Short History of the Policy Strategies," *EU Environmental Policy Handbook* (Brussels: European Environmental Bureau, 2005), 3, 21, http://www.eeb.org/publication/chapter-3.pdf. Also see, Stefan Scheuer, ed. *EU Environmental Policy Handbook: A Critical Analysis of EU Environmental Legislation, Making it accessible to environmentalists and decision makers* (Brussels: European Environmental Bureau, 2005).

27. Thomas Lekan *Imagining the Nation in Nature: Landscape Preservation and German Identity, 1885–1945* (Cambridge, MA: Harvard University Press, 2004); David Blackbourn, *The Conquest of Nature: Water, Landscape, and the Making of Modern Germany* (New York: W. W. Norton, 2006); William Rollins, *A Greener Vision of Home: Cultural Politics and Environmental Reform in the German Heimatschutz Movement, 1904–1918* (Ann Arbor: University of Michigan Press, 1997); Michael Bess, *The Light-Green Society: Ecology and Technological Modernity in France, 1960–2000* (Chicago: University of Chicago Press, 2003); John Sheail, *An Environmental History of Twentieth-Century Britain* (Basingstoke: Palgrave, 2001); Tamara Whited, ed. *Northern Europe: An Environmental History*, (Santa Barbara, CA: ABC-Clio, 2005); J. R. McNeill, *The Mountains of the Mediterranean World: An Environmental History* (New York: Cambridge University Press, 2003); Charles Watkins and Keith Kirby, *The Ecological History of European Forests* (New York; CAB International,1998); Brian Fagan, *The Little Ice Age: How Climate Made History, 1300–1850* (New York: Basic Books, 2000).

28. William Beinart and Lotte Hughes, *Environment and Empire* (Oxford: Oxford University Press, 2007); Richard Grove, *Ecology, Climate and Empire: Colonialism and Global Environmental History 1400–1940* (Cambridge: White Horse Press, 1993); L. Robin and T. Griffith, *Ecology and Empire: Environmental History in Settler Societies* (Edinburgh: Edinburgh University Press, 1997); and Jennifer Anderson, "Nature's Currency: The Atlantic Mahogany Trade and the Commodification of Nature in the 18th Century," *Early American Studies* 2, no. 1 (spring 2004), 47–80.

29. James McCann, *Maize and Graze: Africa's Encounter with a New World Crop, 1500–2000* (Cambridge, MA: Harvard University Press, 2005); Warren Dean, *With Broadax and Firebrand: Destruction of the Brazilian Atlantic Forest* (Berkeley: University of California Press, 1995); Richard Grove, *Ecology, Climate and Empire: Colonialism and Global Environmental History, 1400–1940* (Isle of Harris, UK: White Horse Press, 1998); Reinaldo Funes Monzote, *From Rainforest to Cane Field in Cuba: An Environmental History since 1492* (Chapel Hill: University of North Carolina Press,

2008); and Tamara Giles-Vernick, *Cutting the Vines of the Past: Environmental Histories of the Central African Rain Forest* (Charlottesville: University of Virginia Press, 2002).

30. See. for example, Madhav Gadgil and Ramachandra Guha, *This Fissured Land: An Ecological History of India* (Berkeley: University of California Press, 1992).

31. Robert B. Marks, *Tigers, Rice, Silk, and Silt: Environment and Economy in Late Imperial South China* (New York, Cambridge University Press, 1997); Mark Elvin, *The Retreat of the Elephants: An Environmental History of China* (New Haven, CT: Yale University Press, 2004); and Judith Shapiro, *Mao's War against Nature: Politics and the Environment in Revolutionary China* (New York: Cambridge University Press, 2001).

32. Matthew Frye Jacobson, "More 'Trans-,' Less 'National,'" *Journal of American Ethnic History* (Summer 2006): 74–84. Emphasis in original.

PART I

Nature, Nation-States, and the Regulatory Dilemma

I

Europe's River

The Rhine as Prelude to Transnational Cooperation
and the Common Market

Mark Cioc

In *Seeing like a State*, James C. Scott argued that government-sponsored development projects often fail because administrators misread the landscape and underestimate the complexity of their endeavors. Prussia pumped large amounts of money into forest management in the eighteenth and nineteenth centuries in the hope of achieving a sustainable timber yield, but inadvertently produced ecologically impoverished and disease-ridden tree stands. The Soviet Union (and later China) collectivized its farms in the hope of boosting cereal production, but reaped a harvest of starvation instead. In 1960, Brazil quixotically decided to move its capital from the old and vibrant city of Rio de Janeiro to the new and sterile city of Brasilia, only to discover that most of its citizens did not want to live there. Equally telling were the tragic attempts by Tanzania, Mozambique, and Ethiopia in the 1970s to force their nomadic populations into sedentary villages. "State simplifications" was Scott's term for these failures. Prussian administrators spoke of forests but thought of lumber. Communist planners counted acres, but discounted farmers. Third World governments understood the benefits of urban development, but not the mentality of city life.[1]

Scott focused his attention on large-scale projects undertaken by individual nation-states, but his insights can be fruitfully applied to other large-scale undertakings as well. When diplomats and bureaucrats take a "high-modernist" (top-down) approach, they all too often fail to understand and resolve problems that arise "on location" (from below)—even when these endeavors achieve their primary goals and are therefore judged successful. The record of the Central Commission on Rhine Navigation (hereafter, Rhine Commission)—a transnational agency composed of the major states located on the banks of the Rhine (known as "riparian states")—is one such example. The Rhine Commission behaved in many ways like a sovereign state, exerting a governing control over Rhine affairs for over 150 years, and it embraced "simplifications" in a big way. Commissioners used the term "river," but meant channel and riverbed. They worried about flooding, but not about the floodplains around the waterway. They fretted about water quantities, but not about water quality. What they saw when they looked at the Rhine was not a biological habitat, but a cargo-delivery device; not a river basin, but a water channel; not a place for fishing, but a site for commerce.[2]

Their single-mindedness of purpose—the promotion of trade through improved navigation—allowed the Rhine commissioners to achieve their goals effectively and efficiently; in less than a century, they transformed the Rhine into a world-class commercial waterway. But because they viewed navigation, flood control, water quality, and biodiversity as competing rather than complementary goals, they also embedded a number of failures into their otherwise successful endeavor. The river that existed in the minds of the Rhine commissioners contained no biological life. They engineered the river in such a way that there was little room left for fish or trees. A river, as they saw it, consisted of a long, thin channel. Not surprisingly, they sheared off the Rhine's branches and floodplain, depriving it of its geographical breadth. River water was, for them, a free commodity, useful above all to keep the barges flowing at a steady rate. In the end, they paid a lot of attention to the construction of dams (to regulate the flow) and to the maintenance of ice breakers (to keep channels moving freely in winter)—but no attention whatsoever to the pollutants that were poured into the river along the way.

Today, transnational cooperation is perceived as one of the best avenues for achieving environmental safeguards, so it is worth pointing out that the history of the Rhine Commission offers something of a cautionary tale in this regard.[3] Established by the Congress of Vienna (1814–1815), the Commission is one of the oldest continuous interstate institutions in Europe and was thus an early step in the slow march to the Common Market and European Union. The Rhine Commission has dealt with myriad challenges over the past two centuries, not least the disruptions caused by two world wars (when control of the Rhine provinces of Alsace and Lorraine was in contention), and its composition and goals have been modified many times by European diplomats, most significantly at the Paris Peace Conference in 1919. But environmental protection has never been on its agenda. The absence of an environmental mandate is readily explicable during the early years of the Rhine Commission's existence, before the river had started to show any signs of eco-damage and before the words "preservation," "conservation," and "environment" were part of the civic discourse. But it is far less explicable after 1900, by which time the Rhine's failing biological health was a matter of public concern. So persistently indifferent was the Rhine Commission to ecological issues that in 1950 European governments established the International Commission to Protect the Rhine to counterbalance it.

The Rhine's modern history lends itself to the familiar declensionist model of environmental history writing: economic success came at a high environmental cost. The Rhine Commission set out to control the river as fully as was feasible, only to find itself in a long war of attrition that required extensive manipulations and expensive control measures beyond what was initially anticipated. When engineers reclaimed the Rift Valley floodplain to protect upstream cities such as Strasbourg and Ludwigshafen, the river began to inundate the downstream cities instead. When industries, lured to the Rhine because of its excellent transport network, laced the river with heavy metals and other pollutants, the river emptied the pollutants onto irrigated fields, where they became the problem of Rhine farmers and European consumers. When dams and other human-built structures killed off the salmon and shad populations, the river began to produce roach, bleak, and bream ("garbage" fish) in their place.

"Think globally, act locally" is more a slogan than an analytical tool, but it can be invoked to provide some insights into why the Rhine accrued a reputation as Europe's "romantic sewer" even as it became one of the world's premier commercial routes. The Rhine went from being controlled in the premodern era by a plethora of lilliputian riparian states that "thought locally and acted locally" to being controlled in the modern era by a small group of middle-sized states that "thought globally and acted globally," with no middle ground in between. The ancien régime Rhine—some ninety-seven German princedoms, knightly estates, and ecclesiastical principalities between the Swiss and Dutch borders—was a landscape of petty quarrels. The leaders of these microstates warred with each other over fishing spots and islands. They built diversion dams and other structures that increased the number of forks and sandbars. Above all, they built toll booths, some thirty-four along the lower stretches of the river alone. "The Rhine can count more tolls than miles," went a popular prerevolutionary tune, "and knight and priestling block its path." These leaders were great stewards of the natural resources they valued—riverbank property, islands, fishing holes, and deer—but not of the river's overall economic well-being. By contrast, the Rhine states of the modern era—and the Rhine Commission, which represented their collective interests—thought solely in terms of expanding their global economic reach. They destroyed the toll booths and opened up shipping to all nations. They rectified the main channel and replumbed the feeder streams and tributaries. They usurped ("reclaimed") the riverbanks and floodplains to build farms, towns, and factories. Above all, they decided which enterprises should thrive (coal, steel, chemicals) and which should suffer (fishing, local trade, water utilities) based solely on the profit motive. The Rhine thereby passed from local governance to global governance without any effective institutional link in between.

Put another way, the diplomats at the Vienna Congress created something akin to what the American ecologist Garrett Hardin has called the "tragedy of the commons": all the Rhine states had a stake in maximizing their share of the river's commerce, but none had a stake in preserving it as a riparian habitat.[4] Although the Rhine states were the only political entities in the new Rhine regime in a position to "think globally and act locally," in practice they thought locally only when it suited their budgets and political needs. The state of Hesse, for instance, failed for several decades to dredge a deep channel through the Rheingau (a river widening near the town of Bingen) because it lacked the necessary funds to complete the project properly, not because this type of project endangered the "Romantic Rhine," the stretch of the river from Bingen to Mainz. Similarly, the state of Baden was slow to undertake river improvements between Mannheim and Strasbourg because they threatened the profitability of Baden's railroad network, not because they would wreak havoc on the Baden's expansive floodplain. Only once did the Rhine Commission settle a conflict that involved ecological issues, and even that was more about controlling water than protecting it. During the 1920s, the German government protested the construction of the Grand Canal d'Alsace on the grounds that it would lower the groundwater level, to the detriment of Baden farmers. The dispute was finally resolved in the 1950s by diverting most Rhine water to the canal while allowing some to remain in its original bed, to the benefit of the river's biodiversity.

The Transnational Rhine

The Rhine ranks among the top hundred rivers of the world, as measured by the three most common ways of assessing a river's size: length (775 miles); catchment area or watershed (71,400 square miles); and average delta discharge rate (2875 cubic yards/second). Like most large rivers, the Rhine crosses many borders on its way to the sea. Its headwaters lie in the Alpine regions of Switzerland, Liechtenstein, Austria, and Italy. After leaving the Alps, its path winds northward through French and German territory, picking up some runoff from Luxembourg along the way. It then heads northwest toward the North Sea by way of the Rhine-Meuse delta of Belgium and the Netherlands. This means that nine countries lie partially or wholly within the Rhine's watershed, six of which are riparian states (excepting Italy, Luxembourg, and Belgium). Four of these countries are particularly important to Rhine affairs: Switzerland, where most of the river's headwaters originate; Germany, home to over half the river's watershed; France, which shares the Rift Valley floodplain (including Alsace and Lorraine) with Germany; and the Netherlands, where the Rhine (called the Waal) becomes part of a vast delta.

The Rhine also boasts a transnational character that goes beyond the sheer happenstance of European geopolitics: far more than most rivers, it has been the focus of intense international diplomacy over the past two centuries. The river's modern history began with the French Revolution (1789–1815), when French troops swept away the smaller German states and drove out the Austrian Habsburgs, destroying the Holy Roman Empire in the process. The new riparian states that Napoleon created consisted of middle-sized German entities—among them Baden, Württemberg, Hesse, Nassau, and Westphalia—out of what had previously been myriad independent ones. At the same time, Napoleon created the Confédération du Rhin in 1806, to coordinate the political affairs of the German states; the Magistrat du Rhin in 1808, to oversee engineering projects on the river; and the Convention de L'Octroi, to create a uniform set of commercial codes in the Rhine watershed.

The Napoleonic dream of a unified Rhine died on the battlefields of Leipzig and Waterloo in 1813–1815, but the French vision of treating the Rhine basin as a unified economic entity lived on. The diplomats at the Congress of Vienna dismantled the Confédération du Rhin, but they decided not to restore the microstates of yesteryear. Similarly, they disbanded the Magistrat du Rhin, but then established its mirror image—the Rhine Commission—under the control of the riparian states. Following the same logic, they declared the Convention de L'Octroi null and void, but then incorporated most of its tenets into the Vienna Convention. "Navigation on the Rhine, from the point where it becomes navigable to the sea and vice versa, shall be free, in that it cannot be prohibited to any one" was the precise wording of the free-trade clause that was added to the Vienna accords.[5]

It is easy to see why the Congress of Vienna diplomats adopted these French ideas, even if they disguised their actions as best they could. Austria's foreign minister, Clemens von Metternich, was from the Rhine town of Koblenz. He knew from personal experience the degree to which the ancien régime leaders had stymied commerce and trade on the river, and also how vulnerable they had been to French aggrandizement. Similarly, Prussia's foreign minister, Wilhelm von Humboldt, was eager to bring two of the most important new Rhine states, Westphalia and Rhineland, into Prussia's political orbit, an accomplishment that would not be possible with a restoration of the Rhine ancien régime. Other diplomats were less directly involved in Rhine affairs, but they, too, saw the virtues of political cooperation, knowing full well that a return to the old Rhine would almost certainly mean a restoration of trade barriers that were detrimental to European commerce.

The Rhine is transnational in another sense as well: it was the site of an enormous amount of experimentation in river engineering by a Europe-wide team of hydraulic engineers. To be sure, the two men most closely associated with the creation of the modern Rhine—Johann Gottfried Tulla ("Tamer of the Wild Rhine") and Adolph Eduard Nobiling (inventor of the modern wing dam, or groyne)—were from the German states of Baden and Prussia, but their prominence obscures more than it reveals. The modern Rhine was, above all, a vast joint-engineering project, one that relied on the earlier scientific breakthroughs of Italian engineers (especially Benedetto Castelli and Domenico Guglielmini in the seventeenth century), who developed the formula for accurately determining water flow and who advocated the creation of deep, straight channels; on the political engagement of the prerevolutionary French government, which created the first schools devoted to hydraulic engineering and underwrote the first large-scale, state-directed, rectification projects in the eighteenth century; and on the ingenuity of the Dutch, who knew from centuries of experience how to reclaim land by draining water quickly and efficiently. Tulla's most famous dictum—"No stream or river, the Rhine included, needs more than one bed; as a rule, multiple branches are redundant" (a statement that can still be found in modern engineering textbooks)—was nothing more than the distillation of previous centuries of thinking about river engineering. And Nobiling's wing dams—concave structures about eight yards long and one yard wide, stretching in rows from the river bank toward the center of the stream—were the logical outcome of a tradition that prioritized the creation of a single deep channel.[6]

Common to the zeitgeist of nearly all European water engineers from the eighteenth century on was the idea that a river was "wild" and "unruly" and therefore in need of being "tamed" or "harnessed" or, alternatively, was an "enemy" in need of being "defeated." Tulla, for instance, liked to refer to his flood-control blueprint as a "general operational plan" for a "defense against a Rhine attack." Equally common was the notion that free-flowing rivers were really nothing more than imperfect canals, in need of improvement ("rectification" and "amelioration" in their terms) so that they would become straighter, more predictable, and thus more navigable. With rare exceptions, the national origin of these hydraulic engineers mattered little. They were a like-minded group, who spoke to each other through the language of mathematics; and they were cosmopolitans, willing to crisscross borders at a moment's notice in search of new flood-control and rectification projects. Tulla had received his engineering training in Saxony, the Netherlands, and France, before serving as Baden's representative to the Napoleon's Magistrat du Rhin; he was subsequently appointed as Baden's representative to the Rhine Commission. Nobiling was more of a nationalist, but he had still bounced from the Elbe to the Mosel to the Saar, and then to the Ruhr before becoming Prussia's principal Rhine engineer. Other engineers followed similar trajectories and championed similar projects. One of the reasons modern rivers tend to look alike is that they have all been sculpted by engineers who came out of the same schools and used the same techniques, regardless of their nationality or the geographic location of the river.

The Rhine Commission served as the main political forum for all river projects, and the lead agency for creating unified navigational practices. It standardized transport regulations, police ordinances, and emergency procedures on the Rhine; forced rafts and sailboats off the river when they began to endanger the new steamers and diesels; and regulated the transport of hazardous materials as well as the disposal of ship waste and bilge oil. It also approved all plans and blueprints before any engineering work was begun. The hydraulic engineers, meanwhile, undertook the task of deepening and straightening the main channel, cutting out loops and meanders, reducing the number of braids and branches, and eliminating islands. They removed chokepoints, blasted out canyon walls, and scraped the river bottom. They also reinforced banks, manipulated tributaries, and dammed the Alpine regions. The end result was a river that took on a streamlined, generic appearance, more akin to an interstate highway than a river, geared for efficient transportation but little else. Whereas the river's natural width fluctuated wildly, it was now fixed in cement: 200 meters (656 feet) wide at Basel, 300 meters at Koblenz, 400 meters at Düsseldorf, and 1 kilometer at Hoek van Holland. Its shipping lanes were equally prescribed: minimum depths of 1.7 meters (5.58 feet) in some stretches, 2.5 meters in others. The river's overall length was shortened by over 65 miles, reducing its total size by nearly 10 percent.[7]

To say that these changes brought tangible benefits is to engage in historical understatement, for they were a whopping economic success. In 1810, five years before the Rhine Commission was established, only 328 vessels plied the stretch between the German states and the Netherlands, then as now the most lucrative part of the river. By 2000, there were some 200,000 annual border crossings between Germany and the Netherlands, and the total Rhine fleet stood at over 13,000 ships. In 1840, downstream traffic (typically on rafts) outpaced upstream traffic (typically aided by human or animal tows) by a three-to-one ratio. By the beginning of the twentieth century, upstream travel was outpacing downstream travel by a two-to-one ratio, largely due to the advent of steam and diesel vessels. Total shipping on the Rhine increased year to year as well, rising from 10 million tons in 1825 (before most of the rectification work had begun) to nearly 300 million tons today. The Port of Rotterdam, at the Rhine's mouth, is one of the world's largest ocean harbors (ranking third in terms of cargo and seventh in terms of containers). Duisburg-Ruhrort, where the Ruhr meets the Rhine, is one of the world's premier inland harbors. The Rhine is linked to the Baltic Sea via the Rhine-Herne canal, to France via the Rhine-Marne canal, to the Mediterranean via the Rhine-Rhône canal, and to the Black Sea via the Rhine-Main-Danube canal. Among the rivers of the world, only the Mississippi-Missouri system carries more freight each year, and it is far larger than the Rhine.

There is yet another way in which the Rhine is transnational: it was the progenitor of river commissions around the globe. The first of these were confined to Europe, beginning with the Elbe (1821), Weser (1823), Ems (1853), and Danube (1856). They then spread to North America with the establishment of the Mississippi River Commission in 1879 and the Missouri River Commission in 1884. From there, the idea spread to other large and small river systems in Asia, Africa, and Latin America, most recently to the Indus (1960), Mekong (1995), and Nile (2006). Although not all these commissions were established to promote navigation—for some, flood control and equitable water distribution is the highest priority—the Rhine and its offshoot projects continue to serve as a direct or indirect prototype for many of these river-management agencies to this day. For instance, in 2008 the South Korean government announced plans to build a "grand canal" through its peninsula, modeled not on China's famed Grand Canal but on the Rhine-Main-Danube canal, which (since 1992) has linked the North Sea and the Black Sea.

The Environmental Price of Progress

The Rhine's free-trade regime exacted an environmental toll. These costs can best be assessed by looking at two interrelated issues: flood control and habitat loss.

Collectively, the various hydraulic projects worsened rather than ameliorated the flood danger on the Rhine. There are a variety of reasons for this, but most of them stem from the fact that navigation needs trumped all other concerns. The Rhine's natural discharge rate is steadier than most rivers its size.

Alpine snowmelt in the spring and early summer provides about half its yearly water supply, while non-Alpine tributaries provide the other half during the rainy fall and winter seasons. This seasonal rhythm—Alpine water in spring and summer, non-Alpine water in fall and winter—helps to counterbalance severe fluctuations, allowing for a relatively steady river flow year-round, as measured at the Dutch delta. Over the centuries there were, of course, plenty of "dry" and "wet" years, giving rise to periodic droughts and floods, but for the most part severe flooding was confined to just two stretches: the Rift Valley plain at the base of the Alps (between the Black Forest and Vosges mountains), which was vulnerable to excessive Alpine runoff during the spring months, and the Dutch delta, which swelled to dangerous levels whenever the winter rains persisted too long.

During the nineteenth century, however, river engineers significantly altered this natural regime in ways that fundamentally changed the river's flood patterns. First, they shortened and straightened the main trunk of the river, creating a shorter and swifter flow that carried water from the Alps to the North Sea in far less time. Water that had once taken ten or more days to reach the delta now streamed down in six or seven days. Second, they built artificially high banks along the Rift Valley channel in order to reclaim the floodplain for agriculture, thereby severing the channel from the natural "sponge" that had once absorbed the Alpine excess. Third, they shortened and straightened the non-Alpine tributaries (the Main, Mosel, Ruhr, etc.), which meant that they began to shed their excess water more quickly than before, overburdening the Rhine at a time when it was already running high.

This combination of changes resulted in the creation of a new flood pattern that can be attributed as much to human engineering as to acts of nature. Flood waters that were once confined to the upper stretches of the river often continue downstream to stretches that used to be protected from inundation, turning partial floods into full-scale ones. Inundations struck all or most of the Rhine in March 1983, March 1988, December 1993, and December 1994, to mention only the most recent ones—four so-called hundred-year floods in a span of twelve years. Roughly the same amount of water flows down the Rhine today as it did two hundred years ago. But it now flows differently, and overflows differently, to the detriment of those who reside on the river's lower stretches.[8]

For riverine organisms, floodplain loss is all but synonymous with habitat loss. In 1815, the river had around 2300 square kilometers (888 square miles) of floodplain space in its non-Alpine regions alone, stretching nearly a thousand miles along a continuous river corridor. By the late twentieth century, however, all but 500 square kilometers had been usurped by farms, industries, cities, train tracks, and roads, a loss of more than three-fourths of its original floodplain. With this loss of space came a loss of riverine animals and plants. Among the first to go were the oak, elm, ash, poplar, and beech trees, along with reeds and willows that once lined the river's banks. Next to go were the mammal, reptile, and insect populations that had depended on the riverbanks for their sustenance—from beavers to tree snakes to mayflies. Bird numbers then plummeted, as birds lost their nesting and feeding sites. So, too, did the numbers of fish and other aquatic species, which now had to deal with a channel bereft of the features upon which they most depended for breeding and safety: slow-moving pools, backwaters, loops, and braids. The river's most celebrated fish—the salmon—was a victim of gravel removal (which eliminated its spawning grounds) and dams (which stopped it from reaching the Alpine feeder streams). The river's oldest known continuous inhabitant—the Rhine mussel—was a victim of cement-lined river banks, which compromised its living space while providing an avenue for its competitor, the zebra mussel, to move in. Other native species faced similar challenges. "More faunal changes have occurred in the past one hundred fifty years," noted the biologist Ragnar Kinzelbach in 1984, "than in the previous ten thousand years."[9]

The Missing Middle Ground

River engineering in the early nineteenth century was still more of an art than a science, and some catastrophic failures in previous decades had turned many Europeans into skeptics. It is therefore not surprising that the Rhine Commission had its critics, among them a wide variety of engineers, scientists, politicians, poets, and fishermen who lived and worked along the Rhine and who could see first-hand some of the immediate and long-term consequences of the river straightening that was taking place around them. Two of the most prominent—Fritz André, a hydraulic engineer and contemporary of Johann Gottfried Tulla, and Robert Lauterborn, the most celebrated Rhine biologist of the early twentieth century—can serve to illustrate how easily the Rhine Commission was able to defeat them.

Fritz André was an outspoken critic of the Tulla Rectification Project, which Baden and the Bavarian Palatinate jointly initiated in 1817, shortly after the Rhine Commission was established. Flood control was Tulla's principal objective, but he designed his project so that it would also eventually improve navigation. Following his own dictum ("no river needs more than one bed"), he began straightening and deepening the main river channel, with the intent of cutting out enough curves and oxbows to reduce the river's length in that stretch by over fifty miles, a nearly 15 percent reduction. It was this extensive shortening of the trunk river that caused André the most concern, which he voiced in a widely read scientific broadside, "Remarks on the Rectification of the Upper Rhine and a Description of the Dire Consequences It Will Have for the Inhabitants of the Middle and Lower Rhine," a title that left no doubt as to his point of view. "Thaw winds," he noted, "generally sweep through Germany and its neighboring states at winter's end, causing a general snowmelt and a swelling of the streams." The Kinzig river, for instance, typically reached its peak about three days before Main river. The Main, in turn, peaked nearly two days before the Rhine's swell reached the Main mouth. Similarly, the Neckar had typically already ebbed several days before the Rhine swell reached its mouth. "If the Upper Rhine is rectified as completely as envisaged by the Tulla Project," he predicted, "it will create a shorter and swifter current that will cause all of Germany's rivers to reach their peak discharges at or about the same time. The result will be a significant increase in flooding."[10]

When André's fears were realized with a massive flood in 1824, the Prussian government, acting on behalf of Rhineland and Westphalia, decided to halt the Tulla Project until a scientific inquiry could determine its cause. Initially, Prussia petitioned the German Confederation (the intra-German political forum that had replaced the Holy Roman Empire) rather than the Rhine Commission because the commission had not yet established its headquarters and staff. The German Confederation, in turn, established a special commission composed of diplomats and engineers from all the affected parties—with Prussia representing itself and the Netherlands, which was not a Confederation member—which functioned temporarily as an ersatz Rhine Commission.

In pleading their case, the Prussian diplomats and engineers focused on the long-term implications of river manipulation, arguing that no work should be undertaken unless it had the complete support of all the riparian states. "Every river needs to be viewed as a single entity from its source to its mouth," stated a Prussian legal brief, in remarkably modern language. "It belongs to all of the states through whose territories it naturally flows. Every artificially induced change in its natural conditions that has an impact across the state borders will affect the property of the adjoining state. Negative impacts entail destruction of property and therefore violate interstate law."[11] In defending themselves, Baden and Bavaria's diplomats and engineers did not contest the right of downstream states to halt projects that caused damage to their land and property. Instead, they disputed the notion that the handful of cuts that had been undertaken between 1817 and 1824 could have caused the flood. They pointed out, quite correctly, that 1824 had been an especially wet year that would have caused flooding whether or not the Tulla Project had begun. They also disputed the long-term implications of the rectification work: Tulla's blueprints, they claimed, called for carefully designed river banks that would continue to allow water to inundate the Rift Valley during flood conditions, and thus not be funneled downstream.

The special commission met nearly a dozen times in 1832 to discuss and evaluate the legal briefs and engineering arguments. But after hearing expert testimony from representatives on both sides, the special commission conceded that it lacked sufficient data to render a verdict. Most troublesome was the lack of consensus among the engineers as to the likely consequences of straightening the river. "Theories were pitted against theories, calculations against calculations," Max Honsell noted in his historical account of the 1824 flood, "and the commission ended the negotiations without reaching agreement on a *single* aspect of the dispute."[12]

Stalemate on the legal front did not automatically have to translate into a full-scale retreat by the Prussia-led forces. Had the downstream states continued to mount a concerted diplomatic initiative against the Tulla plan, they might well have succeeded in influencing subsequent events in a manner that would have provided them with greater protection from upstream flooding. Periodic monitoring would certainly have helped to fill in the missing data so that subsequent generations of engineers and jurists could have assessed the Rhine's changing hydraulic conditions in a more clear-cut manner. But instead of turning up the pressure, Prussia, Hesse, and the Netherlands tacitly accepted the commission's final report as a defeat and stood silently by as the Tulla Project resumed in 1832.

The downstream governments decided not to pursue the flood issue after 1832 for a variety of reasons. To begin with, the anti-Tulla coalition was never very strong. The Dutch government, which played little role in the discussions, was preoccupied with its own rectification projects. The state of Hesse, meanwhile, relied entirely on its chief water engineer, Claus Krönke, for advice, who happened to be a close colleague of Tulla. Even as the special committee deliberated, Krönke was preparing to extend the Tulla Project downstream to the Hesse-Palatinate border. The Prussian government, too, was speaking with two voices: as its diplomats argued the legal case against Baden and Bavaria, its engineers were drilling away the Bingen reef to ease shipping through the Rhenish Slate Mountains, a project that potentially augmented the flood danger farther downstream. The coup de grâce came in 1832, when the Rhine Commission entered the fray. "The general feeling is that the cuts should continue," the Prussian representative bluntly told his government in 1832, after returning from a rancorous meeting that pitted him against all his fellow commissioners.[13] André's broadside was conveniently put on a shelf and forgotten, at least until the frequency of floods began to increase in the late nineteenth century, much as he predicted it would. By then, however, there was little the riparian states could do, other than to reengineer the river even more to try to stay ahead of its increasingly volatile flood patterns.

The second major critic of the Rhine Commission, Robert Lauterborn, focused his concerns on floodplain loss rather than on flooding. Born and raised in Ludwigshafen, home to a gargantuan BASF chemical plant, one of the Rhine's most important factories and most notorious polluters he spent his career investigating the quality of Rhine water for the German states of Baden, Hesse, and the Palatinate. No radical anti-industrialist, Lauterborn recognized that some of the Rhine's floodplain had to be sacrificed to economic development, especially in urban areas. As a biologist, however, he also understood that floodplains play a crucial role in maintaining the health and stability of a river, and throughout his life he strove to keep as much of the Rhine's original habitat intact as possible. "Shielding our water resources from 'the wastes of civilization' is one of the most important aspects of nature protection," he wrote in his memoirs: "This became crystal clear to me early in life as I saw the rate at which all traces of a natural environment were disappearing from the vicinity of my home town as it expanded and grew. Back in those days, one could still find a sufficient number of areas on the outskirts of cities that had not yet been denatured. These regions functioned as preserves in which the whole array of local flora and fauna could be found. It seemed to me that one of the most pressing tasks of any natural scientist was to protect those last remaining open spaces so that succeeding generations would have a chance to experience and enjoy them."[14]

Given his prominence, Lauterborn was often called upon as a government and independent expert to assess the environmental impact of various development schemes. But, as he learned from bitter experience, it was far easier to preserve the Rhine's flora and fauna in paintings and photographs than in reality. The issue of floodplain protection came to a head in 1930 over plans to drain a marshy area at Neuhofen Altrhein, an old river branch that was at the time the largest stretch of undeveloped riverscape in the Ludwigshafen vicinity. The request to drain the marshland came from the personnel at the Water Resources Office of Neustadt, whose task it was to promote economic development in the region, and from the mayor of Altrip, who was also the director of the region's largest brick factory and gravel-removal business and who had the most to gain from the drainage scheme. Because the project involved turning a substantial amount of reclaimed land over to brick production, and because the drainage would cause an estimated 1.2 meter (four-foot) drop in the surrounding water table, state and national authorities became involved, as did Lauterborn.

The legal wrangling over the Neuhofen Altrhein project reveals how stacked the cards were against Lauterborn. It mattered little that there were sound ecological arguments against developing the Neuhofen Altrhein, or that the claims of the pro-development forces were specious. The Altrip mayor, for instance, argued that the region was suffering from an acute shortage of arable land. Lauterborn pointed out that Altrip had been a thriving agricultural and fishing village until the brick industry had settled in the region and bought up most of the farmland for use as loam and gravel pits. Twenty years earlier, there had been 423 hectares (1045 acres) under cultivation in the Altrip region. As of 1930 only 150 hectares remained in the hands of farmers; the rest had been bought by the region's two largest brick and gravel factories.

Unable to make headway, the Water Resources Office played the public hygiene card: the marshes were breeding grounds for waterborne diseases. Altrip, so the claim went, was in the grips of a "mosquito plague," putting the local citizenry at risk. Lauterborn, however, noted that the locals hiked and played in the region every day, much as they had in the past, without any discernible changes in their health. His on-site investigations, moreover, revealed that the local mosquito populations bred in the stagnant water in the abandoned loam pits, not in the slow-flowing water in the marshes. Logically, it was the factories, not the marshes, that ought to have been removed.

Economics, however, trumped ecology: the state and city authorities gave the go-ahead for marsh drainage, and then turned the reclaimed land over to the brick factories—without giving much thought to the fact that they had just expunged the last remaining open space in the region. No doubt the Great Depression, which had struck Germany during the controversy, loomed large in the minds of government leaders as they deliberated. But their decision in favor of the brick factories was anything but exceptional. A laissez faire attitude toward environmental matters was the rule: few and far between were Rhine development plans that did not receive approval in one form or another.[15]

It is always risky to generalize from a single case study, but there are few aspects of the modern Rhine's history that clearly resonate beyond the borders of Europe. Two areas in particular are worth highlighting: the Rhine's free-trade regime and the Rhine engineers' relative insulation from public opinion.

That the Rhine's free-trade regime created a top-down approach to riparian management is hard to dispute. Free trade was encoded in the Congress of Vienna treaty that gave rise to the modern Rhine, and free trade has remained the governing doctrine for nearly two hundred years, the Rhine clauses being the only extant feature of the Vienna settlement. This top-down approach brought many benefits, not least a grand vision that allowed the riparian states to coordinate their projects; it also effectively marginalized all issues that did not fit this vision. Environmental protection was one such issue. The logic of free trade pushed in one and only one direction: maximum use of the river for human production and consumption regardless of the long-term consequences for riverine ecology.

It is tempting to think of the Rhine's free-trade regime (and the Vienna settlement in general) as an antiquated relic of the past, but it ought to be kept in mind that a devil-may-care attitude to the environment was very much in evidence when President George H. W. Bush (United States), Prime Minister Brian Mulroney (Canada), and President Carlos Salinas (Mexico) negotiated the North American Free Trade Agreement (NAFTA) in the early 1990s. It was only after Bill Clinton defeated Bush in 1992 that a side treaty was negotiated—the North American Agreement on Environmental Cooperation (NAAEC)—giving rise to the Commission for Environmental Cooperation, whose purpose it was to ensure that environmental laws remain in force. Even this side agreement has done little if anything to stop enterprises from relocating to regions with lax environmental standards or otherwise eluding enforcement mechanisms. Similar problems continue to bedevil free-trade agreements elsewhere in the world, especially those between countries with high living standards and those with low ones, an imbalance that almost always results in a "race to the bottom" in terms of safeguarding the environment. All too often, transnational environmental protection still has a tacked-on quality to it, much as it did when the Rhine states created the International Commission to Protect the Rhine in 1950 as a counterbalance to the Rhine Commission. Such institutions are almost always too weak to fulfill their assigned role as a counterbalance.

One of the principal reasons that nation-states have so willingly embraced river commissions over the past two centuries is that they serve to defuse the political, economic, social, and cultural rivalries that so often arise along riverbanks. River commissions have served as convenient sites of ad hoc diplomacy, where tensions over shared resources are negotiated and resolved to the mutual benefit of the riparian states. From this perspective, the Rhine Commission has functioned as well as can be expected: the riparian states have managed to cooperate on Rhine projects for most of the past two centuries, despite the brief interruptions during the world wars. There was, however, a flip side to this spirit of cooperation: the riparian states largely turned the river over to bureaucrats and engineers, the two groups most likely to think narrowly about a river's role in a landscape. The Vienna Congress simplified matters by telling the riparian states and their bureaucrats that their job was to improve the Rhine as a navigational and commercial artery, not to protect it as a natural habitat. The Rhine states, in turn, handed the river over to the hydraulic engineers, who "simplified" the river through the magic of geometry. Critics of the various

Rhine rectification projects repeatedly encountered an iron-clad mentality that judged the river's health by the number of ships it transported rather than the number of species it supported. The river's biological viability was thus compromised as much by indifference as by design, by a succession of incremental administrative decisions that sacrificed various stretches of the river until most of the entire river's flora and fauna was depleted.

In today's Europe, it would be all but impossible to rectify a river in the way that the Rhine was rectified a century ago. One needs only to look at the Rhine-Main-Danube canal to see the new thinking: when engineers tried to cut a straight channel through the Altmühl Valley, Bavarian conservation groups protested so loudly and persistently that the bureaucrats were compelled to scrap their blueprints and start anew. The end result was an innovatively constructed canal that looks like a river; indeed, one of the ironies of this canal is that it functions in many ways more like a river than the three rivers it connects. Europe and North America, however, are no longer the places where mammoth engineering projects are taking place, not least because most of its rivers and streams were cement-lined and dammed long ago. Construction projects abound in Asia, Africa, and Latin America. China, for instance, is on the verge of completing the Three Gorges Dam on the upper reaches of the Yangtze River, the largest dam project in the world—one that was planned and executed by Chinese bureaucrats and a worldwide team of engineers with almost no input from the local citizenry.

If the Rhine Commission is regarded as a precursor to the Common Market, then the Rhine story is not a hopeful one: environmental protection was added only as an afterthought, and even in recent years, it has continued to lag behind the dictates of economic development in the race to shape the riverscape. The challenge of effectively integrating environmental considerations into the deliberations of international organizations on issues involving free trade and large-scale development remains a daunting one.

NOTES

1. James C. Scott, *Seeing Like a State: How Certain Schemes to Improve the Human Condition Have Failed* (New Haven, CT: Yale University Press, 1998).

2. I develop this idea more fully in Mark Cioc, *The Rhine: An Eco-Biography, 1815–2000* (Seattle: University of Washington Press, 2002). See also David Blackbourn, *The Conquest of Nature: Water, Landscape, and the Making of Modern Germany* (New York: W. W. Norton, 2006); and Piet N. Nienhuis, *Environmental History of the Rhine-Meuse Delta* (Dordrecht: Springer, 2008).

3. Environmental diplomacy is a small but growing field. See especially Richard Elliot Benedict, *Ozone Diplomacy: New Directions in Safeguarding the*

Planet (Cambridge, MA: Harvard University Press, 1991); Robert Boardman, *International Organization and the Conservation of Nature* (Bloomington: Indiana University Press, 1981); Lee-Anne Broadhead, *International Environmental Politics: The Limits of Green Diplomacy* (Boulder, CO: L. Rienner, 2002); John E. Carroll, ed. *International Environmental Diplomacy: The Management and Resolution of Transfrontier Environmental Problems* (Cambridge: Cambridge University Press, 1988); Pamela S. Chasek, *Earth Negotiations: Analyzing Thirty Years of Environmental Diplomacy* (Tokyo: United Nations Press, 2001); Mark Cioc, *The Game of Conservation: International Treaties to Protect the World's Migratory Animals* (Athens: Ohio University Press, 2009); Robert G. Darst, *Smokestack Diplomacy: Cooperation and Conflict in East-West Politics* (Cambridge, MA: MIT Press, 2001); Kurkpatrick Dorsey, *The Dawn of Conservation Diplomacy: U.S.-Canadian Wildlife Protection Treaties of the Progressive Era* (Seattle: University of Washington Press, 1998); John M. MacKenzie, *The Empire of Nature* (Manchester, UK: University of Manchester, 1988); John McCormick, *Reclaiming Paradise: The Global Environmental Movement* (Bloomington: Indiana University Press, 1989); Philippe Sands, ed., *Greening International Law* (New York: New Press, 1994); Lawrence E. Susskind, *Environmental Diplomacy: Negotiating More Effective Global Agreements* (New York: Oxford University Press, 1994); and Mostafa K. Tolba, *Global Environmental Diplomacy: Negotiating Environmental Agreements for the World, 1973–1992* (Cambridge, MA: MIT Press, 1998).

4. Garrett Hardin, "The Tragedy of the Commons," *Science* 162 (1968): 1243–8.

5. This wording was included in Article 5 of the 1814 Paris Peace Treaty, as cited in *Rheinurkunden: Sammlung zwischenstaatlicher Vereinbarungen, landesrechtlicher Ausführungsverordnungen, und sonstiger wichtiger Urkunden über die Rheinschiffahrt seit 1803*, vol. 1 (Munich: Duncker & Humblot, 1918), 1:36. *Rheinurkunden* is the single best source for documentary and historical information on the Rhine Commission during its first century of existence.

6. Johann Gottfried Tulla first enunciated his dictum in "Bericht an das Großherzogliche Ministerium der auswärtigen Angelegenheiten, vom 1.3. 1812," according to Max Honsell, *Die Korrektion des Oberrheins von der Schweizer Grenze unterhalb Basel bis zur Großherzogthum Hessischen Grenze unterhalb Mannheim* (Karlsruhe: Druck der G. Braun'schen Hofbuchdruckerei, 1885), 5. For more on the history of modern hydraulic engineering, see especially Cesare S. Maffioli, *Out of Galileo: The Science of Waters, 1628–1718* (Rotterdam: Erasmus, 1994); and Norman Smith, *Man and Water: A History of Hydro-Technology* (London: Charles Scribner's Sons, 1975).

7. The best source for Rhine statistical data is the International Commission for the Hydrology of the Rhine Basin (CHR), *Der Rhein unter der Einwirkung des Menschen—Ausbau, Schiffahrt, Wasserwirtschaft* (Lelystad: CHR, 1993).

8. On the most recent Rhine floods, see especially International Commission for the Protection of the Rhine (ICPR), *Rhein-Atlas: Ökologie und Hochwasserschutz* (Koblenz: ICPR, 1998).

9. Ragnar Kinzelbach, ed., *Die Tierwelt des Rheins einst und jetzt: Symposium zum Jubiläum der Rheinischen Naturforschenden Gesellschaft und des Naturhistorischen*

Museums Mainz am 9. November 1984 (Mainz: Naturhistorisches Museum Mainz, 1985), 40.

10. Fritz André, *Bemerkungen über die Rectification des Oberrheins und Schilderung der furchtbaren Folgen, welche dieses Unternehmen für die Bewohner des Mittel- und Unterrheins nach sich ziehen wird* (Hanau: C. J. Edlerschen Buchhandlung, 1828), 17–19.

11. For a complete analysis of the proceedings, see Honsell, *Die Korrektion des Oberrheins*, 12–18 (quote on 12).

12. Ibid., 15 (emphasis in original).

13. Cited by Christoph Bernhardt, "Zeitgenössische Kontroversen über die Umweltfolgen der Oberrheinkorrektion im 19. Jahrhundert," *Zeitschrift für die Geschichte des Oberrheins* (Stuttgart: W. Kohlhammer, 1998), 311.

14. Cited by Jörg Lange, "Robert Lauterborn (1869–1952)—Ein Leben am Rhein," *Lauterbornia*, no. 5 (September 1990): 9–10.

15. Ibid., 10.

2

National Sovereignty, the International Whaling Commission, and the Save the Whales Movement

Kurk Dorsey

In the 1970s and early 1980s, when the Save the Whales movement had become a global phenomenon, it was popular to bash the International Whaling Commission (IWC). Environmentalists argued, in the words of Tom Garrett of Friends of the Earth, that the IWC had been "founded on narrow and entirely inadequate concepts." Moreover, the founders had not provided a budget for research, had accepted a veto clause that any member could exercise, and had created an agency with "no definition of moral responsibility."[1] Garrett asserted that "the IWC stands exposed as a tragic farce, discredited and impotent. The whale stocks it proposed to conserve have been reduced, for the most part, to pathetic remnants." In sum, the IWC had "certainly provided an example of everything that an international organization concerned with 'conservation' should not be."[2] While Garrett was an unusually harsh critic, his belief that the Commission had failed to meet its obligations was widely shared. Even Stuart Blow of the US State Department, which was generally supportive of the Commission, agreed that the IWC "has been, to say the least, an imperfect mechanism for the conservation of whale stocks."[3] Throughout the world, opinions about the IWC ranged between Garrett's and Blow's; not many people suggested that the Commission had been even marginally successful.

Of course the Commission had failed to meet the goals laid out in the pre-amble to the 1946 International Convention on the Regulation of Whaling.[4] Those goals were based on a nearly incompatible pairing of the development of the whaling industry and the conservation of whale stocks that were already under duress. Any whale species worth hunting in the twentieth century was less common by the 1970s than when the treaty was signed. For some species, such as blue and humpback whales, postwar whaling had caused commercial extinction and threatened literal extinction. The whaling industry had boomed and then gone belly up, developing so unsustainably that Britain, one of the leading whaling countries in 1946, dropped out of the business in 1963. Norway, the other leader in 1946, was barely clinging to its whaling tradition in the early 1970s. Only Japan and the Soviet Union still pursued whales in any great numbers, and they were reduced to hunting sperm, sei, and minke whales, smaller species that had been relatively unimportant during the industry's heyday.[5]

Yet, the gnashing of teeth about the failures of IWC in the 1970s was not entirely fair. The veto clause that Garrett had panned was probably necessary for the creation of the Commission in the first place, because several potential members were wary of yielding control of the industry to an international body. Garrett might also have acknowledged that the Commission was unlike anything seen before: a conservation agency with the ability to set rules for the use of a valuable resource on the high seas. Negotiators put scientists in prominent positions on the Commission and emphasized the need to make decisions based on scientific data rather than hunches or tradition. There was no transnational conservation movement in 1946 to pressure governments to protect whales or to think about them in terms of moral responsibility, but there were transnational pangs of hunger reminding people that whale blubber made excellent margarine and that whale meat was better than no meat at all. The original framework of the Commission, then, was meant to protect national sovereignty and create an international agency that would have some authority; but it was established at a time when there was not much of a support network or a tradition of global cooperation on conservation. Only when the global environmental movement of the 1970s emerged did it become possible to redefine living whales as creatures having a value beyond their meat and, in some cases, beyond even sovereignty. By then, the IWC had twenty-five years of tradition and established institutional rules that were holding back efforts to bring about such a redefinition. Despite opposition from the states that still whaled, however, environmentalists were able to mobilize an international movement based on the idea that whales were nearly sacred mammals, and they transformed the IWC into an agency that worked for them rather than for the whalers.

The history of efforts to regulate whaling in the last century illustrates the range of responses by states confronted with a transnational environmental problem. States with direct economic interest in a resource almost always support the idea that there should be some regulatory mechanism to sustain the use of the resource for a long time, but they split on the best way to determine sustainability, how to regulate such a system once created, and, most important, how to determine when there is a crisis that demands a response. The sources of those disagreements are a complex mix of internal and diplomatic factors, such as the relative strength of corporations, a state's commitment to cooperate with other states on specific issues, the power and interests of nongovernmental organizations (NGOs), and cultural factors. States without direct economic interest in the resource can get drawn in for a similar variety of reasons, but without the influence of powerful corporations, they are more easily swayed by cultural understandings of nature and by organized NGOs. At times, NGOs cooperate across borders far better than states do, creating transnational thinking outside state straightjackets. As the history of the IWC demonstrates, members of international environmental organizations have a wide range of interests and perspectives, and bringing them to a common understanding of an issue, much less actually getting them to cooperate to solve problems, is sometimes simply impossible. In short, while it has long been fashionable to critique the IWC as a failure, it might be more accurate to express amazement that it came together in the first place and has survived for more than sixty years.

The Origins of the Whaling Commission

The end of World War II presented both an opportunity and a challenge for those who wanted stricter regulation of whaling on the high seas. Since the 1920s, whaling companies had sent expeditions to the seas around Antarctica in pursuit of blue, fin, and humpback whales. In these international waters, they were largely free to do what they wanted, limited only by the weather, their resources, and on odd occasions their consciences, but not the law. Whalers subscribed to an old maxim: below 40° S latitude no law; below 50° no God. In the 1930s, nations interested in whaling signed two conventions agreeing to limitations on their methods; nonetheless, the take of 40,000 whales in the 1937–1938 season was the largest to that point.[6] The opportunity for stricter regulation came courtesy of naval combat and a new commitment to international leadership in the United States. The former sent most of the world's whaling factory ships to the bottom of the sea, while the latter encouraged US scientists and diplomats to lead a charge to create an international agency that would conserve whales through controlled hunting. The challenge to these efforts, though, was far more pressing, because it came in the form of hunger in Europe and Asia, which had to be addressed immediately. In 1945, British officials were projecting a global fat shortage of two million tons in the first year after the war.[7] Because few whales had been hunted during the war, they seemed to be a logical source of fat to fill the growling void in people's guts.

After the war, the United States worked with Britain and Norway to put together a conference to frame a new whaling regime. The conference, which the Americans had proposed in 1943, did not meet until November 1946, partly because US leaders were wrestling with the appropriate whaling policy and partly because they were simply disorganized and overwhelmed. The three governments broadly agreed that there should be a permanent commission with the authority to make a range of basic decisions about whaling based on a schedule of regulations drawn up at the founding conference. They also agreed that scientists should play an important role in the negotiations and at future meetings because they could provide the necessary insights for conservationist measures. But they also were committed to an active whaling industry operating with as few restraints as possible, both because of the food crisis and because of a general belief that resources were meant to be used.

The November 1946 conference to create a whaling commission was remarkably upbeat. Meetings in London during the previous two years had opened with dire warnings about the global food shortage, but this one opened with the acting US secretary of state Dean Acheson calling for global cooperation in the conservation of whales, which he deemed "wards of the entire world." Indeed, the entire US presentation focused far more on the need to cooperate than on the means or the reason for the problem in the first place. An official from the Interior Department spoke later at the meeting about the possibility that scientifically driven cooperation would create "a more peaceful and happy future for mankind." Such optimism came not only from a reading of America's conservation history, but also from the presence around the conference tables of delegates from every continent, including the surprise last-minute appearance of a Soviet delegation that proved very cooperative.[8]

Among the few points of controversy was one with particularly long-lasting consequences—the objection clause, which would later be known as "the veto." The US proposal had included a two-thirds-majority requirement for the passage of any amendment to the schedule of regulations as well as a mechanism by which any member could file an objection to any approved amendment. Filing such an objection would allow that country to ignore the amendment and continue to abide by the old rules. Once filed, an objection would trigger a period within which any other nation could also file an objection, so in effect, one opponent had the ability to veto an amendment. In committee discussions, the two-thirds supermajority was increased to three-quarters, and the objection scheme was also slightly liberalized. The committee chair, British fisheries official A. T. A. Dobson, found himself fighting against his own committee in the plenary session on the day before Thanksgiving 1946. He argued, with support from the Norwegian delegation, against the objection provision, saying that the supermajority requirement was sufficient to prevent ill-considered rules from being approved. If only one country found an amendment unacceptable, it should acknowledge that its interests were too narrow and adjust them. At most, a dissident nation should have the right to call a special meeting with the goal of persuading the majority to overturn the amendment.⁹

With Britain and Norway, the two most important whaling nations, opposing it, the objection system appeared headed for the depths, but it was rescued by an appeal to national sovereignty. The French and Dutch delegations specifically commended the US draft for protecting states' sovereignty; and it is easy to imagine that the Soviets would not have joined any institution that attempted to exert control over their economy, given their general position on economic cooperation with the West. In a committee meeting, US delegates specifically warned that the US Senate would not consent to the new whaling convention unless it contained the objection clause.¹⁰ Given that the Senate's slothlike movement on certain whaling agreements in the past had been one instigator of the permanent commission, this was a serious threat. The British and Norwegian delegations relented, and neither made much of a fuss about the matter in their reports to their governments.

Many of the delegates in Washington in 1946 thought that they had done something noteworthy. Before the war, diplomatic efforts to control whaling had failed, in large part because Japan had not agreed to participate. Without Japan on board, whaling companies from other nations had been able to disrupt conservation measures by arguing that such measures would make it impossible for them to compete with the Japanese. The previous conventions also had fixed terms; updating the regulations required negotiating a new protocol that had to be ratified by each member state, a process that could take years. All the high seas whaling nations signed the 1946 convention, which in turn established the permanent commission. Members of the new IWC, which first met in 1949, brought both business and scientific expertise to solve problems at their annual meetings. The delegates had established what appeared to be a low quota for whaling in the Antarctic—a 33 percent cut from the peak prewar take—that would be shared by any company that could arrange an expedition, which meant that the whaling convention had protected freedom of the seas, economic opportunities for whalers, and the whales themselves.[11]

Establishing a Working System

In the Commission's first few years, members struggled to reconcile their competing interests. Delegates wrestled with compliance problems in the face of overwhelming evidence that Soviet and Panamanian expeditions were breaking rules as a matter of standard operating procedure.[12] They tried to reconcile scientific warnings about declining whale stocks with the global demand for whale products—a considerable challenge given that policy makers and scientists often had sharply different priorities. Britain's fisheries secretary R. G. R. Wall, in passing some of the blame to the scientists, captured the Commission's dilemma:

> The scientists are not, however, quite unanimous on these matters
> and are in any event chary of expressing downright opinions on the
> basis of existing scientific knowledge and the available catch statis-
> tics; and this attitude, which is natural enough to scientists working
> in a field where basic biological knowledge is very incomplete, makes
> it difficult for the Commissioners of the whaling countries to adopt
> as strong a line as some of us would like with our whaling indus-
> tries, who are themselves inclined to take the short view and feel that
> if they can deploy their existing capital equipment to the maximum
> during its period of life, the longer-term future can be left to take care
> of itself. The whaling industry has always been characterised by a
> gambling habit of mind and tends to look for high profits while they
> can be made rather than for an enduring livelihood.[13]

Commissioners were especially nervous, as the industry was expanding faster than they anticipated. Japan returned in 1946; the Soviets launched plans to add extra vessels in the 1950s; the Dutch, British, and Norwegians upgraded and expanded their fleets; and several other countries appeared on the verge of joining them.[14]

As this expansion continued, the data gathered by the Bureau of International Whaling Statistics in Sandefjord, Norway, showed that it was getting harder each year for whalers to find and catch as many whales as the global quota allowed. The average size of the whales caught was getting smaller each year, and the catch was shifting rapidly from blue whales to smaller fin whales.[15] The optimism about the Commission in 1949 began to erode as early as 1951, as such scientists as Birger Bergersen of Norway and Remington Kellogg of the United States decided that the quota agreed to in 1946 was in fact too high.[16] But they were only able to chip away at the quota, bringing it down by about 6 percent by the middle of the 1950s, in the face of industry demands to raise it. When an American diplomat expressed concern in 1951 that commercial whaling would become unprofitable by 1957, his Norwegian counterpart suggested that he was an optimist.[17]

Environmentalists would later dismiss the IWC as a "whalers' club" because of its inability to significantly lower quotas in the face of the evidence of whale population decline. It could more accurately be called "a club of competing interests." Five active members (Japan, the Netherlands, the Soviet Union, Britain, and Norway) pursued whales on the high seas. Several more, including France, Australia, New Zealand, South Africa, and Canada, had important whaling stations on their shores or in their colonies. The final group consisted of consumers of whale oil, such as the United States, Mexico, and Sweden. Further, although each group had its own interests, within each group there were deep divisions. For instance Norway, Mexico, the United States, and New Zealand could usually be counted on to support basic conservation measures, while Australia and South Africa always kept in mind their dreams of establishing pelagic whaling empires. This made it nearly impossible to assemble a three-quarters majority for any major change to the rules, and with the use of the objection clause by France in 1949 and Australia in 1951 to kill amendments, it quickly became apparent that the Commission was not going to be able to change any country's behavior against its will. W. C. Smith, New Zealand's commissioner, rather bluntly summed up Australia's position in one debate: "It is just the same as all the other countries in the Commission; they are all fighting for their own ends."[18]

To be fair to Australia, not all countries behaved in the same way—some consistently broke the rules. In 1955, amid concerns about cheating, the Commission members opened discussions on a plan to improve the inspection system on board whaling factory ships. The founding convention required each vessel to carry two inspectors from the ship's flag state, but the Panamanian and Soviet inspectors appeared to be unwilling or unable to do their jobs. US secretary of state John Foster Dulles observed that the only fix for the troubled Commission was "an inspection system that relies on a corps of inspectors or observers whose conscientiousness, probity and objectiveness are above suspicion."[19] In 1955, members agreed to an annex to the 1946 convention that required the Commission to establish a system for exchanging inspectors, so that each factory ship would have at least one outsider on board. For seventeen years, the Soviets dragged their feet on implementing the agreement, frequently feigning acceptance and then backing off at the last moment. They finally accepted Japanese inspectors on board their vessels in 1972, which, by remarkable coincidence, was also the first year that they had reported accurate whaling data since 1948.[20] The lack of an adequate inspection system during the peak whaling years had made it almost impossible to tighten the regulations because the nations that obeyed the rules refused to accept further restrictions.

As the IWC struggled along, watching whale populations decline but powerless to stop the obvious cheating by some member states, there was an inevitable crisis that threatened its existence. Scientists' exertions in the mid-1950s to reduce the quota and Soviet and Japanese determination to expand their fleets put pressure on the least-efficient whaling expeditions—the Dutch fleet and a few of the older Norwegian and British ones. In 1959 the Dutch, Norwegians, and Japanese decided that the Commission was dysfunctional, and each nation announced that it was leaving. Each also felt the political pressure to appear to be a good global citizen, however, and announced that it would abide by the hunting rules and set quotas for its whalers, but it was clear that their departure would probably kill the Commission if not reversed.

US officials worked hard to save the IWC in large part because they saw it as the best antidote to the extension of territorial waters and exclusive economic zones by individual nations. In 1946, the Commission's power had been limited to protect national sovereignty; yet barely a decade later US officials concluded that the greater threat to the use of pelagic resources came from nations that desired too much sovereignty. In 1952, Peru, Chile, and Ecuador had boldly declared the waters 200 miles out from their shores to be their exclusive economic zones, including waters surrounding islands that they held far out to sea.[21] If many other nations followed suit, it would seriously harm the interests of the major fishing and whaling countries, most of which were members of the IWC. American diplomats pleaded that the IWC was no longer just about whales but was also about how people would manage marine resources. A successfully functioning commission would prove that cooperative governance of the seas was possible; dissolution of the Commission would only reinforce the idea that only unilateral management was possible.

For a variety of reasons, the Dutch, Norwegians, and Japanese rejoined the Commission, which muddled on. But by 1963, the Dutch and British whaling companies were compelled to close because of a lack of targets and declining prices for whale oil. The Norwegians watched their once proud and prosperous industry sink into rust and unemployment. The Soviets and Japanese took over the field more completely and continued to ignore the scientists' advice. As late as 1964, their stubbornness had US diplomat William Herrington repeating the warning about the Commission's importance in controlling the expansion of sovereignty.[22] The IWC was able to take some steps, such as banning the hunting of remnant stocks of blue and humpback whales in the 1960s. But it appeared to have lost enough relevance that New Zealand withdrew in 1968, believing that it no longer had anything to gain from membership.[23]

The Environmental Movement and the IWC

The IWC was, then, clinging to survival when, in 1971, the first waves of the storm of environmentalism broke over it and made the whale a symbol of a planet in peril. That year, people scattered around the world began to seriously consider a proposal to ban all commercial whaling for ten years as the critical step toward saving whales from extinction. In every country with a whaling industry or tradition, except Japan and the Soviet Union, people rallied to the Save the Whales banner. Even in Norway, there was enough sentiment in favor of ending whaling that the government authorized a yes vote on a ten-year commercial whaling moratorium at the 1972 UN Conference on the Human Environment in Stockholm. Generally, Norwegians were not (and still are not) terribly impressed with the logic behind the argument to end whaling altogether. But throughout much of the world a remarkable transnational movement arose that suggested a new way of thinking about whales and the environment in general. As Tom Garrett of Friends of the Earth noted in 1971, "The bankrupt legal doctrine of *res nullius* (belonging to no one) must be abolished. It must be replaced with a doctrine of *res communis* which takes into account the interconnectedness of all life."[24] While few put it that clearly, many agreed that the unique behavior and biology of whales gave environmentalists an opportunity to rethink how humans used their environment.

The anti-whaling movement started out using a broad range of arguments for ending whaling but gradually coalesced around the idea that whales, because of their complex behavior, should be treated as entities roughly equal to humans. In New Zealand, Canada, and Australia, countries with small but active land stations, opponents of whaling had first to convince their governments to end diplomatic and political support for the industry. First, they made a utilitarian argument that the conservation of whales could lead to their recovery as a human food source. Those who were skeptical of the practicality of that idea sometimes settled for the argument that there was no reason to hunt whales because there was a substitute for every product that came from them. But most powerfully, the anti-whalers argued that the latest research showed that whales were sentient beings with claims to something close to human rights.

The experience of the anti-whaling citizens in New Zealand, Canada, and Australia illustrates how the movement developed globally. New Zealanders had a long history of hunting whales and of finding the process fascinating, not repugnant. When New Zealand pulled out of the IWC in 1968, no one seemed to notice because its whaling industry was fading as the humpback population declined. Then, in 1973, the first trickle of concern started to reach Wellington in the form of letters from individuals seeking to get New Zealand back into the Commission and working to end whaling. The next year, these letters began pouring in, and they demonstrated both a wide range of arguments against whaling and knowledge of new ideas about whales around the world, especially in Australia. By 1978, groups that earlier had been willing to list the waste of resources as one reason to end whaling had focused mainly on morality. A newspaper ad that year featuring a peaceful image of a whale and its calf told New Zealanders that whales "talk to each other over great distances, play and make love too." The sperm whale that had overwhelmed Captain Ahab was now considered "gentle" and "intelligent."[25] In June 1976, New Zealand's government decided to rejoin the IWC and follow the lead of the protestors, even if ministers were not really convinced about the merits of the cause.[26]

In 1970 the Australian whaling industry was still very powerful, and the government had long been committed to protecting its interests. Anti-whaling protests started slowly, with an NGO called Project Jonah first gaining traction in 1972. Protestors tried a range of tactics to redefine whales, from letter-writing campaigns to screening movies about whales in public parks on summer evenings. Their first objective was to work toward a ban on imports of whale products, and then toward shutting down Australia's industry, before finally getting the government to work toward a global ban on commercial whaling, their own "white whale" to be pursued at almost any cost.[27] In 1978, prime minister Malcolm Fraser created an independent inquiry headed by Sir Sydney Frost to review the country's whaling practices and recommend a course of action. Not surprisingly, Sir Sydney's recommendation was to end whaling and support a moratorium.[28] Australia has since been one of the most vocal members of the anti-whaling coalition.

Canada's experience suggested how national governments could struggle with transnational environmental developments. Canada was the birthplace of Greenpeace, one of the most successful transnational environmental organizations.[29] In many ways Greenpeace followed in the footsteps of Project Jonah; yet its larger vision and willingness to confront the whalers on the high seas were distinctive and heralded a more aggressive style that would come to dominate the headlines, if not the movement itself. Canada's government was a follower, though, in the IWC, even as Greenpeace became globally known, in part because Canada was also home to a powerful indigenous people's movement. The government supported the First Nations' rights to hunt whales, even as such hunting became increasingly unpopular among environmentalists and within the IWC. With widespread opposition to commercial whaling at home and a stated commitment to whaling by its First Nations, the Canadian government chose to leave the IWC in 1982 rather than walk the tightrope of condemning some whaling while fighting for other types.

The transformation of whaling policy in each of these nations reflected a global turn against whaling. In 1971, the movement for a ten-year moratorium on commercial whaling got its first big boost with passage of a resolution of endorsement in the US Congress. At the 1972 Stockholm conference, the United States introduced a resolution calling for strengthening the IWC. The Japanese led the opposition because the debate quickly centered on the proposal for a ten-year whaling moratorium. Only three nations abstained from the voting (Japan, Portugal, and South Africa), and none voted no. But fifty-three voted for the moratorium, reinforcing the idea that whales "belong to mankind as a whole, not merely to a single industry or nation," in the words of US delegation chairman Russell Train.[30] And yet, because it was only a recommendation, the resolution had no authority unless the IWC accepted it in its meeting in June. The June meeting would include not only two of the three states that had abstained but also Norway, which vacillated but ultimately voted against it. Those three no votes in the IWC meeting, combined with abstentions by countries that were not wholly opposed to whaling like Australia and Canada, turned out to be enough to defeat the moratorium in the Commission and cement the IWC's reputation as part of the problem.

Norway's no vote in the Commission meeting (after its yes vote at Stockholm) attracted the attention of environmental NGOs, who were unsure what to make of Oslo's shifting position. The International Society for the Protection of Animals (ISPA) requested clarification, which set off a minor tiff within the government between the appalled Ministry of the Environment and the only slightly apologetic Foreign Ministry.[31] The diplomats argued that a vote for a moratorium in the IWC would have been pointless because Japan and the Soviet Union would have objected or, worse, withdrawn from the Commission. After six months of contemplating a response that might reveal information better left unsaid, the Foreign Ministry decided just to ignore the matter. But ISPA was not alone in its interest. Before the 1973 IWC meeting, twelve US environmental NGOs sent a joint letter to Norway's prime minister, Lars Korvald, requesting support for the moratorium.[32] Just to reinforce their point, Michael McCloskey of the

Sierra Club reminded the Norwegian Society for the Conservation of Nature that "public opinion around the world now is keeping a watchful eye on Norway in this matter."[33] With Korvald about to head to Canada, where public opposition to whaling was picking up in part because of a book by Farley Mowat, *A Whale for the Killing*, the Norwegian embassy in Ottawa asked the Foreign Ministry for information to respond to the stacks of protest letters. Caught off guard by the surge in anti-whaling opinion, the Norwegian government had nothing to offer.[34]

The letter from the twelve organizations, including such heavyweights as the National Audubon Society and the Humane Society of the United States, was typical of anti-whaling reasoning in 1973. In calling for Norway to back the moratorium, the letter contained a wide-ranging critique of whaling. First, the authors noted that the explosive harpoon was "cruel," recycling an argument that had been used since the 1950s about the inhumanity of whaling. They then noted that "the future existence of several whale species" was at stake, before pointing out that "the delicate balance of life in the world's oceans" also hung in the balance—and that was just in one sentence.

Next, the authors shifted from ecosystem and biodiversity issues to the rational economic arguments, which only left them in a knot of contradiction. They reminded Korvald that the United States had banned the use of whale products without any adverse effects, because whale products were either not necessities or were easily replaced by something else. But in their next sentence they made the fundamentally contradictory argument that whalers had no right to rob future generations "of this irreplaceable resource." In their conclusion they returned to the idea that whales were "fascinating." The letter suggested both the ways in which members of the Save the Whales movement were determined to try almost anything to stop whaling and the inconsistencies in their logic that would eventually evolve into a strident opposition to all whaling.

This letter was part of a larger campaign indicating the transnational nature of the movement as people from several nations mobilized to write letters not just to the offending governments but to the IWC as well. The organizations prized getting a photo of IWC secretary Dr. Ray Gambell receiving a stack of petitions signed by thousands of people or boxes full of letters of protest. Gambell grinned even as he no doubt wanted to roll his eyes, and the activists got to make the point that they could deliver pressure. There seemed to be an inordinate number of letters from school children, presumably reflecting a link between idealistic teachers and the environmental movement. Organizations in different countries ran newspaper ads that included addresses for the Soviet and Japanese embassies or the IWC headquarters, and others sent out postcards that could be mailed to whaling state governments with just a few strokes of a pen and a stamp.[35]

Proponents of whaling in Japan worked hard to defend the industry in the face of letter campaigns and visits from foreign environmentalists, which sent the signal that they were bad stewards of the planet and greedy to boot. Less pressure was put on Norway because its whaling industry was relatively small. Pressuring the Soviets obviously did not work, so Japan became the focus. The main Japanese response was that they thought of whales from an economic standpoint, while foreigners tended to think of whales from a moral standpoint. In a letter to the Norwegian government calling for solidarity, Japanese whalers wrote: "If it is argued that no whales should be killed for human consumption, it must be asked whether man has any more right to kill any of the other animals whose meat he eats."[36] The Japanese government and whaling association insisted that a moratorium lacked a "scientific rationale," and as proof they pointed to the IWC scientists who had rejected the moratorium as too broad an instrument to work. The Japanese government also tried to coordinate with its remaining whaling brethren to keep the IWC debates focused on science rather than "sentiment or emotion."[37] Cooperation was important because as long as the IWC had just fourteen members, the three whaling countries could find a way to block a moratorium, even if they could never move the agenda away from a moratorium for very long. Working as a united front, they could also persuade other members that they had science on their side and at least garner abstentions, if not no votes on the moratorium. For their part, the Soviets dismissed environmental NGOs, whose "actions are sporadic, contradictory and often based on preconceived notions and obsolete information."[38]

Seeing little benefit from appealing to the whaling states, people in the Save the Whales movement found that emphasizing morality was their best card to mobilize the masses in the nonwhaling states, and the members used that angle to expand the Commission's membership. By 1974, when the IWC adopted a new scheme for regulating whaling based almost entirely on scientific estimates of stock size and harvestability, most leaders of the Save the Whales movement were no longer interested in scientific regulation. The time for that had evaporated. As the decade progressed, people were learning about whales through television nature programs, which often ran in multiple countries; recordings of humpback whales, both on popular albums and as an insert in *National Geographic*; whale-watching, particularly in California and New England; and oddities like giant sealife murals on the sides of buildings around the world. As the historian D. Graham Burnett has shown, research sponsored by the US Navy on whale intelligence and acoustics in the 1950s and 1960s played a critical role in creating the idea that whales were intelligent and special, though this idea undermined the Navy's desire to use cetaceans as weapons.[39] Together, these experiences promoted the idea that whales were gentle giants who lived in harmony with the earth, sang to each other, posed no threat to man, and in fact were role models that humans should respect rather than eat. The abstract whale that was one piece of an ecosystem and therefore had to be managed carefully had become a very concrete entity that was too good to kill. The new attitude was perhaps most tellingly revealed in the schemes to identify humpback whales in the Northwest Atlantic by giving them chipper names like Tulip and Bubbles.[40] No one would harpoon something named Bubbles. This definition of a whale got a public rendition in 1979 when John Denver showed up at the IWC meeting's public comment session and crooned "I Want to Live," with its very emotional lyrics about frolicking humpback whales.[41]

Even with all that, it was hard to get the few remaining whaling states to accept a moratorium. As whaling countries became entrenched in their positions, whaling became a matter of pride, not something that could be bargained away. Congress passed the Pelly and Packwood-Magnuson amendments in the 1970s in part to be able to put sanctions on foreign whalers, but they worked slowly and only if the president was willing to risk damaging the freer-trade principle that the United States had championed since 1944.[42] A boycott targeting Soviet products was an exercise in futility. A look at the makes of cars in any parking lot or the products in any appliance store suggested that boycotts of Japanese goods were not especially effective. In Australia and New Zealand, countries that today are ferociously anti-whaling, Japanese automobiles seem to dominate the market more than ever.[43]

The solution was to change the composition of the Commission. Using the shift from *res nullius* to *res communis* as their justification, environmentalists around the world worked to get their own countries and sometimes other people's countries on the Commission and voting for the moratorium. Former member New Zealand came back in 1976 because of domestic demand to help the whales. Germany, which lost its whaling industry in World War II, responded to similar calls. The Republic of Seychelles joined after conservationists raised the money to pay its membership dues, so that it could appoint a scientist who had been a vocal proponent of the moratorium.[44] By 1982, enough new members that were not whaling states had joined the Commission to win a vote on a ten-year moratorium over the objection of the whalers. The anti-whaling movement had succeeded in globalizing the Commission by expanding its membership from fourteen nations, most of which had a direct connection to whaling in the *res nullius* sense, to more than thirty, most of which connected to whales only in the *res communis* sense. In 2012, membership stood at eighty-nine countries, largely because continued Japanese whaling has kept the Commission relevant, and IWC membership is a sign that a nation takes environmentalism seriously—or conversely, receives Japanese development aid.[45] Now the three-quarters majority requirement has locked in the commercial moratorium, as environmentalists take advantage of the tool that they critiqued in the 1970s and 1980s.

Japan has continued to defy the moratorium. Using the legal cover of Commission-sanctioned scientific research, Japanese whalers have hunted minke whales every year since 1982, and some reports say that other species have found their way into the Japanese market.[46] Opponents argue that the scientific research is just a smoke screen to keep the industry alive, but it is at least as important that the Japanese are making a statement that environmentalists have corrupted the mission of the IWC. They argue that the moratorium cannot be justified by science, which was supposed to be at the core of the Commission's decision making. Occasionally, they have fallen back on charges of racism and memories of their long history of whaling, but none of these claims has been especially helpful in changing external perceptions or finding an end to the dispute. Japanese whalers have long lost the public relations battle abroad, and they have boxed themselves into a difficult political position by making whaling a point of national pride. For instance, the Japan Whaling Association has argued that "attitudes toward animals are a part of national cultures. No nations should try to impose their attitudes on others."[47] They are on much more solid ground when they argue that there are plenty of minkes and that the Commission's founding treaty gives them a clear right to pursue plentiful species.

That the whaling commission held its sixty-fourth annual meeting in 2012 is something of a miracle, given all its past problems. The Commission may hardly seem relevant in a world where some fear that melting ice caps will make worrying about the plight of whales seem like a luxury. Still, the Commission's history can serve as a useful historical example if new treaties are proposed to address greenhouse gas emissions or other rising environmental challenges. The Commission structure was a reasonable solution for the problems that its framers imagined; they just failed to imagine the ways in which the food crisis and weakness of the inspection system would challenge their new rules. Any new environmental treaty is likely to encounter similar unexpected challenges and, hence, will have to include both firm goals and flexible means of attaining them. The IWC's founders hoped that a rational discussion of science would lead to harmonizing national positions, which was obviously too optimistic. Future treaties will have to be based on the best scientific findings; despite flaws in scientific methods, there seems no better alternative to achieve unbiased, long-term thinking about the fate of the planet. The Commission's founders correctly understood that a commission that did not include all whaling states was basically useless, but they probably did not fully comprehend the effects of one weak link on the chain. Similarly, a climate treaty that does not include all the industrial countries will never succeed, even if, miraculously, it were to be ratified widely. The diplomats and scientists who created the whaling commission in 1946 certainly made mistakes, but they were not being narrow or unimaginative.

At the same time, it would be useful to think more critically about the Save the Whales movement, with its big heart and moral intentions, rather than just valorizing it. In his essay "The Trouble with Wilderness," historian William Cronon argued that the elevation of the idea of wilderness to its exalted status made it more difficult to justify protecting areas that were not sublime in their beauty and devoid of people. An environmentalism driven by the desire to save wild places has merits, of course, but it cannot serve as a useful model for how to live ethically on the rest of the planet. Cronon urged American environmentalists to step back from the wilderness fetish and place as much value on the tree in the backyard as the tree in the federally designated wilderness area.[48]

Likewise, one can see a fundamental problem in the Save the Whales movement. Whales have drawn an immeasurable amount of attention, and yet all the energy that has gone into saving them has not produced much of a system to deal with the larger global crisis of fisheries depletion and other problems of marine ecosystems. Of course, it is impossible to be outraged over everything that goes wrong on the planet, and, for ethical and ecological reasons, an ocean with whales is far better than the alternative—sometimes saving the top predator means saving the entire ecosystem. Focusing on whales may well have brought about protection for other species and pieces of the larger marine ecosystem. Concern for dolphins, for instance, led to reforms in tuna fishery. Of course, consumers were urged to eat "dolphin-safe" tuna, not "tuna-safe" tuna, so it was just tuna's good fortune that their habits overlapped those of some dolphins (although it was that association that frequently had helped tuna fishermen find their quarry in the first place). If the most persuasive rationale for protecting whales large and small is that they have a moral status based on their intelligence, behavior, and ability to inspire awe, then pity the dumb fish and simple birds, much less the plankton and krill that sustain nearly everything in the ocean.

NOTES

1. Statement of Tom Garrett, wildlife consultant for Friends of the Earth, before the House Foreign Affairs Subcommittee on International Groups and Organizations, July 26, 1971, 25–7.

2. Transcript of Proceedings, Meeting of the Secretary of State's Advisory Committee on the 1972 U.N. Conference on the Human Environment, Washington

DC, November 22, 1971, 36, United States National Archives, College Park, MD, Record Group 40, General Records of the Department of Commerce, Office of the Secretary, Executive Secretariat's Subject File, 1953–1974, box 270, file Fisheries—Whales, (hereafter RG 40).

3. Stuart Blow, Acting Coordinator of Ocean Affairs, Department of State, statement before the House Foreign Affairs Subcommittee on International Groups and Organizations, July 26, 1971, 9.

4. The text of the convention can be found at http://www.iwcoffice.org/ commission/convention.htm.

5. The best history of the industry is J. N. Tønnessen and A. O. Johnsen, *The History of Modern Whaling* (Berkeley: University of California Press, 1982), see chapter 33 on the collapse of the Antarctic industry.

6. Tønnessen and Johnsen, *History of Modern Whaling.* Chapter 20 deals with the expansion of the 1920s, and chapter 26 covers the peak years of the late 1930s; see p. 333 for a brief chart of whaling data. More-detailed charts can be found with any set of minutes from the 1938 whaling meeting, such as those in Record Group 59, General Records of the Department of State, file 562.8 F3, United States National Archives, College Park, MD (hereafter RG 59).

7. IWC Paper No. 5 (1945), Prospective World Supplies of Oils and Fats, Record Group 25, Department of External Affairs, Whale Notes, 1940–49, vol. 3263, file 6120–40, National Archives of Canada, Ottawa, Ontario.

8. Transcripts of the conference can be found in Record Group 43, Records of International Conferences, Commissions, and Expositions, 43.2.32, Files relating to international whaling, National Archives of the United States, College Park, MD (hereafter RG 43). Acheson's speech is in IWC/11, Minutes of the Opening Session, November 20, 1946, and the Interior official's is in IWC/42, Address of the Honorable C. Girard Davidson, November 26, 1946.

9. The discussions can be found in RG 43, IWC/47, November 27, 1946.

10. G. R. Powles, International Whaling Conference, Appendix to Report, December 9, 1946, File "Whaling—General," AAEG 950, PM 104/6/9/1 pt. 5, Archives New Zealand, Wellington, New Zealand (hereafter ANZ).

11. As an example of the sense of satisfaction with the agreement, see the exchange between Birger Bergersen, April 14, 1947, and Remington Kellogg, May 16, 1947, found in the Smithsonian Institution Archives, RU 7165, International Whaling Conferences and International Whaling Commission, 1930–1968, box 11, file 5 (hereafter SIA).

12. The Panamanian expedition, owned by Aristotle Onassis, operated from 1950 to 1955, and it seemed to be free of any oversight from the Panamanian government, which was not active in the commission. The IWC has the complete dossier on the Onassis expedition at file A 541 Olympic Challenger 1956 Papers, IWC Records, International Whaling Commission, Cambridge, England.

13. R. G. R. Wall, Report on the Sixth Annual Meeting of the International Whaling Commission, August 25, 1954, Records of the Foreign Office, FO 371 110654 G6, file 32, National Archives of the United Kingdom, Kew, London.

14. For details on the expansion, see chapter 29 in Tønnessen and Johnsen, *History of Modern Whaling.*

15. See table in Tønnessen and Johnsen, *History of Modern Whaling,* 488.

16. See, for instance, Bergersen to Kellogg, December 4, 1948, RU 7165, box 5, file 11, SIA.

17. William Morgenstierne to Berger Birgersen, June 15, 1951, Fisheries Department, Fangstkontoret, box 24, 1950–53, file V-F-4-b, Riksarkivet, Oslo, Norway.

18. Smith to Secretary of External Affairs, September 17, 1953, file "Economic Affairs: Commodities, Whaling: General," PM 104/6/9/1 pt. 12, ABHS 950, Acc. W4627, ANZ.

19. Dulles to President Dwight Eisenhower, February 6, 1957, RG 59, 1955–59 Central Decimal file 398.246.

20. Two sources on Soviet whaling conduct are A. V. Yablokov and V. A. Zemsky, eds., *Soviet Antarctic Whaling Data, 1947–1972* (Moscow: Center For Russian Environmental Policy, 1995); and Alfred Berzin, "The Truth about Soviet Whaling," *Marine Fisheries Review* 70, no. 2 (March 2008): 4–59.

21. Robert W. Smith, *Exclusive Economic Zone Claims: An Analysis and Primary Documents* (Dordrecht: Martinus Nijhoff, 1986): 26–7.

22. William Herrington to Ron Wall, October 26, 1964, Records of the Ministry of Agriculture and Fisheries, MAF 209/2354 FGB 22242, National Archives of the United Kingdom.

23. P. J. Brooks to Minister, September 9, 1968, File "Intl Whaling Comm General," PM 104/6/9/3, pt. 1, ACC W4627, ANZ.

24. Statement of Tom Garrett, wildlife consultant for Friends of the Earth, before the House Foreign Affairs Subcommittee on International Groups and Organizations, July 26, 1971, 25–7.

25. Undated clipping, July 1978, PM 104/6/9/1 pt. 25, ANZ.

26. For an example of the reasoning against rejoining, see Treasury Memo on IWC, May 27,1976, PM 104/6/9/2 pt. 6, ANZ.

27. Department of Foreign Affairs Press Release, Canberra, June 21,1973, File 51/2/4, Folder 77, Archives of the Norwegian Foreign Ministry, Oslo (hereafter NFM).

28. The Honorable Sir Sydney Frost, *Whales and Whaling: Vol. I, Report of the Independent Inquiry,* Canberra, 1978, 5.

29. For a history of the organization, see Frank Zelko, "Make It a Green Peace: The History of an International Environmental Organization," PhD diss., University of Kansas, 2003.

30. Russell Train, Report of the United States Delegation to the United Nations Conference on the Human Environment, Stockholm, Sweden, June 5–16, Subject Area IV, p. 5, 1972, RG 40, Office of the Secretary, Executive Secretariat's Subject File, 1953–1974, Box 270, File Fisheries—Whales.

31. Clive Deon (?), ISPA, to Mr. Trygve Bratteli, July 6, 1972, file 51/2/4, folder 76, NFM.

32. John Clark, et al., to The Right Honorable Lars Korvald, May 21, 1973, file 51/2/4, folder 77, NFM.

33. Michael McCloskey, Executive Director, the Sierra Club, to Norges Naturvernforbund, May 23, 1973, file 51/2/4, folder 77, NFM.

34. Jan Nyheim, charge d'Affaires, a. i. Ottawa, to Foreign Ministry, November 21, 1972, file 51/2/4, folder 76, NFM.

35. See, for instance, People's Trust for Endangered Species, file H928, in the records of the IWC.

36. Federation of Marine Products Wholesalers Association (Japan) to Norwegian Commissioner, June 14, 1974, file 51/2/4, folder 79, NFM.

37. Embassy of Japan, Oslo, Re: Whaling, June 14, 1974, file 51/2/4, folder 79, NFM.

38. "Whales—A Rational Approach," *Moscow New Times*, March 1974, file 51/2/4, folder 79, NFM.

39. D. Graham Burnett, *The Sounding of the Whale: Science and Cetaceans in the Twentieth Century* (Chicago: University of Chicago Press, 2012), chap. 7.

40. The author saw Tulip and Bubbles on a whale watch in 2002 and had no desire to harpoon them; more on the naming project can be found at http://whale.wheelock.edu/whalenet-stuff/humpcat_intro.html.

41. *The Express*, July 10, 1979, file K 945, Records of the IWC.

42. "U.S. Sanctions against Japan for Whaling," *American Journal of International Law* 95, no. 1 (Jan. 2001): 149–52.

43. Admittedly, this conclusion is based on the author's unsystematic observations in 2000 and 2008.

44. Conversation with Dr. Ray Gambell, former secretary, IWC, January 2002; Gambell did not name the country or the scientist directly.

45. See for instance "Japan Admits Aid Deals Buy Support for Whaling," *Independent*, July 19, 2001 http://www.independent.co.uk/news/world/asia/japan-adm its-aid-deals-buy-support-for-whaling-678208.html.

46. See, for instance, C. S. Baker and S. R. Palumbi, "Which Whales Are Hunted? A Molecular Genetic Approach to Monitoring Whaling," *Science* 265, no 5178 (September 9, 1994): 1538–9; and V. Lukoschek, et al., "High Proportion of Protected Minke Whales Sold on Japanese Market Is Due to Illegal, Unreported or Unregulated Exploitation," *Animal Conservation* 12, no. 5 (October 2009): 385–95.

47. See "Whaling: Question 3," Japan Whaling Association website: http://www.whaling.jp/english/qa.html. For a recent press account of the role of national pride in shaping Japanese whaling attitudes and policy, see *USA Today*, November 17, 2007, available at http://www.usatoday.com/news/world/2007-11-17-whaling_N.htm.

48. William Cronon, "The Trouble with Wilderness; or, Getting Back to the Wrong Nature," in Cronon, ed., *Uncommon Ground: Rethinking the Human Place in Nature* (New York: Norton, 1995), 69–90.

3

Global Borders and the Fish That Ignore Them

The Cold War Roots of Overfishing

Carmel Finley

When nation-states began expanding their territorial seas during the 1980s, economists predicted a vast transfer of wealth from industrialized fishing countries to poorer countries that were poised to develop their own fisheries. This was especially said to be true for the island nations of Micronesia and Polynesia. Only one-sixth of the 31,000 square kilometer region claimed by the island nations is land; the rest is water, home to one of the world's great fish families, the tuna stocks of the western Pacific. The fish are the only significant economic resource for the islanders. About half the annual global tuna catch, more than 2 million metric tons valued at $3 billion (in 2005 USD), is taken in their waters.

The islanders were not able, however, to create a management structure for their waters until 2004, and, less than a decade later, they were questioning whether there would be enough tuna to feed themselves in the future. To be sure, western Pacific tuna are not as critically depressed as their cousins Atlantic bluefin tuna (*Thunnus thynnus*), which since 1969 have been managed by the International Commission for the Conservation of Atlantic Tuna. Scientists declared overfishing of bluefin an "international disgrace" in 2008, when a review committee concluded that the international community deserved better management of the iconic fish.[1]

Yet Pacific tuna management may be headed in the same direction. The escalating problems with tuna raise troubling questions about the ability of governments to manage transboundary resources so that stocks can be sustained. Kurk Dorsey suggests in chapter 2 of this volume that the intent behind the creation of the International Whaling Commission in 1946 was to protect national sovereignty by creating an international agency with limited authority. An examination of the events that led to the creation of the Western and Central Pacific Fisheries Management Commission in 2004 suggests that the national objectives of the major players—in the case of Pacific tuna, the United States and Japan—have not changed. If anything, the desire to bolster national control has strengthened. Moreover, the delay in establishing the Commission enabled new nations, primarily Taiwan and South Korea, to aggressively expand their high-seas tuna fisheries, greatly complicating management.

The problems of effectively managing Pacific tuna go far back in time. Japan took control of the islands and their fish stocks in 1918; the Americans assumed control after 1945. It took until 1982 for the United Nations Convention on the Law of the Sea (UNCLOS III) to be signed, establishing exclusive economic zones (EEZs) of 200 miles and giving coastal nations control of large areas of the ocean. The convention was not ratified until 1995.[2] One reason for the delay was the refusal by the United States and Japan to recognize the authority of EEZs to regulate tuna. Instead, US officials argued that tuna were "highly migratory" and therefore better regulated by an international commission composed of fishing states. This approach ensured that the United States, as well as Japan, would be part of the management process. A fishery management scheme composed of members of the EEZ, by contrast, would have excluded the big powers.[3] The creation of the special "highly migratory" category denied the island nations unilateral ability to manage the stocks off their coasts. Historian Kimie Hara argues that the Cold War has not ended in the Pacific and that the postwar order imposed in the region reflects American desires to have unfettered access to the world's oceans.[4] This is certainly true when it comes to fishing. Both the United States and Japan have strategic reasons for insisting on access to the fish stocks in the region. By insisting on access for themselves, they opened the door for other nations to expand into the fishery.

Ambiguity over when tuna would come under management created the conditions for what Garrett Hardin called the "tragedy of the commons." Hardin's famous essay did not mention fishing, but fishing has come to be the exemplar of how tragedy is set in motion: there is no incentive to conserve fish so they can be caught by other fishermen (or, more importantly, by the fishermen of other countries, since fishing is a form of property rights).[5] The countries that developed a fishery argue they have a right to continue to participate in the fishery. In the case of the western Pacific tuna, US and Japanese actions ensured they would not only continue to fish in the region but continue to catch most of the fish.

Hardin's notion of tragedy centers on the actions of single individuals choosing to graze cattle on the commons. In applying the analogy to fishing, scholars have invoked the example of a single fisherman choosing to fish, a construction that ignores the deliberate role of governments in financing fishing boats and enforcing policies ensuring the rights of their nationals to fish. The announcement that fish will come under future management ensures a rush of boats into a fishery, anxious to be grandfathered in when a license system is established. The possibility of not being able to fish once management is established removes the incentives to conserve stocks. When it comes to tuna, both Japan and the United States acted to safeguard their self-interest, but much more than just fish was at stake. Both countries have a long history of acting to conserve *access* to high-seas stocks. A cornerstone of US postwar foreign policy was preservation of open seas for American naval vessels—and for American fishing boats. The State Department saw restrictions on where American boats could fish as having the potential to restrict passage through those waters by military vessels.[6] For Japan, access to high-seas resources is not only vital to supplying the nation with food but also a key component in the national economy. Giving up access to waters it has traditionally fished is tied closely to issues of national sovereignty.

Other countries have interest in western Pacific tuna as well. The development of super-low-temperature freezing technology allowed tuna to be frozen at sea and delivered to market in top quality, for use as sashimi, to fish markets around the world. Being able to deliver high-quality fish anywhere in the world allowed companies to build processing plants in low-wage countries such as Thailand, the Philippines, and Indonesia in the early 1980s.[7] One result was a new generation of international corporations with unusually complex marketing systems.[8] These evolve continuously to cope with changes in legal ownership, access, and regional and local responsibility for resource management.

Tuna, the Wandering Fish

Almost 100 million years of evolution lie between an ancient fish like salmon and a modern one like tuna.[9] The fourteen species of *Thunnini* within the family Scombridae evolved over thousands of years to live in the high seas, in the warm waters around the equator. The Scombridae family includes about fifty-eight species of tuna and related fish, such as billfish, bonitos, swordfish, and mackerel. The largest of the species are marlins and bluefin tuna, which can grow to be several hundred pounds. The most commercially important species are skipjack (*Katswonus pelamis*), yellowfin (*Thunnus albacares*), bigeye (*T. obesus*), northern and southern bluefin (*T. thynnus*), and albacore (*T. alalunga*). Bigeye is often marketed under its Japanese name, *ahi*.

Tuna are built to swim fast, migrating thousands of miles a year in the upper layers of the ocean, where the water is warmed by the sun and the wind.[10] The Spanish cleric Fray Martin Sarmiento in 1757 dubbed them "wandering fish."[11] It was not until the twentieth century that people developed the skills and technologies to follow tuna through the oceans. Maritime countries had always taken a few tuna in local fisheries, but they lacked the boats and fishing gear to follow the great fish as they migrated swiftly through the oceans. That changed with the development of steam-powered, then diesel engines, and electronics that allowed the fishermen to see into the ocean below their boats.

After 1869, the start of the Meiji era, Japan aggressively expanded its fisheries, bringing new technology from the West and subsidizing the building of larger boats. The Japanese steadily expanded their fisheries through Southeast Asia, becoming by 1900 the dominant fleet throughout the Philippines, Malaya, and the Dutch East Indies.[12] In 1914, having declared war on Germany, Japan occupied German island possessions in the western Pacific, the Marianas, Palau, Caroline, and Marshall island groups.[13]

A further round of subsidies in 1923 paid for the construction of refrigeration facilities, refrigerated boats, and ice-making facilities. Shipments of canned tuna traveled to New York in subsidized Japanese freighters and were sold for only twenty-two cents a case, just a nickel more than it cost to deliver California-caught tuna to New York.[14] By 1923, Japanese fishing boats were catching 330 million pounds of tuna, worth $3 million, from the waters of the western Pacific islands.[15] Japan was the world's leading fishing nation by 1939, with a network of fisheries throughout the Pacific, Indian, and Atlantic oceans. For the imperialistic Japanese government, fishing was a symbol of Japan's modernization and industrialization. "It is no exaggeration to state that the marine industry symbolizes the spirit of the Rising Sun," wrote an official in a 1939.[16]

With the defeat of Japan at the end of World War II came the dismantling of much of its fishing empire.[17] Some of Japan's most profitable fisheries were taken away, including the tuna fishery off the Marshall, Mariana, and Caroline islands. Some of the first policies announced by the Supreme Commander of the Allied Powers (SCAP) focused on rebuilding Japan's fishing industry, to help feed its starving people.

The fishing fleet was initially confined to a small area around Japan, known as the MacArthur Zone. SCAP commander General Douglas MacArthur ordered three successive large-scale programs to build fishing boats. The world's largest fishing fleet had essentially been rebuilt by January 1947, when SCAP announced that it would not authorize any more boat construction but that older vessels would be modernized.[18] Rebuilding the Japanese fishing fleet was one of the success stories of the American occupation.

SCAP opened a trade office in New York in December 1947, and for the next year small amounts of Japanese canned albacore began entering the American market. The trickle soon turned into a flood, prompting the American fishing industry to seek protection from imports through the use of tariffs. The first SCAP-authorized Japanese expedition to the Marshall, Mariana, and Caroline islands (now called the Mandated Islands) to catch tuna for export to the American market came during the summer of 1949.

The United States and the Triumph of MSY

With the end of World War II, the United States planned an extensive series of naval bases through out the Pacific to maintain a system of air and water transit routes for military uses and to assure access to Asian resources.[19] Part of the plan to transform the Pacific Ocean into an American lake involved attracting a fleet of American tuna boats to the region. The Navy had built a fish processing plant in American Samoa during the war. Between 1945 and 1958, the State Department maneuvered to shape international fisheries policy in a direction that would support the overall US position on the freedom of the seas.

Efforts to expand American fishing deeper into the Pacific were given shape by the enormous energies of one man, Wilbert McLeod Chapman (1910–1970). Chapman had graduated from the University of Washington School of Fisheries in 1937 with a degree in ichthyology. He worked for several state and federal fishery institutions before becoming Curator of Fisheries at the San Francisco Academy of Sciences. In 1943, the Office of Economic Warfare asked him to go the tropical Pacific to conduct a survey to locate fish resources to feed American troops.

Chapman spent eighteen months in the equatorial Pacific and returned with a messianic zeal to develop American fishing, especially in the Japanese tuna grounds in the Mandated Islands. In letter after letter to politicians, scientists, canneries, fishing organizations, and labor groups, Chapman poured out his vision of harvesting tuna in large commercial quantities. Development would require island bases, such as the ones the US Navy was planning for the Mandated Islands. He urged officials and the fishing industry to lose no time in staking an American claim "while the international matters in the Pacific are in a state of flux and while the United States has bargaining power."[20]

Chapman saw American boats moving into the Marquesas Islands and French Oceania, as well as the Marshall, Mariana, and Caroline islands. It might be twenty-five years before the vision would be fully realized, Chapman predicted, but he insisted that "foresight now will secure to us a rich resource in the future."[21] He urged the United States to act before the Soviet Union and Japan, both of which knew how important fisheries development would be, took the lead. Furthermore, Chapman explicitly linked fish to national defense, urging the value of "an American industry strongly developed across the tropical Pacific" and pointing out that the expansion of the fishing industry would serve national security goals.[22] Chapman saw the Pacific as the equivalent of the Great Plains, and tuna as plentiful as buffalo had once been.[23]

> In the tropical Pacific we have won an empire of tremendous size.
> It is an empire of great riches, where the land is as nothing and the
> sea is everything—an empire in which the native people are small
> in number and restricted to small points in its vastness; an empire
> which no other nation save the Japanese covets and which no other
> nation save theirs and ours can cultivate and make produce.[24]

In a 1944 joint resolution, Congress directed the US Fish and Wildlife Service to survey the extent and condition of all marine and freshwater fishery resources, including the "high seas resources in which the U.S. may have interests or rights."[25] Representative Joseph R. Farrington of Hawaii introduced a bill in 1945 providing for the study and development of fisheries in Hawaii. The bill included $500,000 for a vessel that would conduct full-scale oceanographic research.[26]

After 1945, many countries in both the Atlantic and the Pacific oceans chafed at the escalating numbers of boats fishing off their coasts. The oceans were a hodgepodge of territorial claims. The Soviet Union claimed a twelve-mile territorial sea, while Iceland and many Latin American countries claimed up to two hundred miles as their exclusive national preserves. The three-mile territorial sea had been strongly supported by the British Navy, but it had never been widely accepted as a principle of international law.[27] By 1955, ten Latin American countries had declared some sort of expanded jurisdiction, from Mexico's claim of nine miles, to Argentina's and Panama's claiming of the continental shelf, to the 200-mile claims of Chile, Peru, Costa Rica, El Salvador, Honduras, Ecuador, and the Dominican Republic.

Chapman's activism in promoting the industry came as a group of West Coast industry representatives were pushing the State Department to pay more attention to fisheries. They argued that fishing involved international treaties and that the rights of American fisheries had to be protected against territorial claims being made by various nations. In 1948, US Secretary of State George Marshall agreed to create an undersecretary post within the State Department to manage fishery affairs. Chapman was named to the position, and the way was cleared for fisheries science to become a tool of US diplomacy.[28]

After the war, the US government sought the advice and services of scientists, part of a general trend toward greater use of expert advice at the highest levels of policymaking.[29] Science was increasingly used to achieve foreign policy objectives, and scientists were deployed to promote the transfer of Western knowledge and technology to other countries. Science was also a vehicle to promote Western ideas about nature and natural resource management. Federal patronage had a powerful impact on the development of many postwar disciplines, but especially on fisheries science and fisheries management, as well as oceanography.[30]

Chapman arrived at the State Department during the summer of 1948, a critical time for American fisheries. The department was negotiating a treaty with eleven European countries and Canada to regulate the depleted North Atlantic fisheries. Mexico, Peru, and Ecuador were seizing American fishing boats, claiming they were fishing illegally. The problems were a legacy of the 1945 Truman Proclamation, by which the United States claimed the right to establish conservation zones for the protection of fish in the high seas contiguous to US territorial waters if fisheries in the area were fully developed.[31] The United States had never actually established a conservation zone, but it asserted the right to do so.

Mexico adopted a 200-mile territorial water zone two months after the proclamation was issued. Argentina, Chile, Peru and Costa Rica quickly followed suit.[32] With the collapse of the California sardine fishery, American boats were fishing off Latin America, drawing complaints that they were depleting local bait stocks.[33] The Americans argued that there was no scientific proof that baitfish were being overfished.

Six months after arriving in Washington, Chapman introduced the US Policy on High Sea Fisheries, which rested on a scientific construction known as "maximum sustained yield" ([MSY], now known as the "maximum sustainable yield"). MSY had been implied in American fisheries policy from the early days of the US Fish Commission, established in 1871 to manage American fisheries.[34] "The policy of the United States Government regarding fisheries in the high seas is to make possible the maximum production of food from the sea on a sustained basis year after year," Chapman wrote.[35] Within days of introducing the new US policy, Chapman signed a treaty with the Canadians and the Europeans to create the International Commission for North Atlantic Fisheries. A second treaty was signed with Mexico a few days later, and a third with Costa Rica in May 1949, creating Inter-American Tropical Tuna Commission.

Such international commissions became the preferred American model for postwar fisheries management—either bilateral or multilateral agreements, generally with limited regulatory and enforcement authority. Fisheries would be managed to attain MSY. There was no scientific discussion of the appropriateness of the goal; Chapman merely made the decision from his position in the State Department.

The creation of a tuna commission did nothing to ease Latin American complaints about American tuna boats. At a series of meetings starting in Santiago in 1952, the governments of Peru, Ecuador, and Chile began discussing a 200-mile regional zone with their own regional fisheries research organization and controlling passage through their waters. The controversy over fishing and territorial claims escalated sharply in late August 1954, when the illegal whaling ship *Olympia Challenger,* owned by Aristotle Onassis, and its fifteen catcher boats arrived off Peru to challenge the actions taken at Santiago.[36]

The freedom to fish was contested on another front as well. During the 1920s, the League of Nations had tried to broker an agreement to define the width of the territorial sea. They were unable to do so, but they created the International Law Commission (ILC) to study the issues. In 1952 the group recommended the creation of an international framework under the Food and Agriculture Organization (FAO) of the United Nations to come up with regulations to protect fish resources from waste and extermination on the high seas. The recommendations included expanding the territorial sea to six miles.[37]

The State Department opposed any expansion of the territorial sea, arguing that it was not necessary to claim expanded jurisdiction to protect fish stocks. Both the State Department and the Defense Department were worried that restrictions on fishing could lead to restrictions on naval vessels. "At stake in the background, and not immediately apparent, are interests of the U.S. Government transcending mere fishing rights, important as those rights are," State Department attorney John Kissick asserted in a 1955 memo. "These include security, naval, maritime, and air transport, for to the extent that areas of high seas are effectively covered into the jurisdiction of a sovereign state, these interests are adversely affected. It is incumbent upon the United States to take every opportunity to maintain the principle that international law does not require a state to recognize more than three marine miles of territorial waters."[38]

At a conference in Rome in 1955, Chapman and his successor at the State Department, William C. Herrington, persuaded the International Technical Conference for the Conservation of the Living Resources of the Sea to adopt MSY as the basis for international fisheries management. The American position was that fisheries conservation could be achieved only through scientific programs set up by international agreements among the concerned states. Sovereignty beyond three miles was, in this view, not needed.[39] There was no need for an international commission with binding authority under the auspices of the UN. The US delegation to the meeting was instructed to shape the recommendations to the ILC as much as possible to reflect the American political objectives. As Herrington pointed out time and again in State Department memorandums, "It is incumbent upon the United States to take every opportunity to maintain the principle that international law does not require a state to recognize more than three marine miles of territorial waters. Beyond this lie the high seas to which freedom of navigation and fishing for all countries appertains."[40]

MSY is an elegant and seemingly simple construction—to avoid taking more fish than can be sustained by that fish population. But as implemented in the postwar fishery commissions established under US influence, it began to incorporate the idea that fishing would not be restricted while a fishery was being developed. Scientists had to prove that stocks were overfished before fishing could be restricted. This interpretation allowed the world's most developed fishing nations to continue to fish off the waters of smaller countries for another two decades, until countries mobilized to claim expanded territorial limits in the 1970s.

The recommendations from the Rome conference were adopted by the Law Commission in 1956 and later became part of the Law of the Sea negotiations in 1958. The Law Commission's actions established MSY in three realms—as science, as policy, and as law. MSY thus had more to do with advancing political and economic agendas than with conserving fish stocks.[41] British scientist Sidney Holt, who played an important role in the development of MSY, wrote in 1978 that it became institutionalized "in a more absolute and precise role than intended by the biologists who were responsible for its original formation."[42]

Questions about fishing jurisdictions had plagued the State Department (and similar departments in other countries) between 1945 and 1958. But by the time the first of three meetings of the UNCLOS conference began in 1958, other Cold War concerns had overtaken the problems of high-seas fisheries. For most of the next two decades, the United States tried to forestall a third UNCLOS meeting, concerned it could not muster the votes to hold the line on a three-mile sea.[43]

Support for a three-mile limit continued to erode as a large number of factory processing ships expanded throughout the world's oceans. The first, the 280-foot *Fairtry,* built by the British, arrived on the Grand Banks of Newfoundland in 1954.[44] Two years later, the Soviets had built two dozen similar ships. When Soviet processing ships showed up on the east and west coasts of the United States during the early 1960s, their presence increased pressure on Congress to expand the territorial sea. At the same time, American tuna boats escalated their fishing off Latin America.

Congress passed the Fisheries Conservation and Management Act in 1976, creating a 200-mile US EEZ. It may have been forced to give up on the concept of the freedom of the seas, but it took steps to retain its investment in high-seas tuna. The legislation included a provision that defined tuna as a "highly migratory" species, a move designed to make the United States part of any tuna regulatory regime in the western Pacific. The policy indicated American interest in the resource, despite the fact that the tuna were not caught in American waters. Over the following decades, the countries of Latin America and the central and western Pacific were offended by what they viewed as American hypocrisy in maintaining a US interest in tuna, yet denying their claims to jurisdiction over tuna within their 200-mile zones.[45]

Chapman had thought it might take twenty-five years for the American tuna fishery to be developed enough to enter into fishing in the Mandated Islands, and he was right. American boats began entering the western Pacific fishery in the 1970s, driven by declining catch rates and deteriorating relations with Latin American countries. Despite the growing number of American boats fishing the island waters, the United States refused to recognize their claims of expanded jurisdiction until 1988. One factor that prompted the United States to capitulate was that some island countries were starting to establish access agreements with the Soviets. Washington agreed to a five-year treaty and to pay approximately 9 percent of the value of the catch as an access fee.[46]

It was not until 1994 that negotiations began in earnest between the distant fishing nations (especially the United States, Japan, Taiwan, and South Korea) and the island governments about the need for sustainable management of tuna and the development of a tuna industry in the islands. The framework for the Western Central Pacific Fisheries Convention was adopted in 2000. The objective of the convention was to ensure, through effective management, the long-term conservation and sustainable use of the region's fish stocks.[47] The island states themselves built boats during the 1980s, hoping to capitalize on their proximity to the fish and to create local jobs. They entered the fishery at a time when the industry was extremely competitive and the harvesting sector was being squeezed by low prices. Between 2000 and 2007, fishing effort (the measure of how many days are fished) increased by 40 percent.[48]

A brief review of the development of fisheries in the Western and Central Pacific Fishery Commission region reveals a number of efforts to control the rate of fishing and the number of boats. The Commission expressed concern that there were too many boats at its meetings in 2005, 2006, and 2007, as it struggled to achieve consensus on how to implement a 25 percent reduction in the bigeye catch and a 10 percent reduction in yellowfin. Economic studies showed that the fishing effort was substantially above optimal levels, making the fishery less profitable than it could have been.[49] More troublesome was the growing use of highly efficient purse seine nets,[50] which substantially changed the age structure of the stocks, resulting in a lowering of the MSY estimate for yellowfin tuna to 4 million metric tons, down from 4.5 million metric tons.[51] Increasingly, implementation of the fisheries convention was slowed by competing interpretations of the text and uncertainty about the extent to which the islanders would be allowed to increase their purse seine fishery. Residents remain disappointed that they have not commanded a greater share of tuna resources.[52]

The failure in the western and central Pacific is the result of overall shape of modern fisheries management, established in Rome in 1955, on a supposed scientific foundation that had been built on political maneuvering, influenced by Cold War concerns. Fishing could not be restricted until there were signs that stocks were overfished; then regulations could be implemented to slow the catch. Despite the voluminous criticism of the failures of MSY, the pattern established at Rome, and the emphasis on freedom of the seas flowing from the Cold War, continues to be embedded in the legal framework for international fishery commissions, making it more difficult to create fisheries that will operate in a sustainable manner.

In "The Tragedy of the Commons" in 1966, Garrett Hardin argued that some problems had no technical solution. He went on to say that it is not mathematically possible to maximize more than one variable at the same time. Part of the postwar promise of international fishery commissions was that that management would ensure fishing and well as the conservation of fish. Hardin was right that there is a tragedy in the commons, but it is not that fishermen fail to control themselves. It is that postwar policies suggested that governments could have it all: access to stocks for foreign policy reasons, yet also conservation in perpetuity. Such policies are supposed to be balanced among the interests of the government, the fishing industry, the government, and the fish. But by insisting that access to tuna stocks be open, the United States and Japan ensured that management would be contentious, expensive, and very hard on the tuna.

NOTES

1. Report of the Independent Review, International Commission for the Conservation of Atlantic Tunas, PLE-106/2008, http://www.iccat.int/Documents/Meetings/Docs/Comm/PLE-106-ENG.pdf.

2. Michael Pretes and Elizabeth Petersen, "Rethinking Fisheries Policy in the Pacific," *Marine Policy* 28 (2004): 297–309.

3. Christopher J. Carr, "Transformation in the Law Governing Highly Migratory Species: 1970 to the Present," in *Bringing New Law to Ocean Waters,* ed. David D. Caron and Harry N. Scheiber (Berkeley: University of California Press, 2004), 55–94, 61.

4. Kimie Hara, *Cold War Frontiers in the Asia-Pacific: Divided Territories in the San Francisco System* (London and New York: Routledge, 2007), 189.

5. Garrett Hardin, "The Tragedy of the Commons," *Science* 162 (1966): 1243–8.

6. Carmel Finley, *All the Fish in the Sea: Maximum Sustainable Yield and the Failure of Fisheries Management* (Chicago: University of Chicago Press, 2011).

7. Rachel A. Schurman, "Tuna Dreams: Resource Nationalization and the Pacific Islanders' Tuna Industry," *Development and Change* 29 (1998): 107–36, 122.

8. Gary D. Sharp, "Tuna Oceanography: An Applied Science," in *Tuna: Physiology, Ecology, and Evolution,* ed. Barbara A. Block and E. Donald Stevens (New York: Academic Press, 2001), 345–89, 354.

9. Keith E. Korsmeyer and Heidi Dewar, "Tuna Metabolism and Energetics," in Stevens and Block, *Tuna,* 35–78, 38.

10. James Joseph, Witold Klawe, and Pat Murphy, *Tuna and Billfish: Fish without a Country* (La Jolla, CA: Inter-America Tropical Tuna Commission, 1988), 3.

11. Ibid., 1.

12. Albert W. C. T. Herre, "Japanese Fisheries and Fish Supplies" *Far Eastern Survey* 12, no. 10 (1943), 101.

13. W. G. Beasley, *Japanese Imperialism, 1894–1945* (Oxford: Clarendon Press, 1987), 154.

14. R. S. Mathieson, "The Japanese Salmon Fisheries: A Geographical Appraisal," *Economic Geography* 34, no. 4 (1958), 352–61.

15. Kamakichi Kishinouye, "Contributions to the Comparative Study of the So-Called Scombroid Fishes" *Journal of the College of Agriculture, Imperial University of Tokyo* 3 (1923): 293–475.

16. Yonematu Mitsui, "Japan's Solid Strength in Present Emergency Traced to Achievements of Fisheries Science," *Japan's Fisheries Industry 1939* (Tokyo: Japan Times and Mail, 1939) 7.

17. Edwin O. Reischauer, *The United States and Japan* (Cambridge, MA: Harvard University Press, 1950), 241.

18. Press Conference Notes, July 16, 1947, US National Archives and Research Administration, RG 331, box 8866.

19. Melvyn P. Leffler, "National Security and US Foreign Policy," in *Origins of the Cold War: An International History,* ed. Melvyn P. Leffler and David S. Painter (New York and London: Routledge, 1994), 15–53, 37.

20. Chapman to Magnuson, April 4, 1945, papers of Senator Warren Magnuson, 3181–3. box 50. folder 21, University of Washington Special Collections.

21. Ibid.

22. Wilbert McLeod Chapman, "Tuna in the Mandated Islands," *Far Eastern Survey* 15, no. 20 (October 9, 1945): 317–9.

23. Wilbert Chapman, *Tuna Fisherman Magazine* vol. 1, no. 2, January, 1948.

24. Wilbert Chapman, "The Wealth of the Oceans," *The Scientific Monthly*, vol. 65, no. 3, (1947), 192–7.

25. Harry N. Scheiber, "Pacific Ocean Resources, Science, and Law of the Sea: Wilbert M. Chapman and the Pacific Fisheries, 1945–70," *Ecology Law Quarterly* vol. 13, no. 38 (1986), 394.

26. Ibid, 407.

27. Hannes Jonsson, *Friends in Conflict: The Anglo-Icelandic Cod Wars and the Law of the Sea,* (London: C. Hurst and Company, 1982), 34.

28. George Marshall to Thor Tollefson, April 23, 1948, box 4, folder 23, papers of Miller Freeman, University of Washington Special Collections.

29. Ronald E. Doel, "Scientists as Policymakers, Advisers, and Intelligence Agents: Linking Contemporary Diplomatic History with the History of Contemporary Science," in *The Historiography of Contemporary Science and Technology*, ed. Thomas Soderqvist (Amsterdam: Harwood Academic, 1997), 215–44.

30. Kristine Harper, *Weather by the Numbers: The Genesis of Modern Meteorology* (Cambridge, MA: MIT Press, 2008); John Krige, *American Hegemony and the Postwar Reconstruction of Science in Europe* (Cambridge, MA: MIT Press, 2006); Stuart W. Leslie, *The Cold War and American Science* (New York: Columbia University Press, 1993); Naomi and Ronald Rainger Oreskes, "Science and Security before the Atomic Bomb: The Loyalty Case of Harold U. Sverdrup," *Studies in the History and Philosophy of Modern Physics* 31, no. 3 (2000): 309–69; Jacob Darwin Hamblin, *Oceanographers and the Cold War: Disciples of Marine Science* (Seattle: University of Washington Press, 2005).

31. Ann Hollick, *U.S. Foreign Policy and the Law of the Sea,* (Princeton, NJ: Princeton University Press, 1981), 20.

32. Charles B. Selak Jr., "Recent Developments in High Seas Fisheries Jurisdiction under the Presidential Proclamation of 1945," *American Journal of International Law* 44, no. 4 (1950): 673.

33. Arthur M. McEvoy, *The Fisherman's Problem: Ecology and Law in the California Fisheries* (Cambridge: Cambridge University Press, 1986).

34. Dean Conrad Allard, Jr., *Spencer Fullerton Baird and the U.S. Fish Commission.* (New York: Arno Press, 1978), 316.

35. Wilbert Chapman, "United States Policy on High Seas Fisheries," January 16, 1949, *Department of State Bulletin*, vol. 20, 67–80.

36. Nicholas Fraser, Philip Jacobson, Mark Ottoway and Lewis Chester, *Aristotle Onassis* (London: Times Newspaper Limited, 1977), 123.

37. FAO Archives, RG 61-1, series C3, November 23, 1953.

38. Kissick to Herrington, memorandum, June 7, 1955, RG 59, box 1538, National Archives.

39. Kissick to W. F. Looney, February 8, 1955, box 1539, folder 398.245-SA6-755,National Archives and Research Administration, RG 59.

40. State Department memorandum, William Herrington to Harold Kissick, June 7, 1955, box 1539, folder 398, 245-SA6–755, National Archives and Research Administration, RG 59.

41. Carmel Finley, "The Social Construction of Fishing, 1949," *Ecology and Society* 14, no. 1, available at http://www.ecologyandsociety.org/vol14/iss1/art6/.

42. Sidney Holt and L. M. Talbot, "New principles for the conservation of wild living resources," *Wildlife Monographs* 59 (1978): 25.

43. Carr, "Transformation in the Law," 58.

44. William W. Warner, *Distant Water: The Fate of the North Atlantic Fisherman,* (Boston: Little, Brown and Company, 1978), 36.

45. Carr, "Transformation in the Law," 69.

46. Schurman, "Tuna Dreams," 113.

47. Quenton Hanich and Martin Tsamenyi, "Managing Fisheries and Corruption in the Pacific Islands Region," *Marine Policy* 33 (2009): 386–92, 384.

48. Adam Langley, Andrew Wright, Glenn Hurry, John Hampton, Transform Aqorua, and Len Rodwell, "Slow Steps towards Management of the World's Largest Tuna Fishery," *Marine Policy* 33 (2009): 271–9, 274.

49. Hanich and Tsamenyi, "Managing Fisheries," 387.

50. Purse seining uses a net that closes at the top and bottom, creating a circle, or purse, that traps schooling fish such as anchovies and tunas.

51. Langley, "Slow Steps," 275.

52. Hannah Parris, "Tuna Dreams and Tuna Realities: Defining the Term 'Maximizing Economic Returns from the Tuna Fisheries' in Six Pacific Island Nations," *Marine Policy* 34 (2010): 105–13, 107.

4

Making Parks out of Making Wars

Transnational Nature Conservation and Environmental Diplomacy in the Twenty-First Century

Greg Bankoff

An unexpected outcome of the global environmental crisis is the emergence of conservation as an important aspect of conflict resolution. Of course, there has always been a strong historical association between conflict and resources, with disagreements arising over their use and ownership. Some even claim that these disputes are set to become more commonplace, fueled by diminishing supplies and unequal distribution. They speak of a violent breakdown of the civil and international order or raise frightening images of anarchic armies of boy-soldiers laying waste to towns and the countryside alike.[1] It is somewhat surprising to find, then, that the new connotation is not about resource use and war but about nature conservation and peace. Peace parks, nature conservation areas that abut or cross international frontiers, are trumpeted by such prestigious institutions and personages as the United Nations Environment Programme (UNEP), the International Union for Conservation of Nature (IUCN), and former South African president Nelson Mandela as a new panacea to solve long-standing internal conflicts, such as on the Korean peninsula; to create bridges between peoples and cultures, as on Cyprus; or to herald in the new African Renaissance. In 2004, the Nobel Peace Prize was awarded for the first time to an environmental activist. Wangari Muta Maathai was recognized for her lifetime's work linking nature conservation to civil rights and peace in her native East Africa.

"Nature abhors fixed boundary lines and sudden transition," wrote Ellen Semple in her seminal article on geographical boundaries in 1907. Not content to limit her remarks to the physical world, she spoke of "debatable zones" of varying and fluctuating width, depopulated "artificial border wastes" that separate contending states or peoples.[2] Scholarly interest in boundaries since Semple's time has largely reflected the wider political and international concerns of the moment, peaking during the interwar decades and then again in the 1990s after the breakup of the Soviet Union and the expansion of the European Union. Debates over nationalism and identity have given way to questions about the territoriality of the state and the importance of boundary-producing practices.[3] Insufficient attention, however, has been paid to border ecosystems and the environmental effects of transboundary movements whether by air, water, or land. State borders may be artificial constructs, but they are etched across the natural landscape and thus inextricably intertwine environmental matters with political, diplomatic, and military ones. As Semple so succinctly observed over a century ago, "Wars belong to borders."[4]

Many of these seemingly disparate threads come together in the concept of the "peace park," two or more designated protected areas in countries sharing a common border and cooperating in some fashion on biodiversity conservation. Over the past few decades, these border conservation zones have gone from relative insignificance to occupying a prominent place in matters of international conflict resolution. But are peace parks the novel phenomena they are claimed to be? What, if any, implications do they have for environmental diplomacy in the twenty-first century? Are conflict and conservation really such strange bedfellows? This chapter explores the provenance of peace parks from the perspective of Paul Martin and Christine Szuter's notion of "war zones" and "game sinks," areas where frequent conflict ensures game is plentiful or where the lack of hostilities encourages human predation.[5] War or its constant threat, though detrimental to the well-being and survival of humans, is not always so for other species, which may actually benefit from conflict situations. Frontier zones or border areas have historically been (or have been made to be) liminal spaces, often contested ones, with transitory or sparse human populations, no-man's lands where wildlife prospers because it is only periodically disturbed by human activities. From this perspective, then, peace parks appear to be only a more formalized and recent manifestation of a phenomenon long established by time and practice.

The Peace Park Phenomenon

There is no single definition of what constitutes a peace park. The term has come to mean different things to different people depending on their perspective and purpose: a route to sustainable development, a space for environmental conservation, or a means of conflict resolution. Thus the World Bank employs the terms "transfrontier conservation area" (TFCA) or "transboundary conservation area" (TBCA) to describe "relatively large areas that straddle frontiers between two or more countries and cover large scale natural systems encompassing one or more protected areas."[6] The IUCN, on the other hand, favors the term "transboundary protected area" (TBPA) to signify land or sea that falls within its various protected-management categories for which the formal and informal mechanisms of cross-boundary cooperation have been developed. The term "protected areas," however, has its critics, who express concern over its historical connotation as "places from which local people are excluded," especially in southern Africa.[7] More recently, the IUCN made a scalar distinction between protected areas, TBPAs, and parks for peace, indicating, respectively: land and/or sea dedicated to the protection and maintenance of biological diversity and natural/cultural resources within a national boundary; such land and/or sea straddling or adjacent to one or more international boundaries; and land and/or sea of the latter sort dedicated especially "to the promotion of peace and co-operation."[8] It is particularly in this last respect that peace parks are heralded by international agencies, national politicians, and environmental groups as an important new international avenue for resolving intractable conflicts.

Part of the definitional problem surrounding peace parks and their utility in diplomacy stems from the different degrees of protection afforded to various areas and the diverse ways peace parks extend across international borders, usually compounded by unresolved issues of sovereignty and long histories of conflict. As early as 1990, the IUCN proposed a ninefold typology to cover all existing combinations and even some that have not yet been realized, such as deep ocean sites and objects in outer space. These categories range from national parks of such unusual scenic, historical, archaeological, or biological value that they can be considered the "common heritage of mankind" to the entire continent of Antarctica with its disputed sovereignty and broad international interests.[9]

A more practical guide to the different types of TBPAs was developed at a workshop organized jointly by the IUCN and the International Tropical Timber Organization in Ubon Ratchathani, Thailand, in February 2003. Five categories of parks were identified: two or more contiguous protected areas across a national boundary; a cluster of protected areas and the intervening land; a cluster of separated protected areas without intervening land; a transborder area including proposed protected areas; and a protected area in one country aided by sympathetic land use over the border.[10] Saleem Ali, a Pakistani-American academic who studies environmental conflicts, points out that some scholars reject categories that limit peace parks to adjoining border zones, noting that such qualifications exclude island states and possibly other more remote areas, and so limit their usefulness in diplomacy.[11]

The uncertainty surrounding what exactly constitutes a peace park, however, has done little to dampen the enthusiasm with which the concept is embraced. The first, and in many ways still the only, truly collaboratively managed TBPA, is the Waterton-Glacier International Peace Park established in 1932 on the border between the United States and Canada. The boundary between these two nations is the longest undefended international frontier in the world, running in a straight line across the continent for 8892 kilometers, cutting through lakes and rivers, passing over mountain ranges, splitting valleys, and crossing through the migration routes and home ranges of wild animals. As such, the park epitomizes both the arbitrariness and artificiality of most international frontiers and the need to cooperate across such boundaries to better effect conservation. It was also very much a local initiative, first proposed by Rotarians in towns on both the US and Canadian sides of the border.[12] An attempt to establish a border park was pioneered by Poland and Czechoslovakia in 1925; however, its implementation was delayed until after 1948.[13] Research on the early history of transboundary parks is sketchy, but there were an estimated fifty-nine such areas in 1988.[14]

Since then, many new parks have been commissioned. Between 1988 and 2007, the number of transboundary park complexes and individual protected areas rose from 59 to 227 and from 70 to 3043, respectively (see table 4.1).[15] This represents a per annum average growth over the twenty-year period of 6.97 percent in the number of complexes and a massive 20.76 percent in the number of protected areas, a clear indication of their growing international importance. Only a small part of this increase can be explained in terms of the emergence of new states. The number of such parks is increasing across the globe; the phenomenon is not just confined to areas in the developing world.[16] One of the most recent and ambitious proposals is the 6800-kilometer greenbelt along the former Iron Curtain running the length of Europe from the Barents Sea in the north to the Mediterranean and Black Sea in the south.[17]

TABLE 4.1. Number of Transboundary Protected Areas 1988–2007[18]

Year	Park Complexes	Individual Protected Areas	Number of Countries
1988	59	70	65
1997	136	488	98
2001	169	666	113
2005	188	818	N/A
2007	227	3043	N/A

FIGURE 4.1 Rocky Mountain goat (*Oreamnos americanus*), Waterton-Glacier
International Peace Park.
Photo courtesy of Alexia Rogers-Wright.

As of 2007, an estimated 4,626,601.85 square kilometers of land lie within
designated TBPAs.[19]

Practitioners and scholars mainly try to explain this increase in terms of the
how and not the why. Thus the IUCN enumerates the benefits that peace parks
confer, namely: promoting international cooperation at all levels; enhancing
environmental protection across ecosystems; facilitating more effective research;
bringing economic benefit to local and national economies; and ensuring better
cross-border control of problems such as fire, pests, pollution, and illicit activities. By creating opportunities for enhanced transboundary cooperation in the
management of the parks, it is argued that they also serve diplomatic ends and
"encourage friendship and reduce tension in border regions."[20]

David McDowell, director-general of the IUCN, made this link even more
explicit in his opening remarks to the Parks for Peace Conference held in South
Africa in 1997, in which he explained the involvement of his organization in
conflict-resolution projects through peace parks. He identified increasingly
scarce natural resources located in ecosystems that are arbitrarily divided by
national borders as the likely primary source of international insecurity and
conflict in the twenty-first century, and added that forms of transboundary
cooperation usually work, fully justifying their label as "peace parks."[21] Saleem
Ali argues that the formation of conservation zones and the sharing of physical
space can "build and sustain peace."[22]

Leaving aside the practicalities of how peace parks work to enhance the environment and to resolve conflicts, looking at why transboundary areas are effective sheds light on their supposed novelty. In fact, the concept of peace parks is a very old and tested one that has been around for as long as there have been complex human societies. One of the ways in which communities historically maintained concord and avoided unnecessary friction was to leave a little space between them. Debunking the myth of what he calls "the peaceful savage," a trope first popularized in Voltaire's *Candide* (1759), archaeologist Lawrence Keeley argues that warfare in traditional societies was far from a relatively harmless, ritualistic game of formalized aggression. Instead, he shows it to have been universally brutal, sanguinary, ruthless, and destructive. War was characterized by high mortality rates and punctuated by frequent massacres. Nor was it a curse whose origin dates from contact with "civilization." The frequency of hostilities led to the creation of no-man's lands, as settlements nearest to an enemy relocated to escape persistent raiding. These "buffer zones" have been reported in Africa, North America, South America, and Oceania, with widths varying according to population density. Where population densities were highest, such as in highland New Guinea, they might only be measured in hundreds of meters, but in more-extensively populated areas of the Americas or on the dry savannas of Africa, they might stretch for tens of kilometers. Keeley goes on to explain how such buffer zones came to function ecologically as game and timber preserves, since it was often too risky to use them for hunting or resource extraction.[23]

The notion that endemic warfare between neighboring antagonistic parties creates buffer zones rich in wildlife and relatively untouched by human activities finds its greatest proponents in the work of paleoecologists Paul Martin and Christine Szuter. Using the diaries of Meriwether Lewis and William Clark, who led the first American overland crossing to the Pacific Ocean and back between 1804 and 1806, Martin and Szuter extrapolated the type and quantity of big game killed during the expedition. From these records, they were able to differentiate areas where animals were plentiful, which they termed "war zones," from those where wildlife was scarce, which they called "game sinks." Big game was abundant in the war zones because these buffer zones between hostile communities were largely free from exploitation by surrounding tribes. On the other hand, wildlife was scarce in the game sinks because of continuous predation. Martin and Szuter argued that, rather than animal population densities in a given area reflecting the changing productivity of habitats, the quantity of game in an area was dependent on human usage. Thus, North American native populations, wittingly or not, practiced a form of nature conservation.[24] While critics allege that such zones were never as distinct as Martin and Szuter claim and that they paid insufficient attention to the role of habitat in their analyses, the central notion about conservation and buffer zones remains intact.[25]

If pre-state buffer zones between warring parties that act as unofficial conservation sanctuaries are well established, the question is whether such zones disappeared during modern state formation; or, if they persisted, did they manifest themselves under slightly different guises? In fact, their continuance is plainly evident in the aggregate nature of what came to constitute the colonial state over much of the developing world. It can still be detected, too, in the fabric of more established nation-states, such as in Europe, if viewed through the prism of their composite historical fractures. In their modern manifestation, these buffer zones are designated as game reserves, conservation areas, national parks, and the like.

The historical link between buffer zones and contemporary protected areas is perhaps more apparent in states whose national territories are largely the product of arbitrary boundaries drawn up by former colonial bureaucrats. Most of these modern nation-states, in fact, are aggregates of lands laid claim to by metropolitan powers and subsequently ordered according to the dictates of perceived racial and social priorities. Internal boundaries in these states, therefore, were just as significant (and contentious) as external ones, more so in some respects since the latter were the product of negotiation, while the former were simply imposed, by force if necessary.

The history of game reserves and national parks in southern Africa illustrates the relationship between buffer zones and the evolution of conservation areas. Namibia, formerly *Deutsch-Südwestafrika* and South West Africa, has one of the highest percentages of land area under state conservation protection in Africa.[26] Conservation measures were first introduced in 1892 when the territory was under German colonial rule, initially to curb excessive hunting of large mammals, and then to establish game reserves. Besides offering some protection to game animals, the reserves "formed buffer zones" and served the twin goals of separating white commercial farmers in the central and southern regions from black subsidence farmers in the north. They also served as a socio-veterinary barrier preventing the spread of livestock diseases, especially rinderpest.[27] During South Africa's colonial period (1915–1990), the local Bushmen population of Hai//om were excluded from the principal game reserve of Etosha, and parks in protected areas in general became intimately associated with apartheid policies.[28]

Across the border in the Republic of South Africa proper, conservation areas were first established in 1898 with the foundation of the Sabi Game Reserve, which was merged into the Kruger National Park when it opened in 1926. As of 2012, South Africa had twenty national parks covering over three and three-quarter million hectares of land, many of which abut what were extremely sensitive international borders during the liberation struggles from the 1960s through the 1990s. Many of these large, thinly populated areas proved to be of strategic value to both sides in the conflict, ideal for infiltration by guerillas based in neighboring states as well as for operations by internal security forces. In the final years of the apartheid government in South Africa, diehard white supremacists even tried to carve out separate white "homelands" by redeploying elite counterinsurgency troops as game wardens to patrol the national parks.[29]

In both the Namibian and South African examples, what are now regarded as conservation areas were equally conceived of as or functioned like buffer or "war" zones, separating antagonistic or hostile parties. Even in the longer-established states of Western Europe, many national parks or protected areas still lie along or adjoin past fractures, even if some of these are now well embedded within the body of the modern nation-state. The creation of national parks in Great Britain, ironically, was the product of wartime exigencies and what one of its early pioneers called the suspension of "the normal British mechanisms for ensuring inaction."[30] A government report in 1945 led to the passage of the National Parks and Access to the Countryside Act in 1949 and to the establishment of a series of national nature reserves.[31] Two of the resulting thirteen national parks adjoin the old historic frontiers that comprise the constituent states of the current nation. The 405 square miles of the Northumberland National Park designated in 1956 encompasses the Cheviot Hills and stretches from Hadrian's Wall to the Scottish border, the landscape of innumerable clashes between ancient rivals and consequently very sparsely populated. Even today, the park only encloses a population of 2200, or less than two persons per square kilometer. Further south, along the Welsh-English border, the 520 square miles of the Brecon Beacons National Park marks a border zone dating back to Norman and even Roman times.[32] More tentatively, a case might even be made that some of the other national parks reflect even older historical divisions within Britain, dating back to the Anglo-Saxon kingdoms of the ninth century: Exmoor and Dartmoor in the old Wessex-Cornish border lands, and the Lake District and Yorkshire Dales on the Strathclyde and Northumbrian divide. The retention of such buffer zones, rich in flora and fauna and with low population densities, only serves to mark the enduring legacy of past enmities.

The link between conservation and buffer zones is perhaps most apparent in the history of military frontier zones in France. An ordinance in 1776 designated the country's border areas as a special *zone frontière* in which militarily sensitive sites such as roads, bridges, waterways, shore lines, marshes, ponds, and forests were entrusted to a special commission. The exact limits of this zone were fixed in 1853 and extended around the entire length of the nation's borders and coastlines, as well as land frontiers. Initially, only limited forest clearing to meet local agricultural and industrial needs was permitted within this zone. However, even this restricted felling so alarmed the military high command that in 1855 all logging was made subject to official authorization. A distinction, however, was subsequently drawn between the whole frontier zone and the land frontiers that were designated *zones reserves*, and where forest clearing was even more strictly supervised. After France's crushing defeat in the Franco-Prussian War of 1870–1871, the frontier zone on the east was extended to include the Seine estuary and an area south of Paris, including the capital city. Within this zone, the military reserved the final say over all forest clearing. In particular, the army rigorously constrained forest clearing along France's frontier with Germany, well into the twentieth century.[33]

Making Parks out of Making Wars

In light of the previous examples, is the recent emergence of peace parks on international relations and conflict resolution agendas novel? While further research is necessary on both the prevalence and extent of these buffer zones across time and cultures and their association with nature conservation, they appear to be a useful expedient in maintaining cordial relations between peoples and for avoiding accidental causes of friction. In fact, modern theoretical models of peace building seem to support such conjectures. Raul Lejano, an academic and advisor to the World Health Organization, shows how both rational game theory based on calculations of individual utility and institutional models of care that encourage relationship-building facilitate conflict resolution. Territory, in his view, is not purely a source of contention leading to war, as usually portrayed, but can also foster cooperation and mutual understanding.[34] That is, he believes that maintaining a buffer zone between neighbors or administering an area jointly promotes peaceful outcomes.

Modern-day buffer zones are surprisingly commonplace even in a world of well-defined international borders. They are the result of hundreds of wars, international and civil, waged during the twentieth century.[35] Many of these no-man's lands may be limited in scope and temporary in nature, with little long-term effect on conservation, but all of them effectively function as unofficial sanctuaries. The 80-kilometer-long UN-patrolled Area of Separation between Syria and Israel in the Golan Heights has existed since 1974 but, because it does not bar nonmilitary activities, has had only limited impact on promoting wildlife and preserving habitats.[36] On the other hand, the more recent

15-kilometer-wide demilitarized zone declared along a 240-kilometer-long stretch of the Kuwaiti-Iraqi border as a result of the 1990 Gulf War encloses a diverse desert ecosystem and effectively extends protection to representative populations of 52 percent of Kuwait's fauna, some of which are regionally or globally threatened. The history of the latter zone shows how even a limited temporal suspension of normal human activities can have surprisingly beneficial environmental results.[37]

Other military buffer zones, however, have become semipermanent features of the local topography. There are places where human activities are more circumscribed or prohibited altogether. The so-called Green Line that separates Greek and Turkish Cypriots splits the Mediterranean island in two along a 180-kilometer-long divide that varies in width from twenty kilometers to a mere three meters at its narrowest stretch, and even runs through the center of the capital city, Nicosia. Until 2003, there was no movement across this border, and rare and endangered species have been observed within its confines, including the Cyprus moufflon (*Ovis ammon orientalis*), an archaic and nearly extinct species of sheep, and two varieties of sea turtles. The caretta-caretta (*Sini kaplumbagasi*) and chelonia-mydas (*Yesil kaplumbaga*) have returned to lay their eggs on the island's northern beaches around the former holiday resort of Varosha, now a ghost town.[38]

Another buffer of somewhat different provenance, though still military in conception, is the Panama Canal Zone. The canal, completed in 1903, remained under sole US or joint US and Panamanian military control until 1999. Its 1432 square kilometers extended the entire length of the canal and included an area five miles (8.1 kilometers) wide extending on each side from the center of the waterway and the two artificial lakes that supply the locks. The zone lies within one of twenty-five recognized world biodiversity hotspots and includes six globally significant bird areas as well as significant stands of lowland tropical moist forest.[39] Ironically, the withdrawal of the US military has exposed one of the world's richest remaining terrestrial biotas to the exigencies of development.[40]

Nowhere is this unforeseen "peace dividend" of military confrontation more apparent than in the Korean demilitarized zone (DMZ). The legacy of the armistice signed at Panmunjom on July 27, 1953, the DMZ and the parallel Civilian Controlled Area (CCA) on the southern side, encloses an area of 2276 square kilometers that has been protected from virtually all human activity for the past fifty years or where any human activities have been severely limited.[41] Running continuously from east to west for 248 kilometers across the center of the Korean peninsula, the zone encompasses a nearly complete cross-section of habitats that includes the rocky east coast, a densely forested mountainous spine, a portion of the central lowlands, and the marshy basin and inter-tidal mudflats where the Imjin and Han rivers debouch into the Yellow Sea.[42]

The DMZ represents one of the world's largest unintentional wildlife reserves, a breeding ground for migratory birds and a sanctuary for many endangered species.[43] So inviolate is the zone to human presence that most assessments of wildlife are based on surveys conducted over the past forty years by scientists in the CCA, which is fully under the control of the Republic of Korea.[44] Even these appraisals, however, give some indication of the overwhelming biological richness of the area, with as many as 1597 plant, 66 mammal, hundreds of bird, and almost 100 fish species noted. In all, 67 percent of all species found in Korea are located in the DMZ, some of which survive only there.[45] There have even been anecdotal sightings of the Siberian tiger (*Panthera tigris altaicia*), not officially recorded in the peninsula since 1923.[46] However, the birdlife has come to characterize the biotic wealth inadvertently conserved in this buffer zone between two opposing armies. The DMZ provides the winter nesting ground for two of the world's most endangered birds, the majestic red-crowned and white-necked cranes (respectively, *Grus japonensis* and *Grus vipio*). About 150 individuals of the former winter in the zone's wetlands, though they have all but disappeared from the rest of the peninsula, while the latter descend every autumn to the area surrounding the truce village of Panmunjom, whose abandoned paddy fields provide them with a much sought-after and increasingly rare habitat.[47]

The preservation of the DMZ's unique biosphere and the treasures it harbors is a dividend of war. Its survival has depended on the continuation of the Cold War in the Korean peninsula long after it has thawed nearly everywhere else. Ironically, the DMZ's future as a wildlife refuge is threatened by peace.[48] It has been proposed that this sanctuary be formalized, and the military buffer zone converted into a TBCA, making parks, so to speak, out of making wars.[49] In one sense, the peace parks of today are simply the war zones of yesteryear, and peace negotiations merge seamlessly with environmental diplomacy.

Peace Parks, Environmental Diplomacy, and Peoples

While there are many proposals to transform military buffer zones into TBPAs, very few have been realized. One that has successfully integrated conservation measures with conflict resolution is in the Cordillera del Cóndor mountain range between Peru and Ecuador. The border dispute between these two nations dates back to Spanish colonial times and focuses on whether the territory of what is now Ecuador extends into the lands east of the Central Cordillera.

Agreement on the frontier was reached in 1942 at Rio de Janeiro, and a border commission was established to supervise its demarcation. The withdrawal of Ecuador from the commission's work in 1948 left a 78-kilometer stretch of the southeastern border unmarked for the next fifty years and led to armed conflicts in 1981 and in 1995, during the three-week-long Cenepa War.[50]

The disputed territory includes the cloud forests of the Cordillera del Cóndor, an area of exceptional biodiversity that has one of the highest concentrations of vascular plants on earth as well as several rare or endangered endemic species of bird.[51] The dispute was only finally settled after international conservation groups persuaded hawkish army officers of the significance of the region's rich biodiversity and the instrumental use of conservation in conflict resolution. In the Declaration of Brasilia of November 1997, the governments of Peru and Ecuador agreed on a number of outstanding issues, including commerce and navigation, measures to promote development, and mutual security. The completion of the outstanding frontier demarcation, however, proved more intractable. Military tensions arose again in 1998 before a final peace treaty, the Itamaraty Accords, was signed that October. As part of this agreement, both parties designated the disputed area for conservation purposes, and national parks were established on either side of the international frontier. Since 2004, moreover, Ecuador and Peru have consolidated their amicable relations by expanding protected areas and incorporating adjacent reserves and intervening lands into the newly created El Condor-Kutukú Conservation Corridor.[52]

The Cordillera del Cóndor is hailed as a test case in how environmental diplomacy can employ conservation to resolve conflict. Its success has greatly helped move the peace park agenda forward.[53] Another project well advanced in this respect is southern Africa's so-called superpark, the Great Limpopo Transfrontier Park (GLTP). Agreement on this park was reached in December 2002, though the idea had first been mooted as early as the 1940s.[54] The jointly managed area that is envisaged includes not only the previously mentioned South African Kruger National Park but also the Gaza province of Mozambique and the Gonarezhou National Park in Zimbabwe. Together, this park will encompass 100,000 square kilometers, an area larger than Portugal and roughly one-third the size of Germany. Again, the park has its origins in protracted border conflicts that were only finally resolved with the end of apartheid in South Africa and the conclusion of the civil war in Mozambique.[55] The GLTP has stalled somewhat in recent years as a result of the implosion of Zimbabwe and her neighbors' continuing suspicion of South African motives.[56] Similar proposals for peace parks, albeit on a less ambitious scale, have been suggested for every major past or ongoing conflict zone across the globe, including the Mesopotamian marshes between Iran and Iraq, Afghanistan, the Siachen

Glacier in northern Kashmir (Pakistan-India), West Africa (Liberia, Guinea, and the Ivory Coast), the Great Lakes Region of Africa, and Indochina, to name only the most obvious.[57]

Border lands, however, are not and probably never have been completely unoccupied. The buffer or war zones stocked with wildlife and with only a transient human presence were models, correct, perhaps, in principle but rarely if ever actualities on the ground. In truth, these in-between lands were never devoid of border peoples in the past and are certainly not uninhabited in the present—even if until recently they have often been treated as such or, worse, on occasion, forcibly emptied to make them so.

The place of people in nature and therefore in conservation remains a contested issue and one that has changed over the decades. Initially, concern over the "protection" of nature was quite narrowly circumscribed and focused on the establishment of national parks and game reserves, and on the active manipulation of the size and movement of mammal populations, especially herbivores and large carnivores.[58] Use of the natural resources by the local inhabitants was restricted and increasingly prohibited. Where colonial or neocolonial rule prevailed, the policy was usually one of outright exclusion.

In Africa, the rights of indigenous peoples were regularly suppressed in order to protect big-game wildlife and to economically exploit the continent's natural resources.[59] In Namibia, for example, the first game reserves were proclaimed in 1907 through the expropriation of tribal lands.[60] Similarly, the establishment of some national parks in the United States has been directly associated with adverse policies toward Native Americans.[61] Even as the concept of conservation continued to evolve after 1940 to include the "rational" utilization of natural resources, the policy of excluding local people from such areas was not lifted. It was still very much a vital force during the IUCN workshop on TBPAs held in Vancouver in October 1988, where border parks were spoken of as helping countries "maintain an uninhabited buffer zone" and assisting in "controlling the spread of diseases," sentiments entirely consistent with former colonial discourses.[62]

Already, though, this vision of national parks as "protected paradises" or "fortresses under siege" requiring an "essentially militaristic defense strategy" to keep them free of people has come under increasing scrutiny, if, for no other reason, than that such a policy might ironically threaten their long-term viability.[63] The presence and even the rights of local indigenous populations have not only been recognized but their involvement in the formulation of policy and the management of parks has increasingly been deemed "essential."

Many communities or subnational groups living on the borders between countries have been divided by arbitrarily drawn political frontiers separating families and peoples. Not only have governments and international conservation agencies increasingly accepted the need for cooperation of local peoples in the running of transboundary parks but their potential role in conflict resolution has also been duly acknowledged.[64] Thus the 8500 or so Achuar people, whose ancestral lands straddle the border between Ecuador and Peru, are seen as vital to the future success of the Cordillera del Cóndor peace park.[65] In southern Africa, the Shangaan and other transnational ethnic groups are seen as "bringing down the fences" between the countries involved in the GLTP. Indeed, the GLTP is cast as part of the African Renaissance, reasserting cultural ties and social exchanges between peoples who have been separated by colonial divisions.[66] That is, people whose existence until recently was denied, whose presence was unwanted, and whose activities were prohibited have been converted in a short space of time into the guardians of wildlife, the custodians of the forests, and stewards of the peace!

Needless to say, this transformation of local people from relative invisibility into the full glare of international diplomacy has not been effected without comment. First, some argue that the new rhetoric only thinly disguises a continuing Western discourse about "good" and "bad" natives. The former are those who live up to Conservation International, the World Wildlife Fund, and similar international and national agencies' deeply held notions about living in a state of "purity," with its requisite degree of "primitivism" and "simplicity."[67] Others simply argue that the current people-oriented approaches to protecting the world's biologically richest areas are failing and that these ecosystems are degenerating apace, often at the hands of their supposed protectors, the indigenous inhabitants. They advocate a renewed emphasis on protection through strict enforcement policies and the exclusion of all human activities.[68]

Old Story, New Diplomacy

Peace parks, then, according to this narrative, are a very old story, one that counsels retaining a certain amount of space between peoples of different cultures, traditions, and languages as conducive to the maintenance of good relations. That such buffer zones should also be wild places, the preserve of game and forest, is simply and literally in the proper nature of things. There is, therefore, no necessary conflict between war zones, TBPAs, and environmental conservation.

There are countless examples of wildernesses that were either maintained or even created as defensive barriers to mark the space between hostile or antagonistic parties. Between the fourteenth and seventeenth centuries, Russian tsars preserved a wide strip of forest for defensive purposes along their southern borders, felling trees so as to create an impenetrable barrier to enemy cavalry, stretching thousands of kilometers in length. Parts of this forest can still be seen today in the Tula region.[69] The Northern Song emperors of China (960–1127), emulating a defensive strategy of even earlier dynasties, planted a dense network of Chinese, or lacework, elm (*Ulmus parvifolia*), called "the elm palisades" (*yusai*), along China's northern borders to create a buffer zone between themselves and the pastoral peoples of the Steppe. These trees grow to heights of up to eighteen meters and, when closely planted, form thickets of broad pendulous branches that prove difficult for cavalry to penetrate.[70]

The idea behind today's peace parks seems surprisingly similar to that behind yesteryear's buffer zones. They are located in much the same sort of geographical spaces, and many also run along or through ecotones, transition zones where mountains meet the plains, forests turn into grasslands, or fields become swamps—areas of rich biodiversity created by adjacent and distinctly different habitats. Flora and fauna are known to flourish in such places. In extreme cases, such as in Tsarist Russia or Song China, humans have even engineered such edge habitats. On other occasions, these zones were primarily defined by human conflict in which hostile or competing groups found it expedient to conserve nature as a defensive measure.

This historical comparison, however, only goes so far. It may be an old story, but today's diplomacy is, in fact, new. Peace parks purposely set out to profit from breakdowns in human relations to try and enhance the natural world, just as "disaster diplomacy" takes advantage of major upsets in the natural world to try and resolve intractable human conflicts.[71] It is new, too, because contemporary international politics diverge significantly from interstate relations in the past. In particular, today's peace parks force us to rethink the nature of national borders, implying instead of sole sovereignty, forms of undifferentiated, multiple, even shifting frontiers. Of course, this idea is not altogether new either and may herald a return to the older notion of borders described by Helen Semple as transition zones of indeterminate width and shifting location. In fact, this development is already happening. As of March 2009, the Italian parliament is studying legislation on redrawing its Alpine frontier with Switzerland, which runs across glaciers that have moved in recent decades as a result of global warming. The idea is that in the future the border will be described as "mobile." Perhaps, in fact, the whole idea of a fixed, immutable frontier and all the problems that implies is only an historical aberration associated with the rise of the nation or colonial state over the last few hundred years, and all that is happening now is a return to concepts of boundaries that have existed between human societies for millennia. Modern diplomacy may only belatedly be taking due cognizance of prior forms of interstate and polity relations.

NOTES

1. Robert Kaplan, "The Coming Anarchy," *Atlantic Monthly* 273, no. 2 (1994): 44–77; Thomas Homer-Dixon, *Environment, Scarcity, and Violence* (Princeton, NJ: Princeton University Press, 1999).

2. Ellen Semple, "Geographical Boundaries: I," *Bulletin of the American Geographical Society* 39, no. 7 (1907): 385, 389, 394.

3. David Newman and Anssi Paasi, "Fences and Neighbours in the Postmodern World: Boundary Narratives in Political Geography," *Progress in Human Geography* 22, no. 2 (1998): 186–207.

4. Semple, "Geographical Boundaries: I," 387.

5. Paul Martin and Christine Szuter, "War Zones and Game Sinks in Lewis and Clark's West," *Conservation Biology* 13, no. 1 (1999): 36–45.

6. *Mozambique: Transfrontier Conservation Areas Pilot and Institutional Strengthening Project* (Washington, DC: World Bank, Agriculture and Environment Division, Africa Region, 1996), 5.

7. Adrian Phillips, "Parks for Peace: Preface," in *Parks for Peace* (Cape Town: Conference Proceedings, International Conference on Transboundary Protected Areas as a Vehicle for International Co-operation, September 16–18, 1997), v.

8. Trevor Sandwich et al., *Transboundary Protected Areas for Peace and Co-operation* (Lavenham, UK: IUCN Publications, 2001), 3.

9. Richard McNeil, "International Parks for Peace," in *Parks on the Borderline: Experience in Transfrontier Conservation*, ed. Jim Thorsell (Gland and Cambridge: IUCN Publications, 1990), 29–32.

10. Further discussion of this typology and examples are given on Global Transboundary Protected Areas Network website, http://www.tbpa.net/issues_04.htm.

11. Saleem Ali, "Introduction: A Natural Connection between Ecology and Peace," in *Peace Parks: Conservation and Conflict Resolution*, ed. Saleem Ali (Cambridge and London: MIT Press, 2007), 8.

12. Bernard Lieff and Gil Lusk, "Transfrontier Cooperation between Canada and the USA: Waterton-Glacier International Peace Park," in *Parks on the Borderline: Experience in Transfrontier Conservation*, ed. Jim Thorsell (Gland and Cambridge, IUCN Publications, 1990), 39–49; Susan Hines, "Can Parks Promote International Peace?" *Landscape Architecture* 98, no. 3 (2008): 40.

13. Jim Thorsell and Jeremy Harrison, "Parks That Promote Peace: A Global Inventory of the Transfrontier Nature Reserves," in *Parks on the Borderline: Experience in Transfrontier Conservation*, ed. Jim Thorsell (Gland and Cambridge, 1990), 5. On the 1925 proposal, see Walery Goetel, "The Great Program of Poland and Czechoslovakia for National Parks," *Zoological Society Bulletin* 28, no.2 (1923): 27–36.

14. Thorsell and Harrison, "Parks That Promote Peace," 4.

15. For a country-by-country list of the UNEP-WCMC Transboundary Protected Areas in 2007, see http://www.tbpa.net/docs/pdfs/2007_UNEP-WCMC_Global_List_of_Transboundary_Protected%20Areas.pdf.

16. Dorothy Zbicz and Michael Green, "Status of the World's Tranfrontier Protected Areas," in *Parks for Peace* (Cape Town: Conference Proceedings, International Conference on Transboundary Protected Areas as a Vehicle for International Co-operation, Sept. 16–18, 1997), 201–33.

17. Jan Cerovsky, "Transfrontier Protected Areas along the Former 'Iron Curtain' in Europe," in ibid., 117–20.

18. Sources: Jim Thorsell and Jeremy Harrison, "Parks that Promote Peace: A Global Inventory of the Transfrontier Nature Reserves," in *Parks on the Borderline: Experience in Transfrontier Conservation*, ed. Jim Thorsell (Gland and Cambridge, 1990), 3; Dorothy Zbicz, "Crossing International Boundaries in Park Management: A Survey of Transboundary Cooperation," in *Crossing Boundaries in Park Managmenet: Proceedings of the 11th Conference on Research and Resource Management in Parks and on Public Lands*, ed. David Harmon (Hancock: George Wright Society, 2001), 198; Dorothy Zbicz, "Imposing Transboundary Conservation: Cooperation between Internationally Adjoining Protected Areas," *Journal of Sustainable Forestry* 17, no. 1–2 (2003): 24; UNEP-WCMC, "United Nations Environment Programme-World Conservation Monitoring Centre Transboundary Protected Area Inventory—2007," http://www.tbpa.net/tpa_inventory.html.

19. UNEP-WCMC, "Transboundary Protected Areas in 2007."

20. Sandwich et al., *Transboundary Protected Areas*, 7.

21. David McDowell, "Opening Remarks by IUCN Director General," in *Parks for Peace* (Cape Town: Conference Proceedings, International Conference on Transboundary Protected Areas as a Vehicle for International Co-operation, Sept. 16–18, 1997), 24.

22. Ali, "Introduction," 1.

23. Lawrence Keeley, *War before Civilization: The Myth of the Peaceful Savage* (Oxford and New York: Oxford University Press, 1996), 111–12, 198.

24. Martin and Szuter, "War Zones and Game Sinks."

25. R. Lee Lyman and Steve Wolverton, "The Late Prehistoric-Early Historic Game Sink in the Northwest United States," *Conservation Biology* 16, no. 1 (2002): 73–85; Paul Martin and Christine Szuter, "Game Parks before and after Lewis and Clark: Reply to Lyman and Wolverton," *Conservation Biology* 16, no. 1 (2002): 244–7.

26. Altogether, Namibia has twenty-one parks and other protected areas accounting for some 114,080 sq. km, or 13.8 percent, of its national territory. Phoebe Barnard et al., "Extending the Namibian Protected Area Network to Safeguard Hotspots of Endemism and Diversity," *Biodiversity and Conservation* 7 (1998): 532.

27. Herbert Schneider, *Animal Health and Veterinary Medicine in Namibia* (Windhoek: Agrivet, 1994); Amy Schoeman, "Conservation in Namibia: Laying the Foundation," *Namibia Environment* 1 (1996): 6–13; Barnard et al., "Extending the Namibian Protected Area Network," 532.

28. Barnard et al., "Extending the Namibian Protected Area Network;" Ute Dieckmann, "'The Vast White Place': A History of the Etosha National Park in Namibia and the Hai//om," *Nomadic Peoples* 5, no. 2 (2001): 125–53.

29. Stephen Ellis, "Of Elephants and Men: Politics and Nature Conservation in South Africa," *Journal of Southern African Studies* 20, no. 1 (1994): 54–55, 65.

30. Max E. Nicholson, *The Environmental Revolution* (London: Hodder and Stoughton, 1970), 158.

31. John Sheail, "Nature Reserves, National Parks, and Post-war Reconstruction, in Britain," *Environmental Conservation* 11, no.1 (1984): 29–34; John Sheail, "War and the Development of Nature Conservation in Britain," *Journal of Environmental Management* 44 (1995): 267–83.

32. For details on the parks, see Northumberland National Park, http://www. northumberlandnationalpark.org.uk/; see also Brecon Beacons National Park, http:// www.breconbeacons.org/.

33. François Reitel, "Le Rôle de l'Armée dans la Conservation des Forêts," in *Forêt et Guerre*, ed. Andrée Corvol and Jean-Paul Amat (Paris: Éditions L'Harmattan, 1994), 49–57.

34. Raul Lejano, "Theorizing Peace Parks: Two Models of Collective Action," *Journal of Peace Research* 43, no. 5 (2006): 563–81. On the probability of territorial disputes leading to military conflict, see John Vasquez and Marie Henehen, "Territorial Disputes and the Probability of War, 1816–1992," *Journal of Peace Research* 38, no. 2 (2001): 123–38.

35. Arthur Westing, "Protected Natural Areas and the Military," *Environmental Conservation* 19, no. 4 (1992): 343.

36. Dan Lindley, "UNDOF: Operational Analysis and Lessons Learned," *Defense and Security Analysis* 20, no. 2 (2004): 153–64.

37. Fozia Alsdirawi and Muna Faraj, "Establishing a Transboundary Peace Park in the Demilitarised Zone (DMZ) on the Kuwaiti/Iraqi Borders," *Parks* 14, no. 1 (2004): 48–55. World War II had a considerable impact on fisheries in the Western Pacific as virtually all deep-sea fishing and whaling came to an end. William Tsutsui, "Landscapes in the Dark Valley: Towards an Environmental History of Wartime Japan," in *Natural Enemy, Natural Ally: Toward an Environmental History of War*, ed. Richard Tucker and Edmund Russell (Corvallis: Oregon State University Press, 2004), 206–27.

38. Anna Grichting, "From Military Buffers to Transboundary Peace Parks: The Case of Korea and Cyprus" (paper presented at the Parks, Peace and Partnerships Conference, Waterton Lakes National Park, Alberta, Canada, September 9–12, 2007).

39. Norman Myers et al., "Biodiversity Hotspots for Conservation Priorities," *Nature* 403 (2000): 853–8.

40. W. Douglas Robinson et al., "Distribution of Bird Diversity in a Vulnerable Neotropical Landscape," *Conservation Biology* 18, no. 2 (2004): 510–18.

41. Kwi-Gon Kim and Dong-Gil Cho, "Status and Ecological Resource Value of the Republic of Korea's De-militarized Zone," *Landscape and Ecological Engineering* 1 (2005): 4.

42. Colin Poole, "The Gift of a No-Man's-Land," *BBC Wildlife* 9, no. 9 (1991): 636; Lisa Brady, "Life in the DMZ: Turning a Diplomatic Failure into an Environmental Success," *Diplomatic History* 32, no. 4 (2008): 585.

43. The DMZ's only rival is the 2826 square kilometer Exclusion Zone straddling the Ukrainian and Belarusian frontier that surrounds the site of the world's worst nuclear accident at Chernobyl in 1986. The human population was evacuated, effectively creating a "nuclear sanctuary." Mary Mycio, *Wormwood Forest: A Natural History of Chernobyl* (Washington, DC: Joseph Henry Press, 2005), 99–126.

44. Ke-Chung Kim, "Preserving Biodiversity in Korea's Demilitarized Zone," *Science* 278, no. 5336 (1997): 242–3.

45. Hall Healy, "Korean Demilitarized Zone Peace and Nature Park (paper presented at the parks, peace and partnerships conference, Waterton Lakes National Park, Alberta, Canada, Sept. 9–12, 2007).

46. Kwi-Gon Kim, *A Study on the Feasibility as well as an Operational Strategy to Develop DMZ Transboundary Biosphere Reserve between DPR Korea and Republic of Korea* (Jakarta: research report submitted to UNESCO, 2001), 5–6.

47. George Archibald, "Cranes over Panmunjom: How Korea's Demilitarized Zone Became a Lush Wildlife Sanctuary," *International Wildlife* 94, no. 4 (1975): 19–21; Bertel Bruun, "Birds, Bombs and Borders," *Explorers Journal* 59 (December 1981): 158–9; Poole, "The Gift of a No-Man's-Land," 636–7.

48. Arthur Westing, "A Transfrontier Reserve for Peace and Nature on the Korean Peninsula," *International Environmental Affairs* 10, no. 1 (1998): 8–17; Healy, "Korean Demilitarized Zone"; Brady, "Life in the DMZ."

49. Ke-Chung Kim, "Preserving Korea's Demilitarized Corridor for Conservation: A Green Approach to Conflict Resolution," in *Peace Parks: Conservation and Conflict Resolution*, ed. Saleem Ali (Cambridge and London: MIT Press, 2007), 239–59.

50. Goetz Schuerholz and Samuel Sangüeza Pardo, "Removing Colonial Barriers for the Benefit of the Indigenous Achuar People of Peru and Ecuador through Conservation Efforts" (paper presented at the parks, peace and partnerships conference, Waterton Lakes National Park, Alberta, Canada, Sept. 9–12, 2007).

51. Hines, "Can Parks Promote International Peace?" 43. The area is the sole remaining habitat to several birds listed on the 2008 IUCN's Red List of threatened species: Cinnamon-breasted Tody-tyrant (*Hemitriccus cinnamomeipectus*), Orange-throated Tanager (*Wetmorethraupis sterrhopteron*), Long-whiskered Owlet (*Xenoglaux loweryi*), Royal Sunangel (*Heliangelus regalis*), Ash-throated Antwren (*Herpsilochmus parkeri*) and Ochre-fronted Antpitta (*Grallaricula ochraceifrons*).

52. Ali, "Introduction," 9–10; Hines, "Can Parks Promote International Peace?" 43–4.

53. Ali, "Introduction," 10.

54. Sir Robert McIlwaine proposed the idea of a continuous game sanctuary crossing from Southern Rhodesia to Bechuanaland in 1943. Rosaleen Duffy, "The Environmental Challenge to the Nation-State: Superparks and National Parks Policy in Zimbabwe," *Journal of Southern African Studies* 23, no. 3 (1997): 443.

55. Anna Spenceley and Michael Schoon, "Peace Parks as Social Ecological Systems: Testing Environmental Resilience in Southern Africa," in *Peace Parks: Conservation and Conflict Resolution*, ed. Saleem Ali (Cambridge and London: MIT Press, 2007), 83–104.

56. Marloes van Amerom and Bram Büscher, "Peace Parks in Southern Africa: Bringers of an African Renaissance?" *Journal of Modern African Studies* 43, no. 2 (2005): 169–71.

57. Thomas Dillon, "Parks, Peace and Progress: A Forum for Transboundary Conservation in Indochina" in *Parks for Peace* (Cape Town: Conference Proceedings, International Conference on Transboundary Protected Areas as a Vehicle for International Co-operation, Sept. 16–18, 1997), 179–94; Annette Lanjouw and José Kalpers, "Potential for the Creation of a Peace Park in the Virunga Volcano Region," in *Parks for Peace* (Cape Town: Conference Proceedings, International Conference on Transboundary Protected Areas as a Vehicle for International Co-operation, Sept. 16–18, 1997), 163–72; Arthur Blundell and Tyler Christie, "Liberia: Securing the Peace through Parks," in *Peace Parks: Conservation and Conflict Resolution*, ed. Saleem Ali (Cambridge and London: MIT Press, 2007), 227–38; Kent Biringer and K. C. (Nanda) Cariappa, "The Siachen Peace Park Proposal: Reconfiguring the Kashmir Conflict?" in *Peace Parks: Conservation and Conflict Resolution*, ed. Saleem Ali (Cambridge, MA, and London: MIT Press, 2007), 277–90; Stephan Fuller, "Linking Afghanistan with Its Neighbors through Peace Parks: Challenges and Prospects," in *Peace Parks: Conservation and Conflict Resolution*, ed. Saleem Ali (Cambridge, MA, and London: MIT Press, 2007), 291–11; Michelle Stevens, "Iraq and Iran in Ecological Perspective: The Mesopotamian Marshes and the Hawizeh-Azim Peace Park," in *Peace Parks: Conservation and Conflict Resolution*, ed. Saleem Ali (Cambridge, MA, and London: MIT Press, 2007), 313–31.

58. Robert Boardman, *International Organization and the Conservation of Nature* (London and Basingstoke, UK: Macmillan, 1981), 21–22, 27.

59. Clark Gibson, *Politicians and Poachers: The Political Economy of Wildlife Policy in Africa* (Cambridge: Cambridge University Press, 1999).

60. Barnard et al., "Extending the Namibian Protected Area Network;" 532.

61. William Beinart and Peter Coates, *Environment and History: The Taming of Nature in the USA and South Africa* (London: Routledge, 1995).

62. Thorsell and Harrison, "Parks that Promote Peace," 5.

63. Gary Machlis and David Tichnell, *The State of the World's Parks* (Boulder, CO: Westview Press, 1985).

64. Sandwich et al., *Transboundary Protected Areas*, 19–21.

65. Schuerholz and Pardo, "Removing Colonial Barriers."

66. van Amerom and Büscher, "Peace Parks in Southern Africa," 173.

67. Malcolm Draper, Marja Spierenberg, and Harry Wels, "African Dreams of Cohesion: Elite Pacting and Community Development in Transfrontier Conservation Areas in Southern Africa," *Culture and Organization* 10, no. 4 (2004): 349.

68. Randall Kramer, Carel van Schaik and Julie Johnson, eds., *The Last Stand: Protected Areas and the Defense of Tropical Biodiversity* (New York and Oxford: Oxford University Press, 1997); John Terborgh, *Requiem for Nature* (Washington, DC: Island Press/Shearwater Books, 1999).

69. Nicholai Smirnov, "The Impact of Conventional War on Natural Areas of the USSR," *Environmental Conservation* 16 (1989): 318.

70. "The Elm Tree Palisades: The Great Wall of the Northern Song," *China Heritage Quarterly* 6, June (2006), http://www.chinaheritagequarterly.org/features.php?searchterm=006_Elm.inc&issue=006.

71. On "disaster diplomacy," see the special section edited by Charlotte Lindberg Clausen in the *Cambridge Review of International Affairs* 14, no. 1 (2000): 214–94.

5

Going Global after Vietnam

*The End of Agent Orange and the Rise of an
International Environmental Regime*

David Zierler

After six years of lobbying government officials, rallying their colleagues
in academe, and studying the effects of Agent Orange in laboratories
and in the forests and villages of Vietnam, a small group of American
scientists dedicated to ending the herbicidal warfare program finally
achieved their goal. By legislative ruling, the Senate Foreign Relations
Committee, under the chairmanship of J. William Fulbright, put an
end not only to the spray program in South Vietnam, but also to the
possibility that herbicides such as Agent Orange would be employed
by US forces in future wars. Operation Ranch Hand, as the Pentagon
called the decade-long herbicide program, became in 1971 an anom-
aly of counterinsurgency strategy in the twentieth century. The tactic
of chemically denuding forests from the air to deny guerilla soldiers
cover had not been employed by any government before the Vietnam
War and has not been employed since.

   This episode, which accounts for at least one case in which nonstate actors were able to influence government policy on the Vietnam
War, came at the intersection of two geopolitical eras in the late 1960s
and early 1970s. The circumstances that led to the end of herbicidal
warfare were both a product and harbinger of a fundamental shift in
the prevailing global concept of international security. It was a shift
away from the ideological divides of bipolar Cold War alliances (and the
requisite primacy of the nation-state) and toward a vision of international affairs that asserted that global challenges, affecting all peoples,
could not be contained within the Westphalian system of nation-state

sovereignty. To growing numbers of Americans and citizens worldwide, the grinding and brutal war in Vietnam had become altogether disconnected from the logic of Cold War containment that had propelled US forces into Southeast Asia ten years earlier. That "consensus," based on the presumption that communism must be checked through political *and* military means before the Soviet Union and its proxies gained control of greater swaths of the globe, had effectively collapsed as a result of the Vietnam War.[1]

At the turn of the decade, the devastation of Vietnam's landscapes—a product of a military strategy ill-equipped to combat a guerilla insurgency that operated without fixed battlefields or civilian-combatant distinctions—was no longer strictly a symbol of collateral (but necessary) damage in the name of waging the Cold War. In the view of the protesting scientists, who focused specifically on what they referred to as the "ecocide" caused by Agent Orange and more broadly on the environmental and public health calamities of the war in its totality, the damage sustained in South Vietnam had little to do with the domino theory or a display of American Cold War resolve. It demonstrated instead humankind's unchecked and seemingly limitless capacity in the industrial-technological age to wreak ecological havoc in all corners of the globe, irrespective of Cold War ideologies or national boundaries.

In this scenario, Vietnam offered a local dystopian warning with global implications as an alarm warning of future global devastation. The scientists' agenda was thus twofold: first, to put an immediate halt to "ecocide" in Vietnam, and second, to ensure that herbicidal warfare, which could be waged easily with cheap and readily available chemicals, would never happen again. The first goal called for an effective lobbying campaign before legislators in Washington; the second would require the involvement of the United Nations Environment Programme, a nascent international body whose leaders sought to confront environmental problems that transcended the decisions of individual nation-states pursuing narrow interests. In both cases, the scientists secured their aims because they were able to couch their critique of America's Vietnam policy within the broader agenda of both the US Congress and the United Nations. The scientific protest against Agent Orange offered American legislators a way to assert greater foreign policy control in the context of an unpopular war, and soon thereafter the scientists offered the UN and its affiliated global actors a platform on which to forge greater international cooperation to address urgent environmental problems as a matter of international security.

As this chapter will demonstrate, the protesting scientists were at the cutting edge of the rise of an international environmental regime. Their agenda, begun in Washington and reaching maturity under the aegis of the United Nations, occurred specifically in the context of changing conceptualizations of international security during the Vietnam era. At a broader level, the scientific protest against Agent Orange illustrated at once rising concerns over global ecological problems and diminishing concerns over geopolitical threats engendered by the ongoing Cold War.

The Accidental End of Herbicidal Warfare in Vietnam

The political process that landed the Agent Orange issue before the Senate Foreign Relations Committee originated from an unlikely and accidental source: Richard M. Nixon. On assuming the presidency in 1969, Nixon moved quickly to place détente and disarmament vis-à-vis the Soviet Union at the center of his foreign policy agenda. Complementing the administration's dramatic moves in the areas of nuclear arms control and new political accommodations with Moscow, Nixon offered another, lesser-known plan to overhaul US policy with regard to chemical and biological weapons (CBW). On November 25, 1969, he issued a sweeping statement on American foreign policy with regard to so-called CBW, based on an interagency review he had ordered under the auspices of the National Security Council, the departments of State and Defense, and the Arms Control and Disarmament Agency. It was the first such review on CBW in fifteen years. In response to this study, Nixon reaffirmed the nation's long-standing pledge not to introduce chemical weapons in war but vowed that the military would maintain its vast chemical stock for retaliatory (and thus deterrent) effect. Citing the "massive, unpredictable, and potentially uncontrollable consequences" of biological weapons, however, Nixon renounced all forms of biological warfare and directed the Pentagon to dismantle its biological weapons inventory.[2] Nixon's words were no understatement: among the biological agents created by US Army scientists was a fungal rust spore designed to wipe out the Soviet Union's entire wheat supply—without any proven mechanism that would limit the attack to communist territory. Nor was Nixon's policy strategically or administratively insignificant: despite the pomp and ceremony surrounding the strategic arms limitation talks (SALT), which did little to halt actual nuclear proliferation, Nixon's biological weapons directive marked the first time in modern history that a nation unilaterally eliminated an entire category of weapons from its arsenal.

The boldness of Nixon's initiative made the president confident that its last provision would quickly and easily codify the CBW policy into law. To that end, Nixon planned to send the Geneva Protocol of 1925 to the Senate for its advice and ratification. The protocol, whose signatories have pledged to refrain from first use of chemical weapons in war, was ratified by most of the great powers in the wake of World War I and the horrific effects of chemical warfare waged on the battlefields of Europe. But the protocol had been blocked in the US Senate in 1926. Although the Senate Foreign Relations Committee had advised ratification of the protocol, a strong lobbying effort comprising private citizens, military officials, and representatives from the chemical industry blocked the vote on the grounds that America's defense capacity should not be constrained in a future, and likely distant, war. The protocol languished in the Senate until 1947, when President Harry S. Truman took it off the table as a general housekeeping measure. Although American presidents since 1925 routinely invoked America's de facto acceptance and adherence to the Geneva Protocol, as a matter of fact the United States was neither governed nor bound by any domestic or international laws relating to the use of chemicals or biological agents in war. Thus, gaining the Senate's ratification on the protocol was to be the strategic capstone to Nixon's CBW initiative.[3]

The administration's decision to reopen the Geneva Protocol to legislative debate proved to be a stunning act of political tone-deafness. Nixon's directive rested on two assumptions: (1) frightening advances in weapons technology rendered obsolete the isolationist claim that war and destruction would never come to American soil; and (2) the United States was not currently engaged in any operations that might complicate its formal adherence to an international treaty that prohibits first use of chemical weapons in war. In fact, the United States was engaged in a massive chemical war in Vietnam. By 1969, Operation Ranch Hand crew members had sprayed coastal mangrove swamps and highland mountain forests in South Vietnam and in border areas of Laos and Cambodia over an area equal to the size of Massachusetts. Many of the areas were sprayed multiple times with herbicides such as Agent Orange, which had a much stronger chemical concentration than any of the commercial products approved under federal guidelines for weed control on American farms. While the human health concerns relating to exposure to Agent Orange were poorly understood, the vast ecological destruction caused by the spray program was readily apparent; it caused one of the protesting scientists at the center of the controversy, Arthur Galston of Yale University, to describe the legacy of Operation Ranch Hand as "ecocide." Together with his colleagues E. W. Pfeiffer of the University of Montana, Arthur Westing of Windham College, and Matthew Meselson of Harvard University, Galston made the termination of Operation Ranch Hand his cause célèbre of the Vietnam Era. Galston, a prominent botanist whose earlier work on soybeans inadvertently helped launched the creation of herbicides, and his colleagues had become vexed by what they considered the cooptation of science for destructive purposes in Vietnam. Yet, faced with a military leadership convinced that Agent Orange was an indispensible tactical weapon necessary to deprive National Liberation Front fighters of their jungle cover—and therefore crucial to ensuring the safety of American and Republic of Vietnam soldiers—the scientists lacked any legal or political mechanism to bring an end to Operation Ranch Hand.

Given Nixon's dismissive and contemptuous attitude toward antiwar protestors in general, it was conceivable at first glance that the president and his foreign policy advisors had assessed the content of the scientists' platform and concluded it could be contained and would not inhibit a swift resolution in the Senate Foreign Relations Committee to ratify the Geneva Protocol. In this imagined scenario, Nixon could have received a legal opinion that the prohibitory boundaries of the protocol were limited to chemicals that killed people, not trees. This opinion could also have considered the fact that protest against herbicidal warfare entered the international arena in 1966, when the Hungarian representative to the UN General Assembly denounced Operation Ranch Hand and declared that it violated the Geneva Protocol.[4] Further, the administration may have concluded that domestic criticisms mounted against Agent Orange were emanating from a very small group; the scientific campaign to end the herbicide program was never more than a "boutique" variety of antiwar dissent. As late as 1969 there were no campus protests or sit-ins geared exclusively to ending Operation Ranch Hand, and the scientists did not encourage such activity in any event. Their fight was waged quietly in scientific journals and in correspondence with various officials in Washington. Wary of politicizing their areas of expertise and getting caught up in the more radical elements of the antiwar movement, Galston and his colleagues were careful to limit their outrage to the ecological destructiveness and legal dubiousness of the herbicide program. In sum, the administration could have plausibly assumed that Agent Orange and the small and relatively quiet group that denounced it would not have posed a threat to the president's CBW initiative.

Yet Nixon's presidential papers yield no evidence to suggest that, in preparation for Nixon's dramatic CBW announcement of November 1969, the White House considered the possibility that Agent Orange would prove problematic in ratifying the protocol. The closest evdence is this: on the same day of Nixon's announcement, the National Security Council circulated National Security Decision Memorandum 35, entitled "United States Policy on Chemical Warfare Program and Bacteriological/Biological Research Program," to top administration officials. The memorandum asserted that administration policy did not consider herbicides or riot control agents to be part of the class of chemical weapons that the United States would formally renounce.[5] No administration official at that juncture voiced concern that this distinction, offered without explanation, could be politically or legislatively knotty. That realization came

after the fact. More than a year later, when the administration was finally prepared to resubmit the Geneva Protocol to the Senate, secretary of state William
P. Rogers successfully urged Nixon to phase out entirely the last remnants of
the herbicide program before the protocol hearings were to begin. He further
counseled that such a move need not change the administration's position that
herbicides did not fall within the prohibitions of the Geneva Protocol.[6]

Rogers's memo was prescient in that he understood the herbicide issue
could derail the hearings. But his strategy assumed that the scientific critics, who
were gearing up to present their arguments before the Senate Foreign Relations
Committee, would be satisfied to know that Operation Ranch Hand was finished.
He did not account for the fact that Galston and his colleagues had broader, more
forward-looking goals in mind. For them, an early yet readily apparent "lesson"
of the Vietnam War extended far beyond the decisions to fight the war or to use
particular weapons. In this view, "ecocide" in Vietnam, if not understood properly, amounted to an environmental dystopia that foreshadowed global environmental disaster. Forcing a change in US policy was a necessary yet preliminary
step to ensure that herbicidal warfare began and ended in Vietnam.

A central premise of the scientists' critique of Operation Ranch Hand was the
ease with which herbicides could be weaponized in hypothetical future wars. The
Nixon administration and the foreign policy establishment in general focused
their efforts at this time on slowing the proliferation of nuclear weapons and
exotic biological agents. By limiting US stockpiles, government officials hoped to
lead international disarmament initiatives by example. While acknowledging that
the administration's impetus to decrease stocks of nuclear and chemical/biologi-
cal weapons was a necessary and positive step toward world peace and stability,
the scientists insisted that the official exclusion of herbicides missed a fundamental point. Herbicidal warfare was a remarkably inexpensive proposition. The
equipment and technological know-how were (and are) readily available to any
farmer with a crop duster. In other words, the herbicide program was not limited
to countries with virtually unlimited war resources. With even a modest budget,
hypothetical combatants the world over thus had at their disposal the means to
wreak widespread ecological havoc. This concern was at the core of the testimony given by Matthew Meselson, one of the key scientists protesting Operation
Ranch Hand, before the Senate Foreign Relations Committee during hearings
on CBW policy that preceded the Geneva Protocol hearings by two years.

Citing the ongoing utility of conventional weapons in warfare, Meselson
asked:

[W]hat sense does it make to maintain constraints on CBW? We
realize that special rules are required for nuclear weapons. The

distinction between conventional weapons and nuclear weapons is a real one, and the importance of maintaining it is generally understood. Chemical and biological weapons share with nuclear ones potentially overwhelmingly destructiveness.... Once developed [they] can be exceedingly cheap, relatively easy to produce, and quick to proliferate.[7]

Within the CBW arsenal, herbicides were unique. And government insistence that Agent Orange and herbicidal warfare were not prohibited by the Geneva Protocol only increased the chances that "ecocide" in Vietnam could and would be replicated wherever foliage and armed conflict intersected. As the protesting scientists saw it, the Nixon administration's stance increased this risk on two levels. By insisting that Agent Orange was merely an agricultural tool that the military had adapted for a particular purpose, the United States had simultaneously advertised and destigmatized the utility of herbicidal warfare. And by tenaciously insisting that herbicidal warfare was an indispensible tactic of counterinsurgency warfare, the United States signaled that Agent Orange was as effective as it was cheap. In short, to any national leader, warlord, or resistance movement operating in forested terrain, the herbicidal weapon offered a perfect—and perfectly legal— tool of war.

An Environmental Critique of Cold War Containment

When the Geneva Protocol hearings began in March 1971, the mood on Capitol Hill regarding Vietnam had turned clearly against the Nixon administration's dogged insistence that the war remained vital to American national security.[8] To its critics in Congress and throughout American society, a conflict that seemed to have no end had upended the strategy of containment. The fear of unchecked global communist domination, first enunciated by George Kennan in the early days of the Cold War, was a pillar of US foreign policy, and foundational to the complex and tortured series of decisions that led to full-scale commitment of American forces to defend the independence of South Vietnam. But to an unsilent majority of the members of the Senate Foreign Relations Committee, led by committee chair J. William Fulbright, the chasm between the goals of the containment strategy and the realities of the situation in Vietnam could no longer be bridged. The importance of maintaining a bulwark against communist takeover from North Vietnam was no longer self-evident.

In broaching the relatively minor issue of herbicidal warfare against this broad intellectual and strategic backdrop during the Geneva Protocol hearings, the scientists effectively exploited a credibility vacuum in the foreign policy establishment. Senator Fulbright and most of his colleagues, who had already dropped out of the Cold War "consensus" under which a broad majority of Americans supported US policy in Vietnam until 1968, were interested in considering new ways to conceptualize national security. The scientists, eager for this opportunity, did not disappoint. Over several days of hearings, most Senators displayed impatience with government officials sent to promote Nixon's policy and barely hid their respect, even reverence, for the scientists. A soliloquy delivered by Arthur Galston during an exchange with Fulbright illustrates the atmosphere during the hearings most dramatically.

> Let me tell you why, as a botanist, I am so convinced of the necessity of banning herbicides and defoliants as weapons of war. These days it is convenient for man to consider himself as master of all he surveys. His ability to reach the bottom of the sea or the surface of the moon, to fly at supersonic speeds, to split the atom, and to construct sophisticated computers makes him feel that there is no problem requiring scientific or technological expertise that he cannot overcome.... But the attitude that I describe I consider a dangerous fallacy which could lead man to overlook his own Achilles' heel.
>
> For man lives in this world only by the grace of vegetation. He is totally dependent on and cannot substitute for that thin mantle of green matter living precariously on the partially decomposed rock we call soil.... In view of the present population of about 3.5 billion people on earth and the estimated doubling of the population every thirty years, it ill behooves us to destroy with profligacy the ability of any part of the earth to yield food for man's nutrition, fiber for his clothes, wood to build and heat his houses, and other products, too numerous to mention.[9]

It was a statement that simultaneously illustrated Galston's opposition to herbicidal warfare in Vietnam and signaled his broader concerns about humankind's capacity to wreak ecological havoc worldwide in the industrial age. Far removed ideologically from environmental preservationists (whose goal was to reduce man's impact on nature), Galston's dismay about "ecocide" in Vietnam centered on the fact that Agent Orange disrupted or destroyed the capacity of humans to exploit the land for their own benefit. It was a concern that Galston extrapolated to a global level—particularly because of the ease with which herbicidal warfare could proliferate.

Fulbright responded that Galston's ideas "ought to be brought to the attention of everybody in the country." The content and context of this exchange deserves extended analysis. What Galston had attempted to do, and what Fulbright accepted wholesale, was to take his specific concerns about herbicidal warfare and weave them into a much broader critique of humankind's relationship with the environment—on a global scale. The immediate effect of Galston's framework was to render narrow—even small-minded—the official legal defense that the US military neither designed nor deployed Agent Orange as an antipersonnel weapon and thus did not believe the Geneva Protocol prohibited it. Remarkably, most independent legal analyses supported that position.[10] The Foreign Relations Committee was not a court of law, however, but a political chamber receptive to replacing and revamping what it had considered discredited conceptualizations of national security. The explanatory power of Cold War containment and the American way of technological innovation to defeat communism had fallen from its halcyon days in the Kennedy administration. Ten years earlier, military strategists, with Kennedy's support, had included herbicides among a broad array of scientific innovations that might tame communist encroachment in Indochina. What is notable in Fulbright's response to Galston's statement—that Galston had a new gospel to preach and everyone should hear it—is the *novelty* he assumed was inherent in the idea that (a) human activity is capable of widespread—even global—environmental destruction, to the point of human self-destruction; and (b) that destruction need not limit itself within national boundaries.

In a sense, Galston used Agent Orange as a pretext to promulgate an environmental philosophy that had been slowly building in the postwar era. He was not the first, of course, to issue a dire warning about the collision between technological advances and environmental health. Had Rachel Carson lived through the 1960s, she surely would have updated and expanded the narrative of *Silent Spring* from heartland America to the jungles of Vietnam. As Galston well understood, the Agent Orange issue offered a politically easy choice on which the Foreign Relations Committee could take a stand; unlike so many environmental debates before and since, there was no trade-off or compromise to make between being "pro-environment" and therefore "anti-economy" because it was only the military value of herbicidal warfare to which boosters of herbicidal warfare could point.

The destruction in Vietnam of hundreds of thousands of acres of trees and wildlife occurred in the name of anticommunism. And against protestations that the use of Agent Orange saved the lives of American soldiers, by 1971, the rejoinder that the soldiers had no business in Vietnam's forests was neither radical nor particularly provocative.

On behalf of the Foreign Relations Committee, Fulbright wrote to the president on April 15, 1971, urging the White House to reconsider its restrictive interpretation of the Geneva Protocol so as to avoid its rejection or total modification in a full Senate vote. Fulbright offered his admiration to Nixon for the great strides the president had already taken in the field of disarmament and for resubmitting the protocol in the first place, making it clear that he did not regard the administration's position on the herbicide issue as indicative of any broader pattern. Fulbright also conceded that the legal merits of the matter with regard to the scope of the Geneva Protocol were ambiguous. Still, he observed, what was immediately obvious and most pressing was that herbicidal warfare was utterly frightening from an environmental perspective and should be banned absolutely for all time. Fulbright closed his letter with an appeal to the president's ego and political instincts.

> If the administration were to take a longer and broader view of
> our own interests, I cannot imagine any serious opposition to that
> decision, either here at home or abroad. On the contrary, I personally believe that were you to take this initiative your action would be
> regarded as truly courageous and possessed of real moral force.[11]

The administration, stung that the president's initiative had stalled on an issue to which it had given almost no initial consideration, sat on the protocol. It was not until four years later that President Gerald Ford took up the matter again as part of his broader mandate to move the country beyond the "national nightmare" of the Watergate scandal and Nixon's consequent resignation. In April 1975 Ford signed Executive Order 11850, "Renunciation of Certain Uses in War of Chemical Herbicides and Riot Control Agents," which disavowed the first use of herbicides in war. The administration had pledged to the Senate Foreign Relations Committee in December 1974 that it was prepared to make this concession, and the Senate moved quickly in January 1975 to ratify the Geneva Protocol based on this understanding. Fifty years after its creation, the legislative and executive branches of the United States had finally reached an accord that allowed the country to be an official signatory to the Geneva Protocol.

Globalizing a Legislative Victory

For Arthur Galston and his colleagues, the ratification of the Geneva Protocol was a tremendous and long-awaited success. In the end, nongovernment actors were able to influence official US policy at the highest levels—a rarity in the broad and convoluted history of antiwar protest in the Vietnam era. But the scientists' work would remain incomplete so long as their impact was limited to the domestic sphere. While America's formal renunciation of first use of herbicides in war gave legal and political heft to the proposition that environmental issues had entered the agenda of international security, the Geneva Protocol itself was not an instrument of international environmental law or policy. Without further work in the global arena to create a broader mechanism of international environmental cooperation—an international environmental regime—the scientists could not feel that their work was complete. To their good fortune, such a regime was in its early stages and was receptive to taking on Vietnam policy— easily the most controversial international issue at that time. The development of the United Nations Environment Programme was directly linked to the international fissures caused and exacerbated by the Vietnam War. Crucially, UNEP offered the scientists a sense of organization and power that had been lacking in more informal associations such as Earth Day, whose organizers invariably shared UNEP's founding vision but lacked its authority. It was in this new forum that the scientists believed their campaign to end herbicidal warfare, as a matter of transnational environmental protection, could "go global."

The impetus to include environmental issues under the aegis of the United Nations came from Sweden, whose representative in 1968 successfully advocated a resolution "to provide a framework for comprehensive consideration within the UN of the problems of the human environment in order to focus the attention of governments and public opinion on the importance and urgency of this question."[12] Two years and several planning committees later, the Canadian industrialist Maurice Strong was appointed Secretary General of UNEP. In debate at the General Assembly and in plenary meetings for the upcoming environmental conference, Strong's use of the now-anachronistic phrase "human environment" had a triple meaning. First, the term suggested the inextricable (yet poorly acknowledged) link between societies and the environs upon which they depend; second, the phrase was deliberately broad so that UNEP, in concert with UN member states, could create wide-ranging policies to mitigate any number of environmental issues whose problems transcended national boundaries; third, the term was deliberately vague because the framers of the Environmental Programme understood that the new body would inherit the classic problems of the Westphalian system, namely, how to balance the national interest of sovereign nations with the common interest of supranational governance.[13]

In one of many speeches Strong gave to drum up support for UNEP and the upcoming Stockholm conference, the secretary general laid out the case that the environmental problems facing mankind required a new kind of global cooperation.

The threats to man's existence from nuclear warfare can be avoided right up until the moment someone pushes the button; but the threat to man's survival which derives from our interventions in our natural environment is of a different nature. Here each of us has his finger on the button, and this responsibility requires us to act now to avoid dangers which will not materialize until the next generation or beyond—but still within the lifetime of our own children or grand-children—and will be beyond remedy by the time they are perceived as imminent threats. To deal with issues which involve cause and effect relationships so far removed from more immediate and press-ing priorities will require a degree of enlightened political will on the part of the peoples and nations of the world that is without precedent in human history.[14]

In June 1972, Stockholm hosted the first annual United Nations Conference on the Human Environment. Sweden's central role in initiating UNEP and its strained relations with the United States over Vietnam were not coincidences. Unique among nations outside the communist orbit, Sweden's leaders had repeatedly denounced the American war in Vietnam since the mid-1960s as a tragic and unnecessary catastrophe.[15] For Swedish prime minister Olof Palme, the UNEP Conference in 1972 was a logical forum in which to advance the cri-tiques of the Vietnam War he had made since joining the Swedish government nearly a decade earlier. As head of government Palme felt no compunction to tone down his rhetoric, knowing full well that his comments could derail the entire conference. In his opening address the prime minister decried the "eco-cide" of Vietnam. "It is of paramount importance," he declared, "that ecological warfare cease immediately."[16]

Since the debacle of the Geneva Protocol in the Senate and the Nixon administration's newfound appreciation for the passions aroused by Agent Orange, the president sent Russell Train, the US representative to UNEP, with instructions to keep all references to Vietnam off the official agenda. The Environmental Programme's promised silence about the environmental destruction in Vietnam was, in fact, a precondition for American participation in the conference. According to one newspaper account, Train became visibly incensed upon hearing Prime Minister Palme's denunciation of the American "ecocide," called Palme's statements a "gratuitous politicizing of our environ-mental discussions," and threatened that the US delegation would abandon the conference.[17] The following day the Chinese delegate followed up on Palme's remarks. According to a State Department telegram, the delegate objected that there was no good reason why America's "poisoning the environment of Vietnam" should be kept off the official record of the conference.[18] Whether or not there was a "good reason," the United States managed to keep all refer-ences to Vietnam out of the record.[19]

Critics of the United Nations Environment Programme have pointed to the official exclusion of "ecocide" as evidence that the organizers of the Stockholm Conference were more concerned with putting on a good show than tackling the most pressing issues of the day. Train's protest against the "politicizing" of environmental issues, if taken to its logical conclusion, would have rendered moot any substantive discussions of any matter. More to the point, Article 21 of the Stockholm Declaration—the executive summary of the conference proceedings—stated that "the sovereign rights of states to exploit their own resources in line with their own environmental policies and the responsibility to ensure that activities within their jurisdiction or control do not cause damage to the environment of other states . . ." As one critic observed of Article 21, "In short, the participating states agreed to cooperate, but they also wanted it to be made absolutely clear that this was not to infringe on any decision-making powers they held."[20] An even blunter assessment is that, despite the lofty rhetoric of its secretary general, UNEP's founding language actually reinforced the notion that environmental problems would remain confined within national boundaries—even though the whole basis of UNEP was that environmental issues are inherently transnational and thus require international cooperation.

Yet the law of unintended consequences—as was the case with the Nixon administration and its miscalculation regarding the relative importance of the herbicide controversy—yielded the most interesting results from the conference. There were actually two parallel conferences occurring at the same time, one under official UN auspices and a much more rambunctious conference held in the adjoining streets and parks. Some participants dubbed this alternative convention "Woodstockholm."[21] The event lived up to its nickname, with thousands of participants erecting tent cities and staging rock concerts and protest marches. Although the participants in the alternative conference could claim a no more unified agenda than their bureaucratic counterparts, they shared the basic premise that the limits placed on the official record would ensure that UNEP would not create meaningful solutions to real transnational environmental problems. On the other hand, the participants of "Woodstockholm" recognized that, from a publicity perspective, the Stockholm conference was a remarkable event: the eleven-day conference attracted some 1200 diplomats and heads of state, several thousand experts on environmental issues and global governance, and an international press corps. It was a rare opportunity for environmental attention-grabbing.

Two of the key scientists who protested herbicidal warfare, Arthur Westing and E. W. Pfeiffer, attended the parallel conference, though they would have much preferred that the United States allow the Agent Orange issue to be aired in the official forum. Still, it was not an opportunity to be lost. Two days before the start of the official conference, Westing and Pfeiffer helped organize a conference on the consequences of "ecocide" in Vietnam and other ravages endured by the Vietnamese landscape and its people as a result of the war. The meeting, which was far more solemn than many of the festivities that would ensue, brought together legal theorists and scientists from around the world.[22] The reason that US officials had worked so hard to keep Vietnam off the official agenda became clear during their presentations, which proceeded as if the war in Indochina had created no environmental problems. UNEP would have otherwise become an impromptu war crimes commission, based largely on the assertion that herbicidal warfare violated the Geneva Protocol.[23] As Arthur Westing recalled, such serious allegations of criminal conduct drew the attention of important officials. Prime Minister Palme, for example, was compelled to broach the "ecocide" issue in his opening address after he was briefed by Westing and Pfeiffer about their work studying the ecological destruction in Vietnam.[24]

Although it is impossible to measure precisely the effect scientists had in influencing international behavior, it is difficult to dismiss their work in explaining the absence of herbicidal warfare from international conflict in the post-Vietnam era. In US deliberations about the Geneva Protocol and then in the United Nations Environment Programme, their efforts combined for a one-two punch. In Washington, the scientists effectively forced government policy to adhere to an international treaty based on an environmental rather than legal argument; in Stockholm, they confronted and neutralized what they saw as a craven attempt by the United States to censor all references to herbicidal warfare in Vietnam—a wartime operation whose effects were possibly the most dramatic intersection of environmental and international issues in modern times.

Still, the scientists' victory remained qualified until the creation of an international mechanism that combined the proscriptions of treaty law with the breadth of an international agreement. That is, neither the Geneva Protocol nor the Stockholm Conference was tailor-made to fulfill the scientists' basic goal—to prevent the deliberate destruction of environments during war. The scientists recognized that laws specifically geared to ban herbicidal warfare could merely compel the fertile minds of the "military-industrial complex" in the United States and elsewhere to develop different technological means to achieve the same ends. The first sign of a fuller resolution of the scientists' efforts came in 1974, when the United States and the Soviet Union explored the possibility of jointly declaring voluntary restraints on environmental warfare.[25] At that juncture President Ford was already prepared to renounce first use of herbicidal warfare. Meanwhile the more generic term "environmental warfare" would be codified in a future treaty that would prohibit herbicides and other weapons designed to damage environments as a wartime tactic. By not explicitly linking herbicides to a treaty to which the United States was a party, government officials avoided the implication that Operation Ranch Hand violated international law retroactively.

This agreement eventually morphed into the UN "Convention on the Prohibition of Military or Any Other Hostile Use of Environmental Modification Techniques," which was opened for signature in Geneva on May 18, 1977.[26] A great majority of the world's nations have signed this treaty. Although at least one of the protesting herbicide scientists has expressed criticism that ENMOD, as the environmental modification treaty is known, has too many holes to ensure stringent verification of compliance, it is difficult to argue with history: whether as a result of the Geneva Protocol, the Stockholm Conference, or a treaty specifically designed to prevent environmental destruction in times of war (or some combination of the three), no major nation has embarked on a systematic and deliberate campaign to harm environments during times of war.[27]

The major exception to this international norm was Saddam Hussein's destruction of the marshlands of southern Iraq in the years after the first Persian Gulf War. The Baathist policy of upriver damming of the Tigris and Euphrates River intentionally devastated the ancient agricultural way of life of the Marsh Arabs, the majority of whom were Shia Muslims who had sought greater autonomy after Saddam's army was routed by coalition forces in Operation Desert Storm.[28] The war against the Marsh Arabs and their ancestral lands has been recognized in the legal literature as an act of "ecocide" and a violation of the terms of the ENMOD treaty.[29] It is notable that Saddam Hussein was both the major perpetrator of environmental warfare since the Vietnam War and, arguably, the greatest violator of the norms of warfare in recent times. Equally notable is that the United Nations Environment Programme spearheaded international efforts to bring the plight of the Marsh Arabs and their environs to the world's attention.[30] Finally, in what may be seen as an environmental component to Washington's ongoing attempt to kick the Vietnam Syndrome in all its forms, the US Agency for International Development launched a resettlement and restoration of the marshlands project only months after the American invasion of Iraq in March 2003.[31] This ongoing project has delivered substantial re-flooding in the region and the return of thousands of refugees to their ancient homeland.[32]

The international community's response to the Iraq marshland crisis stands as testament both to the conception of "ecocide" as formulated by Arthur Galston and his colleagues and to the normative status environmental issues now have among international organizations. Standing apart from environmental degradation that occurs as a by-product of industrial processes and resource extraction, "ecocide" was, and remains, a tactic of war that targets humans through environmental destruction. It is an offense enshrined in international law that will likely be enforced against combatants that attempt to commit "ecocide" in future wars. The scientists' work in the 1970s created a legacy, borne out of a heady mix of antiwar sentiment and rising environmental conscious, in which at least one variant of the antiwar battle-cry slogan "No more Vietnams!" has endured.

NOTES

1. The views, opinions and interpretations expressed herein are those of the author alone and are not necessarily those of the US Department of State or the US Government. This paper is based on fully declassified and open source material.This essay is drawn from *The Invention of Ecocide: Agent Orange, Vietnam, and the Scientists Who Changed the Way We Think about the Environment* by David Zierler. Copyright 2011 by the University of Georgia Press. Reprinted by the permission of the University of Georgia Press.On the intellectual evolution of containment in response to the Vietnam War, see especially Robert Tomes, *Apocalypse Then: American Intellectuals and the Vietnam War, 1954–1975* (New York: New York University Press, 1998), 167–203.

2. For an overview of Nixon's CBW disarmament initiatives see "Ninth Annual Report of the ACDA Transmitted to the Congress," reprinted in United States Department of State *Bulletin* 62 (May 4, 1970), 585–92. See also Jonathan B. Tucker, "A Farewell to Germs: The U.S. Renunciation of Biological and Toxin Warfare, 1969–70," *International Security* 27 (2002): 107–48.

3. The full text of Nixon's "Statement on Chemical and Biological Defense Policies and Programs, November 25, 1969," is available at the *American Presidency Project*, http://www.presidency.ucsb.edu/ws/?pid=2343.

4. Federation of American Scientists, "The Geneva Protocol," http://www.fas.org/nuke/control/geneva/intro.htm.

5. The document was made available through a Freedom of Information Act request submitted through the Digital National Security Archive, posted online at http://www.gwu.edu/~nsarchiv/NSAEBB/NSAEBB58/RNCBW8.pdf.

6. Rogers memorandum to Nixon, "The Geneva Protocol," February 11, 1971, National Archives, College Park, Nixon Presidential Materials Project, National Security files, subject files, box 311, folder 2.

7. Meselson, in testimony before United States, Senate Committee on Foreign Relations, *Chemical and Biological Warfare,* 91st Congress, 1st Sess., April 30, 1969, (Washington, DC: Government Printing Office, 1970), 24.

8. On the role of congressional disaffection with prosecuting the Vietnam War, see especially Robert David Johnson, *Congress and the Cold War* (Cambridge: Cambridge University Press, 2006), 69–104.

9. Galston, in testimony before United States Senate, Hearings, Committee on Foreign Relations, *The Geneva Protocol of 1925*, 1971, 91st Congress, 2nd Sess., 325–6.

10. See, for example, John Norton Moore, "Ratification of the Geneva Protocol on Gas and Bacteriological Warfare: A Legal and Political Analysis," *Virginia Law Review* 58 (March 1972): 419–509.

11. Fulbright letter to Nixon, April 15, 1971, J. William Fulbright Papers, University of Arkansas Libraries, Fayetteville, series 71 box 32, folder 21.

12. UN General Assembly Resolution 2398 (XXIII), December 3, 1968. United Nations *Yearbook*, vol. 22, p. 474. The resolution was passed by unanimous vote. For an analysis of the behind-the-scenes diplomacy for this resolution, see David A. Kay and Eugene B. Skolnikoff, "International Institutions and the Environmental Crisis: A Look Ahead," *International Organization* 26 (Spring 1972): 469–71.

13. E. Thomas Sullivan, "The Stockholm Conference: A Step Toward Global Environmental Cooperation and Involvement," *Indiana Law Review* 6 (1972–1973): 267.

14. Strong, address at the National Foreign Trade Convention, Waldorf-Astoria, New York, November 17, 1971. The Papers of Maurice Strong, Environmental Science and Public Policy Archives, Harvard College Library, Harvard University, box 28, folder 28.

15. Fredrik Logevall, "The Swedish-American Conflict over Vietnam," *Diplomatic History* 17 (Summer 1993): 421–45.

16. Palme, quoted in Tord Björk, "The Emergence of Popular Participation in World Politics: The United Nations Conference on the Human Environment," Unpublished paper presented in the Department of Political Science, University of Stockholm (Fall 1996), 16.

17. Peter Calamai, "U.S. Furious at Ecology Attack," *Ottawa Citizen*, June 8, 1972.

18. United States Department of State, telegram from Washington, DC, to American Embassy Stockholm (June 13, 1972), Strong papers, box 41, folder 404.

19. The full record is titled "Report of the United Nations Conference on the Human Environment, Stockholm, 5–16, June 1972," United Nations Archives, New York, A/Conf.48/14/Rev.1.

20. Lee-Anne Broadhead, *International Environmental Politics: The Limits of Green Diplomacy* (Boulder, CO: Lynne Rienner, 2002), 34.

21. Friedel Ungeheur, "Woodstockholm," *Time*, June 19, 1972, 55.

22. "The Effects of Modern Weapons on the Human Environment in Indochina," *International Secretariat Commission of Enquiry into U.S. Crimes*, Stockholm, June 2–4, 1972.

23. Serious legal scholars took the concept of "ecocide" to its logical endpoint— the framework for a war crimes commission to prosecute American environmental war crimes in Vietnam. Richard A. Falk, a professor of international law at Princeton, was most prominent in these efforts. See especially Falk, "Environmental Warfare and Ecocide: Facts, Appraisal, and Proposals," *Bulletin of Peace Proposals* 4 (1973): 1–17; and Falk, "Adapting a World Order to the Global Ecosystem," in *Patient Earth*, ed. John Harte and Robert H. Socolow (New York: Rinehart, 1971), 245–57.

24. Westing, interview with the author, March 4, 2007, Putney, VT.

25. National Security Decision Memorandum 277: "International Restraints on Environmental Warfare," Gerald R. Ford Library, National Security and Decision Memoranda, box 1.

26. Full text available at http://www.icrc.org/ihl.nsf/FULL/460?OpenDocument.

27. Arthur Westing, "Environmental Warfare: Manipulating the Environment for Hostile Purposes," unpublished paper adapted from a presentation delivered at the Woodrow Wilson Center, May 7, 1996.

28. The best overview of Saddam's war on the Marsh Arabs is Human Rights Watch, "The Iraqi Government Assault on the Marsh Arabs," Human Rights Watch Briefing Paper, Washington, DC, January 2003, available at http://www.hrw.org/legacy/backgrounder/mena/marsharabs1.pdf.

29. Aaron Schwabach, "Ecocide and Genocide in Iraq: International Law, the Marsh Arabs and Environmental Damage in Non-international Conflicts," August 25, 2003, *bepress Legal Series,* working paper 35.

30. United Nations Environment Programme, *The Mesopotamian Marshlands: Demise of an Ecosystem,* Early Warning and Assessment Technical Report, UNEP/DEWA/TR.01-3 Rev. 1 (Nairobi: UNEP, 2001).

31. United States International Aid Agency, "Strategies for Assisting the Marsh Arabs and Restoring the Marshlands of Southern Iraq," October 8, 2003, available at http://pdf.usaid.gov/pdf_docs/PNADD293.pdf.

32. See, for example, Kevin Matthews, "Hope, Economic Transformation, in Iraqi Marshlands," UCLA International Institute, November 11, 2007, available at http://www.international.ucla.edu/article.asp?parentid=82857.

6

The Paradox of US Pesticide Policy during the Age of Ecology

David Kinkela

The late 1960s and early 1970s were a turning point in environmental politics. Influenced by such writers as Rachel Carson (*Silent Spring*, 1962), Paul Erlich (*The Population Bomb*, 1968), Garrett Hardin ("Tragedy of the Commons," 1968), and Barry Commoner (*Science and Survival*, 1966; *The Closing Circle*, 1971), many Americans began to reexamine the underpinnings of postwar consumerism. The seemingly innocuous representations of middle-class America—the suburban home, the car, and the plethora of consumer goods—had come at a tremendous environmental cost. Smog, traffic, industrial waste, and the ubiquitous "bulldozer in the countryside" epitomized the long-term environmental consequences of the American way of life, leading to concern over resource depletion, pollution, despoiled wilderness, and energy consumption.[1] Equally, the dramatic images from the Apollo spaces missions, "Earth rise" (1968) and "Full earth" (1972) revealed the atmospheric boundaries of the planet. The darkened void of space set against the blue, greens, and browns of "spaceship earth" astonishingly captured the limits of earth's resources. Collectively, the shift from a consumer society to one concerned about the environment represented what historians have called the "age of ecology."[2]

Ecology emphasized the concepts of wholeness, interconnectivity, and the interdependence of humans and nature. It also fostered a new brand of politics, aimed at correcting environmental wrongs and conceptualizing the problems of human societies wholly and collectively, rather than in isolation. The social and political upheavals of the 1960s were thus not the discrete expressions of various interest groups; seen through the prism of ecology, they were deeply intertwined events. Critics of the Vietnam War not only condemned the violence and human carnage, but also denounced the massive spraying of Agent Orange as an "ecocide." Counterculture activists returned to the land to find spiritual fulfillment in the natural world. Political leaders embraced ecology to promote a more aggressive environmental agenda and to draw connections between the myriad social and economic problems the nation faced. And, perhaps most importantly, ecology prescribed that certain environmental problems do not stop at political borders but are regional, national, and global in scope. As Barry Commoner suggested in *The Closing Circle*, "Everything is connected to everything else."

These ecological concepts, however, raise a number of significant questions about the role of the nation-state. If, for example, everything is connected to everything, how do nation-states deal with environmental issues outside their political boundaries? What role does the state play in protecting environments within and beyond its borders? And how do states respond to problems caused by environmental factors that lie outside its borders? These questions are difficult to answer as the planet continues to struggle with the problems of global warming, waste, and oil spills. But, as many of the chapters in the volume illustrate, these transnational environmental issues have long and complicated histories. While the age of ecology ushered in a holistic approach to problem solving, it also raised a series of issues pertaining to the limits and responsibility of states in protecting people and environments beyond their borders.

By exploring the era when ecology first took root and people imagined a "world without borders," this chapter examines how the United States determined the appropriate parameters of state regulation within a global context. More specifically, it explores how US policy makers, along with American chemical corporations and environmental groups, refashioned US pesticide policy during the 1970s, a process that exposed the tensions between a global ecological sensibility and the sovereign prerogatives of nation-states.

Regulating the flow of dangerous chemicals across the nation's border created a set of complex issues that proved difficult to answer. These issues were compounded as the economic realities of postindustrial capitalism became increasingly apparent. New regulatory institutions like the Environmental Protection Agency (EPA) made significant strides to limit, and at times prohibit, dangerous chemical pesticides. However, this took place in a rapidly changing political and economic landscape that signaled an end to American postwar prosperity. Deindustrialization, double-digit inflation, and the energy crisis, not to mention the political fallout from the Watergate scandal, challenged political leaders to effectively solve complex environmental problems.

Thus, the regulatory debates over chemical pesticides emerged within a larger discussion about the meaning of industrial capitalism and environmental protection in a global age.

Chemicals in the Postwar World

After World War II, American chemical producers introduced a number of new compounds that revolutionized insect pest control. Beginning with the revolutionary and highly controversial pesticide DDT, first synthesized in 1939 by the Swiss chemist Paul Müller, the number of chemicals entering the market exploded. These included compounds similar to DDT, namely, chlordane (1945), aldrin (1947), dieldrin (1948), hepachlor (1949), and endrin (1951), among others. Classified as chlorinated hydrocarbons or persistent organic pollutants (POPs), they share similar attributes: they are broad-spectrum chemicals that destroy most insect pests; they are insoluble in water, so they persist in the environment; they are inexpensive to produce; and on the whole, they have lower toxicity levels for mammals than other chemical pesticides. Another group of pesticides called the organophosphates is derived from a German nerve gas, and is extremely hazardous to both humans and insects. The two most popular were malathion and parathion, each capable of wreaking destruction on a colony of insects or, as sometimes happened, people. Most pesticide-related poisonings are a result of this chemical group. Unlike chlorinated hydrocarbons, organophosphates break down fairly quickly, and the effect of their residues on agricultural commodities is therefore marginal. Most industrial farms rely on organophosphates. The third major pesticide group is the carbamates. As a group they are not as toxic as malathion or parathion and are less persistent than the chlorinated hydrocarbons. The most popular, carbaryl, was developed in 1958 and sold under the trade name Sevin. Sevin was used extensively in the American South as part of a fire ant eradication campaign that failed to effectively control the invasive species. Throughout the postwar period, chemical control strategies were the predominant form of pest control, diminishing other biological or cultural methods.

Of these pesticides, DDT was perhaps that most famous. Hailed as a "miracle" because of its remarkable success in reducing rates of malaria, typhus, and dengue fever during the war, DDT quickly captured the attention of public health officials, agricultural scientists, international development agencies, and foreign policy experts, many of whom promoted DDT as an instrument to liberate the world from insect-borne diseases. Beginning in 1955, the World Health Organization conducted a massive global malaria-eradication campaign using DDT. Over the next twenty years, use of DDT reduced the global impact of the disease to historic lows.

Within the United States as well, DDT represented a triumph of modern technology. Sprayed for crop protection, deployed for public health purposes, including a failed attempt to halt the spread of polio, and dispatched with unquestioning enthusiasm to sanitize suburban landscapes, DDT represented a new age forged by industrial science.

Disease prevention was just one part of a transformative development project. Another was food production. Following the lead of Green revolutionaries like Norman Borlaug, who developed "miracle" wheat while working for the Rockefeller Foundation's Mexican Agricultural Program in the 1950s, international aid experts believed that technological solutions were the keys to overcoming hunger. For most agricultural experts, pesticides were crucial for crop production. Along with other agricultural chemicals, DDT became part of the technical package advocated by agricultural-development experts. Don Paarlberg, director of agricultural economics for the US Department of Agriculture, encapsulated the idea of agricultural development in the developing world: "Scientific and technological progress in agriculture," Paarlberg stated, "must be accelerated, especially in the poor countries."[3]

As early as 1945, scientists had begun documenting the ecological impact of DDT, first at the local level, and over time at the national and global levels.[4] As a persistent pesticide, DDT migrated across borders; once sprayed, the chemical drifted throughout the natural world, impacting wildlife far away from the site of the spraying, including certain species in the Arctic Circle. Excessive spraying, moreover, hastened a biological reality as insects developed resistance to the pesticide. Although public health officials were acutely aware of this evolutionary process by 1950, they nevertheless championed its use. During the 1950s and 1960s, the *Aedes* and *Anopheles* mosquitoes, which spread yellow fever and malaria, respectively, became resistant to the pesticide. By 1969, because DDT was no longer effective, the global malaria eradication campaign came to an end.

Rachel Carson drew greater attention to the environmental and human health hazards of the pesticide in her landmark 1962 book *Silent Spring*. Her ecological critique exposed the long-term impacts of DDT and other persistent chemicals, while underscoring the human health consequences of chemical technologies. She explained nature's ecological complexity in startling simplicity, describing how chemical pesticides interrupted or damaged ecological processes. Perhaps, more importantly, Carson revealed how human beings were not immune to such ecological disruptions, but as biological beings, they were intrinsically connected to the natural world. In doing so, she uncovered the environmental costs to the postwar consumer republic, the danger to human health, and warned of "a spring without voices."

Carson's book resonated with a great many people. Shortly after its publication, environmental groups, such as the Isaak Walton League and the Environmental Defense Fund (EDF), launched an aggressive legal campaign against the pesticide. Following a series of legal proceedings, including a lengthy nine-month hearing examining the risks and benefits of DDT, the Environmental Protection Agency banned the chemical. In determining those risks and benefits, William Ruckelshaus, the EPA's first administrator, made a calculated decision, but one based on sound science. The statute governing pesticide regulation, the 1947 Federal Insecticide, Fungicide and Rodenticide Act (FIFRA), said little about the export of chemical pesticides. Thus, the decision reflected concerns about DDT's domestic rather than international use. Ruckelshaus determined that the risks of DDT for domestic use far outweighed its benefits. For environmentalists, many of whom had devoted much time and energy over the previous decade to publicizing the ecological dangers of the pesticide, this decision was a major victory.[5] The conclusion of the DDT story seemed at hand.

Pesticides and International Governance

For most environmentalists, and environmental historians for that matter, the EPA ruling represented a successful conclusion to the complicated and contested story of DDT. The decision, however, had both a national and international significance. Ruckelshaus's ruling merely canceled the registration of DDT's domestic use, but did not prohibit the manufacture or export of the pesticide. Thus, the export of this banned substance was perfectly legal.

Over the next the decade, the cross-border flow of DDT and other chemical pesticides challenged lawmakers and environmentalists. Indeed, as the list of compounds unfit for domestic use expanded, the export of banned substances created a complex political and environmental issue that was proving difficult to resolve. As the EPA continued to restrict certain chemical pesticides, the question remained: What political problems would emerge from such regulation?

Rusckelshaus saw the DDT ruling as an opportunity to showcase the Nixon administration's commitment to environmental causes, the inconsistency of the ruling notwithstanding. While he firmly believed in the legality of the DDT ruling, he also understood the larger context in which his ruling would be seen. Along with Russell Train, who was at the time the chairman of the White House's Council on Environmental Quality and would become the next EPA administrator in 1973, Ruckelshaus's announcement on the prohibition of DDT was remarkable not only for what he said but also for where he said it. The location selected for the press conference had much to do with the changing context of postwar environmentalism. Ruckelshaus announced the domestic ban of DDT in Stockholm, Sweden, against the backdrop of the first United Nations Conference on the Human Environment.

The Stockholm conference represented an initial attempt to create an international regulatory framework. At the suggestion of Swedish officials, the United Nations brought together representatives from 114 nations, 16 intergovernmental agencies, and more than 250 nongovernmental organizations to discuss a broad array of environmental issues confronting the world. In their unofficial report of the Stockholm conference, titled *Only One Earth*, the British economist Barbara Ward and the French biologist René Dubos, who coined the phrase, "think globally, act locally," wrote, "There was general agreement among [attendees] that environmental problems are becoming increasingly worldwide and therefore demand a global approach."[6] In particular, conference attendees focused on the environmental problems that confronted the developed world and the developing world disproportionately. At issue were the environmental problems caused by development (i.e., air and water pollution, industrial waste, etc.) and the promise of development to ease environmental problems in the "developing word" (i.e., poverty, famine, disease).[7] Depending upon one's point of view, DDT was either the cause of poor health or the solution to it. For most Stockholm attendees, DDT was more the former than the latter.

The conference laid the groundwork for further international cooperation regarding pesticides. Conference participants agreed "to review and further develop international guidelines and standards with special reference to national and ecological conditions in relation to the use of chlorinated hydrocarbons [DDT], pesticides containing heavy metals, and the use and experimentation of biological controls."[8] It was not until the 2001 Stockholm Convention on POPs that an international framework was established to reduce and/or eliminate threats to human and environmental health. Signatories agreed to curtail the use of persistent chemicals for all agricultural and public health measures. However, countries could use DDT "with the goal of decreasing the human and economic burden of disease" if alternatives could not be developed. As of 2011, the United States had not ratified this convention.

To showcase the nation's commitment to international environmental governance, Ruckelshaus and Train led a sizeable diplomatic contingent. Other American participants included Christian A. Herter, Jr., the deputy assistant secretary of state for environmental and population affairs; Rogers

C. B. Morton, secretary of the interior; Laurence Rockefeller, chairman of the Citizens Advisory Committee on Environmental Quality; and former movie star Shirley Temple Black, who served as a US delegate to the United Nations. According to Train, the early 1970s marked a period when the United States was "the clear world leader...in terms of both domestic environmental policy and international cooperation."[9] This theme was reiterated by the assistant secretary of agriculture, Richard Lyng, who later argued, "The solution to the worldwide concerns about health and environmental matters does not lie in unilateral action by any nation against other nations. It lies in concerted international action...[and] through accelerated international cooperation."[10] By the early 1970s, many US policy makers believed the United States not only was at the forefront of environmental governance but also had an important role in solving global environmental problems.

Yet, when it came to DDT regulation, the United States was not alone. West Germany, for example, banned DDT in 1969. In 1970, Cuba prohibited its use, and Sweden announced it would impose a two-year ban on DDT. That same year, Australia declared it was "rapidly phasing out" the use on DDT to avoid possible restrictions on its produce exports. Indeed, the United States was one on a growing list of nations to prohibit the chemical, a list that would continue to grow.

Nonetheless, Montrose Chemical Corporation, the lone remaining producer of the chemical within the United States, continued to make and export DDT. After its domestic prohibition, US foreign policy officials continued to purchase large quantities of DDT for international public health projects. During the 1970s, US chemical producers steadily increased their presence in the global marketplace, even as they faced stiffer competition from European producers. The discordant strands of US pesticide policy as well as the competing agendas of the EPA regulatory regime, the State Department, and US chemical producers would only become more pronounced throughout the decade. Even though many environmentalists had celebrated the EPA ruling and the nation's participation and leadership at the Stockholm Conference, the meaning of DDT and chemical pesticides in general remained ambiguous at best.

Expansion of the Global Pesticide Market

Despite the EPA's ruling, domestic regulation meant increased profits for Montrose Chemical. Beginning in 1947, the company produced technical-grade DDT at its facility in Torrance, California. At the height of production between

1968 and 1970, the company turned out nearly 80 million pounds of the pesticide, making it the nation's leading DDT producer.[11] By the early 1970s, it held a virtual monopoly on the domestic production of DDT. Olin Mathieson, Allied Chemical, Diamond Shamrock, and the Lebanon Chemical Corporation abandoned the DDT market altogether in the wake of new EPA regulation and shrinking profits.[12] Montrose, on the other hand, established itself firmly in both the domestic and international marketplace, and for a time was able to not only weather environmental regulation but prosper. A major factor for the company's success was that the quality of the DDT it produced far exceeded that of its competitors, making the Montrose brand a more effective and valued insecticide. According to Montrose president Samuel Rotrosen, "The [EPA] decision did not impact us in that it made us stop making DDT. As a matter of fact, we had the most profitable years of our corporate history in the few years following the decision."[13]

Similarly, for many US chemical manufacturers, the expanding global marketplace increased profit margins. Stauffer Chemical Company, for example, which had a 50 percent controlling interest in Montrose, embarked on a ten-year period of tremendous growth. Total sales doubled between 1972 and 1976, from $543 million to $1.1 billion. During that same period, sales of Stauffer's agricultural chemical line rose from $70 million to $198 million, soaring to $299 million by 1979.[14] Stauffer's international sales division increased from $167 million in 1975 to $271 million in 1979.[15] Other chemical corporations followed suit. In 1977, DuPont garnered almost one-quarter of its total sales from the international market. Dow, Union Carbide, and Monsanto reported similar sales figures from foreign sales.[16] Between 1947 and 1978, annual domestic chemical production rose more than 900 percent.[17] In 1975, the International Trade Commission reported that production of pesticides had doubled to almost 1.6 billion pounds over the previous four years. [18]

US manufacturers were not the sole suppliers of chemical pesticides in the world market. European chemical producers played a critical role in internationalizing pesticides as well. Ciba-Geigy (Switzerland), ICI (England), Bayer (Germany), and Rhône Poulenc (France) were the four largest pesticide corporations in the world by the end of the 1980s.[19] Because of the strength of European industries and lack of export regulation in Switzerland, France, and Great Britain, US manufacturers believed that federal regulation of the export market would put them at a competitive disadvantage.[20]

These fears were both well founded and wildly inaccurate. Dow Chemical chairman Carl A. Gerstacker made a highly provocative statement regarding federal regulation and the global chemical market. Speaking at the White

House Conference on the Industrial World Ahead in February 1972, Gerstacker stated:

> I have long dreamed of buying an island owned by no nation…and of establishing the World Headquarters of the Dow company on the truly neutral ground of such an island, beholden to no nation or society. If we were located on such truly neutral ground we could then really operate in the United States as U.S. citizens, in Japan as Japanese citizens and in Brazil as Brazilians rather than being governed in prime by the laws of the United States…. We could even pay any natives handsomely to move elsewhere.[21]

Like the chemical agents that flowed freely across political boundaries, Gerstacker's dream of fluid borders and shifting identities underscores the profound changes in both the global environment and the global marketplace.

Without question, chemicals were rapidly becoming part of the total environment. They were, in fact, inescapable. Within this increasingly toxic environment, each nation held its own ideas about how to protect, consume, or preserve natural environments. Globally, the number of countries with national environmental agencies increased from 26 to 144 between 1972 and 1982, making the national distinctions that much clearer.[22] However, global capitalism and the legacy of conquest and colonialism often impinged on some nations' ability to regulate their natural environments alone. So while Gerstacker's dream went unfulfilled—there is no Dow Island—in the context of understanding the new regulatory landscape, the desire to transcend boundaries to circumvent environmental regulation and shed a specific national identity reflects the rapidly shifting global economy.

Regardless of businessmen's concerns, the global pesticide market exploded during the 1970s. From 1972 to 1985 imports of pesticides increased by 261 percent in Asia, 95 percent in Africa, and 48 percent in South America.[23] In the Philippines, imports of pesticides grew fivefold between 1972 and 1978.[24] In Egypt, the amount of pesticides used in crop production jumped from 2143 tons in 1953 to 12,550 tons in 1963 to 28,340 tons in 1978.[25] India's pesticide use increased at an annual rate of 12 percent during the 1970s and 1980s.[26] The upsurge of the global pesticide market has led to what historian Angus Wright has called "the modern agricultural dilemma." The use of modern technologies, many of which are extremely hazardous to humans and the environment, has transformed agricultural production throughout much of the world. And while food production rates have skyrocketed so, too, have agricultural lands become much more dangerous places.

Burdens and Consequences of US Pesticide Regulation

By 1973, the regulatory climate within the United States had changed considerably. Upon assuming the leadership of the EPA in 1973, Russell Train understood that "the environmental honeymoon had come to an end."[27] The looming energy crisis cast a long shadow over environmental politics as it expressed both the nation's overreliance on foreign oil and the impact of environmental regulation that many business leaders considered an undue hardship for American industry.[28] While many celebrated new emission standards and water safety measures, others were aghast at the regulatory burden imposed on American businesses. "As the economy soured," Train remarked, "environmental programs...became the whipping boy for inflation and job losses."[29] The energy crisis created enormous obstacles for the EPA as it sought to shift from rulemaking to enforcement.

Environmental groups like the EDF continued to press the EPA to control environmentally dangerous pesticides. In 1974, an EDF lawsuit led to a ban of aldrin and dieldrin. This time however, when EPA administrator Train issued the cancellation order, he also suspended production, because aldrin and dieldrin were found to be an "imminent hazard" to the public health.[30] Testimony produced undisputable evidence of the chemicals' carcinogenic effects on mice and rats. A year later, Train ruled against Vesicol Chemical Corporation, manufacturer of heptachlor and chlordane, when he ordered an end to production after studies had shown that those chemicals produced cancers in laboratory animals.[31] Federal regulation ended the domestic health threat associated with the use and production of these pesticides; however, they continued to pose enormous risks overseas. In response, corporations simply moved production and research facilities abroad. The National Pest Control Association claimed, "EPA action in registration and enforcement policy have discouraged continued pesticide research and development in the United States. One major pesticide producer is alleged to have said that in this atmosphere, 40% of its R&D will be conducted abroad by 1980."[32] In another case, Shell moved production facilities from California to the Netherlands and continued to manufacture aldrin.[33]

From a foreign policy perspective, the movement of capital overseas complicated but did not fundamentally alter the ambitions of the US Agency for International Development (USAID) or other aid organizations. Indeed, for many foreign policy experts increasing crop yields was of paramount concern to ensure both the safety and well-being of millions of malnourished people and America's standing abroad. Fear over the environmental and political impact of population growth, or overpopulation as some suggested, elevated once minor concerns about food production to places of prominence within diplomatic circles. Speaking at the World Food Conference in 1974, US secretary of state Henry Kissinger proclaimed, "We are convinced that the world faces a challenge new in its severity, its pervasiveness, and its global dimension." Furthermore, drawing on ecological principles with a forthrightness that would have astonished Rachel Carson, Kissinger told his audience, "We are faced not just with the problem of food but with the accelerating momentum of our interdependence." Indeed, it became increasingly apparent to most foreign policy experts and to Americans more generally that the problems of the world could not be solved by individual nations. Kissinger spoke of "interdependent economies," and suggested that famine "was once considered part of the normal cycle of man's existence, a local or at worst a national tragedy. Now our consciousness is global."[34]

For Kissinger, and for that matter for many international development specialists, the solution to the world food crisis was not to rethink the consequences of modern agriculture but to continue to promote technological solutions. "Existing pesticides must be made more generally available," Kissinger told the assembled crowd: they "are simple and inexpensive" and "could have a rapid and substantial impact on the world's food supply."

US Foreign Aid and Environmental Regulation

Amid these debates, discussion of DDT use within the United States seemed to be a distant memory. Although the chemical was briefly reintroduced in 1974 as part of an emergency measure to control tussock moths in the Pacific Northwest, most Americans considered the matter closed. So it must have come as a shock to find the pesticide making news once again, this time as part of a larger debate over the ethics of exporting banned substances overseas. In December 1976, the *Washington Post* reported that the USAID had been engaged in facilitating the transfer to foreign nations of chemicals banned or considered hazardous within the United States.[35] In 1974, USAID purchased DDT from Montrose Chemical and shipped it to India, Ethiopia, Nepal, Indonesia, South Vietnam, and Haiti for malaria control and agricultural-development projects. USAID also purchased and shipped leptophos, a chemical manufactured by Velsicol Chemical Corporation. Sold under the trade name Phosvel, leptophos had made headlines in 1976, when Velsicol workers experienced dizziness, impaired vision, and partial paralysis. These extreme nervous disorders, which gave rise to the term "Phosvel zombies," shocked the American public when the press reported on the workers' condition. US authorities had given leptophos only a temporary registration in 1971, but the chemical was exported around the world. In one extreme case, 1200 water buffaloes died in Egypt of leptophos poisoning.[36] Passage of the 1976 Toxic Substances Control Act, which prohibited the manufacture or importation of nonregistered chemicals, only confounded the public's trust in the nation's regulatory system. Indeed, it seemed incredible to some that US corporations continued to manufacture and export dangerous chemicals.

In June 1977, public furor further escalated when the Consumer Product Safety Commission removed Tris-treated sleepwear from the market. Tris (2,3-dibromoprophyl), a flame retardant added to children's sleepwear, was found to cause cancer in lab animals. Thankful parents cautiously rejoiced at the decision, but many manufacturers exported their excess inventory to avoid substantial financial losses. Tris-treated sleepwear was later found in Bogota, Caracas, and even Paris.[37] As a result of this public disclosure, in 1977 Congress began holding a series of hearings on the export and re-importation of banned substances. Triggered by the controversy over the Tris-treated sleepwear, the federal government worked to establish procedures to grapple with this complex issue. The report, based on the congressional hearings, underscored the dilemma, reporting, "There is, at present, no consistent, uniform approach to U.S. export policy as it affects products banned by U.S. regulatory agencies." The report also found that there were no procedures in place to deal with re-importation of banned substances and urged that the matter "be considered a potentially serious problem and accounted for in agency decisions."[38]

USAID officials were caught in the crosshairs of competing interests and regulatory confusion. Throughout the 1960s, USAID served an important function in advancing the nation's foreign policy agenda, including underwriting large parts of the Green Revolution, a massive agricultural development project that required chemical fertilizers and pesticides. It also had served as the funding agent supplying foreign nations with American-made DDT for public health programs. Yet domestic environmental regulation, particularly the National Environmental Policy Act (NEPA), created a regulatory hurdle for the State Department. At issue was the requirement established in NEPA that all federal projects undergo a comprehensive environmental review prior to initiation. In conducting such a study, federal agencies could better determine the short- and long-term "impacts" of a particular project. The issue USAID faced, not surprisingly, was that all its projects were on foreign soil. How could the environmental impact of a project be determined in a country where the risk/benefit calculus might be completely different from a similar project undertaken within the United States? "It raises many unanswered questions," Christian A. Herter, Jr., special assistant to the secretary of state for environmental affairs, wrote. "What are the consequences of polluting your neighbors? What are the damages?...the responsibilities?...the liabilities? What is the forum in which they seek redress?"[39] While some State Department officials countered that they were not required to adhere to NEPA regulations since their programs took place beyond US borders, others saw a difficult dilemma.[40]

In light of these controversies, Charles Warren, the Council of Environmental Quality (CEQ) chairman, asked, "What kinds of serious environmental damage can happen—and sometimes has happened—as a result of US government actions outside our borders?...What do we stand to gain from a careful, sensitive application of the National Environmental Policy Act to the conduct of our international programs?"[41] Warren's comments confirmed the dilemma faced by USAID as questions about agricultural development, environmental protection, and US aid became increasingly intertwined. In testimony before the Senate Committee on Foreign Relations in 1976, Russell Train proclaimed, "We are part of an increasingly interdependent and interrelated world.... There can be no thought of a retreat into isolationism." US environmentalism and foreign policy, Train noted, were "interdependent." While these issues were becoming clearer to US policy makers, they remained uncertain about how to construct a regulatory framework that considered national and international environments. "International environmental cooperation," Train continued, represented "an international extension, a global dimension, of our own domestic priorities."[42] Train made a case for the expansion of environmental programs nationally and internationally, but imbued in his comments was the belief that the global was simply a broader canvas on which to extend the "domestic priorities" of the nation.

Indeed, for those who claimed that DDT regulation exposed a deep flaw in US environmental governance, the issues were not as clear-cut as proponents of increased federal legislation believed. On the surface, "dumping" banned substances into foreign markets may seem dangerous and unethical, but environmental and public health factors in other countries may warrant or demand the use of products banned in the United States. Prior to the 1979 UN Vienna Conference on Science and Technology for Development, a *Washington Post* editorial offered an alternative to the "usual platitudes" and oft-stated need for "new 'institutional' mechanisms" that often played out at international conferences. The paper suggested that the conference find a way "to curb runaway industries and [set up] mutually acceptable controls over the export of hazardous substances." More significantly, however, it explored the banned-substances controversy in a highly nuanced way.

It's not as easy to regulate such exports as it might seem. Most health and safety regulations balance risks and benefits, and these judgments reflect values—*our* values—and generally not those of all of us at that. Imposing such decisions on others comes perilously close to stepping on some other country's sovereignty. Also, different environmental conditions may mitigate the nature of the hazard, acceptable alternatives may not be available or conditions may be such that a risk that looks unacceptable here seems well worth taking.[43]

The *Washington Post* reminded its readers of the complexity of environmental regulation in a global age. At a time when many environmentalists embraced the ecological ideas of wholeness and universality, political borders and regional differences, the paper suggested, still mattered.

For the remainder of the decade, Congress continued to tinker with the international dimensions of US pesticide regulation. In 1978, it established mandatory notification to foreign countries in the event hazardous materials were shipped overseas. Likewise, the 1978 FIFRA amendments required new labels that identified the product and producer of the pesticide. They also required the exporter of unregistered pesticides to obtain a written acknowledgment from the foreign purchaser stipulating full disclosure of the transaction. Finally, labels for unregistered pesticides had to be bilingual.[44] However, budgetary constraints prevented proper enforcement of these laws, which required the cooperation of multiple federal agencies.

Ecology, Nation-States, and the End of DDT

On January 15, 1981, just five days before he left office, President Carter signed Executive Order 12264, which prohibited export of banned substances from the United States, including Tris-treated clothing, leptophos, and DDT. Carter's order imposed additional regulatory and reporting responsibilities on the State Department, EPA, the Food and Drug Administration, and the Consumer Product Safety Commission.[45] In signing the order, Carter stated that it "emphasizes to other countries . . . that they can trust goods bearing the label 'Made In U.S.A.'"[46] At a time when America's standing in the world had reached its nadir, Carter attempted to bolster the country's reputation by invoking the terms "trust" and "Made in the U.S.A." When President Reagan moved into the White House and began to reverse Carter's executive orders, Representative Michael Barnes (Democrat-Maryland) said in defiance, "The label 'Made in America' should be taken as a guarantee, not a warning."[47]

Meanwhile, Montrose Chemical entered into an unfavorable global market, as increased competition from companies in France and Italy, unfavorable international exchange rates, and the continued presence of environmental regulation transformed the once lucrative market into a hostile battleground. As a result, Montrose Chemical ended its production of DDT in June 1982. The decision signified the company's unwillingness to compete with foreign manufacturers, falling prices, and the increased burdens of environmental regulations. The plant's closure represented the definitive triumph for environmentalists, a victory that had been twenty years in the making. Yet, the long-term environmental impact of thirty-five years of production left substantial scars. Montrose Chemical was embroiled in environmental litigation over illegal dumping into municipal sewer systems for the remainder of the century.[48]

Although the United States no longer produced DDT by 1982, the ways in which the chemical became part of a much broader discussion about environmental regulation within and beyond state borders remained unresolved. US chemical producers, including Montrose Chemical, had simply sidestepped domestic regulation either by selling their wares overseas or moving production facilities across the border. Moreover, the belief that chemical technologies were (and are) an important part of US foreign policy, especially for improving agricultural yields, also exposed tensions between competing state interests on different sides of the border. By the 1980s American policy makers understood pesticide policy through the complex framework of a global marketplace and questioned the risks and benefits of selling US-made chemicals around the world. Even with the regulatory burdens placed on domestic pesticide manufacturers and users in the early 1970s, chemicals continued to flow freely across borders throughout the decade. Despite the gains made on an international scale, with the 2001 Stockholm POPs Convention, regulating dangerous pesticides across borders remains a complicated and contested process that challenges the actions of the nation in the global environment.

The history of pesticide regulation exposed the limits of environmental governance, the understanding of human health within and beyond US borders, and the complicated politics of popular ecology. Throughout the 1970s, US policy makers, environmental groups, and the chemical industry held different views regarding the risks and benefits of chemical pesticides within and beyond the United States. On the one hand, environmentalists understood pesticides as a global contaminant that needs to be regulated accordingly. On the other hand, American chemical producers viewed the world beyond US borders as an emerging market. The State Department, as I have suggested, lay somewhere in between.

Despite these conflicting viewpoints, all those involved in the pesticide debates shared a common assumption. They all believed that what was in the best interest of the United States were also in the best interest of the world. Environmentalists criticized the seemingly contradictory aspect of US pesticide policy because they saw the world as an interconnected whole. Therefore, identifying DDT, or any other chemical pesticide, as an environmental hazard within the United States meant that that same pesticide was equally hazardous elsewhere, regardless of local political, social, economic, and environmental conditions. For the chemical industry, expanding the global pesticide market meant that pest control problems could be solved universally. Pesticides not only simplified insect control measures around the world, but also undermined local knowledge about insects, food production, and environments.

Americans thought their approaches to insect control, food production, or environmental protection could be universally applied. Yet, the political and ecological realities of the world beyond US borders challenged these universal assertions. In other words, place matters. So while ecology provided Americans with a framework to think about the interconnectivity of "whole" planet, or as Barry Commoner stated, "everything is connected to everything else," they tended to ignore local contexts and ecological variance. These universal impulses ultimately masked significant economic, political, and environmental differences within the United States and other parts of the world.

The pesticide debates were just a small part of a larger political transformation that embraced ecology as a way to understand complicated problems. The concepts of wholeness, interconnectivity, and codependence shaped how environmentalists and foreign policy officials explained a changing world. Environmental issues, they all argued, did not stop at the border and thus could not be solved by any one nation-state. Yet as Americans grappled with the complexity of US pesticide policy in a global age, they did so by placing their interests above those of other nations. Perhaps as we continue to rethink the uses of chemical technologies in our own time, these historical lessons will serve us well.

NOTES

1. This essay is adapted from *DDT and the American Century: Global Health, Environmental Politics, and the Pesticide that Changed the World* by David Kinkela. Copyright 2011 by the University of North Carolina Press. Used by permission of the publisher. www.uncpress.unc.edu. See Adam Rome, *Bulldozer in the Countryside: Suburban Sprawl and the Rise of American Environmentalism* (New York: Cambridge University Press, 2001).

2. See Ted Steinberg, *Down to Earth: Nature's Role in American History* (New York: Oxford University Press, 2002).

3. Don Paarlberg, "Changing World Needs for Grains in the 1970s," January 22, 1973, El Batan Mexico, IX A 1, Special Collections, National Agricultural Library, Beltsville, MD.

4. See Clarence Cottam and Elmer Higgins, "DDT and Its Effect on Fish and Wildlife," *Journal of Economic Entomology* 39 (February 1946): 44–52.

5. John C. Whitaker, *Striking a Balance: Environment and Natural Resources Policy in the Nixon-Ford Years* (Washington, DC: American Enterprise for Public Policy Research, 1976), 134.

6. Barbara Ward and René Dubos, *United Nations Conference on the Human Environment, Only One Earth: The Care and Maintenance of a Small Planet* (New York: Norton, 1972), xv.

7. Because the Soviet Union and other eastern-bloc countries boycotted the conference, much attention was devoted to the environmental consequences of economic and social development along the north-south axis. Björn-Ola Linnér and Henrik Selin, "How It All Began: Global Efforts on Sustainable Development from Stockholm to Rio," paper presented at 6th Nordic Conference on Environmental Social Sciences, Åbo, Finland, June 12–14, 2003, as part of the panel "Johannesburg: A First Anniversary." http://www.cid.harvard.edu/cidbiotech/events/selinlinnerpaper100603. doc. For an earlier summary of the conference see Wade Rowland, *The Plot to Save the World: The Life and Times of the Stockholm Conference of the Human Environment* (Toronto: Clarke, Irwin, 1973).

8. "Recommendations for Action at the International Level," The United Nations Conference on the Human Environment, Recommendation 21, 1972. www. unep.org.

9. Train, *Politics, Pollution and Panda*, 123.

10. Richard E. Lyng to W. R. Poage, October 6, 1970, box 106, file 457, Hyde Murray Papers, BCPM, Waco, Texas.

11. Deposition of Samuel Rotrosen, October 13, 1992, Unites States of America, et al., v. Montrose Chemical Corporation of California, et al., No. CV 90-3122 AAH (JRX) (hereafter, Rotrosen Deposition)

12. DDT: A Review of Scientific and Economic Aspects of the Decision to Ban Its Use as a Pesticide Prepared for: Committee on Appropriations, U.S. House of Representatives, Environmental Protection Agency, July 1975, RG 412, Headquarter Records of the Environmental Protection Agency, National Archives, College Park, MD.

13. Rotrosen Deposition, 409.

14. Stauffer Chemical Corporation Annual Report, 1976, 1979. In 1976, the Stauffer Corporation comprised eight main product lines: Industrial Chemicals, Chemical Systems, Fertilizer and Mining, Specialty Chemicals, Plastics, Food Ingredients, Agricultural Chemicals, and International Operations.

15. Stauffer Chemical Corporation Annual Report, 1979. Sales figures from Stauffer's international sales division consisted of foreign subsidiaries and export. In 1979, export sales totaled $103 million. And for a three-year period ending in 1979, foreign sales increased 2.7 times.

16. Ronie Garcia-Johnson, *Exporting Environmentalism: U.S. Multinational Chemical Corporation in Brazil and Mexico* (Cambridge, MA: MIT Press, 2000), 86. Dow's foreign sales were 35 percent; Union Carbide, 26 percent; and Monsanto, 23 percent.

17. Ruth Norris, ed., *Pills, Pesticides and Profits* (Croton-on-Hudson, NY: North River Press, 1982), 5.

18. Comptroller General's Report to the Congress, "Better Regulation of Pesticide Exports and Pesticide Residues in Imported Food is Essential," (Washington DC, 1979), 1.

19. Barbara Dinham, comp., *The Pesticide Hazard: A Global Health and Environmental Audit* (London: Zed, 1993), 13.

20. Francine Schilberg, "Comment: United States Export of Products Banned for Domestic Use," *Harvard International Law Journal* 20, no. 2 (spring 1979): 350, ff98, 361.

21. Quoted in Richard J. Barnet and Ronald E. Müller, *Global Reach: The Power of the Multinational Corporations* (New York: Simon and Schuster, 1974), 16.

22. Garcia-Johnson, *Exporting Environmentalism*, 87. Of course, while creating a political body responsive to environmental problems represented a significant achievement, enforcement of environmental policies, however, proved to be a difficult task for developing nations due to lack of financial resources.

23. Sandra Postel, *Defusing the Toxics Threat: Controlling Pesticides and Industrial Waste*, Worldwatch paper 79, September 1979.

24. Rafael V. Mariano, "The Politics of Pesticides," paper presented from Peasant Movement of the Philippines, November 11, 1999. Mariano was the then president of the Kilusang Magbubukid ng Pilipinas ([KMP], Peasant Movement of the Philippines). Like many grassroots movements in the "developing" world, KMP understood the ecological and human-health hazards associated with the global pesticide trade.

25. Spilt years represent growing season. See Barbara Dinham, comp., *The Pesticide Hazard: A Global Health and Environmental Audit* (London: Zed, 1993), 142.

26. Ibid., 159.

27. Train, *Politics, Pollution, and Pandas*, 156.

28. Gladwin Hill, "Environment: Reformers Are Undismayed by the Energy Crisis," *New York Times*, December 2, 1973, 80. This article quotes Texaco chairman Maurice Granville, who claimed that the energy crisis could correct "the overreaction to environmental and consumerist concerns reflected in current statutes and regulations."

29. Train, *Politics, Pollution, and Pandas*, 156.

30. The ruling prohibited Shell Chemical Company, the sole domestic manufacturer, from producing nearly 10 million pounds of the chemical in 1975. See Whitaker, *Striking the Balance*, 136.

31. EPA press release, "Train Stops Manufacture of Heptachlor/Chlordane, Cities Imminent Cancer Risk," July 30, 1975. http://www.epa.gov/history/topics/

legal/01.htm. Also see, Charles Wurster, "The Case against Aldrin, Dieldrin," *Audubon*, November 1973, 121–4.

32. Letter from Richard L. Eldredge, Executive Director, National Pest Control Association, to John R. Quarles, deputy administrator, EPA, August 6, 1975, box 7, George Humphreys, Associate Director for Environment, 1975–77, Ford Library, Ann Arbor, MI.

33. Jane H, Ives, "The Heath Effects of the Transfer of Technology to the Developing World: Report and Case Studies," in *The Export of Hazard: Transnational Corporations and Environmental Control Issues*, ed. Jane H. Ives (Boston: Routledge, 1985), 182. In 1985, the nonprofit organization Pesticide Action Network identified DDT, dieldrin, aldrin, heptachlor, chlordane, and seven other chemicals as the "dirty dozen."

34. Address by the Honorable Henry A. Kissinger, Secretary of State before the World Food Conference, November 6, 1974, box 10, papers of Paul Leach, Ford Presidential Library, Ann Arbor, MI.

35. Peter Millius and Dan Morgan, "Hazardous Pesticide Sent as Aid," *Washington Post*, December 8, 1976, A1, A13.

36. David Bull, *A Growing Problem: Pesticides and the Third World Poor* (Oxford: Oxfam, 1982), 40.

37. Mark Hosenball, "Karl Marx and the Pajama Game," *Mother Jones*, November 1979, 47.

38. House Committee on Government Operations, *Report on Export of Products Banned By U.S. Regulatory Agencies*, 95th Congress, 2d session, 1978, H. Doc. 1686, 3, 28.

39. Christian A. Herter, Jr., "Rx for a Cleaner, Healthier World," *Dupont Context* (February 1972), 22.

40. Letter from James R. Fowler, Special Assistant and Executive Director, A.I.D. Committee on Environmental and Development to James Frey, Office of Management and Budget, October 22, 1971, RG 286, Records of USAID, HQ of the Administrator, Subject Files, 1971–72, National Archives, Washington, DC.

41. Charles Warren, "Feeling Uncle Sam's Actions Abroad," *Washington Post*, February 6, 1978.

42. Russell Train, EPA administrator, Testimony Before the Committee on Foreign Relations, May 5, 1976, box 7, papers of George Humphreys, Ford Library.

43. "Trouble for Export," *Washington Post*, August 27, 1979, A26.

44. Andrew B. Waldo, "A Review of US and International Restrictions on Exports of Hazardous Substances," in Ives, *Export of Hazard*, 20–2.

45. Executive Order, "Federal Policy Regarding the Export of Banned or Significantly Restricted Materials," *Federal Register* 46 (January 19, 1981), 4659.

46. Quoted in Joanne Omang, "Carter Limits U.S. export of Banned Items," *Washington Post*, January 16, 1981, D1.

47. Quoted in "Unconcern for Hazards Is Ascribed to Reagan," *Washington Post*, March 13, 1981, A30.

48. Two suits were filed against Montrose Chemical Corporation of California. See Montrose Chemical Corporation of California v. Admiral Insurance Company, Citation: 10 Cal.4th 645. Court: Supreme Court. Docket no: S026013. Also see United States, et al. v. Montrose Chemical Corporation of California, et al. For an overview of Montrose Chemical Corporation litigation see, Terence Kehoe and Charles Jacobson, "Environmental Decision Making and DDT Production at Montrose Chemical Corporation of California," *Enterprise and Society* 4, no. 4 (2003): 640–75.

PART II

Nature, Nation-States, and Global Networks of Knowledge and Exchange

7

The Imperial Politics of Hurricane Prediction

*From Calcutta and Havana to Manila
and Galveston, 1839–1900*

Gregory T. Cushman

During the first week of June 1839, a strong "gale and hurricane" traversed the northern shore of the Bay of Bengal. There was nothing particularly notable about the storm. Far more destructive ones struck the region in 1831, 1832, 1842, and 1864. But this 1839 tempest was carefully watched by Henry Piddington, a retired merchant ship captain at the center of scientific life in British-ruled Calcutta. Inspired by the hurricane studies of colleagues in New England and the British West Indies, Piddington took advantage of his privileged position at one of the nodes of maritime trade in Asia and began to systematically gather information about storms in the Indian and western Pacific Oceans from the logs of other European ship captains, correspondence with colonial officials, and the archives of the East India Company. He was intensely devoted to the belief that the advancement of science and technology was a crucial mechanism of civilization's progress, and a critical measure of Europe's right to rule over colonized territories.[1]

Violent storms presented an enormous hazard to the coastal population, mercantile trade, and British geopolitical interests in the Indo-Pacific. In November 1839, storm surge inundated the port of Coringa, India, destroying seventy vessels, killing more than 20,000 people, and bringing a catastrophic end to the area's export textile trade.[2] In September 1840, a pair of deadly typhoons in the South China Sea sank the HMS *Golconda*, which was carrying 300 Indian Infantry to take part in China's First Opium War. According to Piddington's evaluation for the Marine Courts of Enquiry in Calcutta, the disaster could have been averted if the ship's captain had made use of the latest scientific understanding of these storms.[3] With support from the Indian government, Piddington eventually compiled his insights into a popular handbook that examined the occurrence of maritime storms in various regions of the world, the use of the barometer to detect them, and the phenomenon of storm waves. But its most important advice rested on Robert Redfield's observation in New England that winds blow in a curved pattern around these rotary storms, which spin counterclockwise in the Northern Hemisphere and clockwise south of the equator. Piddington coined the word "cyclone" to describe this behavior, and for decades his work remained a benchmark for sailors and scientists around the world on the nature of this dangerous transnational phenomenon born in the trackless tropical ocean.[4]

Another incident in the history of British imperial science changed the possibilities of communicating knowledge of these storms across the sea. In 1843, a Scottish physician living in Singapore sent a bottle of "milky juice" from a tree common to the rain forests of Malaysia and Borneo back to England, where it was presented to the Society for the Encouragement of Arts, Manufactures, and Commerce. This substance proved to have remarkable qualities as a moldable plastic and electrical insulator. Two bastions of imperial science from this era, Kew Botanic Garden in England and Buitenzorg Botanic Garden in Dutch-ruled Java, organized expeditions to identify the source plant and its distribution. Gutta percha, as this latex is known, turned out to be well suited to the manufacture of undersea telegraph cables. These cables were first laid across the English Channel in 1850–1851 but were extended between Ceylon and the imperial telegraph network on the Indian mainland in 1857–1858 in response to a huge anticolonial uprising. The cables made it technologically feasible to send word of an approaching cyclone the length of the Bay of Bengal.[5]

These two episodes exemplify the importance of science and technology in imperial expansion during the nineteenth century. The development of telegraphic networks played an especially significant role in the progress of meteorology as a science. Even at the molasses-slow transmission rates of the mid-nineteenth century, telegraphs made it possible to construct a synoptic picture of the basic weather each day using information from meteorological observatories scattered over a huge territory. After this data was mapped, it could be used to produce viable forecasts for the next day or two. The United States, with its growing empire connected by railroad and telegraph, developed the first continental-scale network with these capabilities, which became a model for the world's meteorological services. Those at the receiving end of observer networks possessed an enormous advantage in watching weather development. It should come as no surprise that many atmospheric scientists embraced imperial expansion and fought among themselves for supremacy over colonial observer networks to reinforce their privileged positions.[6] The development of marine trade, telegraph networks, and imperial governance also drove advances in the scientific study of electromagnetism, tides, botany, deep-sea oceanography, and seismology.[7] Meanwhile, the prevalence of cholera, dysentery, yellow fever, bubonic plague, "El Niño famines," and other danger-ous border-crossing natural phenomena gave additional impetus to interna-tional efforts to understand and control the environment.[8]

Much the same was true of the science of hurricane prediction. The main benefits in this case, however, did not accrue to the strength and glory of the world's great powers but instead to merchant seamen and a transnational reli-gious order operating across imperial boundaries. Jesuit missionaries took advantage of their privileged positions at the nodes of telegraphic communica-tion networks in two storm-prone regions to develop the world's first interna-tional warning systems for tropical cyclones. They also contributed significant innovations to the understanding of storm circulation and movement, and this work helped the Society of Jesus to both expand its influence internationally during the nineteenth century and regain some of its former strength as an autonomous power within the colonized world. Jesuit organizational leader-ship made hurricane science truly transnational.[9] These accomplishments were similar in many respects to the way geophysicists from Scandinavia used their attachment to the aviation industry to operate across national boundaries and to advance an approach to weather prediction that focused on warm and cold fronts. The "Norwegian school" successfully colonized the meteorologi-cal services of Canada, the United States, and most of Latin America and the Caribbean between the First and Second World Wars.[10]

International businessmen and mariners involved in oceanic trade encour-aged Jesuit efforts and had much to gain from them. The timely communi-cation of storm advisories by undersea telegraph enabled ship captains and investors to act quickly to protect themselves from loss, even across great dis-tances. News of a disaster might also present an opportunity to profit from the misfortune of others. But the relationship between natural disaster and inter-national commerce also had geopolitical stakes. According to historian Sherry Johnson, severe hurricanes in the Caribbean between 1766 and 1780 disrupted the supply of foodstuffs to the region, opened the way to free interimperial trade, and played a significant role in the birth of the United States of America and the outbreak of the Age of Revolution.[11] A century later, a handful of mul-tinational corporations gained notoriety for buying up property and resources in Pacific South America in the wake of El Niño floods, tsunamis, and other catastrophes. In the process, they acquired a transnational base of wealth and power that later became a target for local officials worried about their home-land's dependency on foreign powers.[12] According to historian Kevin Rozario, natural disasters have provided a major stimulus to the growth of American capitalism—an argument that should be extended to include the US relation-ship with the rest of the world.[13]

During the 1890s, undersea telegraph lines became the focus of intense interimperial rivalry, and Jesuit storm-prediction networks were no excep-tion.[14] After colonizing Cuba and the Philippines in 1898 and 1899, the United States gained direct control over telegraphic communications going in and out of the Caribbean and across the South China Sea, including the transmission of storm advisories. However, the differing geopolitical configurations of these two colonized regions prevented the United States from unilaterally dictating the continued place of Jesuit scientists in storm-prediction networks. In the Philippines, the US Weather Bureau bowed to diplomatic pressure from impe-rial powers downwind that were eager to keep Jesuit scientists in positions of authority. But Weather Bureau scientists jealously guarded their monopoly on the communication of storm advisories from Cuba to the US homeland. There is no credible evidence, however, that the marginalization of Jesuit forecasters was somehow responsible for the suffering caused by the 1900 Galveston hur-ricane, still the deadliest weather event in US history.

This chapter presents an early case of international collaboration to obtain protection from environmental harm, highlighting the importance of science and new communication technologies to imperial politics. It demonstrates the impact of competition for geopolitical prominence among nation-states on the development of environmental knowledge, while revealing the ability of missionaries, merchants, scientists, and other nonstate actors to influence international diplomacy for their own ends. Above all, this story reveals some grave dilemmas posed by human engagement with the ocean and atmosphere—the quintessential transboundary environments. It also challenges our faith in the ability of science and technology to protect us from harm. These findings underscore the value of adopting a transnational perspective when researching environmental and diplomatic history.

Imperial Science and Missionary Science

Cuba's size, geographic orientation, and location in the heart of the Caribbean Basin make it especially vulnerable to violent tropical cyclones during hurricane

season (early June to late November). Hurricanes have thus powerfully influenced Cuba's place in world history. For example, three intense storms during
the 1840s devastated Cuba's coffee plantations and encouraged the island's
switch to sugar cane monoculture—to the direct benefit of Brazilian coffee
exporters and the detriment of Brazil's Atlantic rain forest.[15]

Environmental scientists working in Spanish-ruled Cuba also sought to build
meteorological empires of their own. Andrés Poey y Aguirre, the son of Cuba's
foremost zoologist, organized his country's first official physico-meteorological
observatory during the 1850s, with help from the Royal Economic Society of
Havana. He toured Europe's main observatories and, during a stint in New
York City working under the tutelage of storm expert William Redfield, compiled a pioneering historical catalog of tropical cyclones in the Atlantic. But
Poey was not content to imitate northern scientific practices. He was an outspoken proponent of a standardized cloud classification system "applicable to all
latitudes" that included tropical cloud types. He even contended that "the equatorial zone is the point of departure of all great meteorological manifestations
of the globe," which imbued his observations of tropical skies with geopolitical
importance.[16]

During the 1860s, imperial politics presented Poey with an opportunity to
extend his interests far beyond Cuban skies. Spain took advantage of US preoccupation with the Civil War to recolonize Santo Domingo, and it sent an elaborate Scientific Commission to the Pacific that brazenly seized Peru's valuable
guano islands. Commission officials invited Poey to establish a state-of-the-art
geophysical observatory in Lima, but he elected to accept a more appealing
offer from France, the homeland of his slave-trading grandfather. In 1862, with
the support of Mexican conservatives, the French army invaded Mexico and
appointed an Austrian noble as emperor two years later. This action was supposed to strengthen France's influence over the so-called Latin countries of the
Americas, build a territorial connection with French colonies in the Pacific,
and impede Anglo-American expansion in these regions. To accomplish these
goals, France organized its own scientific expedition to Mexico, inviting Poey
and Confederate sympathizer Matthew Maury to staff a new astronomical and
meteorological observatory in Mexico City.[17] "The power of science must form
part of the science of power," Poey wrote to Cuba's governor general defending his decision to go to Mexico.[18] However, during the Battle of Callao in
1866, the Peruvian military sank Spain's hopes of regaining its place as a great
power in the Western Hemisphere. Republican forces in Mexico did the same
to France. The unraveling of these military adventures exacerbated turmoil in
Spain and empowered reactionary forces in Cuba. In September 1868, Spanish
radicals deposed the Bourbon monarchy. Conspirators in eastern Cuba seized

the opportunity to start an anticolonial war. Poey's brother joined the Cuban independence movement, while his father took a controversial, antiracist stand before the Havana Academy of Science in support of Darwinism. Tarnished by these associations, Poey lost his mandate as head of the Havana Observatory and went into permanent exile in 1869. A flood of Cuban intellectuals followed Poey out of the country during the Spanish military's ensuing anti-insurgency campaign. By default, meteorological investigations in Cuba fell into the hands of an entirely different group, the Society of Jesus.[19]

Jesuit scientists have often been trailblazers in meteorology. In 1756, Bohemian Jesuit Juan Rehr published the first systematic measurements of temperature and barometric pressure in Peru after publicly declaring that Galileo had proved "our movement."[20] A year later, a colleague initiated similar observations in Peking. But several imperial states regarded the Society of Jesus as a threat to their sovereignty and forced the worldwide suppression of the order by 1773. During the order's regeneration after 1814, Jesuit missionaries gave paramount attention to education and the establishment of outposts of scientific excellence outside Europe, most notably at Georgetown (United States, 1841), Guatemala City (1851), Manila (Philippines, 1865), Calcutta (India, 1866), Quito (Ecuador, 1870), Zikawei (China, 1872), Tananarive (Madagascar, 1890), La Paz (Bolivia, 1892), Ksara (Lebanon, 1907), Bogotá (Colombia, 1922), and Addis Ababa (Ethiopia, 1957). These institutions helped to rebuild the Jesuit order's international prestige and influence and formed part of a transnational scientific network that was only weakly involved in the geopolitics of state-sponsored imperial expansion. Jesuit observatories were exemplars of a distinct mode of international scientific organization that can be usefully referred to as *missionary science*.[21] The observatories in Lima and Mexico City to which Andrés Poey was connected, on the other hand, were direct prerogatives of the Spanish and French imperial states. They were exemplars of a distinct geopolitical mode that can be usefully referred to as *imperial science*.[22]

In 1854, Spanish Jesuits opened a preparatory school in Havana, the Colegio de Belén, which quickly developed into the most prestigious school for the city's Creole elite. In 1857, a Catalan Jesuit established a small meteorological observatory there to supplement the school's scientific education. In 1862, with help from Jesuit scientists at Stonyhurst Observatory in England, his successor added precision instruments for investigating terrestrial magnetism. The school retained close ties to Stonyhurst and the British Imperial Observatory at Kew for decades. But the Colegio was not immune to the political upheaval of these years. Supporting the Jesuits had become a litmus test of conservatism, and the liberal revolutionary government of 1868 expelled the order from Spain, though not from Spain's overseas empire. In 1871, seven Colegio graduates were implicated in an anticolonial conspiracy at the University of Havana, and two were shot by firing squad. Some blamed the students' Jesuit education for encouraging their aspirations for independence.[23]

Benito Viñes and the Science of Disaster

Benito Viñes Martorell was born in a small, mountain town in Catalonia, Spain, a region that provided fertile ground for the recruitment of Jesuit scientists. Viñes taught physics at the University of Salamanca during the 1860s before being expelled from the country with the rest of the Jesuit order. In March 1870, he received instructions to join the faculty at the Colegio de Belén, where he took over the directorship of the school's struggling observatory. Hurricanes forced themselves into Viñes's consciousness soon after his arrival. In October 1870, three destructive storms passed near Havana, the first of which ripped the zinc roof off the school's observatory. At about this time, Viñes initiated several practices exemplifying the religious dedication to the study of nature for which Jesuit observers are well known. He and his assistants made observations with standardized instruments ten times every day (except on Sundays). Like Piddington, Viñes's understanding of tropical cyclones also rested heavily on vernacular knowledge produced by everyday maritime activities. Viñes kept a storm scrapbook that recorded port news useful for tracking storms, a practice he and his successors maintained for eighty-seven consecutive years. Like Jesuit scientists elsewhere in the world, Viñes's interests extended to earthquakes and other forms of natural disaster.[24]

Viñes also had a powerful new tool at his disposal for tracking the motion of hurricanes. The first undersea telegraph service connecting Havana to Key West and the United States was completed in 1867–1868. By 1875, Havana and several other Cuban ports were also connected by telegraph to Jamaica, Puerto Rico, and the Lesser Antilles. By 1900, European and North American capitalists had laid down over 12,000 nautical miles of undersea telegraph lines connecting the Caribbean islands and the American mainland.[25] Viñes successfully tested the use of telegraphy for tracking storms and producing storm warnings in 1875. On the basis of cablegrams from Spanish naval officials in Puerto Rico and St. Thomas, Viñes issued a public hurricane warning on September 11 that advised ships to avoid sailing out of Havana. This storm grazed the southeastern coast of Cuba, then crossed the island east of Havana on September 13 and 14. One ship, the ironically named *Liberty*, had dared to sail out into the Strait of Florida ahead of the storm and was lost. The storm then continued west across the Gulf of Mexico and strengthened into a major hurricane before making landfall over Indianola, an important port on the north-central coast of Texas. Storm surge destroyed 206 of the town's 257 buildings and killed at least 270 people. The port of Galveston, its main rival, also experienced severe flooding, even though it was nowhere near the eye of the storm. Approximately 500 buildings were destroyed and twenty people drowned in Galveston. This was a harbinger of things to come. Using newspaper reports and ship records, Viñes eventually reconstructed the entire parabolic track of what he called the "perfect type hurricane," from its first appearance east of Barbuda until it headed back out into the Atlantic near Norfolk, Virginia.[26]

Viñes also learned to predict the arrival of hurricanes based on careful observation of the sky. In 1870, he noticed a thin veil of cirrostratus clouds at the edge of hurricanes passing near Havana. This phenomenon was well known to mariners operating in the tropics. The old proverb "red in the morning, sailors take warning" derived from the observation that thin clouds affecting the appearance of the sun or moon can indicate the existence of a tropical storm over the horizon. Following Poey's example, Viñes also gave attention to the type and motion of clouds, which could be used to deduce the activity of upper-level wind currents. Viñes arrived at the conclusion that thin clouds of ice crystals formed at very high altitudes must be responsible for the above phenomena. Storm theorists had already established that surface winds flow around and toward the center of these tempests. Viñes deduced that cyclonic winds must also flow upward and outward from the center of the storm. This explained not only the cirrostratus veil at the outer edge of a hurricane but also the marked drop in barometric pressure at a storm's eye. These physical insights had major implications for estimating the location and path of movement of storms. Viñes concluded that the appearance of elongated "plumiform cirrostratus" clouds at a hurricane's leading edge signaled an approaching storm and indicated the direction of a storm's deadly eye—from as far away as 500 miles. His Jesuit colleagues in the Philippines later marketed a device invented by Viñes that used the movements of different cloud types to enable mariners at sea to calculate the direction of a tropical cyclone's "deadly center."[27] Scientists today consider Viñes's discoveries about the physical nature of hurricanes to be one of the great contributions to modern meteorology.[28]

On October 16, 1876, Viñes used his methodology to accurately predict the path of a storm lurking far to the southeast of Havana almost forty-eight hours before it made landfall. He requested observations from undersea telegraph terminals along Cuba's southern coast to confirm the existence of a large, slow-moving storm, which convinced the Havana Port Authority and Inspector General of Telegraphs to issue a hurricane warning for all of western Cuba on October 17. The storm made landfall over the Zapata Swamp, just west of

Cienfuegos, on the eighteenth and passed directly over Havana later that afternoon, when Viñes sent out a final telegram warning Key West of the storm's progress. His successful forecast made Viñes the darling of Spanish imperial officials, maritime business, and the Cuban public. It dramatically increased the visibility and prestige of the Jesuit order in Cuba and suggested that scientific and technological progress was capable of enabling society to master the wildest manifestations of nature's fury. The intervention of Jesuit scientists in Asia and military scientists in the United States soon turned Viñes into an international scientific celebrity.[29]

Exporting Hurricane Science

The geographical position of the Philippines is very similar to that of Cuba where typhoons are concerned. Jesuit science in the Philippines at this time received far greater support from regional shipping interests and the imperial government than in Cuba. In stark contrast to the Colegio de Belén, the Manila Observatory had one of the finest arrays of astronomical and geophysical instruments in the colonized world, and by the mid-1870s, was connected by telegraph to a network of fourteen meteorological observatories on the island of Luzon. Federico Faura, the Catalan Jesuit who ran the Manila Observatory, began corresponding with Viñes about this time. Following Viñes's example, Faura issued his first typhoon warnings for the Philippines in 1879, and the next year began transmitting meteorological reports and storm warnings to Hong Kong via the new undersea telegraph line across the South China Sea. Faura diverged from the opinion of scientists on the Asian mainland in believing that most typhoons in the region formed far out in the Pacific, similar to the Cape Verde–type hurricanes affecting the Caribbean. If correct, this would magnify the geopolitical significance of Faura's observations, and any future data produced on Spanish-ruled Guam, Japanese-ruled Okinawa, and other outlying Pacific islands once they were connected to a regional telegraph network.[30]

Marc Dechevrens, the Swiss-born Jesuit who directed the new Zikawei Observatory outside Shanghai, also learned of Viñes's work and moved to organize a meteorological empire of his own. Shanghai was a center for Christian missionization and the diffusion of Western science into China and was well situated from that perspective. But the city was far downwind from the main centers of typhoon development. It became connected by undersea telegraph to Japanese-ruled Formosa, Okinawa, and other upwind islands only after 1896, and it depended on Hong Kong for communication with Manila until 1906.[31]

The violent Shanghai typhoon of July 1879 inspired Dechevrens to begin cata-loguing storms and to approach Chinese maritime customs officials about set-ting up a telegraphic storm-warning network for the Chinese coast. In 1882, he began issuing daily forecasts for the port of Shanghai, which were transmitted to ships using a semaphore code of his own design. Dechevrens made some important contributions to the physical understanding of tropical cyclones. He placed even greater emphasis than Viñes on the motion of clouds and steering currents at high altitudes. This led him to invent an anemometer capable of measuring the vertical component of wind speed, which was installed on top of the Eiffel Tower at the 1889 World's Fair. He also pioneered the use of moun-tain observatories to study the vertical structure of storms.[32]

Meanwhile, Viñes had begun exploring ways to establish a formal storm-warning network in the Caribbean. He convinced Spanish imperial offi-cials to maintain the ad hoc group of reporters in the Greater Antilles that had spontaneously sprung to life during the storm of October 1876, and he obtained official support for himself to make an extended tour of hurricane-damaged areas in Cuba, Hispaniola, and Puerto Rico during the subsequent winter. For the moment, however, the US Army Signal Office took the lead by organizing its own small group of meteorological reporters in the Lesser Antilles.[33]

Viñes's vision finally came to fruition during the intense hurricane season of 1886. At least twelve tropical cyclones formed in the Atlantic that year, including seven affecting Cuba and four striking Texas. One of the worst of these hit Grenada and Hispaniola, then crossed the length of Cuba before heading into the Gulf of Mexico on August 17. Army Signal Corps officers based in Washington, DC, passed along Viñes's advisories to observatories on the North American mainland, but they jealously guarded the power to issue official hurricane warnings. Signal officers in Indianola and Galveston belatedly received the order to post warning flags on the night of August 19, long after the two port towns had been caught in the fury of a major hurri-cane. Captain Isaac Reed was killed when the Indianola Signal Office building collapsed around him and caught fire as he tried to secure the observatory's wind-recording equipment. Galveston also experienced severe flooding and collapsed buildings, notwithstanding the city's feeble attempt to create a pro-tective storm barrier in 1878 by planting tamarisk trees on its badly eroded protective dunes. A number of Galveston residents had pleaded for the con-struction of a stronger seawall, but to no avail.[34]

Back in Cuba, the administrator general of communications arranged for all telegraphic stations in the western half of the island to transmit daily meteorological observations to Viñes beginning in July 1886. Two months later, Havana's Chamber of Commerce voted to provide financial and organizational assistance to these efforts, and they convinced insurance agents from the New York Board of Underwriters in Trinidad, Martinique, Antigua, and Puerto Rico to volunteer observations. Viñes was the obvious choice to serve as the central forecaster and administrator, and he imposed the telegraphic transmission code of the US Army Signal Office on the network.[35]

Unlike his colleagues in Washington, Viñes leaned heavily on others to make this transnational network function. Great Britain's consul general in Santiago de Cuba, Frederick Ramsden, obtained the participation of US Army Signal Corps observers in Jamaica and Barbados, and helped negotiate a 50 percent discount on transmissions using British-owned undersea lines. Like many British diplomatic officials of this era, Ramsden was a dedicated naturalist and explorer, and for years he had communicated meteorological observations to Viñes and the Army Signal Office. Geography had not predestined Havana to serve as the central node of this network; in some ways, Santiago was in a more privileged position for hurricane observation. It lay upwind, closer to the heart of the Caribbean, and until the late 1890s, all undersea telegraph traffic heading north and west within the Caribbean Basin had to pass through Santiago. The same was true of Cienfuegos, where the science professor at the city's Jesuit preparatory school, Lorenzo Gangoiti, served as a network observer. But Ramsden and Gangoiti bowed to Viñes's experience and authority as a forecaster and his close relationship with officials in Cuba's colonial capital. On September 10, 1887, the Caribbean Basin's first official storm-warning network went into operation, with additional participants in the Dominican Republic, St. Thomas, Guadeloupe, Dominica, St. Lucia, and Grenada. In 1890, it expanded its services to include daily synoptic weather reports and, despite chronic budget shortfalls, continued operating until the US invasion of Cuba and Puerto Rico in 1898.[36] With governance, communications, and trade divided up among so many competing powers in the Caribbean, a collaborative network of this sort was the only way a formal service could have gotten off the ground. This case again illustrates the ability of scientific internationalism to improve understanding of large-scale environmental phenomena, even during periods of tense geopolitical conflict.[37]

The hurricane seasons of 1887 and 1888 turned out to be even more active, with a total of twenty-eight storms—including two more that passed over the deserted ruins of Indianola. This inspired Everett Hayden, a naval officer, marine meteorologist, and editor of pilot charts for the US Navy Hydrographic Office, to make an "urgent application" to spend time in Cuba learning from Viñes. The Hydrographic Office had been promoting Viñes's work for years, by translating a pamphlet outlining his methods for predicting the motion of West Indian hurricanes, for example. Hayden had the good fortune on his way south to see the backside of a monster hurricane, just after it had passed over Havana in early September 1888. This gave Viñes and Hayden much to talk about regarding the use of clouds to estimate the position of hurricanes. Back in Washington, Hayden publicly endorsed Viñes's hurricane-tracking skill. Hayden's widely disseminated Pilot Charts warned mariners to heed advisories coming out of Havana, which according to Hayden was a locale ideally situated for producing "early, decided, and definite warnings" of the presence of dangerous storms within the great "Bay of North America."[38]

But Hayden strongly disagreed with Viñes's ideas about why storms follow the paths that they do. Viñes's catalog of hurricane tracks demonstrated that hurricanes tend to follow parabolic paths influenced by the earth's gravity and the seasonal position of the sun. Storms in late August and early September, for example, usually wait until they reach 28 to 30 degrees north latitude before "recurving" back toward the north and east. The 1875 and 1886 storms that leveled Indianola and Galveston both followed this basic rule. But many storms do not. Viñes's views on hurricane circulation led him to believe that high-altitude winds play an important role in steering hurricanes by causing them to be attracted to regions of high barometric pressure and repelled by other low-pressure centers. Hayden, on the other hand, thought that extratropical weather systems exercised a strong influence over a hurricane's path. For example, he credited the irregular track of the September 1888 hurricane they had both observed to the existence of a strong "blocking high" (anticyclone) over the southeastern United States.[39]

Their disagreement had geopolitical implications. If Viñes was correct, southern scientists situated in the tropics were in a superior position to directly observe storms and forecast their movement. If Hayden was right, northern scientists with privileged access to continental meteorological data were better situated: "The weather predictor 'cannot explain the weather on any day without casting his eyes over the whole northern hemisphere,'" Hayden concluded. "Let the general government 'cast its eyes over the whole hemisphere'...with our modern telegraphs and cables...and let the local predictor look 'round the little hills and valleys which bound his horizon.'"[40] Imperial politics eventually decided the winner of this controversy.

The Politicization of Hurricane Prediction

In the beginning, the official interests of nation-states played only a minor role in the science of tropical cyclone prediction. Missionaries and merchants working in the interstices of empire led these initial efforts, while military officers and diplomats provided support. Like the "El Niño famines" and the plague and flu epidemics that beset the Indo-Pacific at the end of the nineteenth century, tropical cyclones did not respect the architecture of empire. But this reality did not stop imperial politics from intervening in hurricane prediction efforts.

To understand both the geopolitical context in which hurricane forecasters and telegraph companies operated and the development of international political tensions related to them, it is worth examining the global ecological network that produced undersea cables. The manufacture of these lines was deeply enmeshed in colonial politics. The hilly El Cobre region just west of Santiago de Cuba was one of the world's largest exporters of ore used for producing copper cables in England, until Cuban independence fighters intentionally flooded the mines in 1868. Copper mining quickly moved on to scar the North American West, Southern Andes, and Australia, where it fueled the growth of major multinational firms. Copper mining tended to flourish in neocolonial contexts, where the political power of business enclaves often dwarfed that of local state officials.[41]

On the other hand, the production of gutta percha latex that provided the insulating casing for undersea cables took place on the imperial frontier. Until 1900, gutta percha was produced almost entirely from unsustainable cutting of *Palaquium* and *Payena* trees in Southeast Asia. Merchants of Chinese ethnicity operating out of British-ruled Singapore dominated this lucrative trade, which rapidly extirpated trees from the coastal rain forests of the Malay Peninsula, Sumatra, and northern Borneo. From there, indigenous hunter-gatherers and forest farmers took this extractive industry deep into remote hill regions, in return for trade goods. Gutta percha extraction thus played a significant role in the formal colonization of these lands by European states. Conservationists estimate that 150 million trees were felled during the orgy of wild gutta percha cutting that lasted from 1850 to 1900. In anticipation of an inevitable gutta percha "famine," Dutch imperial botanists working out of Buitenzorg Botanic Garden in Java turned gutta percha into a plantation crop. They had similar success with *Hevea* and *Cinchona* trees, two South American species used for producing rubber and the antimalarial drug quinine, respectively. The Dutch East Indies came to dominate international trade in rubber and quinine. Meanwhile, the rush to secure strategic supplies of tropical commodities from colonized territories dramatically increased the late nineteenth-century rivalry between northern powers, and it played a significant role in the colonization of the Philippines, Puerto Rico, and Hawaii by the United States, as well as the spread of conservationist ideas in tropical forestry through imperial channels.[42]

British botanists working with Kew Botanic Garden failed miserably in their efforts to make tropical plantations within the British Empire into the main producers of gutta percha, rubber, and quinine.[43] A handful of British technological firms dominated the final production of undersea telegraph lines during the first four decades of the industry, however. The Eastern Telegraph and Associated Company used its proximity to these factories, the British Colonial Office, and Maxwellian scientists to build itself into one of the world's most powerful multinational corporations. During the 1890s, advances by France in developing its own autarkic industry, and Great Britain's quest to install an "all-Empire" network dramatically increased interimperial rivalry for control over undersea telegraph networks. The politicization of hurricane advisories flowing through these lines was probably inevitable.[44]

The quest by individual scientists to build their own meteorological empires in the western Pacific started the politicization of tropical cyclone prediction. The problem began when Marc Dechevrens and the Shanghai Chamber of Commerce proposed creating a typhoon warning system for the Chinese coast centered at Zikawei Observatory. Danish-born astronomer William Doberck took offense at this notion. He took command of the new British Royal Observatory at Hong Kong late in 1883—the same year that the colony was connected to Fuzhou and Shanghai by undersea cable. Doberck was a stargazer and disdained meteorology, but he recognized the political value of weather observations for the growth of his observatory. He tried to convince Chinese maritime customs officials to instead make Hong Kong into the central forecasting center for the South China Sea. His crude attempt to turn Manila and Zikawei against each other and subordinate them to his authority enraged Federico Faura to the point that he stopped transmitting storm advisories to Hong Kong for a while.[45]

Military scientists were the first to challenge Viñes's dominion over hurricane prediction in the Caribbean. In 1889, with Viñes's help, the Spanish Navy established its own meteorological observatory at Havana under Cuban-born officer Luis García y Carbonell. This infuriated Cuba's merchant and scientific communities, who viewed it as a wasteful duplication of Jesuit efforts. Cheered on by Everett Hayden, García negotiated an agreement with the US Army Signal Office giving the Havana Naval Observatory free use of American-owned telegraph lines to transmit weather data and storm advisories to the United States. The development of rival telegraphic networks confused the situation even more. To break the British monopoly on undersea communication in the North Atlantic, the French government built its own undersea cable system connecting Guantánamo and Santiago in Cuba to Haiti, the Dominican Republic, and Venezuela; French-ruled Martinique, Guadaloupe, and Guiana; and Dutch-ruled Curaçao and Suriname. In 1896, the French directly connected this trans-Caribbean network to Coney Island, New York, through Cap

Haitien, Haiti. To generate traffic on these new lines, they also offered to transmit meteorological observations free of charge. Not to be outdone, the British completed an "all-Empire" network connecting Jamaica, the Turks and Caicos, Bermuda, and Nova Scotia in 1898.[46]

These changes allowed a cacophony of hurricane observations to reach the United States. Based on cablegrams received from a variety of locales, Viñes began sending out advisories on September 3, 1889, predicting that a storm "of great diameter and intensity" would follow a west-northwest course north of Puerto Rico, Hispañola, and Cuba to Florida, where "according to general rule" he expected it to turn back to the northeast once it reached 27 to 29 degrees latitude. The Havana Naval Observatory seriously botched its track of this storm. García reported that it had passed south of Puerto Rico, then over the Dominican Republic on a northeastern trajectory out into the Central Atlantic. Both sets of advisories turned out to be far off the mark. On the eighth, the storm suddenly showed up again off the New Jersey coast, moving slowly to the southwest. The US Signal Office, Hydrographic Office, and New York Herald Weather Service promptly issued hurricane warnings but were helpless to stop this cyclone from causing "great destruction" and loss of life on the beaches of Atlantic City and other nearby locales. The collapse of telegraph and railroad service along much of the Eastern Seaboard during the storm caused a major breakdown in the communication of these advisories, fueling the spread of a false rumor that the storm was "one of the great hurricanes of the century."[47]

This situation greatly damaged the reputation of the Army Signal Corps. The discovery of a massive embezzlement scheme destroyed the organization altogether. Congress slashed the Signal Corps' budget in retribution, forcing it to withdraw its Caribbean storm observers. In 1891, Congress took control over weather forecasting completely away from the military and handed it over to civilians in the Department of Agriculture.[48] Weather forecasting in Cuba experienced tragedy of its own in 1893. Viñes died of a massive stroke at the height of the hurricane season, while under intense pressure to complete an account of his achievements in time for presentation at the Columbian World Exposition in Chicago.[49] Fortunately, Viñes had been grooming an heir apparent: the long-time head of the Jesuit observatory in Cienfuegos, Lorenzo Gangoiti. In Havana, the public breathed a huge sigh of relief when in late September 1894 Gangoiti precisely forecast the passage of the eye of a hurricane across the city twenty-four hours ahead of time. As a reward, the colonial government ran a direct telephone line from the Colegio de Belén to the Central Telegraph Station and Port Authority of Havana.[50]

Then a political storm struck the island of Cuba. In 1894, a tariff war between the United States and Spain devastated Cuban producers of export goods. The crisis enabled transnational activist José Martí and Afro-Cuban general Antonio Maceo to reorganize the armed struggle for Cuban independence in 1895. Spain's counterinsurgency acquired an abysmal international reputation for human rights abuses and scorched-earth tactics. Propagandists eager to see the United States intervene in the conflict and extend the reach of America's empire to the tropics waged a massive campaign portraying Cubans as helpless victims of Spanish barbarism in need of protection.[51] On May 18, 1898, as the first act of war, three American warships suddenly appeared off the port of Santiago, exchanged shots with the Spanish fort, and began dragging for the undersea telegraph cables that converged on the city. The United States succeeded at cutting the French-owned line connecting Cuba to Cap Haitien and Coney Island, and began censoring all cablegrams sent through Key West. During the first week of July, Frederick Ramsden organized the evacuation of civilians from the blockaded port of Santiago and joined 20,000 desperate refugees in a rain-flooded *campo de concentración*. He fell ill and died a month later. The humanitarian disaster unleashed by war killed an experienced storm observer and talented diplomat who might have tempered international conflict for control over hurricane prediction. In the meantime, Jesuit scientists in Havana completely lost their ability to keep track of Caribbean storms.[52]

In parallel actions, the United States seized Spanish-ruled Puerto Rico, Guam, and the Philippines, deposed the Kingdom of Hawaii, and ramped up its involvement in the Boxer Rebellion in China. In the process, this ascendant imperial power acquired many tropical resources, including its own gutta percha trees, and gained strategic control over key sections of major undersea telegraph networks in both hemispheres. This cleared the way for construction of a trans-Pacific telegraph cable in 1902–1903 connecting US-governed San Francisco, Honolulu, Midway, Guam, and Manila to Hong Kong, Shanghai, and a growing legion of Japanese-ruled islands in the western Pacific.[53]

American imperial aspirations also involved tropical storm forecasting. In 1898, well before the Cuban invasion, the head of the US Weather Bureau, Willis Moore, laid out plans for establishing US hegemony over weather prediction in the Western Hemisphere to President McKinley. Moore sent the head of the Galveston weather station, Isaac Cline, to assist the director general of federal telegraphs in organizing a Mexican version of the Weather Bureau. Cline personally supervised the opening of five Mexican observatories for hurricane surveillance in the Gulf of Mexico, and he made sure that the entire network reported by telegraph to two locales: to the central observatory in Mexico City originally established by Andrés Poey, and to Galveston. In 1900, with the help of the insurance firm Lloyd's of London, the US Weather Bureau extended this empire to the North Atlantic, using a transoceanic telegraph network with stations as remote as the Portuguese-ruled Azores.[54]

On July 22, 1898, Moore sent William Stockman, a long-time fixture at the central forecasting office in Washington, to organize a US-controlled network in the Caribbean. With the help of the British governor in Jamaica, Stockman negotiated discounted telegraph service on British-owned lines connecting observers at Santiago, Santo Domingo, San Juan, St. Kitts, Dominica, Barbados, Curaçao, Trinidad, and Panama. Danish officials in St. Thomas refused to participate, but Luis García y Carbonell faithfully transmitted daily weather reports from Havana as if the war had never happened. On February 1, 1899, Stockman transferred to US-occupied Havana. He first tried to set up headquarters at the Colegio de Belén but gave in to Jesuit protests and moved elsewhere. Stockman also established satellite observatories at Cienfuegos and Puerto Príncipe and hired García as his assistant. This new hurricane prediction network almost immediately faced a difficult challenge. On August 8, 1899, the most destructive hurricane in Puerto Rico's history lashed Cuba's partner to the east. At 11 a.m. on the seventh, the Weather Bureau post at San Juan had ordered the posting of hurricane warnings around the island, but it took six hours for this order to be implemented at Ponce, the city hit first and hardest. This deadly storm greatly exacerbated the tensions that had resulted from the US takeover and reminded everyone involved of the political dangers inherent to hurricane prediction.[55] The storm may have contributed to the occupation government's October 1899 decision to restore the Jesuits' right to send and receive weather observations and storm advisories within Cuba. But the occupation government continued to ban international transmissions.[56]

The imperial politics of hurricane prediction played out quite differently in the Philippines. Territories colonized by Great Britain, France, Germany, Japan, Russia, and Portugal all lay downwind, and the British admiral and US consul in Hong Kong both placed heavy pressure on Admiral Dewey to repair the cut undersea cable to Manila so that transmission of Jesuit storm advisories could resume. William Doberck used the situation to try again to acquire hegemony over typhoon prediction in the region for the Hong Kong Royal Observatory. He wrote a blistering letter to Weather Bureau headquarters in Washington criticizing Jesuit forecasters at Manila and Zikawei. On February 27, 1899, Weather Bureau officials banned José Algué, the Georgetown-trained Catalan Jesuit who had taken over for Faura in Manila, from transmitting weather advisories internationally. This incensed maritime businessmen in Hong Kong and led the British governor to rebuke Doberck and pressure the United States to lift the communication ban, which it did at the end of March. Algué demonstrated great diplomatic skill in dealing with the situation. When the 1899 typhoon season was over, he journeyed to Washington to share plans for expanding his work with Willis Moore. Everett Hayden spent the 1900 typhoon season in Manila to make sure things ran smoothly until Algué returned. In 1901, Algué officially took over as head of the Central Office of the Meteorological Service for the Philippines, and he went on to participate in numerous scientific projects connected to US imperialism in the western Pacific, including the establishment of a meteorological observatory at Guam and a spectacular living exhibition on the Philippines at the 1904 St. Louis World's Fair. In return for agreeing to serve the American empire, the Jesuits gained lasting control over the Manila Observatory and tropical storm prediction in the western Pacific.[57]

Back in Cuba, the imperial politics of hurricane prediction came to a head in 1900. On the first day of September, Lorenzo Gangoiti began tracking a tropical depression as it traveled slowly west-northwest from Danish-governed St. Croix to Santiago, where it dumped over twenty inches of rain. An undersea cable laid down along the southern coast of Cuba in 1895 provided Jesuit and Weather Bureau forecasters in Havana with the chance to follow this slow-moving storm through Cuba, but it was a difficult storm to read. From the confusing mix of reports Gangoiti received on September 4, he concluded that the whole island was being subjected to "many irregularities without a center to regulate them." Reports on the fifth, however, suggested to him that this ill-defined tempest had "greatly increased in intensity" as it passed across the heart of Cuba west of Puerto Principe.[58]

Another Cuban meteorologist had a very different view of the situation. Since 1889, Javier Jover y Anido had operated a lavish private meteorological observatory in Santa Clara, a provincial city near the center of the island. He had once been an integral part of Viñes's hurricane prediction network, but the long war had isolated him.[59] The storm of September 1900 provided Jover with a chance to demand a place for himself in the regional storm warning system. He used the mail, railroad, and newspaper to disseminate his belief that the eye of a "hurricane" headed west-northwest had passed over Santa Clara on the fifth, and to denounce the occupation government's ban on communicating freelance weather observations by telegraph. This inspired a brisk response from the chief administrator of Cuba's telegraph system, H. H. C. Dunwoody. As acting chief of the Army Signal Office back in 1889, Dunwoody had taken a lot of heat for the confusion surrounding the deadly September hurricane that had struck the East Coast, and for many years it had been Dunwoody's job to audit the forecasts of US Weather Bureau employees for trustworthiness. He was in no mood to allow "cranks" to confuse the situation in Cuba, and he asked Stockman to compile a report detailing Jover's mistakes that could be used to undermine his trustworthiness as a weather reporter.[60] Trust is the currency on which modern science operates, and scientists in positions of power have often used this sort of tactic to police the social boundaries of science. This was particularly true of scientific networks operating across international frontiers, where personal relationships provided little help in deciding who qualified as a credible scientist. Modern society's obsession with objectivity, quantification, and expertise is deeply rooted in the quest to develop empires of science.[61]

None of this resolved the question of where this storm was headed next. In those days, the general track of a hurricane over several days provided the best clues to its future behavior. Despite reports of disastrous flooding in central and eastern Cuba, Weather Bureau scientists in Havana and Washington believed the storm had passed far to the south—perhaps below Jamaica—before turning sharply to the north on its way across western Cuba. Based on this desideratum, they concluded that the storm was already in the process of recurving back to the east when it passed over Cuba. Weather Bureau officials therefore issued hurricane advisories for the Gulf Coast of Florida for September 4 to 6. Gangoiti, for his part, also thought the storm had begun "to abnormally recurve" over Cuba. Jover only knew what the storm was doing from what he could see passing over his head.[62] In the absence of close analysis of the archival record in Washington and Havana regarding these forecasts, there is no evidence that imperial scientists suppressed a "correct" forecast by Cuban Jesuits, as Erik Larson has claimed.[63] Tragically, it was indeed possible to make a better forecast with the understanding of the time. This storm turned out to be very similar to the "perfect type hurricanes" that crossed Cuba and devastated Indianola in 1875 and 1886. It waited until it reached 29 degrees north before beginning to recurve, just as Viñes's "general rule" expected. This was the latitude of Galveston, Texas.

Against official expectations, this storm continued westward across the Gulf of Mexico, strengthening as it went. The ensuing maelstrom killed at least 7200 people in Galveston and vicinity. The decisions that doomed this Texas port to destruction were not made in a Weather Bureau forecasting office. Earlier hurricanes had given Galveston residents plenty of evidence that they lived in harm's way. But the desirability of living close to the ocean in a booming port and tourist town seemed to outweigh the risks. The idea that building a weather forecasting empire could significantly improve the security of coastal inhabitants in the southern United States was always deeply flawed. Even if it had received a perfect forecast, turn-of-the-century Galveston had no way to evacuate most of its residents to safer ground. The victims of Hurricane Katrina in New Orleans in 2005 learned a similar lesson.[64]

It is understandable that the survivors of the Great Galveston Hurricane looked to the earth beneath their feet, rather than to the ocean and sky, to find protection. After the storm, the city created an influential new form of local government that, among other things, empowered a commission of engineers to build a massive seawall made from 5200 train carloads of crushed granite, 3700 of stone riprap, 1800 of sand, 1600 of wood piling, 1000 of concrete, and five carloads of steel rebar. These technocrats then inundated the island with ten million cubic yards of sand pumped from the adjacent seafloor. The next major hurricane to strike Galveston in August 1915 demonstrated the value of this environmental intervention: only eleven people died in the protected parts of the island. This apparent success inspired the city fathers of New Orleans to start building earthen levees on a massive scale soon after a similar storm struck their city six weeks later. Gulf residents eventually paid a heavy price for choosing this technological fix: Galveston's once famous beach all but disappeared after it was cut off from its nourishing sand dunes, and New Orleans never weaned itself off its dangerous addiction to levee construction.[65]

Jover confronted Dunwoody about the failed forecast and continued telegraph ban a few days after the Galveston calamity. Dunwoody stood his ground, and the secretary of public instruction got rid of this troublesome critic by appointing Jover director of the Institute of Santa Clara.[66] The United States formally occupied Cuba until 1902, at which point Dunwoody and Moore strongly endorsed handing Cuba's meteorological service over to the Colegio de Belén, with the proviso that the Jesuits "limit their advisories to the Island of Cuba, and not publish advisories that in any manner invade the territory covered by the Weather Bureau." Nevertheless, the liberals who dominated Cuba's first postcolonial government insisted on breaking ties with the Jesuits to create a national meteorological service under the command of García y Carbonell.[67] This national institution later engaged in its own form of imperial science. During the mid-1930s, the Cuban Meteorological Service built overseas weather observatories connected to Havana by wireless telegraph on the British-ruled Cayman Islands and Nicaragua's Cabo Gracias a Dios in order to detect dangerous hurricanes lurking to the south.[68] But the main task of hurricane prediction in the Western Hemisphere remained in the hands of US Weather Bureau scientists on the North American mainland until 1943, when the University of Chicago organized the Institute of Tropical Meteorology at the University of Puerto Rico. This opened a new era in the politics of hurricane prediction in the region. In contrast, Jesuit scientists remained dominant in Philippine meteorology until well after World War II, in part, because they converted to the aforementioned "Norwegian school" of meteorology—the dominant paradigm of the postwar era in atmospheric science—long before their colleagues in Latin America and the United States.[69]

This chapter has traced the amazing geographical reach and international complexity of tropical cyclone prediction networks operating in the second half of the nineteenth century. The geopolitical interests of nation-states did not dictate the pattern of these developments. The extension of undersea telegraph networks and multinational business, the efforts of a transnational missionary order, and the personal aspirations of individual scientists were also critical. At times, these efforts exemplified the possibilities of scientific internationalism to improve human understanding of a hazardous environmental phenomenon operating across national boundaries. It is also important to acknowledge that the politics of hurricane prediction during this era succeeded at making the environment a safer place for human activities in at least one realm, by preventing ships from sailing into dangerous storms on the high seas. However, the horrific storms that struck Puerto Rico and Galveston revealed the naiveté of the imperial notion that centralized control over environmental knowledge would automatically lead to better forecasts that could significantly reduce the vulnerability of coastal populations. The obsession with white ethnic control was the Achilles heel of imperial science.

NOTES

1. Henry Piddington, "Researches on the Gale and Hurricane in the Bay of Bengal," *Journal of the Asiatic Society of Bengal*, 2nd ser. (hereafter *JASB*), vol. 8 (1839): 559 ff, 631 ff; Piddington, "A Sixth Memoir on the Law of Storms in India," *JASB* 11 (1842): 605–6; Henry Blanford, "Catalogue of the Recorded Cyclones in the Bay of Bengal," *JASB* 46, pt. 1 (1877): 332–3; Caroline Blyth, "Piddington, Henry," *Oxford Dictionary of National Biography*, online ed. (2004), http://www.oxforddnb.com/view/article/22221.

2. Henry Piddington, "A Second Memoir with Reference to the Theory of the Law of Storms," *JASB* 9 (1840): 107 ff, 397 ff; P. Swarnalatha, *The World of the Weaver in Northern Coromandel* (New Delhi: Orient Longman, 2005), 18, 28.

3. Henry Piddington, "A Fourth Memoir on the Law of Storms in India," *JASB* 10 (1841): 895–906.

4. Henry Piddington, *The Sailor's Horn-book for the Law of Storms* (New York: John Wiley, 1848).

5. Eugen Obach, *Cantor Lectures on Gutta Percha* (London: William Trounce, 1898), 2–3, 6, 12–8; Daniel Headrick, *The Tentacles of Progress: Technological Transfer in the Age of Imperialism* (New York: Oxford University Press, 1988), 98–102.

6. James Rodger Fleming, *Meteorology in America, 1800–1870* (Baltimore: Johns Hopkins University Press, 1990); Fleming, *Historical Perspectives on Climate Change* (New York: Oxford University Press, 1998), chap. 3; Katharine Anderson, *Predicting the Weather: Victorians and the Science of Meteorology* (Chicago: University of Chicago Press, 2005), chap. 6.

7. Bruce Hunt, *The Maxwellians* (Ithaca, NY: Cornell University Press, 1991); Michael Reidy, *Tides of History: Ocean Science and Her Majesty's Navy* (Chicago: University of Chicago Press, 2008); Richard Drayton, *Nature's Government: Science, Imperial Britain, and the "Improvement" of the World* (New Haven, CT: Yale University Press, 2000); Helen Rozwadowski, *Fathoming the Ocean: The Discovery and Exploration of the Deep Sea* (Cambridge, MA: Harvard University Press, 2005); Gregory Clancey, *Earthquake Nation: The Cultural Politics of Japanese Seismicity, 1868–1930* (Berkeley and Los Angeles: University of California Press, 2006).

8. John McNeill, afterward of this volume; Gregory T. Cushman, *Guano and the Opening of the Pacific World: A Global Ecological History* (Cambridge and New York: Cambridge University Press, 2013); Mike Davis, *Late Victorian Holocausts: El Niño Famines and the Making of the Third World* (London: Verso, 2001); Philip Curtin, *Death by Migration: Europe's Encounter with the Tropical World in the Nineteenth Century* (Cambridge and New York: Cambridge University Press, 1989).

9. Lewis Pyenson, *Civilizing Mission: Exact Sciences and French Overseas Expansion, 1830–1940* (Baltimore: Johns Hopkins University Press, 1993).

10. Gregory T. Cushman, "The Struggle over Airways in the Americas: Atmospheric Science, Aviation Technology, and Neocolonialism, 1919–1945," in *Intimate Universality: Local and Global Themes in the History of Weather and Climate*, ed. James Rodger Fleming, Vladimir Jankovic, and Deborah R. Coen (Sagamore Beach, MA: Science History Publications, 2006), 175–222.

11. Sherry Johnson, *Climate and Catastrophe in Cuba and the Atlantic World in the Age of Revolution* (Chapel Hill: University of North Carolina Press, 2011).

12. Cushman, *Guano*, chaps. 5, 9.

13. Kevin Rozario, "What Goes Down Must Go Up: Why Disasters Have Been Good for American Capitalism," in *American Disasters*, ed. Steven Biel (New York: New York University Press, 2001), 72–102.

14. Headrick, *Tentacles of Progress*, 108–18.

15. Louis Pérez, Jr., *Winds of Change: Hurricanes and the Transformation of Nineteenth-Century Cuba* (Chapel Hill: University of North Carolina Press, 2001); Warren Dean, *With Broadax and Firebrand: The Destruction of the Brazilian Atlantic Forest* (Berkeley and Los Angeles: University of California Press, 1995).

16. Poey, "A Chronological Table, Comprising 400 Cyclonic Hurricanes Which Have Occurred in the West Indies and in the North Atlantic within 362 Years, from 1493 to 1855," *Journal of the Royal Geographical Society* 21 (1855): 291–328; Ramón de la Sagra, *Relación de los trabajos físicos y meteorológicos hechos por Don Andrés Poey* (Paris: Thunot, 1858), 10–1, 19; Poey, *Instructions et considerations synthétiques sur la nature, la constitution et la forme des nuages* (Versailles: Société Météorologique de France, 1865), 4, 9–10; Poey, *Comment on observe les nuages pour prévoir le temps* (Paris: Gauthier-Villars, 1879), 7–8, 40–1, 49, 126.

17. Leoncio López-Ocón Cabrera, "La Comisión Científica del Pacífico (1862–1866) y la Commission Scientifique du Mexique (1864–1867)," in *De la ciencia ilustrada a la ciencia romántica* (Madrid: Ediciones Doce Calles, 1995), 459–69; Marcos Cueto, "La ciencia peruana y la Comisión Cientíifica del Pacífic," in ibid., 451–7; John

Leddy Phelan, "Pan-Latinism, French Intervention in Mexico (1861–1867) and the Idea of Latin America," in *Conciencia y autenticidad históricas* (Mexico City: Universidad Nacional Autónoma de México, 1968), 123–77.

18. Poey's emphasis, quoted in Pyenson, *Civilizing Mission*, 276.

19. Raymond Carr, *Spain, 1808–1939* (Oxford: Clarendon Press, 1966), 260–1, 290–319; Louis Pérez, Jr., *Cuba: Between Reform and Revolution*, 3rd ed. (New York: Oxford University Press, 2006), 88–93; Pedro Pruna Goodgall, "El evolucionismo biológico en Cuba a fines del siglo XIX," in *El darwinismo en España e Iberoamérica* (Madrid: Ediciones Doce Calles, 1999), 71–2; Pyenson, *Civilizing Mission*, 272–9.

20. Gregory T. Cushman, "Humboldtian Science, Creole Meteorology, and the Discovery of Human-Caused Climate Change in South America," *Osiris* 26 (2011): 19–44.

21. Agustín Udías, *Searching the Heavens and the Earth: The History of Jesuit Observatories* (Dordrecht: Kluwer Academic, 2003); Steven J. Harris, "Mapping Jesuit Science: The Role of Travel in the Geography of Knowledge," in *The Jesuits: Cultures, Sciences, and the Arts*, ed. John W. O'Malley et al. (Toronto: Toronto University Press, 1999), 213–40.

22. Historians of science in colonial contexts would benefit greatly from a new set of analytical terms disconnected from Eurocentric modernization and world-systems theory; on *neocolonial science*, see Cushman, "Struggle over Airways."

23. José Luis Sáez, *Breve historia del Colegio de Belén, 1854–1961* (Miami: Belén Jesuit Preparatory School, 2002), 1:11–6, 52–4, 65; *Album conmemorativo del quincuagésimo aniversario de la fundación en la Habana del Colegio de Belén* (Havana: Imprenta Avisador Comercial, 1904), 112–4, 130, 136, 141–2; Carr, *Spain*, 344–6.

24. *Album conmemorativo*, 127–30, 166; Luis Enrique Ramos Guadalupe, *Benito Viñes S.J.: Estudio biográfico* (Havana: Editorial Academia, 1996), 2, 4–5, 9, 17, 42–4, 47, 62–4.

25. Bill Glover, "History of the Atlantic Cable and Undersea Communications: Cable Timeline, 1845–1900," (2009), http://www.atlantic-cable.com/Cables/CableTimeLine/index1850.htm.

26. Benito Viñes, *Apuntes relativos a los huracanes de las Antillas en setiembre y octubre de 1875 y 76* (Havana: El Iris, 1877), 48, 56–9; Ramos, *Benito Viñes*, 18–9, 41; Bronson Malsch, *Indianola: The Mother of Western Texas* (Austin, TX: State House Press, 1988), 228–43; David McComb, *Galveston: A History* (Austin: University of Texas Press, 1986), 29–30.

27. Benito Viñes, *Apuntes relativos*, 37–8, 66–7, 70, 75–6, 90, 101–12, 131–49; Poey, *Instructions et considerations*, 15–6; *Observaciones magnéticas y meteorológicas: Enero-Marzo, 1886* (1887): pt. 1; Ramos, *Benito Viñes*, 64, 68–9; *Album conmemorativo*, 116–7; Ángel Hidalgo, *El P. José Algué, S.J.: Científico, inventor y pacifista (1856–1930)* (Manila: Observatorio de Manila, 1974), 10, 12.

28. Kerry Emanuel, *Divine Wind: The History and Science of Hurricanes* (New York: Oxford University Press, 2005), 7–8.

29. Viñes, *Apuntes relativos*, 49–51, 60–1; Ramos, *Benito Viñes*, 19–23.

30. Hidalgo, *El P. Federico Faura, S.J. y el Observatorio de Manila* (Manila: Observatorio de Manila, 1974), 7, 9–10, 16–8, 27–32.

31. Pyenson, *Civilizing Mission*, 157–60; Glover, "History of Undersea Communications."

32. J. Thirion, "Le typhoon du 31 julliet 1879," *Revue des questions scientifiques* 8 (1880): 270–8; Marc Dechevrens, *The Typhoons of the South Chinese Seas in the Year 1881* (Shanghai: Kelly & Walsh, 1882), preface, 10, 30; Dechevrens "The Vertical Component of the Wind," *Monthly Weather Review* 32 (March 1904): 118–21; *Album conmemorativo*, 200–1; Udías, *Searching the Heavens*, 159–62.

33. Ramos, *Benito Viñes*, 7–9, 14, 16–23; *Album conmemorativo*, 149–50.

34. J. F. Partagás and H. F. Díaz, "A Reconstruction of Historical Tropical Cyclone Frequency in the Atlantic from Documentary and Other Historical Sources, Part III, 1881–1890," (Boulder, CO: NOAA Climate Diagnostics Center, 1996), http://www.aoml.noaa.gov/hrd/Landsea/Partagas; Malsch, *Indianola*, 262–9; McComb, *Galveston*, 30–1.

35. *Album conmemorativo*, 186–90.

36. Frederick Ramsden, "Diary of the British Consul at Santiago during Hostilities," *McClure's Magazine* 11 (October 1898): 580–90, and 12 (November 1898): 62–70; *Album conmemorativo*, 190–1.

37. Gregory T. Cushman, "Choosing between Centers of Action: Instrument Buoys, El Niño, and Scientific Internationalism in the Pacific, 1957–1982," in *The Machine in Neptune's Garden: Historical Perspectives on Technology and the Marine Environment* (Sagamore Beach, MA: Science History Publications, 2004), 133–82; James Fleming and Roger Launius, eds., *Globalizing Polar Science: Reconsidering the International Polar and Geophysical Years* (New York: Palgrave, 2010).

38. Partagás and Díaz, "Reconstruction of Historical Tropical Cyclone Frequency, 1881–1890"; Benito Viñes, *Practical Hints in Regard to West Indian Hurricanes* (Washington, DC, 1885); Karen Linn Femia, "Edward Everett Hayden Family Papers," (Washington, DC: Library of Congress, 2009); US Hydrographic Office, *Pilot Chart of the North Atlantic Ocean* (June 1889, August 1889); US Hydrographic Office, *Hurricane Chart of the Bay of North America* (1890).

39. Benito Viñes, *Investigaciones relativas a la circulación y traslación ciclónica en los huracanes de las Antillas* (Havana: Pulido y Díaz, 1895), 32–47, 55–61; Everett Hayden, *West Indian Hurricanes and the March Blizzard, 1888* (New York: Forest & Stream Publishing, 1889), 15–7; Everett Hayden, *The Modern Law of Storms* (Philadelphia: L. R. Mameroly, 1890), 8–10, 12; Everett Hayden, *Hurricanes in the Bay of North America* (Washington, DC: Philosophical Society of Washington, 1890), 186.

40. Hayden, *West Indian Hurricanes*, 19–20.

41. Walter Harvey Weed, *The Copper Mines of the World* (New York: Hill Publishing, 1907), chaps. 13, 17; Horace Stevens, *The Copper Handbook: A Manual of the Copper Industry of the World* (Chicago: Donohue, 1907), 7:578–9; Thomas R. Navin, "The 500 Largest American Industrials in 1917," *Business History Review* 44 (1970): 360–86.

42. Penoyer Sherman, Jr., "Report of the Special Agent of the Forestry Bureau Sent to Investigate Gutta-Percha and Rubber in the Straits Settlement, Java and Sumatra," in *Report of the Philippine Commission to the Secretary of War* (Washington, DC, 1901), 335–50, see also 38–46; Peter Boomgaard, *Southeast Asia: An*

Environmental History (Santa Barbara, CA: ABC-Clio, 2007), 173, 256; Greg Bankoff, "Conservation and Colonialism: Gifford Pinchot and the Birth of Tropical Forestry in the Philippines," in *Colonial Crucible: Empire in the Making of Modern America,* ed. Francisco A. Scarano (Madison: University of Wisconsin Press, 2009), 479–88.

43. British efforts dominate the historiography, however; Drayton, *Nature's Government*; Warren Dean, *Brazil and the Struggle for Rubber: A Study in Environmental History* (Cambridge and New York: Cambridge University Press, 1987).

44. Headrick, *Tentacles of Progress*, 102–8; Hunt, *Maxwellians*.

45. Mickey Man-Kui Wai, "The Early Tropical Cyclone Warning Systems in Hong Kong, 1841–1899," *Hong Kong Meteorological Station Bulletin* 14 (2004): 49–81; Kevin MacKeown, "William Doberck—Double-Star Astronomer," *Journal of Astronomical History and Heritage* 10 (2007): 49–64; Hidalgo, *Federico Faura*, 41–3.

46. *Album conmemorativo*, 197–9, 202; Headrick, *Tentacles of Progress*, 108–13; Glover, "History of Undersea Communications."

47. "Characteristics for the Weather for September, 1889," *Monthly Weather Review* 17 (1889): 233; "North Atlantic Storms for September, 1889," in ibid., 239–43; *Album conmemorativo*, 200; Partagás and Díaz, "Reconstruction of Historical Tropical Cyclone Frequency, 1881–1890," 27–30.

48. Gary Grice, "The Beginning of the National Weather Service, the Signal Service Years (1870–1891)," http://www.weather.gov/pa/history/signal.php.

49. Published as Viñes, *Investigaciones relativas*.

50. *Album conmemorativo*, 134–5, 219–20; Sáez, *Breve historia del Colegio de Belén*, 56–7; J. F. Partagás and H. F. Díaz, "A Reconstruction of Historical Tropical Cyclone Frequency in the Atlantic from Documentary and Other Historical Sources Part IV, 1891–1900," (Boulder, CO: NOAA Climate Diagnostics Center, 1996), http://www.aoml.noaa.gov/hrd/Landsea/Partagas.

51. Pérez, *Cuba*, 113–38; John Johnson, *Latin America in Caricature* (Austin: University of Texas Press, 1980).

52. Ramsden, "Diary of the British Consul"; Headrick, *Tentacles of Progress*, 115–6.

53. Glover, "History of Undersea Communications."

54. Moore, *Report of the Chief of the Weather Bureau* (Washington, DC, 1898), 7; Moore, *Report* (1900), 6; Moore, *Report* (1901), 3; Cline, *Storms, Floods, and Sunshine: An Autobiography* (1951; Gretna, LA: Pelican Publishing, 2000), 79–84.

55. Moore, *Report* (1900), 8; Stuart Schwartz, "The Hurricane of San Ciriaco: Disaster, Politics, and Society in Puerto Rico, 1899–1901," *Hispanic American Historical Review* 72 (1992): 303–34.

56. Moore, *Report* (1898), 7; Moore, *Report* (1899): 13–6; *Album conmemorativo*, 137–40; William Parker, *Cubans of To-Day* (New York: Putnam's Sons, 1919), 161–2.

57. Hidalgo, *José Algué*, 5–6, 15–6, 32–5, 48–59; Udías, *Searching the Heavens*, 153, 163–4, 308; Fernia, "Hayden Family Papers"; contra James Warren, "Scientific Superman: Father José Algué, Jesuit Meteorology, and the Philippines under American Rule, 1897–1924," in Scarano, *Colonial Crucible*, 508–22.

58. Quoted in Partagás and Díaz, "Reconstruction of Historical Tropical Cyclone Frequency, 1891–1900," 96–8.

59. US War Department, *Report of the Military Governor of Cuba on Civil Affairs* (Washington, DC, 1901), 1:280; "Julio Jover y Anido," *Boletín del Observatorio Nacional* (Havana) 24 (1928): 293–5.

60. "North Atlantic Storms for August, 1889"; Erik Larson, *Isaac's Storm: A Man, A Time, and the Deadliest Hurricane in History* (New York: Vintage, 2000), 72, 106, 111–2, 132–3.

61. Steven Shapin, *A Social History of Truth: Civility and Science in Seventeenth-Century England* (Chicago: University of Chicago Press, 1994); Theodore Porter, *Trust in Numbers: The Pursuit of Objectivity in Science* (Princeton, NJ: Princeton University Press, 1995); Thomas Gieryn, *Cultural Boundaries of Science: Credibility on the Line* (Chicago: University of Chicago Press, 1999).

62. Quoted in Partagás and Díaz, "Reconstruction of Historical Tropical Cyclone Frequency: 1891–1900," 96–8; E. B. Garriot, "A West Indian Hurricane of 1–12 September 1900," *Monthly Weather Review* 28 (1900): 371–7.

63. Larson, *Isaac's Storm*.

64. Susan Wiley Hardwick, *Mythic Galveston: Reinventing America's Third Coast* (Baltimore: Johns Hopkins University Press, 2002), chap. 3; McComb, *Galveston*, 62–5.

65. Hardwick, *Mythic Galveston*, 109–18; Herbert Mason, Jr., *Death from the Sea: Our Greatest Natural Disaster, the Galveston Hurricane of 1900* (New York: Dial Press, 1972), 234–41; Cornelia Dean, *The Battle for America's Beaches* (New York: Columbia University Press, 2001), 1–13; Craig Colten, *Perilous Place, Powerful Storms: Hurricane Protection in Coastal Louisiana* (Jackson: University Press of Mississippi, 2009), 21–4.

66. War Department, *Report of the Military Governor*, 1:618; Larson, *Isaac's Storm*, 114, 289 n.114.

67. Moore to M. Gutiérrez Lanza, October 15, 1901, quoted in *Album conmemorativo*, 137–41.

68. José Carlos Millás, "La estación meteorológica de Caiman Grande," *Boletín del Observatorio Nacional* (Havana) 3rd ser., vol. 1 (1936): 31–52; Millás, "La estación meteorológica de Cabo Gracias a Dios, Nicaragua," *Boletín del Observatorio Nacional* (Havana) 3rd ser., 3 (1938): 145–57.

69. Cushman, "Struggle over Airways"; Udías, *Searching the Heavens*, 154–5.

8

Biological Control, Transnational Exchange, and the Construction of Environmental Thought in the United States, 1840–1920

James E. McWilliams

Farming in late nineteenth-century North America was marked by a willingness to move biomass across transnational ecosystems. The techniques that scientific farmers—farmers who embraced scientific advancements to increase commercial production—employed to boost production required the careful orchestration of foreign plants, animals, and minerals. Guano from South America, honey bees from Italy, Dutch red strawberries from Holland, Shorthorn cattle from northeast England, sparrows from southern England, and parasites from Antigua were just a few examples of biological transfer that kept ecosystems in flux. Each of them suggests how growers diversified agricultural systems through modern methods in order to nurture a globalized biota in the interests of agricultural production and innovation.[1]

The transformation of preindustrial farms into habitats stocked with alien plants and animals reflected the progressive American farmer's growing interest in scientific experimentation and global perspective. Mirroring developments in agricultural science pioneered in England, more and more American growers were, as one Norfolk Agricultural Society speaker put it, "studying the capacities and adaptations of the soils, seasons, weathers, winds, markets," while "keeping an open ear to all suggested improvements." A farmer with an eye on the future "purchases the best stock from foreign lands, and experiments with the most improved implements." He "studies the improved methods of other nations." While these sentiments were by no means universal (they certainly were not prevalent among poor farmers), the idea that "knowledge of what was being done in other parts of the world" could enhance agricultural authority was taking deeper root in American soil by the mid-nineteenth century.[2]

Farmers using scientific approaches increasingly viewed agricultural ecosystems as environments that thrived under constant change. The workable landscape was an entity suspended between wild and sown. Domesticated animals were the evolving outcome of "the transmission of blood" in the ongoing effort to create "a perfect machine." Plants were "so profoundly modified that it is not possible now to recognize their aboriginal parent forms." Soil was changing "frequently and by almost perceptible degrees, from one character to another." The realization that the surrounding agricultural environment was perpetually shifting due to the hand of man established the foundation for a secularized view of nature that accommodated the evolutionary theories of Darwin, the genetic findings of Mendel, and the transnational exchange of species.[3]

Biological control—the purposeful use of natural enemies to control pests—evolved from a scattershot approach to insect control into a federal program of pest management. Farmers had been exploiting insect predation and parasitism since ancient times. However, with the establishment of the US Department of Agriculture (USDA) in 1862 and the Division of Entomology in 1863, the opportunity arose to consolidate authority around systematic biological methods and within agencies that enjoyed an international scope. Since the 1850s, a small cohort of young "economic entomologists" had been traveling the country, working with scientific farmers to streamline control methods. Through the federal government they directed the official course of biological control into the 1880s and 1890s, when it flourished as a dominant form of insect management—reflecting trends in European agriculture. Through the USDA in particular, progressive farmers and government scientists collectively promoted a vision of nature that blended local and transnational influences to serve the economic needs of a predominantly agricultural nation.[4]

No entomologist spoke as persuasively for biological control as Benjamin Dann Walsh, founding editor of the *Practical Entomologist*. In the paper's second year of publication he announced, "It is a remarkable fact that fully one half of our insect foes are not native American citizens but have been introduced here." He insisted that "we must import…parasites that in their own country prey upon the wheat midge, the Hessian fly, and the other imported insects that afflict the North American farmer." Upon this premise, government entomologists would globalize American agriculture while bringing progressive farmers ever deeper into the project of incorporating uncultivated biological relationships into the agricultural environment.[5]

By the 1890s, federally backed biological control programs were well underway. Walsh urged entomologists and scientific farmers across the country to analyze patterns of floral and faunal interaction. While historians have not looked at the emergence of biological control,[6] it has been subsumed under the transition to chemical insecticides in early twentieth century.[7] Given the environmental problems caused by early chemical applications (not to mention the organophosphates and hydrochlorides that followed), this emphasis makes sense.[8] Nevertheless, by rushing through the nineteenth century to capture the chemical turn of the twentieth, historians have missed an opportunity to explore how a transnational conception of insect control shaped perceptions of nature and environmental knowledge in the United States.

The earliest synthetic insecticides were one-size-fits-all technologies that flouted the Acadian assumption that "all the living organisms of the earth [are] an interacting whole."[9] But biological control—in large part because of its eagerness to collapse national borders in the search for natural enemies—operated according to a different set of environmental premises. Not only was it distinctly at odds with chemical methods, but it was an activity that also required a class of farmers to develop an intimate understanding of obscure ecological relationships. This understanding, in turn, came to bear directly on the incorporation of foreign plants and animals into a landscape that, by definition, was constantly being altered to sustain agricultural production. The result was an agrarian view of the environment rooted deeply in both transnational biomass and local ecological sensibilities.

Three preconditions for biological control were directly relevant to the larger argument that preindustrial agriculture fostered a unique environmental mindset. First, biological control was an agricultural technique that tapped into an evolving habit of indigenous ecological observation. Unlike the insect classification methods developed by eighteenth-century naturalists and collectors, agrarian observations about ecological relationships were the direct result of scientific farmers highlighting interactions essential to insect management. These ecological perceptions need to be considered and appreciated for their role in influencing the understanding of the natural world.

Second, biological control demanded an ongoing collaboration between scientists who understood insect relationships in theory and farmers who knew them in practice. This collaboration allowed formal "experts" to blend local knowledge with a globalized view of biomass in order to promote systems that could manage ecological relationships to the farmer's advantage. Charting this relationship sheds light on the social origins of environmentalism and lays the basis for the emergence of federal biological control projects.

Finally, biological control was a form of management that—in part because of its international scope—demanded humility in the face of nature's boundless complexity. The "chaos of experimentation" that characterized biological efforts certainly led to some resounding examples of man controlling nature through biological control. At the same time, however, it constantly reminded farmers and scientists that, while the book of nature may be open to all, its language could never be fully deciphered. The mundane tactics of insect control ensured that farmers could never lose sight of the fact that nature had its own arsenal of relentless weapons. Extermination, as a result, was unthinkable.

Biological control ultimately highlights the paradox that preindustrial agriculture used the conservation of natural relationships to undertake the conquest of nature. It remains undoubtedly true that experiments in biological control between 1860 and 1910 were generally short-lived and less effective in achieving immediate "improvements" than the chemical methods that followed. That said, when the window of opportunity remained open for biological control to flourish, agriculture did not promote an ethic of dominion. Instead, it developed habits supporting environmental perceptions that complemented the conservation-based environmental ethic.

Observation and Experimentation: Insect Control in the Early Republic

Although the American Ecological Society was founded in 1915, ecology as a formal line of academic inquiry did not emerge until the 1950s.[10] Nevertheless, practitioners of biological control before the emergence of the USDA and Department of Entomology were de facto ecologists. Early American farmers had no choice but to deal with chronic insect infestations on their own terms, with their own methods, and in a decentralized and inductive manner. It may be tempting to dismiss these farmers as "a disorganized group of amateurs" confronting questions they were ill equipped to answer.[11] But the provisional solutions they pioneered before 1840, before the rise of economic entomology, included a spectrum of management procedures developed haphazardly, experimentally, and from the ground up. In pursuing such developments, they laid a critical foundation of knowledge for a more formal approach to biological control.[12]

Progressive farmers devised solutions to pest infestations on their own farms, based on indigenous knowledge, and published their observations in the agricultural press. Without access to chemical insecticides, clear taxonomies, or the formal expertise of entomologists, they relied upon their systematic interaction with the natural world. Provisional devices prevailed—devices that mirrored planters' extensive agricultural experience and intimate relationship with the environment they were trying to commercialize. The fact that farmers were reading the landscape in order to enhance their profits should not obscure the fact that they were receiving a thorough ecological education in the process.

Scientific farmers communicated regularly through the agricultural press. A large minority of farmers read farming papers. In contrast to the professionally backed scientific assurance that would later dominate formal entomological work, articles penned by farmers revealed humility in the face of nature's mysteries. What historian Andrew Lewis has argued for naturalists holds just as true for farmers from the same era: they employed a ritualized form of modesty that "admitted and celebrated human limitations in understanding the natural world."[13] Limitations or not, the natural world—and the place of insects within it—remained the unwavering focus of the farmer's investigation.[14]

Farmers worked hard to untangle basic ecological connections. In his discussion of the aphid, a "Genesee Farmer" acknowledged that the pest's winter habits do "not appear to be well understood." He was similarly stumped by the grain worm's "manner of introduction into the [wheat] kernel," noting that the worm, too, "does not yet appear to be fully understood." A gardener from New York expressed frustration over the "vine fretter," admitting that "I have not yet been able to find out where it deposits its eggs" and promising that "as soon as I do, I will make some attempts to destroy them."[15] Beyond acknowledging their own limitations, there is a more subtle point in these common accounts: farmers were intently focused on mapping the basic ecological relationships evolving between insects and plants. An informal catalogue of knowledge was being developed through trial-and-error failures.

By the 1830s, farmers who contributed to agricultural journals were suggesting provisional solutions in a spirit of collective inquiry. "The agriculturalist," writing for *Yankee Farmer*, stressed that his article on the grain worm did not so much aim to "describe a remedy" as "to call attention of our readers to [the worm] and excite inquiry [so] that more light may be thrown upon it." Samuel Deane explained that, in an effort to control garden fleas, he "once applied some clefts of the stems of green elder to some drills of young cabbages." Although the method proved effective (he "could not find that they eat afterwards"), Deane nevertheless erred on the side of caution, concluding, "as I made this trial but once, I dare not positively assert its efficacy."[16] Farmers observed a relevant ecological relationship at work, published their observation of it, waited to see what others witnessed, and adjusted methods accordingly. By 1840, the amalgamation of individual experience into a collective pool of information was critical to insect control strategies.

Occasionally, concrete methods became conventional wisdom. A "border of mustard seed," farmers learned, was a viable remedy for the tobacco fly because, as William Tatham confirmed, "the fly prefers mustard seed, especially white mustard, to any other young plant, and will continue to feed upon that until the tobacco plant waxes strong." A farmer writing under the pseudonym "Senex" advised planters to sow radish and turnips to control for melon pests, and the method quickly became normalized. Chesapeake Bay planters routinely praised the value of allowing weeds to proliferate. Many of them had observed and written passionately about the ability of certain weeds (especially "the juice of arsemart") to repel flies and other insects from an agricultural plot. A sprinkling of hops, farmers learned, could reliably diminish the ravages of the black worm.[17] In a way, successful measures undermined the evolution of ecological understanding. Once an effective natural method became established, the burden of close observation and trial-and-error experimentation was lifted.

Most methods, however, were short lived. Agricultural information at the time was personal, cooperative, haphazard, and unburdened by the imperatives of expertise. Taking on the "peach worm," Senex admitted that "in no system of entomology could I find a description of the insect which has proved so destructive to our peach trees." However, he determined to "rely on my own observations for its history and descriptions." After surveying the relevant entomological information, Senex concluded, with a characteristic note of caution: "I do not presume...to think the above the only or best means of abating the evils we suffer from insects; my object is rather to elicit from others the result of their observation and experience." "Jack Planter" exhorted his colleagues: "If you think the information [they gathered] will be of service to the readers of your paper, please publish it when most convenient." He himself had no idea whether it made sense or not, but vowed to keep experimenting.[18]

Before 1840, expertise was thus conveyed through the endless efforts of enterprising farmers willing to occasionally substitute the pen for the plow. Rarely did a method last. The fact that the ink and sweat yielded few concrete conclusions, however, meant that farmers continued to provide themselves with an ongoing education in ecological interaction that would prove invaluable to a formalized biological control project that would soon place the American farm at the crossroads of transnational exchange.

Economic Entomology and the Embrace of Foreign Insects

Early American expressions of humility, experimentation, ecological thought, and agrarian communication laid a necessary basis for two progressive agricultural developments between 1840 and 1900: the rise of economic entomology as a formal profession linked to international agencies, and the purposeful incorporation of alien plants and animals into traditional farming practices. On the eve of the chemical transition, these developments had become deeply entrenched in the agricultural establishment. At the core of standardized biological control was the long history of ecological knowledge forged by agricultural experimentation, the more recent input of entomological expertise, and the solid backing of a federal government that, while engaged in chemical solutions, was willing to support and fund experiments that relied on collaboration with foreign entomologists and the experimental importation of alien plants and animals.[19]

The rise of biological control led to an altered set of expectations for the progressive farmer. Entomologists and scientists readily acknowledged a shift in perspective. In 1864, conservationist George Perkins Marsh captured this new challenge when he explained, "With the cultivated plants of man come the myriad tribes which feed or breed upon them, and agriculture not only introduces new species but so multiplies the number of individuals as to defy cultivation." Marsh, who lamented the agricultural consumption of natural resources, believed that in tipping the balance of nature the farmer created a host of new problems. Any progressive farmer who failed to conceptualize his farm as a dynamic ecosystem dependant on meticulous management would have found a strong corrective in the work of Charles V. Riley. The young entomologist, writing in 1875, reminded progressive farmers that "we are apt to forget that the system of Nature is a very complicated one—parasite preying upon parasite, cannibal upon cannibal, parasite upon cannibal, and cannibal upon parasite."[20] It was in the midst of this change of focus—one that demanded unprecedented ecological awareness and preparation for repeated failures—that farmers relying on homegrown insect control techniques began to welcome formal entomological expertise into their collective mission.

The relationship that developed between economic entomologists and progressive farmers is an encouraging example of cross-cultural cooperation between disparate professional groups. As the field of economic entomology cohered after 1840, it wisely decided to embrace the farmers' wealth of indigenous knowledge rather than override it with academic theories. Whereas agricultural societies also confronted the problems of insect infestation at mid-century, they did so under the assumption that farmers in general were "a confused and disorganized mob." The first economic entomologists, by contrast, consciously adhered to Joseph Howe's remark: "Could we obtain a record of the experience and practice of [farmers] the result would be invaluable!"[21]

Of course, many farmers distrusted the "experts." A Louisville, Kentucky, paper captured the essence of this skepticism in 1856, writing that "there exists a class of pseudo-scientific professors whose aim it is to take advantage of the willingness of farmers to believe that the revelations of science may be made directly available to them." Farmers feared "self-styled professors" who seemed all too eager "to write a prescription for the whole plantation." Entomologists, however, gradually overcame this legitimate prejudice, worked closely with farmers, and melded the farmer's preexisting depth of knowledge with their own academic ideas of proper insect control.[22]

The first generation of economic entomologists was a cosmopolitan group that had agricultural experience as well as an appreciation for agricultural science. Asa Fitch and Townend Glover—two of the earliest government scientists—were entomologists who had lived and worked overseas before managing large fruit farms in New York state. Benjamin Walsh, one of the most published and opinionated of the early economic entomologists, along with Charles V. Riley, perhaps the most influential entomologist of the late nineteenth century, were both born in Europe and had lasting experience in the field. Albert Cook, a Michigan entomologist, moved to California to oversee an orchard. The first generation of entomologists had experienced foreign ecosystems and gotten their hands dirty as working farmers. They, too, understood the scientific importance of naturalistic observation and the benefits of biological diversity. Most important, entomologists and farmers ultimately based their wealth of insect knowledge on evidence gleaned from direct observation.[23]

The respective bodies of knowledge possessed by these distinct groups began to meld in the 1850s. As a result of their agricultural experience and interests, entomologists were able to seamlessly introduce what may very well have been the most important concept for farmers to comprehend: insect life cycles. The main strategy through which economic entomologists altered pest control methods was by emphasizing the life stages of insects. Asa Fitch, writing in 1859, explained, "In this country, an indication of the external appearance and habits of each species is a great desideratum." Fitch captured the nature of the entomologists' mission when he promised to study only "those insects which are injurious," and in a way that would allow "those who are suffering from these pests to devise the most suitable and effectual modes for combating them." As the editors of *Prairie Farmer* explained, the nation's most destructive insects "must be remembered, and their history and habits become familiar to every young farmer of good observation." The cycles of insect life became critical to everything the entomologists wrote because "success" depended on farmers matching homegrown biological methods with expertise on exactly when insects underwent metamorphosis.[24]

Farmers and entomologists saw eye-to-eye on this matter. Farmers were obviously well aware that different bugs appeared in their crops at different times of the year, but before the involvement of entomologists, they had only the vaguest understanding of the complete sequence of transformations that insects underwent before damaging crops. Knowing where and how an organism bred and laid its eggs, under what conditions it changed into larval and pupae phases, when it became an adult and what it ate when, and the information about the behavioral indices of each phase was critical to achieving greater precision with preexisting control tactics. The entomologist William Le Baron summed it up well: "There is a period in the lives of most...noxious insects...when some one or other of the common remedies...is effective." *The Practical Entomologist* echoed the theme, editorializing that "the transformations of each species...will be faithfully recorded for [the farmers'] information by Entomologists whose time is devoted to this imperfectly understood subject." Only then, it concluded, would the farmer "be enabled from the information thus obtained to determine at what period in the insect's life the greatest quantities can be most readily destroyed by the simplest means." Knowledge of insect life cycles thereby allowed the farmer to pinpoint when and how indigenous biological and cultural methods could be most efficiently employed.[25]

Economic entomologists also succeeded in connecting with farmers because they avoided the academic discussions that had enthralled earlier generations of naturalists. They worked hard to get their messages on life cycles into mainstream agricultural venues.[26] Ambitious economic entomologists began publishing books for wider audiences by the 1850s. Their works reflected T. W. Harris's gently didactic approach in *Insects of Massachusetts* in which he promised that "this report is designed for the use of persons who may not have elementary and other works on this branch of natural history at their command." Nowhere were the effects of this symbiotic relationship between farmers and entomologists more evident than in the agricultural journals that had traditionally served as the scientific farmers' exclusive arena for conversation. Entomologists were warmly welcomed into their pages. A *Michigan Farmer* piece on the curculio insect referred to four well-known economic entomologists and, highlighting the single finding that the beetles "oviposite in the young fruit" in June, concluded that this discovery "may lead us to most important results." Increasingly, scientific farmers came to realize, it did.[27]

This triumph of discourse between progressive farmers and economic entomologists established the basis for the importation of foreign biomass for the purpose of controlling invasive insects in the United States. Popular efforts to promote the biological control of insects began with the importation of foreign birds. In 1855, a group of US and Canadian ornithologists and entomologists established the Society for the Acclimatization of Foreign Birds (SAFB). Their effort was consistent with a larger European effort to introduce nonnative species to colonized (or formerly colonized) lands. By 1900 importing and nurturing foreign birds had become a standard method of insect control on American farms. Unlike with fertilizer (which has been studied much more extensively), the impact of bird importation would extend beyond the farm itself to impact regional biodiversity as a whole. Birds consumed select insects, the absence of those insects altered the nature of the soil, and the altered soil attracted a new array of fungi, nematodes, and insects. Farmers noted the ecological repercussions of these changes and adjusted their methods accordingly.[28]

Aligning itself with the USDA in the 1860s, the SAFB began to actively establish transnational connections that would shape the American agricultural environment. It started by importing English sparrows to control moths that damaged orchard fruit on the east and west coasts. Such efforts built upon corresponding attempts by the Division of Entomology, which also worked closely with foreign official scientists, to document the insect contents of birds' stomachs, and record how those contents might influence agricultural production. In 1872 alone, over 1000 birds were imported from Europe to Ohio to control for a plague of caterpillars. By 1899, the Division of Economic Ornithology had collected over 32,000 birds, examined the contents of almost 20,000, and made extensive recommendations about which birds farmers should continue to introduce in order to manage specific pests. Farmers actively followed ornithological advice through their extension agents, experiment stations, word of mouth, and agricultural newspapers.[29]

Agricultural writers and government entomologists spread the word about the benefits of a diversified bird population. "I wish to add my testimony," the entomologist Mary Treat wrote in the introduction of *Injurious Insects of the Farm*, "in favor of the various birds that visit our gardens and orchards in the capacity of helpers, as they feed upon some of the most noxious insects that we have to contend with." Treat went on to say that the purple martins take "rose bugs from the grape vines," the orioles "pull the bag worm from his case," and the catbird eats "the unsavory pear slug." In Massachusetts, Charles L. Flint reported that after introducing a range of foreign birds into his kitchen garden, "I did not see a slug on my asparagus all summer." The entomologist Stephen A. Forbes, after conducting experiments on an Illinois apple orchard, wrote that "birds of the most varied character were either detracted or detained here by the bountiful supply of insect food, and were freely feeding upon the species most abundant." These local accounts affirmed the transnational work of the SAFB, and kept American farmers attuned to the keen power of observation and the necessity of calling on the relevant federal organizations to broaden their international ties.[30]

Joining these observations of avian biological control were extensive and vivid accounts of insects controlling insects—which would lead, by the 1880s, to the dispersal of federal entomologists across the globe to consult with scientists and import relevant insect enemies. As early as 1864, Flint noted of the plant lice that "were it not that their insect enemies tend to reduce their numbers materially, and keep in check this vast army of suckers, we might reasonably apprehend the speedy destruction of all our crops." A farmer living near Columbus, South Carolina, wrote to the *Southern Planter* about "the operations of the numerous qualities of ants...that were lying in wait for the grass-worm," doing little more than acting upon the "natural desire for a fresh supply of food." Building on Fitch's work on predaceous insects, editors of the *Southern Planter* noted, "We have heard from two distinct sources that the ants have been observed in large numbers feeding greedily on the chinch bugs." By 1871, A. S. Packard was declaring that "insects are a most powerful agency in nature."[31]

Other reports were even more encouraging. When aphids covered Michigan wheat crops and were quickly countered by an unidentified insect, entomologists seized the opportunity to publicize the virtues of biological control and the importance of making it a conscious strategy. Their editorial in *Science* explained, "The importance of parasitic and predaceous insects in overcoming our insect pests has long been recognized by the practical entomologist. He sees the destroyers swept off as by a flood, and sees in these prolific friends the easy solution of the problem of insect years. He knows that, were it not for these friends, the destroying hosts would make our earth a desert, and replace plenty with famine. He knows that adversity among these tiny helpers means success to the swarms of insects that devour the crops, and so is rejoiced when he sees these little helpers active and numerous."[32]

The Michigan case was "a vivid illustration of this important and interesting fact"—the fact that insects were their own worst enemies. The aphids had been "rapidly blighting the grain," but even then, "when the lice were countless in numbers, and when the winged forms were easily spreading to the oat-fields, the hand of deliverance was discerned in the comparatively few but wondrously prolific enemies of the lice, which had already sounded a halt in the march of destruction." Summarizing the destructive power of grasshoppers, one entomologist remarked that, "fortunately there are a considerable number of species of animals"—namely the blister beetle and ground beetle—"that depend to a greater or less extent upon grasshoppers for substance.... All combine in keeping the pests in check." Charles Riley agreed, writing that "there are some instances which there can be no doubt whatever as to the good which would flow from the introduction of beneficial species." A. S. Packard added, "It is quite as essential for one to know what insects are beneficial to agriculture as what are injurious."[33] By the 1880s, the sentiment was that insect-based biological control should become a fundamental goal of the US Division of Entomology and its umbrella organization, the USDA, was well established.

That this emphasis would demand that American entomologists develop tight transnational connections is best exemplified by the itinerary of L. O. Howard, head of the Bureau of Entomology from 1894 until 1927. When Howard undertook efforts to control the gypsy and brown tail moths in 1905, he visited and collaborated with scientists in France, Italy, Austria, Hungary, Germany, and Russia. His efforts came to naught, but his globe-trotting behavior reflected the USDA's expanding scope of inquiry. Other biological control efforts were quite effective. During the final quarter of the nineteenth-century entomologists imported, bred in insectaries, and released (among hundreds of other insect species) the seven spotted ladybird beetle (obtained in North Africa and India) to control the mealy plum aphis, the mite-eating ladybird from Western Australia to control for red spiders, the black ladybird beetle from eastern Australia to control for black scale, parasites from Antigua to control for the soft scale, and the Asiatic ladybird beetle to prey on the San Jose scale.

Of course, not all these efforts bred desirable results. One might consider the importation of the green lacewing to California orchards, a metallic ground beetle from Italy to Massachusetts, a ladybird beetle from Northern China to Sacramento, and flesh flies from New South Wales to take on plague locusts in the Midwest. Riley, who as head of the Division of Entomology throughout the 1880s spent most summers overseas, surveyed these efforts and explained (with perhaps strained optimism), "Nature will, with the new conditions induced by these importations, come to the relief of the fruit-grower." Observing the spread of foreign insect biomass a few years later, James Bradford Olcott tellingly wrote that "our neighbors thousands of miles away are brought as near as adjoining farms."[34]

Although the Division of Entomology arranged for the importation of many hundreds of insect species, one grabbed international headlines and placed biological control on the map of effective management measures. In 1886 an insect called the cottony-cushion scale, which had been imported accidentally from Australia, proliferated to the point of collapsing the California citrus industry. At the behest of Riley, the State Department sent Albert Koebele, an insect enthusiast and collector, to Australia in 1888 to research the cottony-cushion scale's natural predators. Koebele quickly discovered the Vedalia beetle, a ladybird beetle that consumed the scale with impressive voracity. In January of 1889 he sent three boxes holding a total of 129 Vedalia beetles to California, where state entomologists bred them for experimentation in citrus fields. In June 1889, entomologists released 10,555 Vedalia beetles.[35]

Entomologists had already seen clear evidence of the success of biological control, but nothing prepared them for what followed. In the course of a breeding season, the scale "ceased to be a major pest." The positive results were hard to overstate. Shipments of oranges from California tripled within a year. "We fully expect," editorialized *Insect Life*, "to learn of the increase and rapid spread of this new introduction, as well as of the other predaceous species which have been introduced." The Vedalia story, according to E. O. Essig, an early twentieth-century entomologist, "furnished to the world the first demonstration of effective natural control."[36]

Biological control thus appeared poised to play a defining role in the twentieth century. By the early 1890s it was enjoying unprecedented popularity. F. M. Webster, the state entomologist of Ohio, reported in a study of the Hessian fly that "it is proper to say here that the pest suffers much from the attacks of several minute parasites, which attack and destroy it in both the egg and larval or maggot stage." A USDA survey noted that "the boll worm was scarce during the past season," with the surmised reason being "a common species of Soldier bug [that] was found devouring a large full-grown boll worm." A test pupa placed "on a branch of cotton with some newly hatched boll worms" proved that the worms indeed had fallen "victim to its beak." While Koebele was solving the cottony-cushion scale problem, other entomologists in California were reporting that "the larva of a little moth...is also known to feed on the eggs." Yet others were encouraged by a scale-eating chalcid fly, explaining that "this little friend was introduced from Australia with its host." Two of Riley's last reports for the Division of Entomology crowned the achievements of biological control with an overview of its many accomplishments. His final assessment was that "there can be no doubt whatever as to the good that would flow from the introduction of beneficial species."[37]

Riley's dream would go unrealized. Throughout the 1880s and 1890s, as the USDA collaborated with scientists internationally to foster a transition to biological control, American farmers nurtured close relationships with government entomologists. The entomologists, in turn, continued to rely on the agriculturalist's keen powers of observation to refine control strategies. USDA fieldwork at home and abroad during this period reached a peak. Given the nature of the relationship between farmers and government scientists and government scientists and their foreign counterparts, and the exchange of ecological information at the heart of it, the likelihood that nineteenth-century agriculture was acting as a crucible of environmental thought seems strong enough to warrant further investigation. This is not, however, to challenge the fact that this broad web of international and local relationships was short-lived.

The chemical transition that transpired between 1900 and 1920 had legitimate justifications—insecticides were evidently needed to prevent malaria and fight a war—but the impact on biological control was devastating. The bureaucratic reengineering of the Bureau of Entomology to support the proliferation of lead-, kerosene-, and arsenic-based insecticides gutted the funding for biological-control experimentation.. At the same time, it erased a generation's wealth of ecological knowledge. Later in the century, after "the age of ecology" began, environmentalists would lament the environmentally insensitive remarks of politicians like the Republican senator from Utah Jake Garn, who famously declared, "I frankly don't give a damn if a 14-legged bug or woundfin minnow live or die." The reason Garn could posture so successfully was that the rise of chemicals rendered useless the ecological awareness once endemic to agricultural practice. Nineteenth-century practitioners of biological control would not have known much about fourteen-legged bugs, but they certainly would have appreciated the myriad consequences of the disappearance of a species.[38]

An emphasis on biological control highlights a less obvious manifestation of "transnational" environmentalism. Viewing agriculture in terms of markets, supply chains, and systems of finance, American farms are traditionally thought to have become globalized as they industrialized after 1920. However, examining agriculture through the less obvious lens of moving biomass, such a trajectory is complicated. Agriculture on the cusp of industrialization enjoyed its own kind of transnational interaction. Federal entomologists affiliated primarily with the USDA cast their nets internationally to capitalize on the potential of biological control. When they crossed borders, plants and animals followed. The result was the purposeful and increasingly international exchange of species, a development that had a direct impact on cultural conceptions of nature.

Chemicals brought these developments to a halt. They blunted biological diversity, sidestepped ecological relationships, laid the basis for monoculture, and industrialized farming in environmentally stressful ways. The possibility that preindustrial biological exchange might have fostered opposite outcomes—and in so doing strengthened the key tenets of an early environmental ethic—is one worth our ongoing attention.

NOTES

1. This chapter is adapted from *American Pests*, by James E. McWilliams. Copyright 2008. James E. McWilliams. Reprinted with permission of Columbia University Press.Charles L. Flint, "Secretary's Report," *Fifth Annual Report of the Secretary of the Massachusetts Board of Agriculture* (Boston: Williams White, 1858), 78.

2. Donald Worster, *Nature's Economy: A History of Ecological Ideas* (Cambridge: Cambridge University Press, 1977), xv; "From the Report on Stock," *Eleventh Annual Report of the Secretary of the Massachusetts Board of Agriculture* (Boston: William White, 1863), 185; A. W. Cheever, "Various Views of Farming," Seventeenth Annual report of the Secretary of the Connecticut State Board of Agriculture (Hartford, CT: Case, Lockwood, and Brainard, 1884), 217.

3. "Report on Stock," 188; R. L. Allen, *The American Farm Book: or, Compend of American Agriculture* (New York: C. M. Saxton, 1849), 14; Charles Darwin, *The Variation of Plants and Animals under Domestication*, vol. 1 (London: John Murray, 1888), 322; Ari Aukusti Lehtinen, "Modernization and the Concept of Nature," in Timo Myllyntaus and Mikko Saikku (eds.), *Encountering the Past in Nature* (Athens: University of Ohio Press, 1999), 29–45; Worster, *Nature's Economy*, 50–5.

4. Overviews of biological control include Richard Sawyer, *To Make a Spotless Orange: Biological Control in California* (Ames: Iowa State University Press, 1996); James Whorton, *Before "Silent Spring": Pesticides and Public Health in Pre-DDT America* (Princeton: Princeton University Press, 1994).

5. Benjamin D. Walsh, "Fighting the Insects," *The Practical Entomologist* (September 29, 1866), 1.

6. See Sawyer, *To Make a Spotless Orange*; Whorton, *Before "Silent Spring"*; and Thomas R. Dunlap, *DDT: Scientists, Citizens, and Public Policy* (Princeton, NJ: Princeton University Press, 1981); John H. Perkins, *Insects, Experts, and the Insecticide Crisis: The Quest for New Pest Management Strategies* (New York: Plenum, 1982); W. Connor Sorenson, *Brethren of the Net: American Entomology, 1840–1880* (Tuscaloosa: University of Alabama Press, 1995).

7. Edmund P. Russell, "Speaking of Annihilation": Mobilizing for War against Human and Insect Enemies, 1914–1945," *Journal of American History* (82) 4 (1996): 1505–1529; James E. McWilliams, "The Horizon Opened Up Very Greatly": Leland O. Howard and the Transition to Chemical Insecticides in the United States, 1894–1927," *Agricultural History* (82) 4 (fall 2008): 468–96; Steven Stoll, "Insects and Institutions: University Science and the Fruit Business in California," *Agricultural History* 69 (spring 1995): 216–39.

8. Edmund S. Russell, "War on Insects: Warfare, Insecticides, and Environmental Change in the United States" (PhD diss.: University of

Wisconsin-Madison, 1999); V. G. Dethier, *Man's Plague? Insects and Agriculture* (Princeton, NJ: Darwin Press, 1976).

9. Worster, *Nature's Economy*, xiv.

10. Joel B. Hagen, "Teaching Ecology during the Environmental Age, 1965–1980," *Environmental History* 13 (October 2008): 705.

11. The phrase comes from George H. Daniels, *American Science in the Age of Jackson* (New York: Columbia University Press, 1968), 7.

12. A. Hunter Dupree, *Science in the Federal Government: A History of Policies and Activities to 1940* (Cambridge, England: Harvard University Press, 1957), 8. On the virtues of experimentation, see Wilson Flagg, "Plan of a Series of Experiments for Investigating the Potato Disease," *Transactions of the Essex Agricultural Society for 1859* (Newbury, MA: William H. Huse, 1959), 129. Lewis, "A Democracy of Facts, An Empire of Reason," 668; Lewis, "A Democracy of Facts, An Empire of Reason," 668–9.

13. Lewis, "A Democracy of Facts, An Empire of Reason," 668–9.

14. A Genesee Farmer, *The Farmer's Cabinet* (1) 2 (August 1, 1836), 25–6; Samuel Deane, *The New England Farmer* (Worchester, 1814), 183; Mary Griffith, *Our Neighborhood or Letters on Horticulture and Natural Phenomenon* (New York, 1831), 30–1; H. C. Giddens, "To Kill Lice on Swine," *Southern Cultivator* (X) 1952, 294; from "Bucks County Intelligencer," printed in *Farmer's Cabinet* (1) 12 (Jan. 1, 1837), 185; Lewis, "Swallow Submersion and Natural History," 668; Sally McMurray, "Who Read Agricultural Journals? Evidence from Chenango County, New York, 1839–1865," *Agricultural History* (63) 4 (Fall 1989): 1–18.

15. Genesee Farmer, *Farmer's Cabinet*, August 1, 1836, 25.

16. Samuel Deane, *The New England Farmer*, 181; "Destructive Insects," *The Farmer's Cabinet* (1) 1 (July 1, 1836), 5–6; "The Wheat Fly," *The Farmer's Cabinet* (1) 10 (December 1, 1836), 145; "Remedy for the Culicue, or Plum Weevil," *Southern Cultivator* (X), 301; McMurray, "Who Read Agricultural Journals?" 2–5; Donald B. Marti, "Agricultural Journalism and the Diffusion of Knowledge: The First Half Century in America," *Agricultural History* 54 (January 1980): 37–8.

17. "Turnep Fly," *Farmers Cabinet* (1) 6 (October 1, 1836), 88; ibid (1) 2 (August 1, 1836), 25; ibid (1) 12 (January 1, 1837), 181. The "arsemart" reference is in Ann Leighton, *Early American Gardens: "For Meate or Medicine"* (Amherst, MA: University of Massachusetts Press, 1986), 242.

18. "The Agriculturalist," "The Agriculturalist," *Yankee* farmer (1) IV (January 6, 1838), 1.

19. Charles E. Rosenberg, "Science, Technology, and Economic Growth: The Case of Agricultural Experiment Station," in *No Other Gods: On Science and American Social Thought* (Baltimore: Johns Hopkins University Press, 1978), 153–72.

20. Charles V. Riley, *Potato Pests: Being an Illustrated Account of the Colorado Potato Beetle…* (New York: Orange Judd Company, 1875), 34; Myllyntaus and Saikki, *Encountering the Past in Nature*, 33.

21. Joseph S. Howe, "Progressive Farming," in Charles L. Flint (ed.), *Abstract of Returns of the Agricultural Societies of Massachusetts* (Boston: Wright & Potter, 1872), 19.

22. "Chemistry as Applied to Agriculture," *Southern Planter* (XVI) 10 (October 1856), 298.

23. Mallis, *American Entomologists*, 38–41, 43–9, 69–79, 139–42; Sorenson, *Brethren of the Net*, 67–8; Mallis (ed.), "The Diaries of Asa Fitch, M.D.," *Bulletin, Entomological Society of America* 9 (1963): 264; A. S. Packard, "Injurious and Beneficial Insects," *American Naturalist* 7 (September 1873): 525; Packard quoted in Mallis, 299; A. S. Packard, "Moths Entrapped by an Asclepaid Plant (Physianthus) and Killed by Honey Bees," *Botanical Gazette* (5) 2 (February 1880): 19.

24. Herbert Osborn, *Fragments of Entomological History, Including Some Personal Recollections of Men and Events* (Columbus, OH: self-published, 1937), 11; Asa Fitch, *Noxious, Beneficial, and Other Insects of the State of New York* (third, fourth, and fifth reports) (Albany: C. Van Benthuysen, 1859), iv; Hae-Gyung Geong, "Exerting Control: Biology and Bureaucracy in the Development of American Entomology, 1870–1930" (PhD diss.: University of Wisconsin, 1999), 8; "A String of Bugs," *Prairie Farmer* (XI) 8 (August 1851), 1.

25. Sorenson, *Brethren of the Net*, 104; William LeBaron, *Second Annual Report on the Noxious Insects of the State of Illinois* (Springfield, 1872), 7; "Introduction," *The Practical Entomologist* (1) 1 (October 30, 1865), 4.

26. "I am aware," Thaddeus Harris wrote to the old-school naturalist Nicholas Hentz, "that the 'New England Farmer' is not likely to be much circulated among men of science, and will therefore not be considered the best authority." T. W. Harris, letter to Nicholas Hentz, November 19, 1828, Museum of Science, Boston, archives.

27. "The Curculio," *Michigan Farmer* (XVI) 16 (June 1858), 175; "Bugs on Apple Buds," *The New England Farmer* (1) 7 (July 1867), 332, 346–7 (Walsh quote); "The Wheat Aphis," *New England Farmer* (16) 1 (January 1864), 16; "Dr. Fitch's Report on the Insects of New York," *Southern Planter* XVI (7) (July, 1857), 437.

28. Matthew Evenden, "The Laborers of Nature: Economic Ornithology and the Role of Birds as Agents of Biological Pest Control in North American Agriculture, ca 1880–1930," *Forest and Conservation History*(39) 4 (October 1995): 172–83.

29. Robin W. Doughty, "Sparrows for America: A Case of Mistaken Identity," *Journal of Popular Culture* (14) 2 (Fall 1980): 212–28; Virginia DeJohn Anderson, *Creatures of Empire*.

30. Department of Agriculture, *Report of the Commissioner of Agriculture for 1881–1882* (Washington, DC: WPO, 1882), 158–9; Matthew Cooke, *Injurious Insects of the Orchard, Vineyard, Field, Garden... With Remedies for their Extermination* (Sacramento, CA: Crocker, 1883), 402, 420.

31. A. S. Packard, *First Annual Report of the Injurious and Beneficial Insects of Massachusetts* (Boston: Wright and Potter, 1871), 1; "Pissant vs. Chinch Bug," *The Southern Planter* (XVII) 7 (July 1857), 437; "The Grass Caterpillar," ibid., 439.

32. "Enemies of the Plant Louse," *Science* (XIV) 340 (August 9, 1889), 100–1

33. Dernier, *God's Plague?*, 135–6, 142 (Walsh quote); Clarence M. Weed, "On the Injurious Locusts of Central Illinois," printed in S. A. Forbes (ed.), *Miscellaneous Essays on Economic Entomology* (Springfield, IL: H. W. Rokker, 1886), 51; C. V. Riley, *Parasitic and Predaceous Insects in Applied Entomology* (Washington, DC: Government Printing

Office, 1893), 141; Packard, *First Annual Report of the Injurious and Beneficial Insects of Massachusetts*, 28.

34. E. O. Essig, *A History of Entomology* (New York: Macmillan, 1931), 274–397.

35. L. O. Howard, *A History of Applied Entomology* (Washington, DC: The Smithsonion Institution, 1930), 154–7; Ian Tyrell, *True Gardens of the Gods: Californian-Australian Environmental Reform* (Berkeley: University of California Press, 1999), 181.

36. V. G. Dethier, *Man's Plague?*, 144–5; E. O. Essig, *A History of Entomology* (New York: MacMillan, 1931), 125; Albert Koebele, "Report of a Trip to Australia…to Investigate the Natural Enemies of the Fluted Scale," *Bulletin No. 21* [U. S. Department of Agriculture: Division of Entomology] (Washington, DC: Government Printing Office, 1890), 6. *Insect Life* quotation is from Koeble's report; "How Hawaii Got Rid of Insects," *New York Times* (August 8, 1897), 18.

37. C. V. Riley, "Annual Address of the President," *Proceedings of the Entomological Society of Washington* (II) 4 (Washington, DC, no publisher given, 1893), 2; F. B. Webster, "The Hessian Fly," *Bulletin of the Ohio Agricultural Experiment Station* (IV) 7 (November, 1891), 133; F. W. Malley, "The Boll Worm of Cotton," *Bulletin No. 24* [U. S. Dept. of Agriculture: Division of Entomology] (Washington, D.C.: Government Printing Office, 1891), 27; C. V. Riley, "The Icerya or Fluted Scale," *Bulletin No. 15* [U. S. Department of Agriculture: Division of Entomology] (Washington, DC: Government Printing Office, 1887), 13; S. A. Forbes, "On a Bacterial Disease of the Larger Corn Root Worn," *Seventeenth Report of the State Entomologist on the Noxious and Beneficial Insects* (Springfield, IL: Rocker State Printer and Binder, 1891), 72–3; Riley, "Parasitic and Predacious Insects in Applied Entomology," *Insect Life* (VI) 2 (1893), 131–41; Riley, "Parasitism in Insects," *Proceedings* of the Entomological Society of Washington (II) 4 (1893), 1–35.

38. Garn, quoted in Shannon Peterson, *Acting for Endangered Species: The Stauatory Ark* (Lawrence: University Press of Kansas, 2002), 51.

9

Bird Day

Promoting the Gospel of Kindness in the Philippines during the American Occupation

Janet M. Davis

In March 1900, William Howard Taft, the newly appointed head of the new Philippine Commission, arrived in Manila to draft a blueprint for American civilian governance of a country that was now roiling under US martial law. Prompted by the imminent specter of a permanent US occupation, the long and brutal Philippine-American War began on February 4, 1899, when the Filipino nationalist Emilio Aguinaldo and his allies attacked the American garrison at Manila. Two days later, the US Senate narrowly voted to annex the islands. After a raucous debate over the racial politics of empire building, a lone senatorial vote provided the constitutionally mandated two-thirds majority (57 to 27) needed to ratify the Treaty of Paris. Yet just months earlier, the US military had helped liberate the Philippines from Spanish colonial rule during the Spanish-American War. Now, in an unexpected blow to Philippine sovereignty, Taft declared the people of the 7100 ethnic and linguistically diverse islands that constituted the Philippines to be "unfit" for self-government: "The great mass of them are superstitious and ignorant.... The idea that these people can govern themselves is as ill-founded as any proposition that [William Jennings] Bryan advances." As evidence that Filipinos were incapable of self-rule, Taft asserted, "They are cruel to animals and cruel to their fellows when occasion arises. They need the training of fifty or a hundred years before they shall even realize what Anglo-Saxon liberty is."[1] The humane treatment of animals was cast not just as a mark of civilization but also as a criteria for political autonomy.

During the US occupation of the Philippines (1899–1946), American beliefs about the moral treatment of animals were exported to US territories, disguised as ideas about civilization and self-determination. In turn, a constellation of new animal welfare laws helped define the ideological and operational contours of America's empire at the municipal, provincial, and territorial levels. Legislation, in tandem with animal-centered activities in local Filipino schools, playgrounds, parks, and streets provided a powerful window on the daily life of empire as well as the circulation of American exceptionalist ideologies concerning humanitarianism, uplift, proper moral comportment, racial savagery, and the rhetoric of Filipino readiness for citizenship. These ideological flows were primarily transnational rather than international. Instead of recognizing and reinforcing discrete national boundaries through international treaties and organizations, American animal welfare activities in the occupied Philippines were symbiotic, not simply unidirectional. As a transnational imperial project, US humane initiatives streamed dialogically across national boundaries in a mutually constitutive process of exceptional nation building at home and abroad.[2]

American animal humanitarians in the Philippines paid special attention to wild birds. As fleeting objects of visual and aural beauty, liminal "pets" on the wing, whether encaged in the home, in the nest, or dismembered and arranged flowerlike on a hat, birds performed critical cultural and political work as gendered metaphors for family, home, and nation. Animal advocates argued that the act of caring for birds encouraged civilized habits of body and mind. This work was no less important than the work James E. McWilliams covers in chapter 8 of this volume. McWilliams demonstrates that birds also performed essential agricultural labor during the nineteenth century. The use of birds was a common biocontrol tactic among entomologists. American and Canadian groups such as the Society for the Acclimatization of Foreign Birds (1855) imported foreign birds to combat insect pests that were decimating domestic farm fields—thereby complicating binary notions of nature and civilization as avian ecological workers collapsed the distinction between "wild" and "cultivated."

Furthermore, wild birds wedded the separate ideological agendas of the fin de siécle American conservation and animal welfare movements as no other animal had done before. Both movements cared deeply about animals but rarely came together on the activist field because their worldviews were parallel, rather than intersectional. Animal welfare advocates generally focused on acts of cruelty to individual animals, often in highly affective and anthropomorphic terms. The conservation movement, on the other hand, largely conceived of animals in the aggregate, treating whole species and their ecological relationship to the environment, rather than focusing on individual animals.[3] While American government officials and conservationists acknowledged that wild birds had both cultural cache and economic value, each conceded that "wild" colonial subjects had neither.

A consideration of wild birds and animal welfare activities in the US-occupied Philippines also highlights the complex ways in which nation-states managed the transnational environment through their promotion of "civilization" campaigns. As this chapter demonstrates, the American occupation government directly shaped environmental policies and animal welfare activities in the Philippines through traditional expressions of state power: legislation, appropriations, and policing. Moreover, American officials colluded with private entities, such as humane societies and missionaries. These non-state actors shared the colonial state's universalizing moral assumptions about environmental stewardship and animal kindness as key building blocks for a future Philippine nation-state that mirrored American values. Yet one should not assume that these nonstate actors worked in ideological lockstep with US authorities. For example, Society for the Prevention of Cruelty to Animals (SPCA) leaders readily condemned the Philippine-American War, and missionaries loudly criticized aspects of occupation policy, such as the changeable legal status of the cockfight, when they undermined their goals.

American Popular Culture, Race, Animals, and Imperial Ideologies of Uplift

William Howard Taft's coupling of animal cruelty with the inability to self-govern echoed a common ideological refrain among animal advocates in the United States and abroad in the late nineteenth and early twentieth centuries. Animal welfare politics and humane education programs were important moral platforms for expansionist principles, particularly in the Philippines, where occupation officials left a detailed historical record of animal activities. Ideologies of American uplift also circulated widely in such popular forms as international expositions, vaudeville, the circus, periodical literature, sports, and movie actualities. Aided by improved transportation technologies, such as the transcontinental railroad and the steamship, these mass US cultural forms promulgated American expansion in teleological terms as the inevitable culmination of the nation's manifest destiny: a beneficent beacon of democracy, civic virtue, and modern progress that would uplift the world. Those who commonly worked in mass entertainment, and not coincidentally, with animals, made such connections explicit. The circus proprietor Peter

Sells, for one, declared in a show program that America's recent victory over Spain heralded a triumphal new age: "We have placed an object lesson before the world that will cause tyrants tremble [*sic*] and inspire the oppressed with hope. We have taken our place at the very head in the front rank of nations. We have taught the whole world a lesson that has started every nation on earth to meditating upon the figure America is to cut in the world's politics of the future."[4]

The politics of animal welfare and imperial uplift complemented contemporary racial theories and corresponding popular representations of animalized human savagery. In Sells's circus program, one also could find plentiful images of animalized performers at the circus sideshow, the so-called "ethnological congress of strange and savage tribes," and the animal menagerie. Moreover, midways at world's fairs, such as Chicago's World Columbian Exposition in 1893, featured a constellation of "missing links" and "savages" juxtaposed with animals from their country of origin. Popular media represented African American celebrities like the boxer Jack Johnson in brutish, animalistic terms.[5] The sociologist William Graham Sumner used Spencerian and social Darwinian notions of the survival of the fittest to explain human differences and social inequality. Melding evolutionary theory with contemporary ideas about race, the psychologist G. Stanley Hall forged his unified theory of recapitulation, the notion that human beings acted out earlier stages of evolutionary development at different life stages. According to Hall, people of color (and all females) were essentially trapped in a "lower" evolutionary phase than white males. Although these popular and theoretical couplings of race and animality were representational, they had enormous political and social heft in supporting regimes of Jim Crow violence and disenfranchisement. In the early twentieth century, they also helped shape the ideological contours of on-the-ground encounters between people and animals in America's overseas empire. Yet before such ideas could be exported, they had to be developed and tested on home ground.

The US Animal Welfare Movement: A Brief Historical Overview

Imbued with a universalistic vision of humanitarian mission and moral uplift, nineteenth- and early twentieth-century animal welfare organizations strove to civilize America's urban, animal-powered industrial economy. An odd fusion of faith (in the form of Protestant perfectionism born during the antebellum Second Great Awakening) and war (in the shape of the Civil War, Reconstruction, and the growth of the US empire) catalyzed and sustained this social movement. The nation's earliest humane society was founded in 1866, after the Civil War's grinding, cataclysmic violence brought abolition and suffering to the center of America's consciousness. This new organization boldly called itself the American Society for the Prevention of Cruelty to Animals (ASPCA), even though its activities were limited to New York state. Based in New York City, the ASPCA was vested with the powers of arrest through its state charter. Subsequent state SPCAs were identified by their specific state names (such as the Massachusetts SPCA, or MSPCA), and were likewise deputized by individual state authorities to police the populace. By 1874, there was an animal welfare society in virtually every medium and large city north of the Mason-Dixon Line.[6] After Reconstruction, the animal welfare movement spread throughout the nation. Armed with police-like badges and uniforms, humane society officers—who were often the local elites—patrolled bustling city streets, stockyards, railroad yards, tenements, and alleys, on the prowl for a drunken hostler flogging his beleaguered cart horse, or a group of immigrant boys cheering on a dog fight. Other areas of concern included the transportation of cattle and sheep to stockyards; adulterated milk; and the checkrein, tail-docking, and blood sports. Virtually everyone in the movement supported the euthanasia of stray dogs and cats as a humane alternative to a life of suffering on the streets. Humane officers also targeted wealthy scientists and doctors who performed vivisections. They condemned rich sportsmen who engaged in urban pigeon shoots, but generally paid limited attention to hunting outside the city. They focused the majority of their surveillance activities on working-class people (often immigrants) whose labor was dependent on animals—in other words, on a constituency that many well-to-do animal advocates deemed to be incapable of self-governance.

American animal activists were especially critical of working-class women who adorned their heads with dead bird bodies in a voluminous turn-of-the-century millinery confection known as the "bird hat." Denouncing feather fashions as "the vanity of silly women,"[7] elite members of new Audubon societies and other organizations turned to intimate associations of family and home to describe the decimation of herons, egrets, and songbirds for the millinery trade, in which bird parents were snatched and butchered, leaving vulnerable orphan hatchlings abandoned in the nest. According to the *New York Times*, "The most expert plume hunters...prefer to net or trap the birds and tear the plumes from the backs of their living victims, leaving them to die lingering deaths in the swamps. Often their last moments are further harassed by encounters with water-rats and snakes that lie in wait for their defenseless prey. Foxes and wildcats also run riot among the young birds, which literally fall from their nests into their jaws."[8]

The historian Jennifer Price observes that the bird protection movement was a women's movement. New Audubon societies in the late 1890s
were started and sustained by women who were doubly active in the women's
club movement and other areas of Progressive era reform.[9] Women activists
reserved special contempt for those bird-hat-loving women whose moral standing should have prompted them to know better. A letter to the editor of the
New York Times published in 1897 captured this sentiment well: "Then, too,
how can Sunday-school teachers, who are supposed to teach the children to
be kind to God's creatures sit with hats ornamented in this way and expect the
little ones to listen to their teachings?"[10] Through the metaphors of family and
home, bird advocacy helped legitimize women's political presence in the public
sphere in an era before the ratification of the Nineteenth Amendment. Their
sustained lobbying paid off. Activists rejoiced at the passage of the federal Lacey
Act in 1900, which created the nation's first wildlife refuges and strengthened
existing state laws by prohibiting the interstate commerce of specific birds and
game that were poached in one state and sold in another. Other legislation
banned the sale of domestic American songbirds for the cage trade.

Americans experienced the urgency of bird welfare on both the macro- and
microlevels. Massive bird die-offs and extinctions transformed abstract ideas
about the degradation of animal life during the Gilded Age into an immediate
and concrete reality. Until the late nineteenth century, millions of Americans
shared the spectacular sensory experience of witnessing mountainous clouds of
billions of passenger pigeons darkening the skies, creating wind through their
sheer flapping air mass, and reportedly changing the weather as they flew.[11]
And then they were gone. In 1914, the last bird, a single specimen housed at
the Cincinnati Zoo, curiously named Martha, died, and the passenger pigeon
was officially extinct, a victim of mass slaughter as a result of commercial hunting and new transportation technologies in the exploding industrial marketplace that expanded consumer access to this delicious game bird.

Americans also encountered birds in more immediate ways. The bird's
power as a symbol of domesticity was intimately felt because the caged songbird
was a ubiquitous pet in the nineteenth-century home. The historian Katherine
Grier points out that in an age before recorded sound, pet songbirds provided
pleasing music in domestic spaces that would otherwise be unfathomably silent
to modern ears.[12] Nonetheless, at the turn of the twentieth century the caged
songbird was fast becoming another potent symbol of animal cruelty. Using the
common metaphor of the birdcage as prison, the English animal welfare writer
Ernest Bell—a frequent voice in American humane literature—denounced the
cage trade: "We know that human prisoners will try to beguile the monotony of
their cells by singing the songs learnt in happier times. Invalids in a sick-room

will often sing, not because they are happy, but because they feel their lives dreary....The singing of birds is an instinct, and its exercise is no doubt a relief, just as when silence is exacted, but it can in no way be taken as a sign of enjoyment of prison life in one case more than the other."[13]

Given the global scale of profligate market hunting and habitat loss, the imperative of bird protection was hardly limited to the United States. Other nations were increasingly alarmed about the rapid disappearance of birds and other wildlife. In 1900, for example, delegates from European countries with colonies in sub-Saharan Africa convened in London and signed the Convention for the Preservation of Wild Animals, Birds and Fish in Africa, which set forth a series of regulations to prevent "indiscriminant slaughter," and promote conservation. Although enforcement was haphazard, the Convention became a blueprint for conservation legislation in other parts of the world, such as British Malaya.[14]

The American animal welfare movement was born in urban streets, but as Englishman Ernest Bell demonstrates, its activist field quickly encompassed the world. George T. Angell, the founder and president of the MSPCA, worked directly with nongovernmental actors such as missionaries, political bodies like municipal councils, and individual government officials abroad to expand the geographical reach of what would otherwise be a local organization. Shortly after creating the MSPCA in 1868, Angell, a wealthy lawyer with a hardscrabble upbringing, personally financed the publication and distribution of 200,000 free copies of the organization's new journal he hoped would give voice to the birds and animals he so wanted to save. It was appropriately titled *Our Dumb Animals*.[15] The Boston police helped deliver complimentary copies of the journal to nearly every household in Boston. The MSPCA also mailed *Our Dumb Animals* to influential citizens around the world. Over the next several decades, the journal commanded an impressive monthly readership of between 50,000 and 100,000.[16]

Angell worked closely with American missionaries who had joined his transnational children's organization, the Bands of Mercy (1882), to propagate the gospels of Protestantism, biblical stewardship, and animal kindness to a youthful audience in every continent. In the United States alone, there were 131,688 Bands in 1921, comprising public school classes, church groups, and youth organizations affiliated with the Woman's Christian Temperance Union (WCTU), and the National Association of Colored Women, among others.[17] Missionaries overseas reported their activities to *Our Dumb Animals*, with tales of transforming savage headhunters and dog-eating bullies into docile, animal-loving Christians. As president of the WCTU, Frances Willard included animal welfare in her transnational "Do Everything" platform. She contended that,

"Nothing has made men madder in their rage toward the defenseless than the drink delirium, hence to teach the ethics of kindness to animals is germane to the white-ribbon gospel. God speed the Band of Mercy. Let not a guilty man or scape-grace boy escape its blessed teachings!"[18] Willard and other American animal welfare supporters embraced an urgent and sweeping mission to uplift a volatile nation—and indeed, a violent world—in accord with humane principles. Yet these principles were often rigidly universalistic, dismissing culturally specific social practices and values in favor of an abiding faith in the self-evident truth and moral superiority of their civilizing mission.

"Brutes in the Shape of a Man": Animal Welfare and the Dawning of the American Empire in the Philippines

When William Howard Taft arrived in Manila in 1900, he was ideologically equipped with well-established American notions of animal cruelty, kindness, civilization, and savagery and ready to impose them on Filipinos. After he became the first civil governor of the Philippines on July 4, 1901, Taft's administration—working in cooperation with Filipino elites—established an elaborate municipal code for the entire country that structured the legal minutia of local governance. On February 6, 1902, just seven months after the installation of civilian rule on the islands, the Municipal Board of Manila's Ordinance for the Prevention of Cruelty to Animals became law. In five detailed sections, the ordinance mandated new modes of comportment and surveillance, replete with stiff fines of $100.00 USD (or $2,485.96 in 2010)[19] and imprisonment of up to six months for those who failed to comply:

> Section 1: No person shall overload, overwork, cruelly beat, torture, torment, mutilate, or cruelly kill any animal; or carry, drive or lead any animal in an unnecessary cruel manner; or abandon or cruelly work any old, maimed, infirm, sick or disabled animal; or cause or knowingly allow any of the same to be done. Section 2: No person shall fail to provide any animal in his charge or custody, as owner or otherwise, with proper food, drink and shelter. Section 3: No person shall give or permit, or aid, abet or encourage, by his presence at an exhibition or otherwise, the giving or permitting of any exhibition of bull fighting, dog fighting, cock fighting or fighting of any animals. Section 4: Any person violating any of the provisions of this ordinance shall, upon conviction thereof, be punished by fine not to exceed one hundred dollars ($100), or imprisonment not to exceed

six (6) months, or both, for each offense. Section 5: All ordinances, orders and regulations, and parts thereof, inconsistent herewith, are hereby repealed, and this ordinance shall take effect and be in force on and after the fifteenth day of February, 1902.[20]

Manila's animal cruelty ordinance (and countless others like it across the islands) brought Progressive era routinization and order to the daily governance of public life in the occupation capital.

Tellingly, revised versions of the Philippine municipal code included animal cruelty, in a section called "Offenses Against Public Morals," which dealt specifically with bodily and moral comportment. In 1908, for instance, this section also contained laws against obscene advertising, intoxication, vagrancy, the maintenance or possession of gambling devices, playing games of chance, the use of the US flag in advertising, and a whole litany of "indecent acts," including "indecent or lewd dress... any indecent exposure of his or her person, or be guilty of an unseemly, obscene, or filthy act, or any lewd, indecent, immoral, or insulting conduct, language, or behavior; or shall exhibit, circulate, distribute, sell, offer or expose for sale, or give or deliver to another... any lewd, indecent, immoral, or obscene book, picture, pamphlet, card, print, paper, writing, mold, cast, figure, or any other thing; or shall exhibit or perform... in any house, building, lot, or premises owned or occupied by him, or under his management, or control, any lewd, indecent, or immoral play or other representation." In addition to separate laws dealing specifically with prostitution, liquor, and gambling, other sections covered myriad "offences," including prohibitions against noisemakers in public, firecrackers, bells, kite flying, and the use of multicolored confetti (only solid colors could be thrown). Other ordinances treated barbering, stipulating that barbers be neat, "with short, well-trimmed nails," and wear a "clean white shirt." And still others prohibited eyelid scraping, ear cleaning, and other modes of grooming in public.[21] The municipal ordinances were remarkable for their intrusiveness and breadth in policing virtually all aspects of personal comportment and leisure. The codes were meant to impose order on a supposedly unruly and "uncivilized" population.

Such laws had more practical concerns for military officers as well. The popular blood sport of cockfighting was particularly problematic for American authorities trying to pacify insurgent Filipinos. As war raged against the US military in the provinces of Batangas and Laguna, Brigadier General J. F. Bell issued a cockfighting ban on Christmas Eve, 1901, to take effect immediately and last for the duration of the insurrection. In Bell's words, cockfighting was "a source of very considerable revenue to insurgents and a convenient means of enabling the insurgent element to secretly mingle, impose upon and intrigue with the portion of the people who may prefer to be peaceful. Upon receipt of these orders, all commanding officers will forbid further cockfighting until authority to renew the same is obtained from these headquarters."[22] Amid continued unrest, Manila's first municipal animal cruelty ordinance also banned cockfighting outright when it became law on February 6, 1902. Military officials primarily used the ban on cockfighting as a practical measure of social and political control. The cockfight, particularly on saint festival days, was a raucous, ritualistic, masculine spectacle, replete with gambling, drunkenness, and occasional fistfights. And as Brigadier General Bell observed, it was also a potent occasion for sharing information and spreading the insurrection.

American officials, SPCA activists, travel writers, and Protestant missionaries denounced cockfighting as indicative of long-standing social corruption. For many, it was a manifestation of Spanish Catholic decadence and native "bloodlust." The president of the ASPCA, Alfred Wagstaff, declared, "It was the fervent hope of the friends of humanity that whenever the flag of the United States was planted, the dumb animals might share in the benefits of an advancing civilization."[23] Bruce Lesher Kershner, a missionary with the Disciples of Christ who was in the Philippines from 1905 to 1917, observed that men took their game cocks to church and fed them Holy Water and the Communion wafer as a means of fortifying the birds for battle: "Not unfrequently he would slip the wafer from his tongue where it had been placed by the priest when at Communion, and putting it in his handkerchief, carry it to his chicken. He believed that the chicken which had eaten the body of Christ was invincible."[24] Americans disdained this cultural practice as an animistic, "savage" twist on transubstantiation—a teaching that many Protestants also rejected.

Yet American officials were primarily guided by practical, rather than moral, concerns. Despite rhetorical denunciations of the cockfight as a barometer of Filipino "cruelty," American officials readily reinstated it (complete with taxes and municipal regulations) across the Philippines once fighting had slowed. Just weeks after Manila's new anticruelty law took effect in 1902, the Philippine Commission amended the municipal code to permit cockfighting on legal holidays. Subsequent revisions regulated and taxed the cockfight even further, but it was never again banned outright.[25] American officials argued that regulation—rather than prohibition—was prudent and cost effective in a country where cockfighting was wildly popular. They reasoned that it was better to contain it and use it as a source of municipal revenue, than to waste valuable government resources trying to enforce the ban, likely a futile endeavor in any event. Officials pointed to American policy in Cuba as a cautionary tale.[26] In 1900, US Brigadier General Adna R. Chaffee had signed Order 165 on behalf of the military governor of Cuba, which banned cockfighting across the islands.[27]

However, enforcement proved costly and politically dangerous. When José Miguel Gomez, the chief opponent of the American ban on cockfighting, was elected president of Cuba in 1909, the Cuban Congress quickly repealed it.[28]

The American occupation government spearheaded a range of animal welfare legislation during its tenure in the Philippines. Laws provided for the incorporation of deputized SPCAs, prohibited horsetail docking, established provisions for the feeding and watering of animals in transit by railroad or ship, created bans on hunting, and specified standards of veterinary care for milch animals, instituted dog muzzling and leashing ordinances, set a ban on gambling on horse races except on Sundays and designated holidays, and new ordinances codified the right of the police to shoot on sight any stray dog.[29] Humane activists in the United States petitioned (without success) for a ban on vivisection, specifically targeting Philippine monkeys, which were being used to test experimental small pox vaccines. Mrs. Elizabeth Stuart Phelps Ward wrote to President Roosevelt, a personal acquaintance, protesting the practice as "bad precedent" for the treatment of animals in the new empire, especially since many major American research institutions had begun to regulate vivisection. Ward and other activists feared that US scientists were essentially moving vivisection offshore as a way to avoid criticism at home.[30] In general, US animal welfare legislation in the Philippines represented a significant cornerstone of the American occupation government's exceptionalist mission to conquer and civilize through a legislative program of benevolent assimilation and tutelage, predicated upon ordering public comportment and policing moral conduct. Yet animal advocates also argued that American scientists should remain legally accountable, and that the laws of the Philippines should regulate their behavior as well as that of the less "civilized" Filipinos.

Although most of the anticruelty legislation during the occupation focused on encounters with individual domestic animals like dogs and carabao, birds were primarily treated in the aggregate, appearing most frequently in the legal record in conservation legislation, and as the subject of scientific research. The ornithologist Richard McGregor reported in 1909 that American scientists had already collected approximately 8000 Philippine bird specimens (with roughly 150 others yet to be captured) during a series of expeditions across the islands for the occupation government's Bureau of Science.[31] (Paradoxically, in addition to its conservation activities, the Bureau of Science also did a brisk business in bird skins with museums around the world.)[32] Advocacy groups such as the American Ornithologists' Union urged the passage of laws against the export of birds and plumage.[33] The War Department's Bureau of Insular Affairs politely forwarded such requests to the Philippine Commission, which enacted a series of bird-related acts that established closed hunting seasons on specific birds, and also dictated how birds were to be killed: with a gun, spear, lance, or bow and arrow. Trapping, baiting, and the use of artificial light to entice a protected bird or mammal were strictly prohibited under the law.[34] The Philippine feather trade, however, remained unregulated until 1916, when Act 2590, An Act for the Protection of Game and Fish, declared it unlawful to kill, wound, or sell any protected bird, mammal, or bird's nest or eggs, to include "insect-eating birds, song birds, game birds and generally all wild birds," with the exception of those proving to be "injurious" to one's property. Moreover, Act 2590 declared it illegal "to sell or have in possession for sale any part of either [protected bird, fish, shellfish, or mammal]," unless one had received a permit from the Secretary of the Interior "for scientific purposes only."[35]

The legislation designated the Philippine Constabulary, local police, extension agents, and other officials, as deputy game wardens, "with full authority to enforce the provisions of this act and to arrest offenders against it."[36] Instituted shortly after the establishment of a civilian US government in the Philippines in 1901, the Philippine Constabulary was a powerful, insular, police force that reported directly to the Philippine Commission. In the words of the historian Paul Kramer, the Constabulary "would in many ways function as a colonial army in police uniform, waging war in areas otherwise designated as 'pacified.'"[37] As deputy game wardens, the Constabulary now played a direct role in policing animal activities on the islands. An Act for the Protection of Game and Fish was sweeping in its environmental scope. (Indeed, much of the law remains on the books in the early twenty-first century.) In deputizing the Constabulary, extension agents, local police, and others as game wardens, Act 2590 ensured that such unprecedented environmental surveillance—specifically with regard to tamping the Philippine feather trade—was now finally possible in a way that it had never been before.

Occupation legislation transformed public spaces, such as playgrounds, schools, parks, and cemeteries into bird sanctuaries. In November 1931, *Philippine Public Schools, A Monthly Magazine for Teachers* reported on a new administrative order from the Department of Agriculture and Natural Resources that echoed Act 2590 of 1916: "(1)…all botanical gardens, public parks, public-school sites, public playgrounds, government experiment stations, public-building sites, and cemeteries are hereby declared game refuges and bird sanctuaries, and it shall be unlawful for any person to hunt, take, wound, or kill, or in any manner disturb or drive, from the places mentioned above, any wild birds or wild animals, or take or destroy the nests or eggs of such birds in the said places. (2) Any person violating this order shall be punished for each offense by a fine of not less than ten pesos nor more than two hundred pesos."[38] Such conservation efforts paralleled similar efforts in the

United States and represented the success of legislation in imposing a particular kind of state-sanctioned order in the Philippines.

The Philippine Classroom as Bird Sanctuary

Designating public schools as game refuges and bird sanctuaries in conservation legislation complemented the pedagogical mission of US occupation authorities: to uplift and build potential Filipino citizens by teaching American educational content related to US history and political institutions, and American literature, domestic science, and agricultural methods as well as the English language. The following discussion focuses on the relationship between occupation pedagogies and ideological production, rather than on the myriad ways in which Filipino children undoubtedly received these messages of uplift. The occupation government passed compulsory attendance laws, funded the expansion of public schools, and sponsored humane education programs that appeared in a surprising range of curricula: art projects, hygiene lessons, grammar exercises, school gardens, annual achievement tests, agricultural training, etiquette manuals, festivals, and civics courses. During the Wilson administration, the process of Filipinization in the Bureau of Public Instruction (and other areas of the civil service) began in earnest, which reflected the educational and political interests of the elite, educated, urban Filipinos (*ilustrados*) who worked closely with American occupation authorities. Any consideration of humane education during the occupation must acknowledge the significant role that Filipino *ilustrados* played in the project of collaborative nation building.[39] Outside the classroom, contemporaneous US expeditions across the islands helped shape the ideological content of occupation pedagogies: wildlife expeditions promoted environmental stewardship and provided new flora and fauna for the classroom. In this way, the occupation government attempted to educate all those under its control in what it deemed to be the appropriate use of animal resources.

Pedagogical discourses of kindness must be viewed within the larger historical context. Concurrent military expeditions, for instance, provided a striking doppelganger of brutality alongside the more humane educational message children received in their primers. During the Philippine-American War, the US military and its Filipino allies used the "water cure" (or waterboarding in today's parlance), military impressment, corvee labor, burning out entire communities, and starvation rationing in reconcentrated villages to terrorize and subdue insurgent groups. (150,000 Filipinos vanished in the Batangas region alone.)[40] In 1901, Brigadier General Bell specified the terms of the shoot-on-sight orders that had been issued to station commanders in the field: "Any able bodied male found by patrols or scouting detachments outside of protected zones without passes will be arrested and confined, or shot if he runs away. No old or feeble man or any woman or child will be shot at pursuant to this rule."[41]

Some critics of American militarism, such as Jane Addams, denounced the war as a profound contradiction of US ideals of self-determination; whereas others, like W. E. B. DuBois, saw the war as a logical extension of racial violence in the United States. George Angell echoed the anti-imperialists, using *Our Dumb Animals* as a platform to condemn the war. Angell contended that a commitment to animal kindness would create a totalizing moral imperative for world peace and gentle stewardship. He paid special attention to the war in the Philippines because he felt that Filipino resistance to the US occupation bore a striking resemblance to that of American patriots during the Revolution. Articles such as "The Present War Craze," "The Philippines Are Expensive," and "Shooting Boys in the Philippines" sharply illustrated his interconnected beliefs in pacifism, benevolence, sovereignty, and animal mercy:

> It seems to be admitted now that a high army officer has ordered that all Philippine boys over ten years of age, in the Province of Samar, should be shot because they were liable to fight for their country and for what they believed to be its highest welfare, *just as American boys would have done under similar circumstances*. To be sure we paid Spain twenty millions of dollars for the privilege of shooting them, and so shifted from Spain's shoulders to ours a war *which she was mighty glad to get rid of* and which saying nothing of the loss and suffering of human and animal life, has cost us up to the present moment more than six hundred millions of dollars [emphasis in original].[42]

Angell cared about both human and animal subjects under US control and hoped the government would act accordingly. He viewed US militarism in the Philippines as a brutal form of empire building that fundamentally contradicted American exceptionalist ideals.

Angell, however, was no isolationist. He had no qualms about the establishment of an American moral empire in the Philippines. Targeting the Philippine classroom as the primary location for spreading the gospel of animal kindness, the MSPCA and its sister organization, the American Humane Education Society, mailed thousands of complimentary copies of *Our Dumb Animals* and such best-selling children's books as *Black Beauty*, and *Beautiful Joe* to Philippine public schools. The MSPCA also funded new Bands of Mercy, promoted missionary work, and publicly supported other animal welfare activities on the islands as peaceful expressions of uplift.

The aims of the teachers resonated with Angell's vision of an empire of kindness. On August 21, 1901, 509 future American public school teachers landed at the islands on the U.S.S. *Thomas.* The "Thomasites," as they were subsequently known, were eager to fill available positions in the occupied Philippines public schools, where compulsory attendance laws had dramatically expanded enrollment; municipal governments provided significant funding for local schools; and, after 1907, the Philippine Assembly made generous annual appropriations for public education. Public school attendance in 1901 totaled 150,000 elementary-age Filipinos. Just five years later, that figure had ballooned to 372,465.[43] Given the breathtaking linguistic diversity on the islands, coupled with the problematic political legacy of Spanish, which was spoken by elite *ilustrado* collaborators during the Spanish colonial regime, English was quickly adopted as the language of public instruction.[44] According to one Thomasite, the teachers' mission was "to carry on the education that shall fit the Filipinos for their new citizenship."[45] At the end of the first year of the occupation government, the secretary of public instruction reported to the Philippine Commission that a curriculum of animal kindness was imperative, particularly because native teachers were skipping school to attend the cockfights[46]: "Instruction of children in the wickedness of cruelty to animals I need only to mention to commend to your attention. May the day soon come when Filipino cattle will not be starved for three days previous to slaughter and when chickens will not be plucked before they are killed."[47] Despite such dismissive commentary, within the next two decades Filipino teachers would play a central part in propagating occupation humane education programs.

By contrast, humane education initiatives received uneven support in the United States. Animal welfare organizations viewed the exploding American student population at the turn of the twentieth century as a receptive—if unwieldy—audience for pedagogies of kindness. With the advent of new compulsory attendance laws during the Progressive Era, the numbers of students attending US schools, public and private, swelled. According to US Census figures for 1901, in 1900 there were 17,072,000 children in grades kindergarten through twelfth grade enrolled in school. By 1920, that number had climbed to 24,049,000.[48] Seeing an opportunity in this expanding population of school children, animal welfare advocates began vigorously lobbying state legislators to pass mandatory humane public education laws. Yet by 1920, only eighteen of the forty-eight states had passed such laws. Moreover, only three of those states—New York, Oklahoma, and Illinois—included punitive enforcement measures, cutting state funds for salaries and school budgets as punishment for ignoring the law.[49]

Animal welfare activities, however, were still a part of American classrooms, even in states without compulsory humane education laws. The American Humane Association instituted its annual Be Kind to Animals Week in 1915. Generally held in April, Be Kind to Animals Week included educational outreach activities, such as poster and essay contests, speeches, lantern slideshows, parades, radio addresses, pageants, and film. A Sunday church service known as Humane Sunday, or Mercy Sunday, inaugurated the annual event. English animal welfare supporters had instituted Humane Sunday in 1865; thereafter, this Sunday sermon dedicated to animal welfare and biblical stewardship became increasingly popular among US animal advocates at the turn of the twentieth century.[50] Taken together, compulsory humane education programs and "Be Kind to Animals Week" promulgated animal mercy as a cornerstone of American civilization. Animal advocates argued that these educational initiatives helped assimilate the millions of southern and eastern European children who immigrated to the United States from 1890 to 1920 and would do likewise for those children living in occupied territory.

Similarly, American educators in the Philippines stressed that a curriculum of animal kindness and environmental stewardship would prepare Filipinos for possible independence—if, and when, occupation officials deemed them ready. After 1901, humane education became an established part of the Philippine public school curriculum, and when the public schools gradually became Filipinized starting in the 1910s, it continued to figure prominently in lesson plans. Despite the US-mandated secularism in public education in the Philippines, Christian Filipino teachers played an important role in educating a far-flung pantheon of non-Christian Philippine islanders, such as Muslim Moros and animistic Igorots. In the words of Paul Kramer, "The Americans had bequeathed to Filipinos the tools for civilizing their own internal others, tools Filipinos now had the capacity to employ."[51] Humane education thus represented a key tool of uplift—an essential part of American empire building and Filipino nation building in a diverse society where *ilustrados* were often agents of internal colonialism.

Bird Day, as a prominent feature of the yearly school holiday calendar, encouraged children to think humanely and ecologically.[52] First instituted on May 4, 1894, by Charles Almanzo Babcock, the superintendent of schools in Oil City, Pennsylvania, Bird Day blossomed into an international phenomenon and was often celebrated in conjunction with Arbor Day, a holiday for tree planting that began on the treeless, windswept plains of Nebraska on April 10, 1872, when more than one million trees were planted. By the 1920s, Bird and

Arbor Day was one of many holidays intended to promote America's higher humanitarian purpose in its empire.

The ubiquity of this dual holiday, in particular, was a testament to the popularity of two contemporaneous educational currents in the United States: the nature-study movement, which emphasized the study of plants and wild animals in an urban, industrial society as a way to combat alienation from the natural world, and John Dewey's pragmatic educational philosophies. Both cast a long shadow in the Philippines, where American and Filipino educators stressed the pedagogical and therapeutic power of hands-on, active learning. (Indeed, Dewey and other pragmatic philosophers and progressive educators dominated the recommended reading lists of American and Filipino teachers.)[53] Consequently, Bird and Arbor Day was filled with tree planting, gardening, and birdhouse construction, activities that required direct soil-grubbing physical engagement with the learning process.[54]

Art courses promoted animal kindness and gentle comportment through a dual aesthetic emphasis on the harmony and beauty of the natural world. Art manuals highlighted the importance of radiating lines, rhythm, symmetry, and color harmony in creating pleasant, tranquil representations of animals and the larger rural world: "Repetition or rhythm is a principle or rule in design. It is the music of which Nature repeats her lines and colors and thereby produces harmony and beauty.... Radiation is also everywhere in nature. It is really a form of repetition or rhythm. Example:—fingers on the hand; wings of birds...By radiation is meant graceful growth of the various parts of a design from a common spot or axis...Drill on the color harmonies. These should be memorized as thoroughly as fundamentals in arithmetic."[55] Educators used animals, arts, music, and activity to reinforce "civilizing" lessons.

Birds and animal-powered agricultural labor were common subjects for visualizing a harmonious outdoor world in a pacified agrarian society, and teaching about them was meant to insure a kind and educated citizenry. Manuals directed teachers to assign the construction of bird posters out of paper silhouettes, crayons, or paint, along with suggested captions that reinforced ideologies of animal kindness: "Protect Bird Life"; "Save the Birds"; "Birds Help the Farmers"; "Birds Beautify"; "Feed the Birds"; and "Birds Save the Crops."[56] Education manuals stressed the importance of aesthetic appreciation in fostering a commitment to animal kindness: "An interest in and a love of birds may be created by emphasizing their beauty of song or color, the way they help us by killing the worms that destroy plants, etc....It is for the teachers to stimulate the children to take such an interest in nature, and in birds in particular, that it will be impossible for them ever to kill the small, harmless birds which are far too scarce now."[57] A dutiful child who refused to kill an innocent bird could grow up to be a compliant citizen.

Bird literature in the classroom augmented aesthetic pedagogies of animal kindness and conservation. Students studied Philippine bird species and habitat requirements, in addition to bird observation in garden classes, caring for injured birds and cataloging abandoned nests and eggs. Official publications urged teachers to stress how insectivorous and rodent-eating birds were the "farmer's friend," in addition to directing boys, in particular, to monitor each other's behavior around birds:

> In rural communities, the garden class may form a "police" organization for the protection of birds, having each member of the class act as a policemen to watch and report other boys who wantonly shoot birds. Such mischievous boys should be given a heart-to-heart talk by the garden teacher or by the principal of the school or in some other way to feel the ill effects of their acts.... For lack of something else to busy themselves with, boys usually spend their vacation on farms killing birds with sling shots, blow guns, shot guns, and every other conceivable means of taking life. For this reason, something about the protection of birds should also be included in the closing programs of schools.[58]

It is readily apparent that such lessons were motivated by more than concern over animal well-being. Idle boys who knew how to use guns threatened more than birds, they threatened the well-being of a new national project.

Grammars of animal kindness formed another key component of humane education in Philippine public schools. The act of learning the American English language was saturated with imperatives for animal mercy, from the importance of feeding one's dog to the example of gentle children who hosted a funeral for a deceased pet bird named Yellow Bill. Comma-placement exercises, capitalization and punctuation drills, along with practice sheets transforming the present tense into past tense forms, helped transmit and structure ideas about bird protection and civilized comportment. A typical exercise for seventh graders required students to transform appropriate verbs into the past tense in the following exercise, "The Boy Who Robbed Birds' Nests":

1. I know a boy who is fond of catching birds. He sometimes even
2. takes the eggs out of the nest. He does not think about how sorry the
3. mother bird will be when she finds that her pretty blue eggs are
4. gone.

5. This boy goes to the forest to find birds. On his way he meets
6. two of his friends. He tells them what he intends to do and asks
7. them to go along. They tell him that God punishes naughty boys
8. who rob birds' nests. He says that he doesn't care and that he intends
9. to go anyway. He goes farther and farther into the deep
10. woods, so far that he loses himself and can't find his way out. He
11. sits down and cries and wishes he had not come.[59]

Grammars of kindness unfailingly described the moral consequences of bad behavior, as in the case of the cruel boy who got lost in the forest, or a man who was riddled with a lifetime of guilt for wantonly killing a bird.[60] Furthermore, seatwork exercises related to animals were constantly in conversation with grammars of American patriotism, Philippine hygiene, industry, and the process of readying oneself for possible sovereignty. In close proximity to cheery sheet music for a "Song of Cleanliness," "I Have Two Hands," or "Philippines, My Philippines," one could find eclectic—yet complementary—seatwork exercises that explained the heroic deeds of American Revolutionary patriots and exhortations to perform one's patriotic part by joining the army. In juxtaposition with exercises telling "small" and "slight" Filipino boys to enjoy vigorous exercise and the wholesome outdoors, one comprehension exercise depicted Thomas Jefferson as a ruggedly masculine patriot: "This American youth was tall, raw-boned and hardened because he lived almost constantly in the open air."[61] Another exercise took the form of a Home Improvement Card containing a student checklist for proper, sanitary home life, and used the presence of animals in Philippine domestic life as a barometer of personal hygiene. The Home Improvement Card quizzed students about the cleanliness of their homes, the existence of a private bathroom, any animals wandering nearby, and the presence of a fence to keep said animals (especially destructive foraging pigs) and strangers away from the sanctified domestic world.[62] Student posters declaring that "Birds Beautify Our Town," and school efforts to keep itinerant domestic animals off the premises complemented municipal animal welfare ordinances to control local environments.

The relationship between animal mercy and readiness for self-government represented an important preoccupation in education materials, just as it had in legislative endeavors earlier in the occupation period. Instructions for art posters, for one, consistently included kindness to animals as a major topic for any "Good Citizenship" project. (Other subjects included exercise, fresh air, pure food, patriotism—loyalty, obedience, and politeness—care of flowers, birds, trees, and property.)[63] Exercises in rhythm and inflection for Philippine educational achievement tests spanned the pantheon of kindness—animal mercy, good manners, beauty, self-control, neatness—and love of country (the Pledge of Allegiance to the US flag was omnipresent). Students were tested on their cadence and inflection as they repeated the following: "1. Do an act of kindness every day. Manners make the man," or "3. The Philippines is a free country, although it is not yet an independent nation. Its people are a free people....35. "Hundreds of birds that go singing by, hundreds of birds in the sunny weather."[64] Filipino students got the message they would never be truly free until they learned how to act appropriately according to a set of moral and conservation laws set up by an occupation government and modeled by *ilustrado* teachers. Such evidence makes us question the very meaning of freedom in this sense. Occupation authorities defined, freedom as the ability to become free yeoman farmers in accord with a desired division of labor on the Islands, rather than envisioning Filipinos as framers of their own government. The imposition of such ideas was not necessarily welcome by Filipino officials—even as they worked together with US officials in a shared project of Philippine nation building.

Throughout such contradictory declarations of Filipino freedom and eventual independence, American and *ilustrado* educators envisioned an animal-powered agricultural future for the majority of their students. These teachers and administrators saw the proper care of carabao, pigs, poultry, and pets, in conjunction with a personal regimen of thrift, obedience, industry, personal cleanliness, sobriety, patriotism, and environmental stewardship, as preconditions for nationhood. Nonetheless, as a legislative foundation for independence took shape in the 1930s, Filipino lawmakers rejected important aspects of the American-sponsored animal welfare movement on the islands. After Filipino legislators drafted a new Constitution in 1935 that would lead to eventual independence with official American approval, they slowly dismantled various forms of US power, including the SPCA Philippines. Seen as an arm of an occupying force, during the sessions of the First Commonwealth National Assembly in 1936, legislators voted to abolish the considerable policing authority of the SPCA Philippines, as well as its power to collect fines—thus rendering the organization subordinate.[65]

Yet educational programs of animal kindness remained an enduring aspect of the American occupation in the Philippines. Wild birds, as this essay has suggested, were an important part of an American project of benevolent assimilation. Occupying a liminal cultural and ecological space between pet and wildlife, birds populated the pages of educational materials as paragons of natural harmony, and anthropomorphized nuclear families comprising attentive mothers and cozy children in the nest. Textbooks urged pupils—as future agriculturalists, conservationists, and citizens—to treat birds as the good friend of the farmer.[66] Nonetheless, sustained pedagogies of animal kindness served yet another civilizing purpose for American officials and educators in the Philippines: to rewrite and therefore revise the violent legacies of conquest with a symbiotic program of uplift and environmental stewardship, thereby ostensibly civilizing the American occupation itself in the eyes of the Filipino people and the rest of the world.

NOTES

1. Correspondence from Taft to E. B. McCagg, April 16, 1900, quoted in Peter W. Stanley, *A Nation in the Making: The Philippines and the United States, 1899–1921* (Cambridge, MA: Harvard University Press, 1974), 64.

2. For helpful treatments on transnationalism, see Nhi Lieu, *The American Dream in Vietnamese* (Minneapolis: University of Minnesota Press, 2011); Benedict Anderson, *Imagined Communities: Reflections on the Origins and Spread of Nationalism*, 2nd ed. (New York: Verso, 2006); Aihwa Ong, *Flexible Citizenship: The Cultural Logics of Transnationality* (Durham, NC: Duke University Press, 1999); Robin Cohen, *Global Diasporas: An Introduction* (New York: Routledge, 1997); Arjun Appadurai, *Modernity at Large: Cultural Dimensions of Globalization* (Minneapolis: University of Minnesota Press, 1996).

3. In many respects, the historical differences in these movements mirror those of the fields of animal studies and environmental history more broadly: emerging out of the fields of literature, philosophy, anthropology, cultural studies, and the law, animal studies is deeply vested in ontological, epistemological, and ethical questions of animal representation, agency, and power. Drawing from interdisciplinary considerations of history, the biological sciences, geography, and culture, environmental historians typically explore the symbiotic relationship between the animal and its ecology. See Andrew C. Isenberg, "The Moral Economy of Wildlife," in *Representing Animals*, ed. Nigel Rothfels (Bloomington: University of Indiana Press, 2002): 48–64; Jan E. Dizard, *Going Wild: Hunting, Animal Rights, and the Contested Meaning of Nature*, 2nd ed. (Amherst: University of Massachusetts Press, 1999); Lisa Mighetto, *Wild Animals and American Environmental Ethics* (Tucson: University of Arizona Press, 1991).

4. Peter Sells quoted in Janet M. Davis, *The Circus Age: Culture and Society under the American Big Top* (Chapel Hill: University of North Carolina Press, 2002), 192.

5. For classic treatments, see Robert Rydell, *All the World's a Fair: Visions of Empire at American International Expositions, 1876–1916*, (Chicago: University of Chicago Press, 1984); and Gail Bederman, *Manliness and Civilization: A Cultural History of Gender and Race in the United States, 1880–1917* (Chicago: University of Chicago Press, 1995).

6. James Turner, *Reckoning with the Beast: Animals, Pain, and Humanity in the Victorian Mind* (Baltimore: Johns Hopkins University Press, 1980), 52.

7. G. O. Shields, letter to the editor, "The Slaughter of Birds," *New York Times*, April 27, 1900, 8.

8. "Points Way to End Slaughter of Birds," *New York Times*, January 2, 1911, 20.

9. Jennifer Price, *Flight Maps: Adventures with Nature in Modern America* (New York: Basic Books, 1998), 64.

10. A.A.C., "A Plea for the Birds," letter to the editor, *New York Times*, November 16, 1897, 6.

11. Price, *Flight Maps*, 1.

12. Katherine Grier, *Pets in America: A History* (Chapel Hill: University of North Carolina Press, 2006), 46–8.

13. Ernest Bell, *The Other Side of the Bars: The Case of the Caged Bird* (London: Humanitarian League, 1911), 16; J. Frank Dobie Collection, Harry Ransom Center for the Humanities, University of Texas at Austin (hereafter, HRC).

14. Harriet Ritvo, *The Animal Estate: The English and Other Creatures of the Victorian Age* (Cambridge, MA: Harvard University Press, 1987), 284–5.

15. Sydney H. Coleman, *Humane Society Leaders in America* (Albany, NY: American Humane Association, 1924), 99–100.

16. James Turner, *Reckoning with the Beast*, 50.

17. Coleman, *Humane Society Leaders in America*, 105.

18. Frances E. Willard, "President's Annual Address," Temperance and Prohibition papers, Series 3 (hereafter, WCTU Series), Roll 3: Annual Meeting Minutes, 1889–1892, "Minutes of the National Convention: 1889," Chicago, November 8–13, 1889, 147.

19. "The Inflation Calculator," www.westegg.com/inflation/infl.cgi, accessed December 18, 2011.

20. "Ordinance for the Prevention of Cruelty to Animals," Ordinances City of Manila (Manila: Bureau of Printing, 1902), 115, 112.150, Philippine Materials Collection, V 376, Entry 95, Record Group 350 (hereafter, RG 350), Stack Area 150, 58:20:2, National Archives and Records Administration, College Park, Maryland (hereafter, NARA II).

21. Ibid., 117, 123; and "Offenses against Public Morals," in George A. Malcolm, *The Manila Charter as Amended and the Revised Ordinances of the City of Manila* (Manila: Bureau of Printing, 1908), 229–39; 112.150, Philippine Materials Collection, V 377, Entry 95, RG 350, Stack Area 150, 58:20:2; Ordinance No. 267, *Ordinances City of Manila* (1916), Nos. 265–740, 1–2; 112.150, Philippine Materials Collection, V 375, Entry 95, RG 350, Stack Area 150, 58:20:2, all at NARA II.

22. Brigadier General J. Franklin Bell, "Telegraphic Circular No. 19," *Telegraphic Circulars and General Orders* (Bantangas: Headquarters, Third Separate Brigade, 1902), 17–8.

23. Correspondence from Alfred Wagstaff to Governor Magoon, February 18, 1907, Cockfighting Prohibition (Cuba), box 213, file 1660, General Classified Files, entry 5A (1898–1913), RG 350, Stack Area 150, 56:8:6, NARA II.

24. Bruce L. Kershner, *The Head Hunter and Other Stories of the Philippines* (Cincinnati, OH: Powell and White, 1921), 68–9.

25. No. 364, An Act Amending Section 40 of Act No. 82 Entitled "A General Act for the Organization of Municipal Governments in the Philippines Islands,"

February 20, 1902; and No. 635, Amendment to No. 82, and No. 364, February 11, 1903, Cockfighting (Philippines), box 454, file 6633, General Classified Files, Entry 5A (1898–1913), RG 350, Stack Area 150, 56:13:5, NARA II.

26. Correspondence from Brigadier General Clarence Edwards, chief of Bureau of Insular Affairs, to Ansel E. Johnson, First Congregational Church, Monrovia, Calif., November 29, 1910, Cockfighting (Philippines), box 454, file 6633, General Classified Files, Entry 5A (1898–1913), RG 350, Stack Area 150, 56:13:5, NARA II.

27. General Orders No. 165, Havana, Cuba, April 19, 1900, General Classified Files, Entry 5A (1898–1913), box 213, file 1660 (Cockfighting Prohibition, Cuba), RG 350, Stack Area 150, 56:8:6, NARA II.

28. Inclosure to Dispatch No. 992: An Act Legalizing Cock-Fighting," translated from the Official Gazette, July 3, 1909, Cockfighting Prohibition (Cuba), box 213, file 1660, General Classified Files, Entry 5A (1898–1913), RG 350, Stack Area 150, 56:8:6, NARA II.

29. See Law No. 1285, Act of Incorporation for Society for the Prevention of Cruelty to Animals in the Philippines, January 19, 1905; Second Philippine Legislature, Law No. 2101, "An Act to Prohibit Certain Cruel Practices on Horses, and for Other Purposes," January 24, 1912; Section 40 (i), Philippine Commission, *Municipal Code and the Provincial Government Act, as Amended by the Acts of the Philippine Commission Down to and Including May 31, 1905* (Manila: Bureau of Public Printing, 1905) 112:135, vol.352, Entry 95, RG 350, Stack Area 150, 57:20:1, Bureau of Insular Affairs, Library Materials, Philippines—Miscellaneous; No. 55, "An Act to Provide for Wholesome Food Supplies and to Prevent Cruelty to Animals in Transportation," *Public Laws Passed by the Philippine Commission, September 1, 1900-August 31, 1902*, v. 266 (Manila: Bureau of Printing, 1902), 73–4; Section 969, "Examination; Condemnation of Milch Animals, 520, in George A. Malcolm, ed., *The Charter of the City of Manila and the Revised Ordinances City of Manila* (Manila: Bureau of Printing, 1927), 112.150, Philippine Materials Collection, V 379, Entry 95, RG 350, Stack Area 150, 58:20:2; Section 781, "Unlawful Acts in Parks," 330, in Malcolm, ed., *The Charter of the City of Manila and the Revised Ordinances of the City of Manila* (Manila: Bureau of Printing, 1917), 112.150, Philippine Materials Collection, V 378, Entry 95, RG 350, Stack Area 150, 58:20:2; No. 1537, "Horse Races Act, amended" 142–143, in Malcolm, ed., *The Municipal Code and the Provincial Government Act Compiled and Annotated Being Acts Nos. 82 and 83, as Amended by Acts of the Philippine Commission and Legislature Down to February 3, 1911* (Manila: Bureau of Printing, 1911) 112:135, vol. 354, Entry 95, RG 350, Stack Area 150, 58:20:19:6, NARA II.

30. Correspondence from Elizabeth Stuart Phelps Ward to President Theodore Roosevelt, February 5, 1904, Animals, Cruelty to (Philippines), General Classified Files 5A (1898–1913), box 622, file 10795, RG 350, Stack Area 150, 56:17:1, NARA II.

31. Richard C. McGregor, *A Manual of Philippine Birds, Part One: Galliformes to Eurylaemiformes* (Manila: Bureau of Printing, 1909), 2.

32. "Price and Exchange List of Philippine Bird Skins in the Collection of the Bureau of Science, Manila, Philippines, Effective 1911," 1–2, General Classified Files, Entry 5A (1898–1913), Ornithology (Philippines), box 429, file 5817, NARA II.

33. Correspondence from chief of Bureau of Insular Affairs to American Ornithologists' Union, Committee on Foreign Relations, February 9, 1903; Correspondence from William Dutcher, chair of the Commission on Foreign Relations of the American Ornithologists' Union to Clarence R. Edwards, chief of the Bureau of Insular Affairs, February 11, 1903; Correspondence from Acting Executive Secretary to Clarence R. Edwards, March 26, 1903, Ornithology (Philippines), box 429, file 5817, General Classified Files, Entry 5A (1898–1913), RG 350, Stack Area 150, 56:13:1, NARA II.

34. Section 3497–3498, *A Compilation of the Acts of the Philippine Commission* (Manila: Bureau of Printing, 1908), 1050, Philippine Materials Collection, Entry 95, V. 263–80, 111.54 Executive Orders and Proclamations, and Public Laws, RG 350, Stack Area 150, 58:19:3–5, NARA II.

35. Act No. 2590, "An Act for the Protection of Game and Fish," Enacted February 4, 1916, Philippine Laws, Statutes and Codes, Chan Robles Virtual Law Library, http://www.chanrobles.com/acts/actsno2590.html, accessed April 9, 2009.

36. Ibid.

37. Paul A. Kramer, *The Blood of Government: Race, Empire, the United States, and the Philippines* (Chapel Hill: University of North Carolina Press, 2007), 155.

38. "New Rules and Regulations," *Philippine Public Schools, A Monthly Magazine for Teachers*, v. IV, n. 8 (November 1931): 406, 121.195, Philippine Materials Collection V677, RG 350, Stack Area 150, 58:22:5–6, NARA II.

39. Kramer, *The Blood of Government*, 379–81; Dean C. Worcester, *The Philippines Past and Present* (New York: MacMillan, 1930), 402–3.

40. Kramer, *Blood of Government*, 157.

41. Bell, "Telegraphic Circular No. 14," December 21, 1901, 14.

42. "Shooting Boys in the Philippines," *Our Dumb Animals* (hereafter, ODA), vol. 35, no. 1 (June 1902): 2; "The Present War Craze," ODA, vol. 30, no. 11 (April 1898): 134; "The Philippines are Expensive," ODA, vol. 33, no. 4 (September 1900): 38.

43. Encarnacion Alzona, *A History of Education in the Philippines, 1565–1930* (Manila: University of the Philippines Press, 1932), 208.

44. Ibid., 210–2.

45. Adeline Knapp, quoted in Kramer, *Blood of Government*, 168–9.

46. "The Filipino Teachers," in *Report of the Secretary of Public Instruction of the Philippine Islands for the Year Ending October 15, 1902* (Manila: Bureau of Printing, 1902), 873, Reports Secretary of Public Instruction and Director of Education, etc., 1900–1910, Philippine Materials Collection, Entry 95, V680, RG 350, Stack Area 150, 58: 22:7, NARA II.

47. John A. Staunton, "The American Teacher in the Community," presented at American Teachers' Institute at Cebu, June 16, 1902, in ibid., 947.

48. Census figures provide a detailed portrait of the nation's educational demographics: for 1900, the total number of children in grades K–8 and 9–12, respectively, was 16,422,000 and 650,000; the same year, the total number of children exclusively in public school was 15,703,000, with 15,161,000 in grades K–8, and 542,000 in grades 9–12. In 1900, the percentage of 14- to 17-year-olds enrolled in

school compared to the total population in that age group was 10.6 percent. In 1920, the total number of children in grades K–8 was 21,292,000, and 2,757,000 for grades 9–12. The total public school population in 1920 was 22,409,000, with 19,872,000 in grades K–8, and 2,537,0000 in grades 9–12. In 1920, 35 percent of all 14- to 17-year-olds in the United States were enrolled in school. "Mini-Historical Statistics," *U.S. Census Bureau, Statistical Abstract of the United States: 2003*, 33–4, http://www. census.gov/statab/hist/HS-20.pdf, accessed September 5, 2009.

49. Bernard Oreste Unti, "The Quality of Mercy: Organized Animal Protection in the United States, 1866–1930," PhD diss., American University, 2002, 582.

50. Ibid., 590–4; Dean Wilson Kuykendall, "The History of Humane Education," MA thesis, University of Texas, August 1935, 151.

51. Kramer, *Blood of Government*, 381.

52. Other school holidays included Mother's Day, the Fourth of July, and Rizal Day, which honored the slain Filipino nationalist and author, José Rizal, who resisted Spanish rule.

53. See, for example, "For the Teacher's Home Library," *Philippine Public Schools: A Monthly Magazine for Teachers*, v. 1, n. 3 (March 1928): 146–7, *Philippine Public Schools* (January–December, 1928): 121.195, Philippine Materials Collection V675, RG 350, Stack Area 150, 58:22:5–6, NARA II.

54. One can see the influence of progressive pedagogy in the monthly column, "Helpful Lesson Plans," in the educational journal *Philippine Public Schools*, where teachers shared tips for effective teaching. In March 1930, Abner Racelis shared his successful hands-on activities on Arbor Day at Leuban Elementary School in Tayabas, which included tree planting, writing essays about favorite trees, and more. *Philippine Public Schools, A Monthly Magazine for Teachers* 3, no. 3 (March 1930): 127; *Philippine Public Schools* (January-December, 1930–1931); 121.195, Philippine Materials Collection V677, RG 350, Stack Area 150, 58:22:5–6, NARA II.

55. "Nature," *Course of Study in Drawing for Normal Schools* (Bureau of Education) (Manila: Bureau of Printing, 1929), 16, 25, Philippines Materials Collection, Entry 95, V654, 121.143, Courses of Study, RG 350, Stack Area 150, 58:22:5, NARA II.

56. Ibid., 25.

57. *Drawing Course of Study for Primary Grades* (Manila: Bureau of Printing, 1926), 23, Philippines Materials Collection, Entry 95, V654, 121.143, Courses of Study, RG 350, Stack Area 150, 58:22:5, NARA II.

58. *Philippine Public Schools*, v. 4, n. 4 (July 1931): 197–8, *Philippine Public Schools* (January-December, 1930–1931); 121.195, Philippine Materials Collection V677, RG 350, Stack Area 150, 58:22:5–6, NARA II.

59. "Exercise 29: Change Present-Tense Forms to Past-Tense Forms," *A Workbook in Language for Grade VII*, v. I (Manila: Bureau of Printing, 1935), 55, Philippine Materials Collection, Entry 95, V654–5, 121.143, Courses of Study and Textbooks, English, RG 350, Stack Area 150, 58:22:5, NARA II.

60. "Lesson for Fourth-Year English," *Philippine Public Schools*, v. 2, n. 6 (September 1929): 265, *Philippine Public Schools* (January-December, 1929); 121.195, Philippine Materials Collection V676, RG 350, Stack Area 150, 58:22:5–6, NARA II.

61. "Thomas Jefferson," *A Work Book in Language*, v. 2 (Manila: Bureau of Printing, 1935), 46, Courses of Study and Text Books, 121.143, and 121.16, Philippine Materials Collection, Entry 95, V654–5, 657–8, RG 350, Stack Area 150, 58:22:5, NARA II.

62. "Pupil's Home Improvement Card," *Philippine Public Schools*, v. 4, n. 7 (October 1931): 202–3, *Philippine Public Schools*, (January-December, 1930–1931); 121.195, Philippine Materials Collection V677, RG 350, Stack Area 150, 58:22:5–6, NARA II.

63. Course of Study in Drawing for Normal Schools—Bureau of Education, (Manila: Bureau of Printing, 1929), 23, Philippine Materials Collection, Entry 95, V654, 121.143 Courses of Study, RG 350, Stack Area 150, 58:22:5, NARA II.

64. *Manual of Directions for the Philippine Educational Achievement Tests* (Manila: Bureau of Printing, 1926), 23, 29, Philippine Materials Collection, Entry 95, V654, 121.143 Courses of Study, RG 350, Stack Area 150, 58:22:5, NARA II.

65. "Commonwealth Act No. 148," Public Laws of the Commonwealth enacted by the National Assembly, December 21, 1935 to March 9, 1937, vol. I, Acts Nos., 1–232 (Manila: Bureau of Printing, 1939), 706, Record Group 350, Philippine Materials Collection, Entry 95, V 308, 112.111 Public Laws; RG 350, Stack Area 150, 58:19:5, NARA II.

66. Antonio Nera, *Nature Study Readers, Book Four* (Rizal, P.I.: Oriental Commercial Co., 1933), Philippine Materials Collection, Entry 95, V658, 121.16, Catalogue—Course of Study; 121.144 Textbooks, RG 350, Stack Area 150, 58:22:5, NARA II.

10

Salmon Migrations, Nez Perce Nationalism, and the Global Economy

Benedict J. Colombi

In *The Art of Not Being Governed*, James C. Scott examines the world of self-governing peoples whose culture and social organization was a "history of deliberate and reactive statelessness."[1] His account is largely focused on the hill peoples of Southeast Asia in a geographic area he calls *Zomia*, a swath of mountainous, high-altitude lands that extend from the Central Highlands of Vietnam to northeastern India. His argument is both controversial and suggestive of people who have not been fully conscripted or incorporated by the nation-state, and provides what he calls an anti "civilizational discourse" of peoples who he claims are "best understood as runaway, fugitive, maroon communities who have, over the course of two millennia, been fleeing the oppressions of state-making projects in the valleys—slavery, conscription, taxes, corvée labor, epidemics, and warfare."[2]

Although the Nez Perce in the Pacific Northwest are a world away from the territories of the hill peoples and Southeast Asia, Scott's work helps us contextualize the story of their interactions with nation-states and global environments. The Nez Perce story forces us to think about what a nation-state is, who belongs to it, and how nature and political culture are linked in dynamic yet inseparable ways. Cross-regional salmon migrations, for instance, help constitute Nez Perce sovereignty and nationalism, which in turn represent influential forces determining how the Nez Perce have dealt with outsiders, including corporations, state governments, and even other nations in an ever-changing political climate. Salmon migrations also help highlight why the Nez

Perce belong in a book about globalization and social and environmental change.

For the Nez Perce, economic, political, and environmental change in the twentieth century has been particularly troubling. The relationship between global, transnational actors and state and nonstate local actors in the form of Nez Perce nationalism is evident in the way state power has been extended with severe ecological impacts on Nez Perce life, particularly through twentieth-century dam building and its impact on migrating salmon. Moreover, the global effects of trade link the exertion of state power to state-sponsored dam building before and after World War II. The increasing lack of state-sponsored controls after World War II and in the twenty-first century expanded globalizing forces through neoliberal economic policies and trade with emerging global economies, such as China. Even the United States since World War II has shifted from sponsoring socialist-oriented dam-building projects that were generally viewed as public works projects for a public good to state-sponsored projects of dam building for the purpose of expanding free-market capitalism and trade, particularly with regard to connecting resources on Nez Perce lands to consumers in East Asia in the decades following the Second World War.

Over the years, a collision between an ecologically based community (that is, not "national") with the demands of the nation-state for rationalized production and economic development has occurred. While the Nez Perce know they can work through the nation-state to (partially) realize their demands for restoration or compensation, they also realize the difficulty of doing so given the pressures of the global economy. In short, the Nez Perce's salmon restoration efforts have a social, legal, and economic purpose and are their tools of cultural preservation, environmental preservation, and national definition. Escalating demand for salmon on both sides of Pacific has threatened the species' very existence and undermined the Nez Perce's historic claims to salmon.[3] The Nez Perce feel that salmon help define who they are, but their sense of identity can be attacked or reinforced on a number of different levels: local, national, and international.

This chapter first considers how the Nez Perce people developed a stateless, salmon-centric way of life that profoundly shaped the region and the environment. They did so with the building of extensive social relations and the modification of their homeland, and also through the formulation of expansive trade and commerce networks. Tracking Nez Perce historical change presents a new way of understanding cultural and political space and challenges the civilizational discourse of the Western concepts of progress, development, and modernization. Rather, the Nez Perce built their indigenous society and culture around features of their own tribal cosmology and by the engineering of cultural landscapes since the end of the last Ice Age, and perhaps even before that time.

The question facing the Nez Perce today is more immediate: How do they maintain themselves as a sovereign tribal nation with a salmon-centric culture in light of the dramatic remapping of their homeland? Central to understanding the largest problems facing contemporary Nez Perce is the way the nation-state and global capitalism, working together, have profited enormously from the opening of the Pacific Northwest and by exerting global economic forces on Nez Perce people and resources. The Nez Perce's nature-salmon economy was critical to their ability to exercise a genuine sovereignty consistent with their identity across millennia. This chapter shows that the encroachment of the nation-state and global capital altered, but did not destroy, the connection between migrating salmon and Nez Perce life and culture.

This approach transcends national political boundaries and looks at the historical and ecological connections between humans and the natural world on the global level. It highlights and examines the strategies of the United States government's efforts to settle Nez Perce people and lands and shows how the nation-state achieved their goals, initially through violence, treaty negotiations, and allotment, and later through dam building and the development of a global agricultural empire. Consequently, this chapter draws attention to the political and environmental impacts of development by national and global actors operating on Nez Perce lands, and how this has shaped and continues to shape the natural world and nonhuman migrations of salmon.

The Organization of Nez Perce Society

The Nez Perce encountered the nation-state and western expansion as a consequence of the Lewis and Clark expedition in 1805. The two parties met on the upper reaches of the Clearwater River in the Bitterroot Mountains of what is today north-central Idaho. Lewis and Clark represented the colonization of the American West through the demarcation of boundaries of state power and trade. They connected the developing nation-state to people and lands via a network of rivers and a swath of diverse territories and cultures that were systematically different from early US settler society.

A snapshot of the Nez Perce homeland and adjacent territories in 1805 would have shown dozens of interactions of autonomous tribes with long histories and great diversity. Anthropologists have shown that the tribes of the interior Northwest were egalitarian, stateless societies that maintained themselves and their tribal economies by deliberately shaping their environments, including ensuring abundant returns of migrating salmon.

Contemporary Nez Perce culture is therefore rooted in a small-scale, egalitarian, and democratic society that had successfully lived in the Columbia and Snake River drainages for millennia. The Nez Perce organized their society primarily to support and reproduce households while safeguarding the environment. Population densities remained relatively low, and the Nez Perce organized themselves into linguistically affiliated bands, interspersed throughout the region by correlating watersheds, or sub-basins. Prior to contact and colonization, Nez Perce subsistence required deliberate, seasonal migrations and demanded a broad utilization of rich, subsistence resources. In turn, a cultural complex of water, salmon, game, and roots became the ideological and material foundations on which the Nez Perce built their society and economy.[4]

Salmon have not always been a rich and predictable food source. The drainages of the Columbia and Snake Rivers experienced great flooding and climatic change throughout much of history, impacting the predictability of returning salmon. About 10,000 years ago, summers in the region became warm and dry, and winters were unusually cold. This pattern persisted for nearly 4000 years and by about 6000 years ago the Northwest climate gradually cooled and began to offer an optimal environment for people to shape and ensure abundant salmon runs.

There are several theories about how salmon became a primary food source. Many argue that to utilize salmon, indigenous societies must have developed economies that invested in efficient fishing technologies and highly developed social organizations.[5] This system was designed around the harvesting, procurement, and trading of several salmon species. The Nez Perce, for example, developed a complex fishing technology harvesting species of chinook, coho, chum, and sockeye salmon; cutthroat, lake, dolly varden, and steelhead trout; and different varieties of whitefish, sturgeon, suckers, lamprey eels, and pikeminnows. The archaeological record and early ethnographic account supports pre-contact fish consumption for Nez Perce adults at roughly 500 pounds per year.[6]

Ultimately, the Nez Perce use of fish resources led to subsistence intensification, the building of extensive kinship networks, and the formulation of an expansive trade and commerce network of Nez Perce use and intertribal influence.[7] With the addition of the horse around A.D. 1700, the Nez Perce emerged as a powerful tribal entity in the interior Northwest. The Nez Perce were the largest tribal society in the region, with population estimates of nearly 6000 by the contact period in the late eighteenth century.[8] Without doubt, early Nez Perce society exemplified the smallest-scale condition of indigenous lifeways, but late pre-contact Nez Perce social practices centered on a complex and democratic system of communal housing, food storage, village life, named positions of leadership associated with the redistribution of resources, and encampments of more than 1000 people made up of various aboriginal groups linking the Nez Perce both symbolically and economically with other tribal entities on the Columbia Plateau.

Contact, Violence, Treaty Negotiations, Allotment

In the Nez Perce homeland, contact meant that a stateless society was caught up in the "play of forces larger and more powerful than themselves."[9] This interplay among contact, violence, and treaty negotiations, then on to the allotment of Nez Perce lands and, finally, to dam building illustrates Scott's statement that "the modern state, in both its colonial and its independent guises, has had the resources to realize a project of rule that was a mere glint in the eye of its precolonial ancestor: namely to bring nonstate spaces and people to heel."[10] By viewing native and nonnative encounters this way, colonization serves to integrate and bring a monied economy to people, lands, and resources on the margins of the nation-state so that they become contributors or *rentable* to foreign exchange and gross national product.[11] Therefore, whenever and wherever it could, the United States, in combination with the global economy, made certain that resources and people were made available for capitalist modes of production and consumption.

Notwithstanding this, Nez Perce interactions with global capitalism began long before dam building, with their active fur trading with the Canadian-based North West Company in the early nineteenth century, resulting in considerable changes to Nez Perce social life and economy. By the early 1800s, fur-trading companies were encouraging Nez Perce men to marry more wives and become "chiefs" to increase the pace at which pelts were trapped, processed, and bought from native producers, and sold for greater profit to nonnative consumers. The fur industry depleted vast populations of beaver and other fur-bearing animals, and by the mid-1840s few animals of value remained in the region. The fur trade brought relative prosperity to a minority of Nez Perce, and trade with the newcomers was in the form of voluntary exchange rather than coercion. While some benefited, however, such encounters were also directly responsible for an unprecedented depopulation of Nez Perce people. Epidemics brought in by nonnative trappers ravaged various Nez Perce villages, and by 1841, population estimates had dwindled to 2000 from the 1805 estimate of 6000.[12]

Many Nez Perce suffered the impact of pandemic disease. In the late eighteenth and early nineteenth centuries, missionaries provided food and medical care to sickly Nez Perce individuals, and in turn were able to successfully convert large numbers of Nez Perce to Christianity. By the 1830s, the Presbyterian missionaries Henry Harmon Spalding and Asa Bowen Smith had established successful missions along the confluence of Lapwai Creek and the Clearwater River and further upstream on the Clearwater River in Kamiah. Moreover, this new form of enclosure prohibited religious converts from engaging in most forms of Nez Perce culture or religion.

In the 1850s, increasing pressure on the US government to acquire Nez Perce land and resources prompted the nation-state to respond with policies of removal and treaty agreements. The treaties codified unequal power in two ways: first, in the domestic undermining of Nez Perce sovereignty and nationality; and, second, in making sure the Nez Perce ceded large amounts of tribal traditional lands to the larger, more powerful US government. They also drew the ungoverned Nez Perce from the periphery into newly formed provincial territories and encouraged them to develop alternative modes of subsistence (i.e., monocrop agriculture). This incorporation meant a radical change to Nez Perce traditional lifeways, impacting their seasonal rounds of fishing, hunting, and foraging. Even so, the Nez Perce notions of the sovereignty and the importance of fish were preserved in the 1855 treaty:

> The right of taking fish in all the streams where running through or bordering said reservation is further secured to said Indians; as also the right of taking fish at all usual and accustomed places in common with citizens of the Territory; and of erecting temporary buildings for curing, together with the privilege of hunting, gathering roots and berries, and pasturing their horses and cattle upon open and unclaimed land.[13]

Idaho became a territory in 1863 and US officials ratified the 1855 treaty. With ratification came an extreme reduction in Nez Perce land, reducing the treaty's original boundary of almost 5 million acres to roughly 800,000 acres.[14] Ratification produced a schism within Nez Perce tribal community,[15] pitting pro-Christian tribal members against non-Christian traditional factions. Acculturated forces decisively split the Nez Perce into antagonistic entities. Nez Perce acculturation, however, to some extent changed tribal attachments to natural resources, including land, but attachments to salmon prevailed.

In the meantime, native and nonnative violence continued to escalate, and in 1877 the Nez Perce War was waged by the US Army against the non-treaty bands to "root-out" all the nonacculturated factions of Nez Perce resistance.

Battles were fought at Whitebird near the Salmon River and across the Bitterroot Mountains in the valley of the Big Hole. US military policy was to kill all Indians—including women and children. The war on Nez Perce factions appalled warriors, since traditional warfare strategy never involved the direct killing of civilians. Chief Joseph realized his people could fight no more and surrendered forty miles from the Canadian border at the Bear Paw Battlefield in northern Montana. The survivors of Joseph's band were eventually detained in Oklahoma, where more lives were lost due to the extreme heat of a foreign climate.[16] It was not until 1885 that Chief Joseph and his people were permitted to return to the Pacific Northwest and the Nez Perce homeland and reservation.

With most Nez Perce now confined to reservation life and subject to federal oversight, the US government came up with a highly effective strategy to reduce communally owned reservation land. Designed by federal policy makers, the Dawes Act of 1887 allotted each head of an Indian household 160 acres of land; individuals over eighteen years of age, eighty acres; and those under eighteen, who were mostly orphans, forty acres. The Dawes Act, or "allotment," was a carefully crafted policy aimed at dividing up communally owned land and destroying tribal traditional relations.

During this period Nez Perce populations dropped to an all-time low, making large portions of communally owned reservation land available to nonnative individuals. Before 1800, the Nez Perce successfully managed more than 28 million acres of ancestral territory. After the allotment, the Nez Perce received a sum of $1,626,222 in exchange for roughly 500,000 acres of unallotted land—nearly 75 percent of the reservation. Of the 800,000 acres of reservation land, the Nez Perce were left with a only 204,587 acres, or 27.4 percent of the land base within the reservation.[17] Over the next century, they continued to suffer staggering land losses. By 1975, Indian-owned land on the Nez Perce reservation was down to a meager 80,000 acres. Within only a few generations, Nez Perce land considered too sacred to be bought and sold was mostly in the hands of nonnative individuals and under federal oversight.

What happened to Nez Perce interactions of salmon and water during the nineteenth-century governmental campaigns of contact, treaties, and allotment? To be sure, treaties are documents signed and negotiated between two nations. Thus, one can read these events as negotiations between two nations. On the one hand, the Nez Perce were not easily drawn into the larger nation-state and world economy: the production, consumption, and trade of salmon had remained a primary occupation throughout the nineteenth century, even during allotment. Moreover, the great salmon rivers of Nez Perce ancestral territory remained dam-free throughout the nineteenth and early twentieth centuries. The challenge facing the Nez Perce throughout much of twentieth century became how to maintain their sovereign status and nationhood, with its salmon-centric culture, in light of the dramatic remapping of their homeland.

Large Dams as a Global, State-Making Process

The hegemony of large dams came about via a combination of statecraft and the remapping of the Nez Perce homeland by global economic forces. As a consequence, state control over Nez Perce land increasingly led to the control of Nez Perce people. In turn, the abundance of arable farmland in the homeland led to the development of fixed-grain agriculture, and by the 1890s, wheat became the region's most important agricultural commodity.

The story of the cultivation and transportation of wheat, along with the construction of hydroelectric dams, is one of appropriating Nez Perce land and redefining the relationships between salmon migrations and the larger world economy. Monocrop agriculture bound Nez Perce cultivators to monotonous rhythms of long, hard labor. Fishing, on the other hand, involved constant movement alongside migrating salmon. It also created symbolic and material ties to human and animal relationships of antiquity.

Wheat cultivation and large dams transformed the Nez Perce salmon-centric society in profound ways. First, global economic forces and the nation-state converted the Nez Perce reservation from a site of small-scale hunting, fishing, and agrarian enterprise to a large-scale, global agribusiness. Second, large dams were part of a state-making enterprise of controlling rivers, supporting regional populations, and encouraging growth in the global agricultural economy. Dams were an expression of twentieth-century economic growth and represented national defense. Regional and national actors used hydropower to support defense-related industries, supplying ample amounts of energy for the production of aluminum (i.e., Alcoa) and aircraft (i.e., Boeing), and to the Hanford site, a US nuclear-production complex during World War II and the Cold War.

In particular, the key technological changes from small- to large-scale farming involved the replacement of naturally reproducing, self-sufficient farm inputs of human labor and horses with fossil-fuel-powered farm machinery and agricultural chemicals. Factory farming produced higher yields and greater surpluses. From 1910 to 1987 wheat yields in the Nez Perce homeland nearly tripled.[18] Agricultural intensification destroyed more than two-thirds of the small-scale farms and replaced them with fewer and more powerful large-scale farms. Economies of scale resulted in the removal of nearly 14,000 people from small-scale farming and damaged the economic self-sufficiency and viability of many small towns throughout the Nez Perce reservation.

As a result, the Nez Perce suffered economic disparities produced before and after World War II. Beyond global economic forces, the Nez Perce faced an increasing demographic presence of nonnatives owning and controlling a large majority of reservation land. They lacked the financial muscle to meet the capital-intensive requirements of factory farming. Large-scale agribusiness required the use of fossil fuels and globally manufactured products. The costs of fuel and farm machinery and the increasing use of chemical fertilizers and pesticides were economic impossibilities for most Nez Perce. Strikingly, the Nez Perce reservation consumed virtually no chemical fertilizers or fossil fuels 1910, but those chemicals accounted for 31 percent of all farm inputs thirty years later.

Dams had the second greatest impact on Nez Perce nationalism and salmon. New Deal era dams were designed to meet increasing demands of national defense, hydroelectric production, and agricultural intensification. Before World War II, regional farmers and the transportation industry moved wheat largely by railcar, and before that, by steam-powered river barges. From its inception, wheat production in the Inland Northwest was aimed for global export. Agricultural commodities left the Nez Perce reservation in great quantities, heading in a downriver, westward direction to Portland, Oregon, and from there to global markets (i.e., Great Britain, Japan, and later China). Thus, during the 1860s steam-powered river barges and then railcars transported grain from the Nez Perce homeland to global industrial centers.

The concentration of labor and of political and economic power have enabled the United States to build more than 200 dams and water diversion projects in the drainages of the Columbia and Snake Rivers over the past 150 years of nonnative development. Four dams located on the lower Snake River, adjacent to the Nez Perce reservation and along the lowest reach of the river in southeast Washington, are the primary focus of Nez Perce dam removal policy. The nation-state convinced private and public interests that placing dams on the lower Snake would help meet the growing demands of a maturing world economy and national defense by supplying defense-related contractors and the Hanford Site regional hydropower from Snake and Columbia basin dams. Even so, the lower Snake River is at the heart of the Nez Perce homeland and serves as a bottleneck for all the great salmon-producing rivers of central Idaho, including the Clearwater and Salmon Rivers and the main-stem Snake River, which originates from deep cold-water springs hundreds of miles upriver in the Greater Yellowstone ecosystem. It is not surprising, therefore, that this region is also rich in early archaeological sites, including some dating back

11,500 years. Prior to contact, the Nez Perce claimed the lower Snake River as a central place in their ancestral territory and homeland. It remains a critical source of power and cultural continuity in the maintenance of Nez Perce tribal relations—in part due to the importance of salmon.

Despite the fact that the lower Snake River as a central Nez Perce fishing site and way of life, the nation-state appropriated the necessary funds in 1947 to construct four large dams. This plan required that the US Army Corps of Engineers form the largest construction district in its history.[19] The dams on the lower Snake River merited this project for two important reasons: first, to increase the scale of agricultural commodities by river transportation and, second, to intensify the production of hydropower for consumption by regional homes and businesses and by large-scale industry. Once the dams were built, Lewiston, Idaho, would become a year-round inland seaport. More importantly, agriculture commodities would meet the demands of newly expanding global markets in East Asia, including China.

Beyond growth in the world agricultural economy and regional industry, proponents of dams also touted their use in national defense. Dam supporters launched an aggressive campaign to convince others that hydroelectric dams on the lower Snake River would solve Hanford's growing energy needs.

From the Nez Perce perspective, the dams on the lower Snake River were and are a significant obstacle to sovereignty, treaty rights, and cultural well-being. Since time immemorial the Nez Perce have revered migrating salmon and healthy watersheds as a paramount symbol of their cultural and religious identity. This ancient relationship was built upon three main elements: salmon as food, as an object of trade, and as a necessary component of traditional religious expression. After 1975, the Nez Perce began to push for the removal of all four dams on the lower Snake River. This effort fulfilled a larger campaign based on treaty rights and twentieth-century legal precedents to restore salmon and other endangered fish to the Columbia and Snake Rivers basins. Furthermore, the Treaty of 1855 guaranteed the Nez Perce and other Columbia Basin tribes the "right of taking fish" at their "usual and accustomed" fishing sites. Roughly a century later, in *Washington v. Washington State Commercial Passenger Fishing Vessel Association,* the US Supreme Court ruled that the original treaties entitled Northwest tribes to one-half the total Columbia Basin salmon harvest and approved the use of modern fishing equipment.[20]

Nez Perce policies on salmon are based on the belief that restoring populations to harvestable levels is the best solution to meeting federal treaty obligations and, more importantly, to maintaining tribal identity, culture, and sovereignty. The Nez Perce realize that if harvestable stocks are not restored, the federal government and US taxpayers may be obligated to compensate the tribes for lost cultural and legal rights to harvest salmon.

More recently, the Nez Perce and other Columbia Basin tribes have refused on religious grounds to estimate an appropriate monetary amount, but the repatriation dollar value may be between $6 and $12 billion. Furthermore, the Institute for Fisheries Resources conducted a study in 1996 entitled "The Cost of Doing Nothing" using widely accepted economic methods to calculate a net asset value of $13 billion for Columbia Basin salmon.[21] Historically, Snake River salmon accounted for half of all salmon in the Columbia Basin. Therefore, a net asset value for salmon in the Snake River Basin has been pegged at $6.5 billion. Tribal claims of the Nez Perce and others could also include lost land value because, by the late 1800s, Northwest Indian tribes had ceded over 6 million acres of communally managed land to the United States. The Institute for Fisheries Resources attached a value of $2,000 per acre and estimated that the value of tribal land cessations to be an additional $12 billion. In short, if harvestable stocks are not restored, the federal government and its taxpayers could be responsible to compensate the tribes for roughly $23 billion. Compensation ties into a discussion of sovereignty by reinforcing it, and is one of the reasons the Nez Perce continue fighting for sovereign tribal nation status.

In the 1990s, Nez Perce leaders set a legal precedent when they instituted their fight for healthy watersheds, and the Nez Perce Tribe and the federal government "spent $10 million preparing their water case for trial and will spend an additional $2 million per year in the years ahead."[22] The two major legal battles facing the Nez Perce Tribe are securing adequate flows of water in the Snake River basin and upholding a duty of fiduciary trust on behalf of the US government. The Nez Perce support free-flowing rivers because, without adequate habitat, salmon and other anadromous fish fail to successfully reproduce and survive. Furthermore, the failure to restore free-flowing rivers demonstrates the federal government has violated its responsibilities as a benevolent guardian of the Nez Perce Tribe. The damming of the Snake River and Columbia River basins disregarded several promises enshrined in the Treaty of 1855. The Nez Perce Tribe has promised that it will if necessary pursue litigation against the federal government for breach of trust. Tribal leaders conclude that the federal Snake River management plan is geared to protect dams and the status quo, rather than salmon. In sum, dams are unacceptable to the Nez Perce Tribe because they violate their 1855 treaty rights and harm migrating salmon.

While these environmental battles are fought in court, the Nez Perce continue to witness the collapse of a once-plentiful salmon fishery. Prior to Euro-American settlement, 10 to 16 million adult salmon entered the river each year.[23] Of those, roughly 8 to 10 million were adult Chinook salmon. In early summer large runs of eighty-pound Chinook salmon, appropriately named "June hogs" by early Euro-American settlers, would enter the Snake River each year. For countless generations the Nez Perce fished for these giant salmon, but now the June hogs are extinct and have not returned to the rivers of the Nez Perce homeland since the last dam was completed on the lower Snake River in 1975. Moreover, fishery biologists failed to acquire hatchery stocks prior to the total disappearance of June hogs from the Columbia and Snake drainages. In 1993, remaining Chinook salmon counts were at an all-time low. Only 450,000 fish returned to the Columbia River basin, and roughly 250,000, or half of the total run of Chinook salmon, were harvested.

As a result, large sums of money are currently being invested to restore salmon throughout the Pacific Northwest. In the Columbia Basin this has resulted in skyrocketing costs and few tangible results. Well-intentioned fishery managers have relied on hatcheries and fish passage systems to solve the problem of declining salmon brought on by international trade and the polities of US government. However, neither approach is solving the current salmon crisis. A retired Army Corps of Engineers fishery biologist recently stated that roughly 8 to 10 billion dollars has already been spent to improve fish passages on the lower Snake River.[24] A fish screen was put in at McNary Dam to facilitate juvenile salmon returning to the Pacific Ocean. This improvement cost the federal government and US taxpayers roughly 18 million dollars.

Given such data, the key question becomes who benefits from the maintenance and perpetuation of large dams in the Nez Perce homeland? To be sure, the nation-state, individual actors, and private institutions benefit exponentially from the dams, while the majority of the native and nonnative population pays enormous costs in the form of "perverse subsidies."[25] These subsidies are "perverse" in that economic growth through subsidies harms both the environment and the nonelite majority. Agribusinesses, large-scale industry, electricity-generating corporations, and resource-management institutions receive a federal subsidies with state-sponsored dams and in turn derive exponential sources of revenue and even social power at the expense of migrating salmon and social well-being in the Nez Perce homeland.

Moreover, on the Snake and Columbia Rivers, a transnational river-barge industry continues to transport wheat and other agricultural commodities to global markets. Of the total amount of grain produced on Nez Perce reservation lands by nonindigenous farmers, more than 90 percent is exported from the United States.[26] Those who profit argue that any discussion of dam removal on the lower Snake River must consider that the increased cost of shipping grain by railroad and highway versus river barge would raise the price per bushel of wheat, for example, by 8 percent to 10 percent. Unless the federal government is willing to cover these costs, farmers will be forced to pay higher prices to ship their commodities to the consumer. Thus, large-scale farmers, a transnational shipping industry, and other agribusinesses that profit enormously from the maintenance of dams on the lower Snake River resist dam removal and, in so doing, resist alternative forms of development in the Nez Perce homeland as well as Nez Perce sovereignty.

In combination with the agricultural economy, several federal agencies, including the Bonneville Power Administration, have an interest in maintaining dams in the Pacific Northwest. Dams on the Columbia and Snake Rivers produce more hydropower than any in other river system in the United States and the world. Since the late 1930s, Bonneville Power Administration has held a monopoly over the sale of energy produced by large dams in the Pacific Northwest. This monopoly, in turn, gives Bonneville Power Administration tremendous power over others, including tribal campaigns of dam removal on the lower Snake River. Furthermore, the transformation of the Nez Perce homeland to a system of large-scale farms, dams, and declining numbers of salmon is an example of how the nation-state, according to Scott, "tames nature" and "gradually gets a handle on its subjects and their environment."[27]

Nez Perce Futures

The Nez Perce embrace their salmon-centric culture to ensure a more resilient, alternative future, and they are developing strategies to tackle the long-term effects of more than 200 years of external policies of state-making and global-scale development. Contemporary Nez Perce policies are designed to address environmental issues by solving salmon-related problems, including those historically brought on by dam building and agricultural development in the region as well as those that anticipate the increasing vulnerabilities of global climate change and other environmental disasters. In doing so, the Nez Perce are actively managing resources of great cultural importance at all the "usual and accustomed places" associated with traditional-use areas, both on and off the reservation. The Nez Perce are effectively building a strong sovereign nation and shaping a vigorous future economy.

The primary goal of Nez Perce environmental programs is to restore several species of migratory salmon in the Nez Perce homeland. In collaboration with the Columbia River Inter-Tribal Fish Commission, Nez Perce Fisheries provides scientific, technical, and policy inputs to protect reserved rights of salmon and water in the Columbia River basin. Moreover, the Nez Perce Tribe operates fifteen fish hatcheries, both on and off the reservation, and monitors the harvest of half the available adult salmon migrating in the Columbia and Snake drainages each year.

The Nez Perce and other Columbia Basin treaty tribes have also provided recommendations for the protection and restoration of all salmon populations listed under the federal Endangered Species Act. Consultation about shared resources between the Columbia River treaty tribes and federal agencies has resulted in federal court mandates and the issuance of biological opinions on the survival and recovery of listed salmon species.

The aim of biological opinions is to ensure that any federal action (i.e., dams on the Snake and Columbia Rivers) is not likely to reduce the survival and recovery of the listed species. The Nez Perce and Columbia Basin treaty tribes therefore generally oppose large dams and other water development projects that negatively affect migrating salmon and water quality.

Water remains a central concern for the Nez Perce. In 2005 the Nez Perce negotiated an agreement between nonnative water users, the Idaho State Senate, and the US Congress in the Snake River Basin Adjudication—a water rights case initiated in 1986 to settle more than 150,000 outstanding claims to water in the Snake River drainage. The Nez Perce Tribe, in return, drew from its cultural connections to salmon and water and formed an agreement under which the Bureau of Reclamation may lease up to 427,000 acre feet of water from the state to increase flow in the Snake River drainage and help endangered salmon. Additional water in the Snake River facilitates salmon migrations and improves Nez Perce fish and habitat projects.

Even so, the greatest vulnerability to both salmon and people in the twenty-first century stems from the projected impacts of global environmental change, including global warming (i.e., climate change). In the Pacific Northwest, the Nez Perce and other native nations are reacting to climate change by adopting novel and innovative policies while simultaneously asserting tribal sovereignty.[28] First, adjudicating water rights for salmon is a powerful tool in a modern reality of increasing demands and declining supplies. Second, the federal Endangered Species Act is a valuable legal framework for the Nez Perce and other native nations aiming to protect salmon populations. Additional legal structures, such as contract law, may provide another means by which to secure in-stream flows for migrating salmon. Furthermore, in the spirit of protecting salmon, the Nez Perce and other tribes are implementing policies to designate off-reservation landholdings as federally protected National Parks, National Monuments, and Wild and Scenic Rivers.

Intergovernmental and intertribal cooperation has resulted in the Nez Perce and other tribes participating in the co-management of salmon-based resources through the Columbia River Inter-Tribal Fish Commission and other collaborations with such federal agencies as the National Oceanographic and Atmospheric Administration and the National Fish and Wildlife Service. In salmon restoration, these partnerships are effective in co-managing hatchery programs and in developing long-range management strategies of problems at the nexus of the nation-state and environmental problems. The Nez Perce, for example, have developed and implemented strong policies on future dams and related irrigation projects, have lobbied to enforce dam operators to release more water when needed to improve fish passage, and, when necessary, have litigated for the decommissioning of dams as a measure of last resort.

To counteract climate change, the Nez Perce tribe has committed to twenty-nine forest-restoration projects and set aside nearly 5000 acres for carbon seques-tration as a means to have forestry and reforestation practices remove carbon dioxide from the atmosphere. Tribal efforts to plant Douglas fir and ponderosa pine saplings are projected to absorb a year's worth of carbon dioxide from nearly 500,000 cars, trucks, and SUVs.[29] The Nez Perce tribal government also aims to have corporations offset their greenhouse gas emissions by paying the Nez Perce to keep trees growing and for forests to remain intact. Few American companies are presently mandated to curb greenhouse emissions with carbon sequestra-tions. The Nez Perce efforts are models of the value in keeping forests alive, thus providing integrity to salmon watersheds and critical habitat.

Regional and Global Socio-Environmental Change

Salmon and water lie at the heart of the Nez Perce homeland, characterized by its spectacular forests, abrupt topographical changes, and freshwater resources. Continued stress, however, from more than two centuries of commercial growth in the present global economy, and the projected impacts of global cli-mate change, presents the Nez Perce with urgent and challenging problems. The Nez Perce know that their response to such problems will influence both salmon stocks and their own survival in an uncertain and unknown future.

The Pacific Northwest presently has 10 million inhabitants—three orders of magnitude greater than the total native population in was in 1750.[30] By the late nineteenth century the immigrant population exceeded the indigenous population, and by the early twentieth century the total population of the region was more than one million people. Before World War II, economic expansion and population growth fueled state-expansionist projects to build large dams in the Columbia basin. After World War II per-capita energy consumption in the Pacific Northwest increased dramatically, with the regional economy nearly doubling between 1985 and 2003.

Two centuries of state-sponsored commercial growth degraded ecosystems, diminished the opportunities for many small-scale ranching, farming, and forest-based communities and partially destroyed the great Columbia River salmon fishery.[31] Moreover, massive change in historic ecosystems has removed from 80 percent to 90 percent of the old growth coniferous forests in the Nez Perce homeland, and timber cutting, grazing, and fire suppression have made the remaining forests prone to disease and fire. Ninety percent of the sagebrush steppe in the Inland Northwest and 99 percent of the Palouse Prairie steppe, a unique grassland ecosystem in the heart of Nez Perce ancestral territory, have been removed, mostly for urban and agricultural development. In addition to the looming extinction of salmon, dramatic environmental changes in native habitat have led to the extinction of fourteen bird and mammal species from Washington and Oregon, and Oregon lists forty-two additional mammals and birds and as "species of concern."[32] In coming decades the social and environmental sustainability of the entire region will be further challenged by the combined effects of population growth, large-scale development, and the projected impacts of global climate change.[33]

For the Nez Perce, salmon ecosystems define cosmology, labor, energy, and economy. Salmon link biodiversity and productivity because salmon store in their bodies and transport and move "materials, and energy and nutrients between marine, aquatic, and terrestrial ecosystems."[34] Historically, spawning salmon transported more than 100 million kilograms of energy and materials from marine to terrestrial ecosystems (10 to 16 million fish) annually in the Columbia River basin, making it the world's richest inland fishery.[35] Before the arrival of European-American settlers, these rich ecosystems supported some 200,000 indigenous peoples diversified into forty-seven cultural subareas and representing eleven language families.[36] Factoring in the impact of European disease, the pre-contact population may have been twice this size.[37] As the indigenous population declined, so did the salmon. Columbia Basin salmon runs measure 20 percent of their historic levels of 10 to 16 million before 1805, with as few as 200,000 fish returning annually.[38] The current decline in Columbia Basin salmon—and the Nez Perce population—can be attributed to the impacts by hydroelectric dams, irrigation projects, and overall habitat loss.[39] Saving one may be a way to preserve another.

How will global climate change affect salmon and in turn a salmon-centric Nez Perce culture? Climate change in the Columbia and Snake Rivers is projected to redistribute stream flows and reduce the amount of annual freshwater cycling.[40] Sharp variations in water are affected by the reduction in annual snow pack.[41] Pacific Northwest average annual air temperatures warmed by between .7 and .9 degrees Celsius in the twentieth century, and climate models suggest that additional increases from 1.5 and 3.2 degrees Celsius will occur by the mid-twenty-first century.[42] These higher air temperatures could harm salmon during spawning, incubation, and rearing stages of their life. Warmer temperatures create earlier snowmelt and less moisture falling as snow. Increases in rain versus snow will lead to increased winter peak flows that scour stream and riverbeds and obliterate salmon eggs. A reduction in snow pack results in diminished flows in summer and fall, decreasing the availability of suitable spawning habitat and expediting increases in water temperatures.

Little is known about the ability of salmon to adjust to global climate change. The negative effects of climate change are projected to be most pronounced in the higher and more pristine tributaries of major river systems. In the Nez Perce homeland, rivers and streams are markedly cooler and higher, and they provide a more suitable habitat for spawning salmon than warmer, lower-elevation streams further downstream in the lower Columbia River basin. Perturbations in climate and increases in average temperatures will likely challenge the remaining salmon stocks in the next 50 to 100 years. Recent research in the Pacific Northwest on chinook salmon populations suggests declines between 20 percent and 40 percent by 2050.[43] The Nez Perce and other Columbia Basin tribes depend on chinook salmon for their large size and high fat content. A significant decline in chinook salmon and other fishes threatens Nez Perce's future food security and salmon-centric, autonomous culture.

Conclusion

First, it is critical to consider how migrating salmon have shaped the history of an entire region and how a rapidly expanding global economy altered but did not destroy the relationship between salmon-centric environments and Nez Perce life and culture. The United States made every effort to make subjects out of the Nez Perce and to convert and utilize their homeland for the expansion of the global economy. The Nez Perce, recognizing the human right to cultural expression and survival, exercised genuine sovereignty in both historical and modern contexts, in spite of state-sponsored efforts to bring them and valuable resources under firm control.

Second, it is critical to connect the hegemony of large dams and a global agricultural economy and economic growth in the twenty-first century. China is the newest actor in this regard. The recent growth of China's economy and the renewed importance of Snake and Columbia dams as shipment corridors links the two powerful, global economies for some time into the future. Nearly ten years ago, in 2004, the *Seattle Post-Intelligencer* reported, "Already this year, China has accepted 1.8 million metric tons of US wheat—nearly 17 times as much as all of last year. And about 60 percent of it was funneled through Columbia River ports. For the first time in 30 years, China has entered the Pacific Northwest wheat market on a dramatic scale."[44]

Larger structural changes shape this trend, too. China has a substantial wheat economy, but internal demands of rapid urbanization and an increasing affluent population has encouraged China to import more wheat than any other country in the world. China's wheat imports account for roughly 10 percent to 15 percent of the world trade.[45] Beyond affluence and consumption, China has decreasing farmlands and increasing problems associated with drought and water shortages. Without doubt, the magnitude of China's environmental and economic disasters associated with food production is staggering.

China, in turn, has become the newest consumer of Nez Perce wheat. Transnational shipping industries move wheat by river barge through dams to international shipping ports in Portland, Oregon. From there, Hanjin Shipping, among other large shipping companies, transport Northwest wheat to East Asian consumers. China, in the present century with its unprecedented growth and consumer demand has enormous political and environmental impact on Nez Perce cultural and natural resources. Development by national and global actors therefore shapes and informs the future of dams and salmon-related resources and the sustainability of the Pacific Northwest region.

Furthermore, transnational actors at both local and global levels have greatly challenged Nez Perce nationalism and sovereignty with the dramatic remapping of their homeland. For most of their existence the Nez Perce avoided living in a world in which stratification and development were the norm. Rather, their social structure encouraged subsistence routines that maximized well-being and freedom for the largest numbers of people. They lived in a homeland that, until 200 years ago, was out of the reach of state intervention. Considering the size of the tribe, the Nez Perce have been remarkably successful in resisting full encroachment of the nation-state and global capital by not allowing transnational forces to completely alter or destroy their connections to migrating fish and their salmon-centric way of life.

NOTES

1. James C. Scott, *The Art of Not Being Governed* (New Haven, CT: Yale University Press, 2009), x.

2. Ibid., ix.

3. Benedict J. Colombi and James F. Brooks, *Keystone Nations: Indigenous Peoples and Salmon across the North Pacific* (Santa Fe: School for Advanced Research Press, 2012).

4. Allan Gould Marshall, "Fish, Water, and Nez Perce Life," *Idaho Law Review* 42 (2006): 763–93.

5. Gordon W. Hewes, "Indian Fisheries Productivity in Pre-contact Times in the Pacific Salmon Area," *Northwest Anthropological Research Notes* 7 (1973): 133–55; Schalk, Randall F. "Structure of an Anadromous Fish Resource," in *For Theory Building in Archaeology*, ed. Lewis R. Binford (New York: Academic Press, 1977), 207–49; Deward E. Walker, Jr., "Mutual Cross-Utilization of Economic Resources in the Plateau: An Example from Aboriginal Nez Perce Fishing Practices," in *Report of Investigations* (Pullman: Washington State University Laboratory of Anthropology, 1967), no. 41.

6. Hewes, "Indian Fishery"; Walker, "Mutual Cross-Utilization."

7. Alan Gould Marshall, "Unusual Gardens: The Nez Perce and Wild Horticulture on the Eastern Columbia Plateau," in *Northwest Lands, Northwest Peoples: Readings in Environmental History*, ed. Dale D. Goble and Paul W. Hirt (Seattle: University of Washington Press, 1999), 173–87.

8. Deward E. Walker, Jr., "Nez Perce," in *Handbook of North American Indians*, ed. Deward E. Walker, Jr. (Washington, DC: Smithsonian Institution, 1998), 420–38.

9. John W. Cole and Eric R. Wolf, *The Hidden Frontier: Ecology and Ethnicity in an Alpine Valley* (New York: Academic Press, 1974), 1.

10. Scott, *Art of Not Being Governed*, 4.

11. Ibid.

12. Walker, "Nez Perce."

13. Horace Axtell, et al., *Treaties: Nez Perce Perspectives* (Lewiston, Idaho: Confluence Press, 2003), 117.

14. Archie Phinney, "Numipu among the White Settlers" *Wicazo Sa Review* 17 (2002): 21–42.

15. Deward E. Walker, Jr., *Conflict and Schism in Nez Perce Acculturation: A Study of Religion and Politics* (Pullman: Washington State University Press, 1968).

16. J. Diane Pearson, *The Nez Perces in the Indian Territory: Nimiipuu Survival* (Norman: University of Oklahoma Press, 2008).

17. Emily Greenwald, *Reconfiguring the Reservation: The Nez Perces, Jicarilla Apaches, and the Dawes Act* (Albuquerque: University of New Mexico Press, 2002).

18. John H. Bodley, *The Power of Scale: A Global History Approach* (New York: M. E. Sharpe, 2003).

19. Keith C. Petersen, *River of Life, Channel of Death: Fish and Dams on the Lower Snake* (Lewiston, Idaho: Confluence Press, 1995).

20. Charles F. Wilkinson, *American Indians, Time, and the Law: Native Societies in a Modern Constitutional Democracy* (New Haven, CT: Yale University Press, 1987), 73.

21. Hans D. Radtke and Shannon W. Davis, *The Cost of Doing Nothing: The Economic Burden of Salmon Declines in the Columbia River Basin* (Eugene, OR: Institute for Fisheries Resources, 1996).

22. Daniel McCool, *Native Waters: Contemporary Indian Water Settlements and the Second Treaty Era* (Tucson: University of Arizona Press, 2002), 79.

23. Jim Lichatowich, *Salmon without Rivers: A History of the Pacific Salmon Crises* (Washington, DC: Island Press, 1999).

24. Conversations with the author, April 25, 2003.

25. Norman Myers and Jennifer Kent, *Perverse Subsidies: How Tax Dollars Harm the Environment and the Economy* (Washington, DC: Island Press, 2001).

26. Benedict J. Colombi, "Dammed in Region Six: The Nez Perce Tribe, Agricultural Development, and the Inequality of Scale," *American Indian Quarterly* 29 (2005): 560–89.

27. James C. Scott, *Seeing Like a State: How Certain Schemes to Improve the Human Condition Have Failed* (New Haven, CT: Yale University Press, 1998).

28. Jonathan M. Hanna, "Native Communities and Climate Change: Protecting Tribal Resources as Part of National Climate Policy," in report published by the Natural Resources Law Center (Boulder: Colorado Law School, University of Colorado, 2007).

29. Joshua Zaffos, "Tribes Look to Cash in with 'Tree-Market' Environmentalism," *High Country News* 13 (2006): 5.

30. John H. Bodley, "Scale, Power, and Sustainability in the Pacific Northwest," paper presented at the annual meeting for the Society for Applied Anthropology, Vancouver, British Columbia, March 27, 2006.

31. Xanthippe Augerot, *Atlas of Pacific Salmon: The First Map-Based Status Assessment of Salmon in the North Pacific* (Berkeley: University of California Press), 2005.

32. Constance Iten et al., "Extirpated Species of Oregon and Washington," in *Wildlife-Habitat Relationships in Oregon and Washington*, ed. David H. Johnson and Thomas A. O'Neill (Corvallis: Oregon State University, 2001), 452–73.

33. Edward A. Parson et al., "Potential Consequences of Climate Variability and Change for the Pacific Northwest," in *Climate Change Impacts on the United States: The Potential Consequences of Climate Variability and Change*, ed. National Assessment Synthesis Team, U.S. Global Change Research Program (Cambridge: Cambridge University Press, 2001), 247–80.

34. Jeff C. Cederholm et al., "Salmon and Wildlife-Ecological Contexts, Relationships, and Implications for Management," in *Wildlife-Habitat Relationships in Oregon and Washington*, ed. David H. Johnson and Thomas A. O'Neil (Corvallis: Oregon State University Press, 2001), 628–84.

35. Lichatowich, *Salmon without Rivers*, 180.

36. Alfred L. Kroeber, *Cultural and Natural Areas of Native North America* (Berkeley: University of California Press, 1939).

37. Robert T. Boyd, "The Introduction of Infectious Diseases among the Indians of the Pacific Northwest 1774–1874," PhD diss., University of Washington, 1985, 324–413.

38. Augerot, *Atlas of Pacific Salmon*, 2.

39. Michael Blumm, *Sacrificing the Salmon: A Legal and Policy History of the Decline of Columbia Basin Salmon* (Den Bosch, Netherlands: BookWorld Publications, 2002); Lichatowich, *Salmon without Rivers*.

40. Edward A. Parson et al., "Potential Consequences of Climate Variability and Change for the Pacific Northwest," in *Climate Change Impacts on the United States:*

The Potential Consequences of Climate Variability and Change, ed. National Assessment Synthesis Team, U.S. Global Change Research Program (Cambridge: Cambridge University Press, 2001), 247–80.

41. Philip W. Mote et al., "Preparing for Climatic Change: The Water, Salmon, and Forests of the Pacific Northwest." *Climatic Change* 61 (2003): 45–88.

42. James Battin et al., "Projected Impacts of Climate Change on Salmon Habitat Restoration," *Proceedings of the National Academy of Sciences of the United States of America* 104 (2007): 6720–5.

43. Ibid.

44. Brad Wong, "State Wheat Supply in Demand: China's Appetite for Grain Could Be Northwest's Gain," *Seattle Post-Intelligencer Reporter*, November 23, 2004.

45. Jikun Huang et al., "China's Food Economy to the Twenty-First Century: Supply, Demand, and Trade," *Economic Development and Cultural Change* 47 (1999): 737–66.

II

The Brazilian Amazon and the Transnational Environment, 1940–1990

Seth Garfield

Something unusual has happened in the Brazilian Amazon over recent decades. Under an aggressive development project unleashed by the military government between 1964 and 1985 and pursued by its democratic successors, the Amazon has witnessed massive land enclosures, the expansion of road networks and hydroelectric projects, rapid demographic growth, and violent conflict. The region today boasts some 21 million people (two-thirds of whom are urban), as well as 65 million head of cattle.[1] An estimated 16 percent of the Brazilian Amazon has been deforested. A lesser-known, perhaps equally remarkable fact is that, of the total area of the Brazilian Amazon, which accounts for between 70 percent and 80 percent of the total area of the Amazon Basin, approximately 22 percent is demarcated as indigenous lands; another 10 percent is designated as conservation units.[2] Concomitant with such dramatic changes, the Brazilian Amazon, the sovereign territory of one South American nation, has become the object of intense international scrutiny. It has come to embody the challenge of natural resource management that has mobilized and confounded contemporary nation-states. But how exactly did this region—a place most residents of the Northern hemisphere and Brazil have never visited—end up as the cause célèbre of over 200 NGOs worldwide?[3]

For students of international relations, the answer is simple: the fate of the Amazon, the world's largest remaining rain forest, epitomizes the tug of war in the so-called North-South divide in environmental politics. For Northern conservationism, which historically has been premised on removal of native populations from "wilderness" preserves, Amazonian ecosystems are bulwarks against species depletion and global warming.[4] For Southern policy makers, tropical nature serves as a resource for poverty remediation and national development. Such divisions notoriously erupted at the United Nations Conference on the Human Environment in Stockholm in 1972, at which Brazil and other developing countries challenged calls for environmental conservation, calling them impediments to economic growth.

Yet, for complex societies and globalized economies like Brazil or the United States, to reduce Amazonian ecopolitics to a North-South dichotomy is both instructive and misleading. The notion of a monolithic Southern or Northern bloc separated by a Green Curtain is belied by the World Bank's bankrolling of policies promoting Amazonian deforestation and by Brazilian grassroots movements for environmental and social justice. Policy rifts over tropical-forest conservation as a strategy to combat greenhouse gas emissions have divided the United States and European governments, just as Brazilian state ministries have bickered over the merits of foreign credits for avoided deforestation.[5] Indeed, historian Donald Worster suggests that understandings of nature are not distinctly national (or natural), but philosophical, pitting conservationists, who advocate natural resource management under technocratic/ scientific principles as a resource for human use and capital gain, against preservationists, whose "biocentric" view recognizes a moral obligation to the innate value of nature itself.[6] Alternatively, attitudes toward nature can be seen as riven, not by an equator, but by the class-based experiences of work and leisure.[7] To understand Amazonia's contested space in the transnational arena requires exploring how the historical uses and meanings of tropical forest are mediated through processes that are preeminently social.

Historians who are inclined to see past as prologue might assert that there is nothing terribly new about the Amazon's (trans)national intrigue. Since the colonial period, Amazonian populations have been producers and consumers of global commodities, targets of assimilationist policies, and objects of inter-imperial rivalries.[8] As a morality tale pitting nature against culture and heavily overlain with racial innuendo, the Amazon has long accommodated Northern presentiments of apocalypse or salvation: well before it was deemed the "lungs of the earth" for an asphyxiated or overheated planet, the forest was cast as a Malthusian breadbasket, a refuge for European hordes, or a dumping ground for African Americans before the Civil War.[9] The Amazon's geopolitical nerve also runs quite deep among Brazilian nationalists, even if its articulation heretofore lacked the jingoistic pithiness of the more contemporary slogan, "the Amazon is ours." In other words, the Amazon has long been defined as an environmental problem or a solution that has galvanized an array of transnational actors.

Yet the current scale of things is quite distinct. Amazonia's flora and fauna may have always been of interest to a band of foresters and scientists, but this is a far cry from today's mass panic over tropical deforestation. And while the jungle has always made for a sensational tale and sale, the commodification of the Amazon in the media and in the leisure, food, cosmetic, and tourist industries reached new dimensions in mass-consumer societies of the late twentieth century. Few in the United States may know how many countries in South America contain the Amazon rain forest, but many believe it is their duty to save it. Likewise, if the conflict over resources and power is no novelty in Amazonian history, the "greening" of its social movements, reworking local vocabularies of class struggle as well as mythical or spiritual perceptions of nature into new political identities, is.[10]

This chapter offers an historical analysis of the reframing of the Brazilian Amazon in contemporary international affairs. It explores how the socioeconomic and ecological change unleashed under Brazilian military rule and its aftermath collided with the contemporaneous popularization of environmental politics in the North to transform public policies and local conflicts in Amazonian forests into (new) transnational fields. Novel scientific disciplines, technologies, and cultural vocabularies remade the Amazon in the popular and political imaginary in the North and in Brazil; shifting ideologies, in turn, impelled and sustained conservationist initiatives at the local and international levels. Yet the contemporary ruckus over the management of the Amazon also demonstrates the forest's long-standing entanglement with industrial consumerism and civilizing projects. An examination of natural resource management in the Amazon during World War II offers a revealing comparison. In sum, to understand how governments have grappled with environmental problems that defy the capabilities of any single nation, it is important first to explore why these problems have come to be perceived that way.

The Forest for the Trees: Amazonian Rubber during World War II

A shifting trade in tropical forest commodities has marked the Amazon's fitful integration into the world economy since the colonial period. In the late nineteenth century, prize latex had been extracted almost exclusively in the wild from *Hevea brasiliensis,* a tree native to the Amazon. By the 1910s, however, Britain had established more cost-efficient rubber plantations in its Asian colonies using seeds smuggled out of Brazil several decades earlier.[11] On the eve of

Pearl Harbor, annual US imports of crude rubber topped 1 million tons (more than the rest of the world combined); 98 percent came from Southeast Asia, whereas only 4 percent of prewar US rubber consumption was synthetic.[12]

To offset US rubber dependency, critics advanced three principal options: domestic stockpiling, development of a synthetic industry, and geographic diversification of markets. Railing against the European "cartels" that controlled US access to rubber, in 1923, secretary of commerce Hebert Hoover obtained from Congress an appropriation of $500,000 for the Departments of Commerce and Agriculture to fund the exploration of opportunities for rubber cultivation in the Western Hemisphere.[13] Heartened by the potential for rubber cultivation in the Amazon that US government reports outlined, Henry Ford acquired a 2.5-million-acre concession on the Tapajós River in Pará in 1927, which the Companhia Ford Industrial do Brasil named Fordlândia. Production at Fordlândia and its sister plantation Belterra was snagged by labor autonomy and resistance, leaf blight, and soil erosion. Ford's multimillion dollar Amazon fiasco surely gave pause to the large tire companies contemplating market diversification.[14] Indeed, none of the proposed alternatives to Asian rubber succeeded before US entry into the war. President Franklin Roosevelt, hobbled by isolationist sentiment, moved haltingly to build up stocks; the fear of over-expansion and contraction haunted business leaders; and the US population, reeling from economic depression, failed to mobilize for substitutes.[15]

Following the Japanese invasion of the Malayan peninsula in February 1942, the United States lost more than 90 percent of its sources of latex. Unlike many other commodities derived from tropical flora, rubber was indispensable for modern warfare.[16] From airplanes, army trucks, tanks, battleships, motorcycles, gun mounts, bullet-sealing gasoline tanks, submarine storage battery jars, blimps, and barrage balloons to life rafts, hoses, raincoats, boots, and gas masks, rubber was key to ensuring the mobility, speed, and efficiency critical for military defense.[17] The Roosevelt administration prioritized the manufacture of synthetic rubber, tasking chemists, business leaders, academics, and government officials with the breakneck-speed development of a state-subsidized industry.[18] Maximum development of wild rubber in Latin America was secondarily endorsed. In a bilateral agreement in March 1942, Brazil agreed to sell its exportable surpluses of wild rubber to the United States for a fixed, five-year price; US plant scientists would also struggle unsuccessfully to cultivate rubber trees resistant to South American leaf blight, a fungus that ravaged plantation-grown rubber trees in the Amazon and other areas of the Western Hemisphere.[19] Brazil's dictator, Getúlio Vargas, sought to leverage wartime alliance with the United States to revive the Amazon rubber trade and promote the broader economic development of the backwater region.

The loss of a critical raw material amid global warfare provoked renewed American interest in Amazonia's natural resources and the unparalleled involvement of the US government in the region. As one author noted in 1944: "It is probable that the past two years have seen more actual exploration of the basin, more knowledge gained about its physical nature, than have all the four centuries since that early conquistador, Francisco de Orellana, was the first white commander to traverse it." Although he rehashed the threadbare image of the Amazon as newly discovered territory, he was correct on several fronts: over the previous years, the United States had sent hundreds of clerks, administrators, engineers, and agricultural technicians into the Amazon to increase rubber output.[20] The Amazon surfaced in monographs, travelogues, films, and wartime propaganda, reflecting the broader campaign of US officials to solidify an inter-American alliance, however distorted by romantic idealism or ingrained prejudice. Indeed, in conjunction with the Brazilian government, the United States invested $10 million to boost infrastructure alone in the Amazon—the equivalent of $110,490,000 for the year 2000.[21]

The documentation from the Amazon wartime rubber campaign offers an interesting window onto the evolving resonance of the forest in the US imaginary. As US officials labored to overhaul the unregulated work conditions of wild latex extraction, the rubber technicians inevitably bristled. The field reports of the US government's Rubber Development Corporation, for example, often blasted tappers for improper care and extraction of *Hevea*. Based on an eight-week survey of wild rubber properties (*seringais*) in the western Amazon, C. J. Alexopoulos denounced the pervasive "wounding" of rubber trees, which occurred when tappers scraped off the cambium, or fine growth tissue between the bark and the wood, causing the formation of excrescences composed of stone cells covered by a thin layer of bark with few or no latex producing cells. He considered good tapping to be that which left one millimeter of bark outside the cambium: less depth represented a loss of latex, while greater depth was apt to result in wounding and permanent damage to the tapping surface.[22] Technicians on the Javary River likewise reported that "the trees have been ruined by deep and severe tapping with the *machadinha* [hatchet] and the Amazonas knife in the past and have become very unproductive."[23] In the Muaná District, a municipality near Belém, E. B. Hamill noted that over 100 trails had been reopened in October 1943, but the rubber trees had been so badly mutilated over the years that it was impossible to employ a knife for a low panel; in many cases ladders were being used to tap at a height of ten feet.[24] Such denunciations are a far cry from contemporary environmentalist tributes to tappers' capacity "to support themselves and to preserve the continuing vitality of the forest with only small-scale cutting of the trees."[25]

US rubber technicians, many of whom were former inspectors on large rubber plantations in Asia, had a distinctly utilitarian view of nature.[26] They followed a long line of scientific and agricultural "experts" who sought to conserve and control nature (and workers' access to the natural environment) to foster economic growth. Never mind that Amazonian workers toiling under exploitative systems of commercial exchange hardly imagined that a new type of knife or tapping style was their magic bullet.[27] Redolent of the progressivist tradition of conservationism, the rubber technicians had little faith in the capacities of poor people, whom they generally viewed as ignorant and incapable of managing natural resources. Although it was tinged with a heavy dose of ethnocentrism, their condemnation of predatory tapping had also long been echoed by Brazilian elites.[28] In this rendition of political ecology, extractivism accelerates natural resource degradation and underdevelopment.[29]

In contemporary anthropological literature, there is debate over whether "traditional peoples," such as rubber tappers, instinctively exhibit a greater protectiveness toward the environment or whether the notion that nonindustrial peoples possess an innate ecological wisdom is a myth cultivated by environmentalists in industrial society. Some insist that it is important to distinguish between what people think and what they do. According to such criteria, societies that have had little impact on the environment due to geographic isolation, low population density, and limited technology are not inherently ecologically benign.[30] Others differentiate between destructive and sustainable forms of extractivism.[31] Yet counterposing wartime representations with contemporary green discourse elucidates how dominant frameworks have informed outsiders' understandings of Amazonian nature. Clearly, disparate uses of the forest have colored distinct visions of its significance. Rubber Development Corporation technicians could hardly see the forest for the rubber trees, at least inasmuch as Amazonian ecosystems and mindsets were hampering output for the US war machine. In 1945, author Henry Albert Phillips asserted that Brazil's failure to create rubber plantations in the Amazon reflected and revealed "something elemental, deep down in the core of Brazilian character and conduct as a whole. Brazilians are not realists, and never will be, to anything like the same degree that Anglo-Saxons can be and often are."[32] In 1992, environmentalists troubled by deforestation could not but enshrine Amazonian tappers' "dependence on a productive, sustainable ecosystem [that] taught each family to remove from the forest enough natural resources necessary for their survival.... In this way, over the last 100 years, they became a part of the forest's ecology." [33] Tapper "traditionalism," once deplored as congenital sloth or predatory hacking that endangered Allied military preparedness, was now seen as safeguarding the global environment.

Yet even as Amazonia's importance in the global economy and imaginary has evolved, basic underpinnings of this interrelationship endure. Just as the crisis in industrial capitalism after Pearl Harbor precipitated US intervention in the Amazon, the excesses of that capitalism have stoked US and European concerns with tropical deforestation and global warming. In both historical periods, Northerners, as temperate subjects, claim the technical knowledge and moral quotient to dictate or discern the proper management of tropical resources. In both moments, science has been marshaled to delineate and defuse problems of resource production and consumption that are rooted in local socioeconomic conflicts and global inequalities. In both eras, proper resource management in the Amazon has been defined as a transnational concern, even as dramatic postwar changes have modified, in part, the bases for such preoccupation.

The Brazilian Military and the Remaking of Amazonia

The Amazon acquired a new geopolitical resonance under Brazilian military rule (1964–1985). Since the Vargas era, the Brazilian military had chafed at the unfortified borders, precapitalist modes of production, and tenuous state presence in the Amazon. And like the Vargas regime, which had welcomed US investment in the wartime Amazon, the military dictatorship recognized that the environmental challenges of "conquering" the forest defied the capability of one developing nation. Yet even as it wooed foreign capital for megaprojects and mineral exploration in the Amazon, the military transformed the outsize territory into an outsize nationalist mission: a bunker for national security, treasure trove for economic development, panacea for social injustice, marker of national character, and litmus test for good government.[34] The concomitant emergence of a mass environmental movement in the North Atlantic and later in Brazil, however, tugged Amazonia in a different direction.

In a region that accounts for roughly 60 percent of Brazilian territory, state investment in highway construction, heavily bankrolled by foreign loans, aimed to facilitate the rapid movement of goods and people and to lessen dependency on river travel. Through offers of tax breaks, fiscal incentives, and liberal credit, government agencies and state banks lured private investors. Cattle ranches alone received an estimated $5 billion in subsidies between 1971 and 1987, and highly skewed patterns of land ownership were reproduced in the region.[35] The Amazon's population increased by 13 million between 1970 and 2000, as migrants from southern and northeastern Brazil acquired land through both official and private colonization projects.[36] With land titling careless and corrupt in a booming market, landowners and speculators employed fraud and intimidation to evict long-standing occupants as well as recent migrants. Violence spiked in the aftermath of democratization as landowners mobilized to quash rural labor activism, while hyperinflation encouraged investors to seek speculative profits in land. In 1986, 64 percent of all land conflicts in Brazil occurred in Amazonia.[37]

What most aroused international condemnation during military rule and its aftermath was deforestation. The causes of deforestation in the Amazon have included highway construction (85 percent of all deforestation occurs within thirty miles of a road), land use for pasture (as of 1989, livestock occupied more than 85 percent of the area cleared), large hydroelectric projects, colonization and land speculation, mining, wood production, and soybean cultivation.[38] Although large landowners accounted for the bulk of deforestation, smallholders also contributed to the destruction of forest resources because of insecure land tenure, reliance on swidden agriculture in low-yield production systems, and lack of government support or sustainable economic alternatives.[39] These forces have also evolved over the past three decades. Economic pressures fueled by soya exports (to feed Chinese and European farms animals) are a much greater threat now than in the 1970s and 1980s, when a larger share of clearing was driven by a weaker lobby of ranchers and land speculators.[40] Moreover, internal frontier migration is primarily responsible for smallholder deforestation, reflective of the drop in interregional population movements.[41] Whereas in 1975 less than seven million acres of land in the Brazilian Amazon had been altered from its original forest cover, by 1988 an estimated 40 million acres of forest had been destroyed.[42] Using Landsat data and satellite information from the US National Oceanographic and Atmospheric Administration, Philip Fearnside estimated total deforestation through 1988 at 8 percent; a World Bank–commissioned study arrived at a higher figure of 12 percent.[43] Levels vary significantly by state, with deforestation highest in longer-settled areas such as Maranhão (66 percent) and Tocantins (40 percent) and lower in Amazonas (2 percent) in the 1990s.[44]

Estimates of Amazonian deforestation have been highly contentious. The discrepancies are in part due to the varied criteria used to measure deforestation: the level of conversion to other land uses (whether complete or partial), modification in vegetation, alteration in forest cover, damage to the ecosystem, or changes in climate function. For example, the U.N. Food and Agricultural Organization considers deforestation to be a complete conversion of open and closed forest to agricultural land "with depletion of tree cover to less than 10 percent," a far more conservative criterion than that employed by environmental groups.[45] More broadly, a newfound geopolitical setting has been determinative in reframing land use change in the Brazilian

Amazon, repositioning local power struggles over resource management in transnational environmental terms.[46]

Ecopolitics and the Framing of Amazonia

In the 1970s, as the Brazilian military unleashed rapid social and ecological changes in the Amazon, a broad, transnational environmental movement emerged among more affluent residents of the northern hemisphere who were preoccupied with problems of transborder acid rain and nuclear proliferation. The origins of a popular "age of ecology," underscoring human beings' fundamental interdependence with other biological species, can be traced back earlier, to the publication of Rachel Carson's *Silent Spring* (1962), with its exposé of the toxic effects of pesticides on the environment; to the 1960s "flower power's" repudiation of consumerism and militarization; and to postwar horror at Hiroshima. Yet the 1970s, inaugurated with the April 1970 launching of Earth Day, marked a quantitative shift. Some of the decade's environmental milestones included the creation of the Environmental Protection Agency in the United States and the subsequent passage of key environmental legislation; the U.N. Conference on the Human Environment, UNESCO's Man and the Biosphere Programme and establishment of the U.N. Environmental Programme; and the founding of the Green Party in West Germany in 1979. Environmental history emerged as a subdiscipline in North American universities, and the decade also witnessed the publication of influential books focusing on the problems of species depletion, catastrophic climate change, and human depredation of the environment. The term "environment," with its social-scientific connotation, came to replace the more Romantic-sounding "nature," while "eco" became a common prefix signaling this newfound consciousness.[47]

By the dawn of redemocratization in Brazil, environmental groups had proliferated worldwide. Between 1985 and 1990, for example, membership in the Environmental Defense Fund doubled (and doubled again between 1990 and 1991). Both the Natural Resources Defense Council and the Nature Conservancy grew over two and a half times between 1985 and 1990. World Wildlife Fund–US grew fivefold, and Greenpeace membership jumped from 400,000 to 850,000. Transnational environmental networks increased from two groups in 1953 to ninety in 1993, or to less than 2 percent of total international nongovernmental organization (NGO) groups to nearly 15 percent. The development of computerized databases to employ direct mail techniques for fundraising and to manage membership lists helped US environmental organizations to mushroom over the course of the 1980s.[48]

The allure of the pastoral was nothing new in Western thought: it tapped into deep-seated religious, philosophical, and artistic traditions that romanticized the natural realm as a font of divine contemplation or redemption, shelter from political tyranny, and refuge from industrial consumerism. But the embrace of environmentalism by vast sectors of the middle class beginning in the 1970s was novel and reflective of socioeconomic changes in advanced industrial nations. As the number of educated Americans expanded in the postwar economy, filling the public sector, the arts, and the service industries, a larger proportion of the working-age population became disengaged from processes of industrial production. Moreover, the economic boom in North America and Western Europe during the 1980s meant that fewer people objected to environmental protection based on financial concerns.[49] The democratization of automobile ownership widened access to "wilderness" areas, liberating city dwellers from the drabness of urban life. Bedrocks of industrial production and pollution, cars became vehicles for nature worship and pastoral fantasy.[50] For the American Left, disillusioned by Vietnam and Watergate and demoralized by the Soviet model of socialism, ecological movements sustained Marxism's subversive transnational critique of materialism and individualism.[51] Others point out that environmental degradation, which had long victimized poor people and people of color, only became a white, middle-class political concern in the 1970s, when the decline in industrial production and the growth of private transport (purportedly) democratized issues such as pollution.[52]

In Brazil, a confluence of factors led to the growth of environmental politics in the 1980s: the rapid increase in pollution and environmental degradation in large urban areas that sensitized sectors of the middle class; the political reintegration of the Left following defeat of the guerrilla movements and the democratic opening initiated by the military; the emergence of new social movements and public debate; and Brazil's role as a developing nation with strong ties to the international market and media amid the worldwide proliferation of ecological movements.[53] The 1980s also witnessed the spread of environmental NGOs in Brazil, many of which received funding from foreign embassies and North American and European philanthropic organizations. These organizations would serve as a critical link in gathering and disseminating information and developing a network of individuals and organizations concerned with Amazonia.[54]

Tropical-forest depletion, of course, has a long history.[55] In the seventeenth century, for example, the Portuguese Crown protected various Brazilian timbers deemed critical for shipbuilding from felling, whether they were located on public or private property.[56] Eighteenth-century British officials, alarmed by the perceived climatological and pluvial effects of forest depletion in their tropical island colonies, reserved tracts of forest land.[57] Yet, as political scientists Margaret Keck and Kathryn Sikkink point out, the term "tropical deforestation" first gained widespread use among environmentalists only in the early 1970s. Before then, concern about tropical-forest loss fell under the rubric of habitat protection. The 1968 Latin American Conference on Conservation of Renewable Natural Resources had no session on forests, and the index of the *Bulletin* of the International Union for the Conservation of Nature and Natural Resources (IUCN) for 1967–1971 did not have an entry for "forest," "deforestation," or "tropical forest." The IUCN first took up the issue of tropical deforestation in 1972 in response to the Brazilian military's project to sponsor mass colonization in the Amazon. In 1973, the Organization of American States and various U.N. agencies cosponsored international meetings on the economic development of Latin American tropical-forest areas.[58]

Yet, if shifting economies, ecologies, vocabularies, and ethics helped give rise to international environmental movements, this still does not explain why combating Amazonian deforestation became one of their enduring causes. Does it reflect an old tendency of residents of the northern hemisphere to view tropical nature as lusher or purer than its temperate counterpart?[59] Does the very denomination of "deforestation" as shorthand for the multifaceted environmental and social changes in the Amazon prompted by massive land enclosures reveal the Western hallowing of trees, whose size, "prehistoric" origins, and self-regenerating energy embody the dignity and transcendence of nature that heirs to the Romantic tradition cherish, or is it an affirmation of life in death-denying industrial cultures?[60] Might this explain why popular incantation of the Amazon as a "rain forest" has supplanted other terms once widely used to describe the region, such as "valley," "basin," or the more nefarious-sounding "jungle?"[61] Is it, as Bruno Latour argues, that political ecology claims to speak on behalf of "the Whole," but can succeed in shaping public opinion and altering power relations only by "focusing on places, biotypes, situations, or particular events?"[62] Does Americans' overriding focus on tropical deforestation in South America—rather than on corresponding processes in Sumatra, Borneo, Congo and West Africa—reflect the Amazon's importance as the world's largest remaning tropical forest, or does it stem from an historical pattern of policing their nation's "backyard" in the Western Hemisphere?[63] Or perhaps, in media-driven, information-saturated societies, the burning of the rain forest has made for a riveting news report or a successful environmental fundraising campaign.[64] "Fire," notes Brazilian environmental scientist Alberto Setzer, "has a strange effect on people's minds. It attracts their attention."[65] Not to mention that putting a "Save the Rain Forest" bumper sticker on a car as a gesture of environmental consciousness represents far less of an inconvenience than opting for public transportation.

Science and the Remaking of the Amazon

The Amazon's geopolitical greening derives from more than socioeconomic and political transformations, environmental changes, media representations, and cultural-linguistic turns. It is also a story of how science and technology during the Cold War and its aftermath served not only to destroy the forest but also to recreate it. An early scientific breakthrough on tropical-forest ecologies occurred during the 1960s, when the US Atomic Energy Commission began to investigate the effects of a nuclear war or accidents on forests. Systems ecologist Howard Odum, subjecting tropical forests in Puerto Rico to radiation tests, found that wounding the ecosystem allowed for a greater understanding of the structure and functions of the forest, providing the first comprehensive study of a tropical forest and the emergence of a new generation of influential tropical ecologists. These specialists' new studies would underscore the ways in which nutrients are derived from and exchanged from the forest and its litter and held in the tissues of living organisms rather than in its shoddy soils.[66] The Brazilian military government's Projeto Radam, an aerial radar survey carried out for the benefit of mining companies and other potential investors, provided information on Amazonian geology and soils, while the more comprehensive and detailed data collected through the Landsat remote-sensing satellite program would be used to track deforestation.[67] Advances in remote sensing and GPS technologies, facilitating the demarcation of protective reserves, have automated processes previously carried out by field cartographers and surveyors.[68]

Conservation biology has also been key in reframing (and renaming) the significance of land-use change in the Amazon. Formalized in the 1980s, the discipline aimed to preserve ecosystems and habitats rather than simply species and to promote policies to reverse degradation. As historian of science David Takacs points out, the term "biodiversity" was a neologism coined by conservation biologists. Less tainted by connotations of class or geopolitical privilege than "wilderness protection," dissociated from the negative connotations of "nature," and uncompromised by the triage of the older endangered-species approach, biodiversity incorporated the conservation goals toward which many biologists really aimed (preservation of intact ecosystems and biotic processes) while still allowing the public to maintain the emotional grasp on charismatic icons. Whereas in 1988, "biodiversity" did not appear as a keyword in *Biological Abstracts*, in 1993 the term appeared seventy-two times.

Symbiotically linked to multiculturalism, which was also popularized in the 1980s, the notion of biodiversity spread across various academic disciplines as well as into the mass media.[69] Biodiversity was one of the major items on the agenda at the United Nations Conference on Environment and Development in Rio de Janeiro in 1992.

In this context, species depletion in Amazonia became a transnational problem. Researchers admonished that "barely 20 per cent of rainforest species had been catalogued" and warned that "up to 50 per cent of all animal and plant species, mostly of rainforest origin, will have vanished" by the late twenty-first century."[70] Had the Amazon forest been clear-cut 150 years earlier, as happened in the eastern woodlands of the United States, warned biologist Margery Oldfield, the immense value of *Hevea brasiliensis* might have been lost to posterity.[71] Oldfield's comparison highlights both the long-standing and shifting importance of Amazonian resources for the global economy: rubber trees, once the motor of the Amazon's economy and a critical input for US wartime industry, had become mere symbols of the preciousness of tropical biodiversity.

Climate science has likewise reframed the Amazon in the transnational arena by implicating deforestation in the process of global warming. Over the course of the twentieth century, the world's population quadrupled, as did the use of energy, resulting in a sixteenfold increase in the rate of carbon dioxide emissions. Still, the discovery of global warming has itself been the product of a circuitous scientific and political journey, as has its relationship with tropical deforestation. During the Cold War, the US government increased research funding for physical geoscience and meteorology in the interest of national defense and the potential waging of climatological warfare. The use of satellites to monitor global weather was first launched by the US Department of Defense in 1960 and significantly improved in the following decade. Radiocarbon, which came under intense study in the US amid wartime efforts to build nuclear weapons and postwar detection of radioactive fallout from Soviet nuclear tests, could be used to track the movement of carbon in the atmosphere. In 1951, the World Meteorological Organization was created at the United Nations, while the International Geophysics Year (1957–1958) drew together scientists from a dozen different disciplines and many nations to collaborate on research projects. Although tracking climate change per se remained a low national priority, technological innovations allowed scientists to measure carbon dioxide levels in the atmosphere, while new institutional forums enabled interdisciplinary and globalized research projects in previously balkanized fields of meteorology, oceanography, hydrology, geology, glaciology, and plant ecology. Funding and research on the implications of long-term climate change remained sparse well into the 1970s (and continued to examine as well the prospect of global cooling), yet a number of scientists increasingly argued that the heating of the atmosphere caused by the emission of carbon dioxide and other greenhouse gases might precipitate the melting of polar ice, a rise in water levels and inundation of productive lands, changes in the ozone layer, and increases in ultraviolet light radiation.[72]

With the 1980s witnessing the six hottest years then on record, talk of global warming migrated from arcane scientific journals to political forums, media reports, and everyday conversation. Anticorporate groups latched on to the cause as a bane of government deregulation. The environmental movement, which had taken only an occasional interest in the topic, took up global warming as a key plank, as groups with other objectives, such as preserving tropical forest, reducing air pollution, promoting renewable energy sources and removing government subsidies on fossil fuels, or slowing population growth could now find common cause. A 1981 survey found that only 38 percent of Americans had heard of or read about the greenhouse effect—the topic first made the front page of the *New York Times* that year—but by 1989, 79 percent of Americans were aware of it. Most notably perhaps, researchers and laypeople began to speak of or re-envision climates, no longer in the traditional sense of regional weather patterns, but as planetary systems. Northern populations and politicians became sensitized to the idea of global warming—even if many remained perplexed by its ramifications and unmoved by calls for lifestyle overhauls in response. Significantly, 1988 marked the creation at the United Nations of the Intergovernmental Panel on Climate Change (IPCC) to assemble and coordinate scientific information and recommend policy measures to reduce the emission of greenhouse gases.[73]

Land-use change in the Amazon has contributed to the greenhouse effect through the burning and decomposition of biomass; the repeated burning of pasture and secondary forest; methane emissions from cattle; the decomposition of plant matter in anaerobic conditions in areas flooded by hydroelectric dams; and logging.[74] In 1991, the World Bank estimated that deforestation in the Brazilian Amazon accounted for 4 percent of total carbon dioxide emissions, while the total contribution of deforestation worldwide to global warming, primarily from the release of carbon, was estimated at 14 percent in 1990. As a percentage of carbon dioxide emissions from fossil fuel burnings, deforestation worldwide accounted for 27 percent in 1989–1990, while the Brazilian Amazon, according to the Brazilian government, represented between 4.4 percent and 7.6 percent.[75] By the early 1990s, land-use change in Brazil accounted for the largest source (nearly 60 percent) of the nation's annual carbon dioxide emissions.[76]

During the 1980s, industrialized countries, which contained 26 percent of the world's population, accounted for 81 percent of energy consumption.[77] In 1990, the United States remained the world's single largest emitter of greenhouse gases, with a baseline emission of 1.6 billion tons of carbon that year from fossil fuel and cement.[78] Two-thirds of petroleum usage in the United States in the 1980s was by transport vehicles; carbon dioxide emitted by cars is believed to have contributed 55 percent to global warming between 1980 and 1990, with automobiles producing 65 percent of world emissions of carbon monoxide and 47 percent of nitrogen oxide.[79] Nevertheless, in the late 1980s and early 1990s, a number of politicians and members of the public in advanced industrial nations defined Amazonian deforestation as critical to the problem of global warming. In 1989, the German parliament held hearings on tropical deforestation and climate change and identified reduced deforestation as a priority to avoid global warming. Reports published by Greenpeace and Friends of the Earth–UK over the next two years contended that the most cost-effective mechanisms to counter the greenhouse effect were tropical reforestation and the slowing of deforestation. Prior to the U.N. Conference in Rio de Janeiro in 1992, tropical deforestation was considered a major contributor to global warming by European governments and European-based NGOs.[80]

Following the return to democracy in 1985, as Brazil faced the challenges of massive foreign debt, hyperinflation, and neoliberal reform, its political elite became increasingly sensitive to foreign censure and incentives to encourage environmental policy making in the Amazon. At the G7 Summit in Houston, Texas, in 1990, for example, the Pilot Program to Conserve the Brazilian Rainforest was launched, largely at the initiative of the German government. The Program consisted of a $300 million aid package administered through the World Bank (as trustee) and the Brazilian Ministry of the Environment, designed to support conservation and sustainable development in the Amazon and the Atlantic rain forest, while strengthening institutional capacity and environmental policymaking in Brazil.[81] In hosting the Eco-92 Conference in Rio de Janeiro, President Fernando Collor aimed to showcase Brazil's commitment to environmental protection.

The reframing of land use change in the Amazon as a transnational environmental problem in the 1980s stemmed not only from Brazilian state policies promoting frontier expansion but also from shifts in the North Atlantic and Brazilian political economy, the emergence of a global ecological movement, new technologies and forms of scientific knowledge, and media representation and cultural perceptions of the forest. Amazonian resources and populations had long been intrinsic to the processes of global development and scientific

knowledge, not to mention foundations of Brazilian nationalism, yet new material demands, ideological beliefs, and symbolic meanings have reinvented the
rain forest in international politics. Yet echoes of Malthusianism, which has
informed one strand of imperial and environmental policy making, resonate
in the Northern panic that developing nations are putting the entire world at
risk through deforestation or species depletion. Alternatively, the promotion of
tropical forest "carbon sinks" as an antidote to climate change can deflect political pressure and financial costs from the energy, manufacturing, agricultural,
and automobile industries in the United States and their advocates to promote
or invest in environmentally-friendly technologies.[82] Apocalypse, once again,
hinges on proper use of the Amazon's resources.

"Traditional Peoples": New Identities, Old Tropes

The greening of Amazonian politics is also the result of appropriation of environmental discourse by poor rural Brazilians confronting endemic violence
and social marginalization. In the mid-1970s and 1980s, as land closures
intensified in the Amazon, thousands of rubber tappers were expelled. Under
Brazilian law, squatters who consistently utilized an area for more than a year
without conflicting claims from other parties were granted possession, but
landowners used "legal" titles and violence to displace long-term residents.
With the assistance of the National Confederation of Rural Workers and the
Catholic Church, tappers brought a number of successful lawsuits demand-
ing indemnification of property, title for contested land, or allocation of land
parcels on government colonization projects.[83] Tappers in the state of Acre also
resorted to direct action in the form of the *empate,* or "standoff," in which they
would physically impede ranch workers from clearing forest for pastureland.
Between 1975 and 1988, forty-five *empates* were carried out, one-third of which
were successful. The repression that ensued was also staggering: 400 arrests,
40 cases of torture, and several assassinations.[84]

When the National Plan of Agrarian Reform was unveiled by the Brazilian
government in 1985, tappers founded the National Council of Rubber Tappers
to ensure that regional plans for the Amazon would accommodate the specific needs of extractivists.[85] The Council advocated the creation of extractive
reserves on federal land, with use regulated by a local community association
of tappers and other "traditional forest dwellers." The model for the communal
land use of federal territory was inspired by existing legislation covering indigenous reserves in Brazil; yet unlike indigenous peoples, whose constitutional
right to land is based on their status as original occupants, the rights of rubber

tappers and other "traditional peoples" would be contingent upon environmental stewardship.[86]

As tappers moved beyond the parameters of local politics to engage national and multinational actors in their struggles, they faced a crisis of political legibility.[87] The Amazonian population primarily comprised mestizos and acculturated Indians, as well as mixed-blood Northeastern migrants or their descendants. The miscegenated population of the Amazon, attesting to a long history of colonial rule, religious conversion, sexual violence, and migration, destabilizes master narratives of "unspoiled" landscapes. They have long been rendered invisible in historical and ethnographic accounts, as well as in developmentalist discourse.[88] Tappers' ballads, in fact, have celebrated their contributions to the nation-state: "Let's honor the tapper / let's honor the nation / cause thanks to the work of these people / we have automobiles and aviation."[89]

As "traditional peoples," tappers could stake their claim to a new form of symbolic capital and social status. Affirming the "desire to establish the broadest possible alliances with traditional peoples in Amazonia," the Tappers' Council called for "models of development that respect the way of life, cultures and traditions of forest peoples without destroying nature, and that improve the quality of life."[90] The link to indigenous peoples was more than organizational. Alongside the greening of social movements in the Brazilian Amazon in the 1980s came a "reddening" of cultural identity in a nation that had long enshrined whiteness.

With backing from international environmental NGOs and Brazilian anthropologists, rubber tappers gained leverage. Since the early 1980s, US and British environmental activists had begun to target ecologically destructive projects funded by multilateral banks, which were particularly vulnerable to pressure from the US Congress due to greater American financial contributions and voting shares. In Brazil, the World Bank had helped to fund aggressive road-building programs in the Amazon, and one of the first targets of the environmentalists was the Polonoroeste project in Rondônia in western Amazonia. Between 1983 and 1986, the US Congress held seventeen hearings related to multilateral development banks and the environment.[91]

The success of the campaign rested, in part, on the courtship between Northern environmentalists and battle-hardened rubber tappers in western Amazonia. In 1985, environmentalists established contact with Chico Mendes, a tapper and labor organizer who had been involved for more than a decade in organizing rubber tappers in Acre to oppose eviction. The relationship allowed tappers to gain international allies in their struggle for social justice, while for environmentalists, the tappers put a human face on the woes of deforestation, offered an alternative to large-scale development projects, and a defense against accusations that the destruction of the rain forest was only of concern to privileged foreigners.[92] In 1987, Mendes traveled to the United States to meet with members of Congress and staff of the World Bank and the Inter-American Development Bank to oppose the Brazilian government's efforts to secure funding for a proposed road-paving linking Porto Velho to Rio Branco under the Polonoroeste project. Lobbying by environmentalist groups led to the suspension of more than half of World Bank disbursements for Polonoroeste, representing the first time that the Bank had halted a loan for environmental reasons.[93]

Grassroots activism was met with violence and political concessions. In 1988, Mendes was assassinated by a rancher, one of ninety rural workers killed in Brazil that year.[94] The following year, however, an amendment to Brazil's National Environmental Policy Act formally established extractive reserves as a distinct type of conservation unit that allows for extraction of natural resources by residents. Community associations received the contract for exclusive land use, granting free concessions for sixty years to individual members who have resided in the area for at least one year. As of 1994, the total area of the nine extractive reserves (eight of which were in Amazonia) was 22,007 square kilometers, with a total population of 28,460.[95]

The embrace of a "traditional" identity inseparable from environmental calling allowed tappers to score important political and territorial victories, yet it came with its own traps. The reserves premise the sustainability of communities on the maintenance of precarious extractive activities. The removal of federal subsidies for rubber in the 1990s and the inability of Amazonian latex to compete with its Asian rivals have resulted in hardship for residents of extractive reserves. The lack of adequate housing, education, health care, and transportation has led to out-migration.[96] Neither as the rear guard against the Axis nor as the safeguard against global warming have tappers been able to escape crushing poverty.

If Iberian conquest inserted the Brazilian Amazon into the world economy, the region's bumpy integration owes to the varied and contested uses of natural resources whose management has both driven and defied the initiatives of individual nation-states. An overview of the Amazon's wartime and postwar history elucidates such trends. Facing a rubber shortage, US wartime policy makers viewed and demanded Amazonian latex as a key industrial input to buttress global democracy. Reckoning with postwar deforestation, environmentalists, scientists, politicians, and media recast the Amazon as the preserve of an imagined global environmental community. And confronting ecosystems that stymied the consolidation of state power and capital accumulation, the Brazilian government repeatedly turned to transnational actors for assistance.

The contingency of forest resources, however, cannot be understood solely in terms of material use or depletion. The reincarnation of the Amazon as a transnational ecological sanctum has emanated as well from shifts in industrial economies, scientific and technological innovations, emergent political and grass roots movements, and novel cultural values and vocabularies. All the while, struggles in and over the Amazon have remained rife with recriminations over the nature of civilization in the tropics.

As historian Roger Chartier notes, the fundamental object of a history resides in the "tension between the inventive capacities of individuals or communities and the constraints, norms, and conventions that limit—more or less forcibly according to their position in the relations of domination—what is possible for them to think, to express, to do."[97] Histories of the Amazon are haunted by such tensions, which have threaded the colonial and postcolonial webs of power that enmeshed tropical landscapes and peoples. Indeed, it is precisely because the Amazon is not just a site for accumulation or a set of ecosystems or policy points, but a flashpoint for notions of morality, race, and nation, that knowledge of its nature (and the nature of knowledge about it) will continue to stir controversy for some time to come.

NOTES

1. Mark London and Brian Kelly, *The Last Forest: The Amazon in the Age of Globalization* (New York: Random House, 2007).

2. David Cleary, "Extractivists, Indigenes, and Protected Areas: Science and Conservation Policy in the Amazon," in *Global Impact, Local Action: New Environmental Policy in Latin America*, ed. Anthony Hall (London: Institute for the Study of the Americas, 2005), 199–216.

3. For an overview, see Ans Kolk, *Forests in International Environmental Politics: International Organisations, NGOS, and the Brazilian Amazon* (Utrecht: International Books, 1996); and Luiz C. Barbosa, *The Brazilian Amazon Rainforest: Global Ecopolitics, Development, and Democracy* (Lanham, MD: University Press of America, 2000). For British NGOs, see Andréa Zhouri, "Árvores e gente no ativismo transnacional: As dimensões social e ambiental na perspectiva dos campaigners britânicos pela Floresta Amazônica," *Revista de Antropologia* 44, no. 1 (2001): 9–52.

4. See Antonio Carlos Diegues, *O Mito Moderno da Natureza Intocada*, 5th ed., (São Paulo: Hucitec; NUPAUB/USP, 2004).

5. Philip M. Fearnside, "Global Implications of Amazon Frontier Settlement: Carbon, Kyoto, and the Role of Amazonian Deforestation," in Hall, *Global Impact*, 36–64.

6. Donald Worster, *Nature's Economy: A History of Ecological Ideas*, 2nd ed., (Cambridge: Cambridge University Press, 1994). For Brazil, see José Augusto Pádua, "Natureza e Projeto Nacional: As Origens da Ecologia Política no Brasil," in *Ecologia*

e Política no Brasil, ed. José Augusto Pádua (Rio de Janeiro: Espaço e Tempo; IUPERJ, 1987), 11–62.

7. Richard White, "Are You an Environmentalist or Do You Work for a Living? Work and Nature," in *Uncommon Ground: Rethinking the Human Place in Nature,* ed. William Cronon (New York: Norton,1996), 171–85.

8. See Roberto Santos, *História econômica da Amazônia, 1800–1920* (São Paulo: T. A. Queiroz, 1980); and David G. Sweet, "A Rich Realm of Nature Destroyed: The Middle Amazon Valley, 1640–1750," PhD diss., University of Wisconsin, Madison, 1974.

9. See Susanna Hecht and Alexander Cockburn, *The Fate of the Forest: Developers, Destroyers, and Defenders of the Amazon* (New York: Harper Perennial, 1990), 55–72.

10. See Margaret E. Keck, "Social Equity and Environmental Politics in Brazil: Lessons from the Rubber Tappers of Acre," *Comparative Politics* 27, no. 4 (July 1995): 409–24; and Elizabeth Dore, "Capitalism and Ecological Crisis: Legacy of the 1980s," in *Green Guerrillas: Environmental Conflicts and Initiatives in Latin America and the Caribbean,* ed. Helen Collinson (Nottingham: Russell Press, 1996), 8–19. On environmentalism as a "vocabulary of protest" for the poor, see Ramachandra Guha and Juan Martinez-Allier, *Varieties of Environmentalism: Essays North and South* (London: Earthscan Publications, 1997).

11. See Barbara Weinstein, *The Amazon Rubber Boom, 1850–1920* (Palo Alto, CA: Stanford University Press, 1983).

12. Jonathan Marshall, *To Have and Have Not: Southeast Asian Raw Materials and the Origins of the Pacific War* (Berkeley: University of California Press, 1995), 23; William M. Tuttle, Jr., "The Birth of an Industry: The Synthetic Rubber 'Mess' in World War II," *Technology and Culture* 22, no. 1 (January 1981): 65; and K. E. Knorr, *World Rubber and Its Regulation* (Palo Alto, CA: Stanford University Press, 1945), 46.

13. E. L. Demmon, "Rubber Production Opportunities in the American Tropics," *Journal of Forestry* 40, no. 3 (March 1942): 209; Dean, *Brazil and the Struggle for Rubber,* 69; Stephen D. Krasner, *Defending the National Interest: Raw Materials Investments and U.S. Foreign Policy* (Princeton, NJ: Princeton University Press, 1978), 101.

14. On the Ford plantations, see Greg Grandin, *Fordlandia: The Rise and Fall of Henry Ford's Forgotten Jungle City* (New York: Metropolitan Books, 2009); John Galey, "Industrialist in the Wilderness: Henry Ford's Amazon Venture," *Journal of Interamerican Studies and World Affairs* 21, no. 2 (May 1979): 261–89.

15. See Alfred E. Eckes, *The United States and the Global Struggle for Minerals* (Austin: University of Texas Press, 1979), 103–4; and Stephen D. Krasner, *Defending the National Interest: Raw Materials Investments and U.S. Foreign Policy* (Princeton, NJ: Princeton University Press, 1978), 101–6.

16. Austin Coates, *The Commerce in Rubber: The First 250 Years* (Singapore/ New York: Oxford University Press, 1987), 137–9.

17. Charles Morrow Wilson, *Trees and Test Tubes: The Story of Rubber* (New York: H. Holt and Company, 1943), 222–5; Alfred Lief, *The Firestone Story: A History of the Firestone Tire & Rubber Company* (New York: Whittlesey House, 1951), 264.

18. Tuttle, "Birth of an Industry," 62–5. On the role of chemists and botanists in contributing to global inequalities, see Daniel R. Headrick, "Botany, Chemistry, and Tropical Development," *Journal of World History* 7, no. 1 (1996): 14.

19. Warren Dean, *Brazil and the Struggle for Rubber: A Study in Environmental History* (Cambridge / New York: Cambridge University Press, 1987)

20. Earl Parker Hanson, *The Amazon: A New Frontier?* (New York: Foreign Policy Association, 1944), 14.

21. Roberto Ribeiro Corrêa, "BASA: Seis Décadas de Mudança Institucional," in *Amazônia: Terra e Civilização,* vol. 2, ed. Armando Dias Mendes (Belém: BASA, 2004), 557.

22. Harold E. Gustin to B.V. Worth, Manaus, September 4, 1942, Princeton University Library (hereafter, PUL), Rubber Development Corporation, Amazon Division (hereafter, RDCAD), box 3, Rubber Tapping and Production Methods 11/6–7.

23. Constantine J. Alexopoulos and H. Caldeira Filho, Special Report no. 1: The Seringaes of Raymundo Bessaa on the River Javary, Benjamin Constant, January 23, 1944, PUL, RDCAD, box 5, Technician Reports 5/2.

24. E. B. Hamill to All Technicians, "Excerpt from a memorandum of Field Technician Becker on the Muaná District," Manaus, October 11, 1943, PUL, RDCAD, box 8, Tech Reports 4/8.

25. Environmental Law Institute Staff, *Brazil's Extractive Reserves: Fundamental Aspects of Their Implementation* (1992), 7. While extractivism can range from collection to annihilation, rubber tapping has been more typically defined in the contemporary literature as the former. See Mary Helena Allegretti, "The Amazon and Extracting Activities" in *Brazilian Perspectives on Sustainable Development of the Amazon Region,* ed. Miguel Clüsener Godt and Ignacy Sachs (Paris: UNESCO and Carnforth, UK: Parthenon Publishing, 1995), 158–62.

26. On American rubber plantations in Southeast Asia, see Richard P. Tucker, *Insatiable Appetite: The United States and the Ecological Degradation of the Tropical World* (Berkeley: University of California Press, 2000), 226–82.

27. "New Area Report on Upper Solimões Region: Rio Itecoarí and Affluents: Rio Branco and Rio das Pedras" by Constantine J. Alexopoulos, field tech, and Herculano Caldeira Filho, March 25, 1944, MML, RDC, ADR, box 9, Folder Technicians Report ALEXOPOULOS HERCULANO CALDEIRA FILHO.

28. See Pádua, "Natureza e Projeto Nacional," 39.

29. See Stephen Bunker, *Underdeveloping the Amazon: Extraction, Unequal Exchange and the Failure of the Modern State* (Urbana: University of Illinois Press, 1985).

30. See Kent H. Redford, "The Ecologically Noble Savage," *Orion Nature Quarterly* 9, no. 3 (1990): 24–9; Shepard Krech III, *The Ecological Indian: Myth and History* (New York: Norton, 1999); Douglas J. Buege, "The Ecologically Noble Savage Revisited," *Environmental Ethics* 18, no. 1 (spring 1986): 71–88; and Larry Lohmann, "Green Orientalism," *Ecologist* 23, no. 6 (1993): 202–4. For an overview of the debate, see Kay Milton, *Environmentalism and Cultural Theory* (London / New York: Routledge, 1996), especially chaps. 4 and 6.

31. See Allegretti, "Amazon and Extracting Activities."

32. Henry Albert Phillips, *Brazil: Bulwark of Inter-American Relations* (New York: Hastings House, 1945), 28–9.

33. Environmental Law Institute Staff, *Brazil's Extractive Reserves,* 7.

34. See Hecht and Cockburn, *Fate of the Forest*; Dennis Mahar, *Frontier Development Policy in Brazil: A Study of Amazonia* (New York: Praeger, 1979); Marianne Schmink and Charles H. Wood, eds., *Frontier Expansion in Amazonia* (Gainesville: University of Florida Press, 1984.

35. Environmental Law Institute Staff, *Brazil's Extractive Reserves*, 14 no. 8.

36. Hervé Théry, "New Frontiers in the Amazon," in Hall, *Global Impact, Local Action*, 65; Anna Luiza Ozorio de Almeida, *The Colonization of the Amazon, 1970–1980* (Austin: University of Texas Press, 1992).

37. David Goodman and Anthony Hall, introduction to *The Future of Amazonia: Destruction or Sustainable Development*, ed. Goodman and Hall (New York: St. Martin's Press, 1990), 10.

38. Kolk, *Forests in International Environmental Politics*, 72–5; London and Kelly, *The Last Forest*, 147, 179.

39. See Charles Wood and Roberto Porro, eds., *Deforestation and Land Use in the Amazon* (Gainesville: University of Florida Press, 2002); Lee J. Alston, Gary D. Libecap, and Bernardo Mueller, *Titles, Conflict, and Land Use: The Development of Property Rights and Land Reform on the Brazilian Amazon Frontier* (Ann Arbor: University of Michigan Press, 1999); Hecht and Cockburn, *Fate of the Forest*

40. Fearnside, "Global Implications," 41.

41. João S. Campari, *The Economics of Deforestation in the Amazon: Dispelling the Myths* (Cheltenham, UK / Northampton, MA: Edward Elgar, 2005).

42. Hecht and Cockburn, *Fate of the Forest*, 54.

43. Kolk, *Forests in International Environmental Politics*, 79–81.

44. Anthony Hall, "Environment and Development in Brazilian Amazonia: From Protectionism to Productive Conservation," in *Amazonia at the Crossroads: the Challenge of Sustainable Development*, ed. Anthony Hall (London: Institute of Latin-American Studies, 2000), 100.

45. Kolk, *Forests in International Environmental Politics*, 65–6.

46. Margaret E. Keck, "Social Equity," 409–24.

47. See John McCormick, *Reclaiming Paradise: The Global Environmental Movement* (Bloomington: Indiana University Press, 1989); Worster, *Nature's Economy*, 339–48.

48. Margaret E. Keck and Kathryn Sikkink, *Activists beyond Borders: Advocacy Networks in International Politics* (Ithaca, NY: Cornell University Press, 1998), 10–1; 128.

49. Mary Douglas and Aaron Wildavsky, *Risk and Culture: An Essay on the Selection of Technical and Environmental Dangers* (Berkeley: University of California Press, 1982), 157–64.

50. Guha and Martinez-Allier, *Varieties of Environmentalism*, 16–7. See also Paul Sutter, *Driven Wild: How the Fight Against Automobiles Launched the Modern Wilderness Movement* (Seattle: University of Washington Press, 2002)

51. Douglas and Wildavsky, *Risk and Culture*, 157–64; Eduardo Viola, "O movimento ecológico no Brasil (1974–1986): Do ambientalismo à ecopolítica," in Pádua, *Ecologia e Política no Brasil*, 68–70.

52. Peter Thompson, "New Age Mysticism, Postmodernism and Human Liberation," in *Green Thought in German Culture: Historical and Contemporary Perspectives*, ed. Colin Riordan (Cardiff: University of Wales Press, 1997), 112.

53. Viola, *O Movimento Ecológico no Brasil*, 108.

54. Marianne Schmink, "Amazonian Resistance Movements," in *Ecological Disorder in Amazonia: Social Aspects*, ed. Leszek Kosinski (Paris: UNESCO), 157.

55. See Michael Williams, *Deforesting the Earth: From Prehistory to Global Crisis* (Chicago: University of Chicago Press, 2006).

56. Shawn William Miller, *Fruitless Trees: Portuguese Conservation and Brazil's Colonial Timber* (Palo Alto, CA: Stanford University Press, 2000).

57. Richard H. Grove, *Green Imperialism: Colonial Expansion, Tropical Island Edens, and the Origins of Environmentalism, 1600–1860* (Cambridge: Cambridge University Press).

58. Keck and Sikkink, *Activists beyond Borders*, 133–5.

59. See Candace Slater, *Entangled Edens: Visions of the Amazon* (Berkeley and Los Angeles: University of California Press, 2002); Nancy Stepan, *Picturing Tropical Nature* (Ithaca, NY: Cornell University Press, 2001).

60. Laura Rival, "Trees: From Symbols of Life and Regeneration to Political Artefacts," in *The Social Life of Trees: Anthropological Perspectives on Tree Symbolism*, ed. Laura Rival (Oxford / New York: Berg, 1998), 1–36; and Angie Zelter, "Grassroots Campaigning for the World's Forests," in ibid., 221–32.

61. Slater, *Entangled Edens*, 137–9.

62. Bruno Latour, *Politics of Nature: How to Bring the Sciences into Democracy*, trans. Catherine Porter (Cambridge, MA: Harvard University Press, 2004), 21.

63. Shawn William Miller, *An Environmental History of Latin America* (Cambridge: Cambridge University Press, 2007), 194.

64. Eduardo Gudynas, "The Fallacy of Ecomessianism: Observations from Latin America," in *Global Ecology: A New Arena of Political Conflict*, ed. Wolfgang Sachs (London: Zed Books, 1993), 171.

65. Quoted in Andrew Revkin, *The Burning Season: The Murder of Chico Mendes and the Fight for the Amazon Rain Forest* (Boston, MA: Houghton Mifflin, 1990), 236.

66. Hecht and Cockburn, *Fate of the Forest*, 41.

67. Roger D. Stone, *Dreams of Amazonia* (New York: Penguin Books, 1986), 149.

68. Cleary, "Extractivists, Indigenes," 212.

69. David Takacs, *The Idea of Biodiversity: Philosophies of Paradise* (Baltimore, MD: Johns Hopkins University Press, 1996), 37– 83.

70. Goodman and Hall, introduction, 2.

71. Stone, *Dreams of Amazonia*, 153.

72. Spencer Weart, *The Discovery of Global Warming* (Cambridge, MA: Harvard University Press, 2003), 21–35, 110.

73. Ibid.,116; 142–60.

74. Fearnside, "Global Implications," 36.

75. Kolk, *Forests in International Environmental Politics*, 84.

76. Pew Center on Global Climate Change, *Climate Change Mitigation in Developing Countries: Brazil, China, India, Mexico, South Africa, and Turkey* (October 2002), 15, www.pewclimate.org/docuploads/dev_mitigation.pdf.

77. Arturo Escobar, *Encountering Development: The Making and Unmaking of the Third World* (Princeton, NJ: Princeton University Press, 1995), 212.

78. Fearnside, "Global Implications," 50.

79. See Julia Meaton and David Morrice, "The Ethics and Politics of Private Automobile Use," in *Environmental Ethics* 18, no. 1 (spring 1986): 42–5.

80. Fearnside, "Global Implications," 45–51.

81. See Hall, "Environment and Development," 102.

82. See the discussion in Fearnside, "Global Implications."

83. Keck, "Social Equity and Environmental Politics," 413.

84. Chico Mendes, *Fight for the Forest: Chico Mendes in His Own Words* (New York: Monthly Review Press, 1992), 81. See also Revkin, *Burning Season*.

85. Keith Bakx, "The Shanty Town, Final Stage of Rural Development? The Case of Acre," in Hall, *Future of Amazonia*, 52.

86. See Mary Allegretti, "Extractive Reserves: An Alternative an Alternative for Reconciling Development and Environmental Conservation in Amazonia," in *Alternatives to Deforestation: Steps toward Sustainable Use of the Amazon Rain Forest*, ed. Anthony B. Anderson (New York: Columbia University Press, 1990), 257–8; Manuela Carneiro da Cunha and Mauro W. Barbosa de Almeida "Populações Tradicionais e Conservação Ambiental," in *Biodiversidade Amazônica—Avaliação e Ações Prioritárias para a Conservação, Uso Sustentável e Repartição de Benefícios*, ed. João P. R. Capobianco et al., (Instituto Socioambiental, 2001), 184 n.1.

87. On the question of "legitimacy" in Amazonian political discourse, see Beth A. Conklin, "Body Paint, Feathers, and VCRs: Aesthetics and Authenticity in Amazonian Activism," *American Ethnologist* 24, no. 4 (1997): 711–37.

88. See Stephen Nugent, *Amazonian Caboclo Society: An Essay on Invisibility and Peasant Economy* (Providence, RI / Oxford: Berg, 1993).

89. "Hino do Seringueiro" excerpted from *Frutíferas e Plantas Úteis da Vida Amazônica*, ed. Patricia Shanley and Gabriel Medina (Belém: CIFOR and IMAZON, 2005), 284.

90. Quoted in Hecht and Cockburn, *Fate of the Forest*, 262–3.

91. Keck and Sikkink, *Activists beyond Borders*, 137–9.

92. Keck, "Social Equity," 409–24.

93. Goodman and Hall, introduction, 14–15.

94. See Keck, "Social Equity," 409–24.

95. Environmental Law Institute Staff, *Brazil's Extractive Reserves*, 11–31.

96. Ibid., 46–7; Anthony Hall, "Did Chico Mendes Die in Vain? Brazilian Rubber Tappers in the 1990s," in Collinson, *Green Guerrillas*, 97; London and Kelly, *Last Forest*, 200–04.

97. Roger Chartier, *Forms and Meanings: Texts, Performances, and Audiences from Codex to Computer* (Philadelphia: University of Pennsylvania Press, 1995), 96.

12

International Trash and the Politics of Poverty

Conceptualizing the Transnational Waste Trade

Emily Brownell

In 2008, Sugule Ali, a spokesman for the Somali pirates, attempted to invert the developing news narrative about the recent string of attacks on merchant ships off the coast of Somalia. "We don't consider ourselves sea bandits," he said. "We consider sea bandits those who illegally fish in our seas and dump waste in our seas and carry weapons in our seas. We are simply patrolling our seas. Think of us like a coast guard."[1] Although they were portrayed internationally as criminals preying on global commerce in the wake of a failed state, these pirates portrayed themselves as fishermen who can no longer fish. In the twenty years since Somalia collapsed, foreign firms capitalizing on the nation's precarious statehood have dumped toxic waste and illegally fished along the coast, decimating fish populations and ruining local economies. Januna Ali Jama, a spokesman for the pirates in Puntland,[2] explained that the ransom for the pirates is a way of "reacting to the toxic waste that has been continually dumped on the shores of our country for nearly 20 years...the Somali coastline has been destroyed, and we believe this money is nothing compared to the devastation that we have seen on the seas."[3] The United Nations confirmed that the practice of dumping had occurred since the civil war in the 1990s, when European firms realized it was far cheaper to dump illegally off the coast of Somalia, at a cost of about $2.50 a ton, than to pay waste disposal costs in Europe that could be as high as $1000 a ton.[4] One of the complicated narratives highlighted by Somalia's recent history is the vulnerability of transnational environments to the political geography of nation-states.

Transnational environments are often defined, not by commonalities and continuities that transcend political borders, but by how cultural, legal, and political differences among these borders leave room for exploitation. Countries, corporations, and even individuals who exploit the gap in the cost and regulation of waste disposal across borders are seeking a path of least resistance for waste storage. In the absence of safeguards for protecting the environment and public health, waste often settles into the unseen margins. In the past thirty years, as disposal has been transformed from a local into a global problem, the international waste trade has become a complex aspect of globalized commerce. Environmental and legal scholar Daniel Etsy tells us that this kind of transformation of scale is not usually the result of a trend becoming global, but of industries in a few regions seeking out cheaper costs and lower regulations. Shipping waste across the world to dispose of it cheaply typifies the potential ramifications of this uneven geography of production and disposal. With liberalized trade and global competition for shares in markets, each nation's environmental regulations become essential in determining how competitive different industries within its borders will be.[5] The end result of this market competition is the increased transboundary movement of industries and objects, leading often to local problems writ large in global economies and environments.[6]

This chapter broadly suggests that looking at the international waste trade provides not just a compelling case for examining these transboundary processes, but can also reveal a compelling method for considering transnational environments. In the pages that follow, I propose a framework for examining biological, political, and conceptual transformations of waste across borders. Specifically, I examine different permutations of the transnational waste trade, focusing on Africa and how waste, along with the people and environments it affects, has been transformed in manifest ways through global exchange. I then provide three brief examples of this flow of discarded goods: hazardous waste trade, the used clothing industry, and food "dumping." These exemplify three different conceptions of waste: waste that is jettisoned because it is a potential hazard and faces expensive disposal back home; items that have been used by their original owners but are sent abroad to be resold; and unused commodities that are sent abroad to protect their domestic market value. The trade of all three, along with the waste trade in general, has been variously considered benevolent or encumbering. I use these examples to highlight the different potential fates of jettisoned objects and to suggest that thinking about the movement of objects as much as the cargo itself, forces a reckoning with moral questions about global and local environments and economies.

Theorizing Waste as Transnational Environmental History

Ironically, one of waste's most salient characteristics, and which so often provokes the interest of scholars, is its mutability. Historians, anthropologists, and sociologists have all written about its ability to change categories and characteristics with apparent ease, to be defined based on its context rather than its content. Sociologist Zsuzsa Gille, in her book on waste in socialist and postsocialist Hungary, stresses that waste, by its very nature, is liminal, and she goes so far as to compare it to transitional people, objects, and/or events such as, "hermaphroditism, or ritually marked points in an individual's or a group's life, in which they are suspended between two states."[7] Because it occupies a "no-man's-land" wedged between objecthood and oblivion, much is at stake in the way different individuals, groups, or nations classify or name waste. Waste issues thus always force a confrontation with real or conceptual boundaries, especially if we foreground the moral, political, and social dimensions of waste categorization and disposal in that analysis.[8]

Richard Foltz recently challenged historians of world history and environmental history to follow "the principle of reintegration [and] transcend our fragmented ways of knowing."[9] He urged that both fields confront the new collective reality of the global environment and realize that "we can never throw anything away because on an ever-shrinking planet there is no such place as 'away,'" and furthermore, that "we can never 'do only one thing,' because no action occurs in isolation, and containment is an impossibility."[10] Essentially, Foltz is advocating that a good environmental ethos makes for good historical practice. Transnational environmental historians must trace histories latitudinally as well as longitudinally, paying attention to the conservation of matter across space when histories cannot be contained within national borders. There is, then, a natural synergy to reconsidering the boundaries of waste trading and environmental history together: both force us to reckon with where things go, the multiple reverberations of any single action, and how these objects (and their stories) change in their new milieu.

International waste trading has evolved since the 1970s based on the very notion of creating an "away" vast enough and cheap enough to meet the West's consumption. The waste disposal industry relied on exploiting the notion of "away" long before the 1970s, but in North America waste disposal remained mainly within national borders. Ultimately though, domestic disposal reached a crisis point in the face of a growing environmental-justice movement, bad publicity, and increasing government regulation that pushed waste into the as yet unregulated and vastly cheaper world of international dumping. As Gille writes, since waste "as any form of matter . . . cannot be made to disappear . . . the next best thing is getting it out of sight—that is, lifting it from the actual milieu in which it was generated."[11] Yet, through the act of displacement, waste tends to proliferate.[12] Urban historians looking at how municipalities confronted the dilemma of waste disposal in rapidly growing American cities have written on the issue of proliferation before transnational waste dumping. As urban historian Joel Tarr reminds us, confronting waste's propagation in one area leads to further displacement, usually requiring even more sophisticated solutions.[13] It also displaces the dilemma of disposing waste on a population that did not generate it. An example of the complex fallout of displaced waste, the Goshute Indians in Utah who, after being given barren land (in essence, wasted land) by the US government that they could not use for anything else, leased acreage for the storage of "forty thousand metric tons of high-level radioactive waste," to the chagrin of local and state governments who did not want to deal with the potential environmental fallout.[14] Epitomizing the NIMBY (not in my backyard) syndrome that evolved in the United States during the 1970s and 1980s, both the distance and the connection between waste generation and waste disposal began to grow, its geography and trajectory dictated by those powerful enough and vociferous enough to redirect it out of their own backyards.[15]

To narrate a history of waste in a transnational context, then, requires seeking out these attempts to create an "away" and reincorporating them into the narrative. Geographer Caitlin Desilvey's work on observing the transition of cultural objects into biological ones provides a model for dealing with the mutability of things over time, which we can apply across space as well.[16] While working as a preservationist on an old farmhouse in Montana, she began to ask herself if she should really be rescuing old pots and books from decay, enforcing their role solely as objects with distinct cultural meanings. As both a historian and an ecologist, DeSilvey wrestled opposing urges: to preserve objects from obsolescence and to defer to natural processes. Abandoning the preservationist impulse, she began to imagine a purpose in considering different interpretations of these objects if she scrutinized them as they decayed. This approach, she writes, encourages "engagements with degraded and fragmented things."[17] Like Gille, DeSilvey was interested in the social effects objects produce in their destruction as opposed to their preservation. In toying with these questions, DeSilvey remembers Rebecca Solnit's observation that, "thinking about natural history and human history is like looking at one of those trick drawings, a wineglass that becomes a pair of kissing profiles. It's hard to see them both at the same time."[18] Solnit's observation holds true for waste as well: though they are one in the same, it is difficult to simultaneously see the former object of value and the present discarded object. Looking anew at discarded and forgotten objects forced Desilvey to blur the boundary between an artifact and "ecofact," provoking questions about the social effects of crossing (and in the case of waste, often crisscrossing) this cognitive barrier.[19]

By "observing decay," or engaging with the declension of objects, we can perhaps see more clearly the range of possible reverberations and reincarnations they can have in a new location. As an object with a certain cultural designation, such as a children's toy or a computer, is disarticulated in one context, it becomes rearticulated elsewhere, in an array of possible cultural and biological incarnations, from ending up in a landfill to being resold, recycled or remanufactured, affecting local and national markets, to leaching chemicals into groundwater. DeSilvey concludes, "objects have to fall into desuetude at one level in order to come more fully into their own at another."[20] From a state of desuetude, objects become a range of new incarnations, from the highly hazardous to the ecologically sound and useful. The toxic waste trade, the used-clothing industry in East Africa, and food dumping in West Africa are different "ecofacts," each displaying different permutations of "decay" upon their arrival in Africa.

Africa as the "Wasted" Continent

> The Russian astronauts flying in space
> Radioed a puzzle to their Moscow base
> They said we are flying over Nigeria
> And we see high mountains in built-up area
> Right in the middle of heavy traffic
> Is this space madness, tell us quick
> The facts were fed to their master computer
> Which soon analyzed the mystery factor
> "that ain't no mountain," the computer said, snappish!
> It's just a load of their national rubbish!"[21]

When Lawrence Summers was chief economist for the World Bank in 1991, he wrote a memo on what to consider when deciding where to dump pollution and waste. "Health impairing pollution," he wrote "should be done in the country with the lowest cost, which will be the country with the lowest wage....I think the economic logic behind dumping a load of toxic waste in the lowest wage country is impeccable and we should face up to that."[22] Furthermore, Summers added, "The concern over an agent that causes a one in a million change in the odds of prostate cancer is obviously going to be much higher in a country where people survive to get prostrate cancer than in a country where under 5 mortality is 200 per thousand."[23] While he later dismissed his memo as sarcastic, for environmental activists—and African politicians—Summers's language confirmed their suspicions that waste dumping was brokered and executed with conscious disregard for the communities it polluted. For the governments and industries of the West, getting rid of garbage represented little more than an economic calculation of risk that saw poverty and its accompanying problems as a justification for dumping, rather than a deterrent. Receiving waste, or wasted products, is part of a much longer history than the explicit trade itself, and is part of a larger narrative of Africa being perceived as a wasted continent. When African nations are offered sums of money nearly equaling their GDP to house toxic waste, the psychological and political dimensions of poverty cloud any potential judgment of whether the exchange is benevolent or encumbering, ingenious or desperate.

The administration of International Monetary Fund and World Bank Structural Adjustment Programs (SAPs) in the early 1980s compounded this new flow of waste from the industrialized world. Among other prescriptions and restrictions, SAPs required African countries to abide by trade agreements that encouraged foreign consumer goods to flood urban markets. In 1992, political scientist Gwyn Prins noted that in the past twenty years the predominant agents of change and arbiters of the relationship between the developing and the developed world have been these large commercial lending agencies and other "non-state actors."[24] And yet the aggregate impact of these nonstate agents has worked in opposition to the stated political goals of development.[25] "Sustainable growth," "conservation," and "environmental stewardship" were popular buzzwords in international politics as new approaches to development, but the pressures of loan repayment dictated a very different reality. Waste dumping during the 1980s is just one part of the broader economic transactions that repayment often outlined. Along with the waste that was coming off of boats, a tide of domestically produced rubbish began mounting in tight urban spaces owing to a marriage of struggling economies and cheap consumer goods. All the while, SAPs were dictating funding cuts for the municipal programs and services that would have to deal with this influx in waste. The poorer residents of cities surviving in the urban margins went from creating little inorganic waste, to sometimes living off of waste—building their houses out of it, collecting recyclables to sell, and refurbishing discarded goods.[26] In a matter of a few decades, a confluence of factors had dramatically reconfigured the developing world's relationship with waste. Across the continent, Africans did not fail to notice and remark upon their new polluted landscape.

Scholars have since begun unpacking what this period has bequeathed Africans culturally as well as economically. For example, literary theorist Sarah Lincoln's work examines how African writers have responded to the "continent's continued status as a 'remnant' of globalization—a waste product, trash heap, disposable raw material." Invoking the work of previous literary critics, she employs the term "excremental vision" to explore how African authors, poets, and filmmakers have reflected on these transformations in their communities and environments.[27] The recent toxic waste spill in Abidjan, Cote d'Ivoire, for example, had the media charting the city's descent, from the promise of "Abijan la belle" to "Abidjan la poubelle" (Abidjan the trash can), as it was forced to reckon with the real health consequences signaled by this new turn of phrase:

> The stench of gasoline and rotten eggs that announced the arrival
> of the European sludge only confirmed this diagnosis of the radical
> failure of the country's dreams of integration into global networks of
> production and exchange;' instead of production, or even productive
> consumption, Cote, D'Ivoire had joined the rest of Africa in its busi-
> ness of consuming, willingly or unwillingly, the toxic remainders of
> those processes.[28]

This characterization echoes anthropologist Stanley Diamond's 1963 observation that "Africans are being forced to substitute a mere strategy of poverty and survival for authentic cultural expression."[29] "Put another way," Diamond added, "they are being rapidly converted into marginal producers and marginal consumers on the remotest fringes of contemporary industrial society."[30] Beyond authors and playwrights, Africans have developed profoundly interesting forms of cultural expression and economic ingenuity for coping in these extreme circumstances. And yet, there is always the risk of imbuing these practical choices with more explanatory power and agency than they deserve.

One source of anecdotal evidence of Africans responding to the degradation and destruction of their cities came from the now defunct blog, "Africa Have Your Say," which appeared on the BBC website, where Africans living on the continent and abroad weighed in on pertinent issues. One question posed in this forum in September 2006 was "How well is your town run?"[31] Jaochim Arrey from Douala, Cameroon, wrote, "My city is the biggest garbage bin in the world. In the seventies and eighties, Douala used to be a good example for other African cities, but today this city is almost not habitable. There is garbage everywhere." In another forum entitled, "Is Africa drowning in rubbish?"[32]

Ayan, a Somali now living in Seattle remembers growing up with her siblings: "We used to go through the rubbish hoping to find something valuable. We would find bottles and used them to store water. The thing was, we had nothing and the rubbish was our source of food and shelter. The saying goes 'one man's garbage is another man's treasure.'"[33] Morfaw Rene, a Cameroonian currently living in Belgium writes, "I think the high mountains of rubbish you find in the streets is due to the fact that the politicians are too rich and live in mansions in the Nation's capitals. They are far removed from the man on the street who lives in the rubbish. Hygiene and sanitation is scarcely on the agenda of African politicians."[34] Such comments demonstrate the social reverberations of perceiving oneself as a "global remnant," and these men and women seem all too aware of the ubiquity of garbage in the average African's life and across the African landscape.

As these descriptions suggest, the waste trade is just one piece in the proliferation of waste on the continent. Considering the waste trade implicitly invites an examination of the longer history of how transnational relationships have created "wasted" African environments and economies. As historians have noted, transnational colonial environments were forged through confrontations between colonial ambitions for productive cash crops and local realities of land and labor.[35] Conversely, an examination of postcolonial environments suggests that both urban and rural environments have been in part shaped by the goods foisted upon the continent and their mitigating effects on productivity and innovation. To note this process, we need look no farther than three permutations of waste arriving on African shores.

Hazardous Waste Trade

In summer 1988, the question of toxic waste dumping in Africa came to a head as brokered deals between the Western world and Africa were revealed in the press. It seemed as if an unholy alliance had emerged between the two. In June, Blaine Harden of the *Washington Post* wrote, "Africa, a pre-industrial continent in urgent need of hard currency, has awakened with a start in recent weeks to the equally urgent need of the industrialized West to get rid of its toxic waste."[36] Nigerian officials uncovered 4000 tons of PCBs from Italy that were stored in a residential backyard in Koko, and senior government officials in the Congo were arrested for allowing the dumping of 50,000 tons of toxic waste from various sources, including a New Jersey waste management firm. The Norwegian government was also forced to recoup 15,000 tons of incinerator ash from Guinea that one of its vessels had dumped. By July, "from Morocco to the Congo," wrote columnist James Brooke, "virtually every country on West Africa's coast reports receiving offers this year from American or European companies seeking cheap sites to dispose of hazardous waste." Labeled "toxic terrorism" in the news, these deals seemed ubiquitous enough at the time to signal a new and particularly vile neocolonial relationship between the Global North and South.[37]

The strains of colonialism were particularly strong in the case of France and Benin exchanging economic relief for toxic waste. The former colony was in debt to France and to several international banks in the 1980s, the same time that many African economies were imploding. The French Government arranged a deal with Benin where, in exchange for a down payment of $1.6 million and thirty years of economic assistance, the West African nation would house France's radioactive and industrial waste.[38] The same year, Benin also contracted with a European company, Sesco Waste Dumping, to take between one and five million pounds of toxic waste a year for ten years, paying the government of Benin $2.50 per ton of waste, and with an additional fifty cents per ton being invested in local agriculture, mining, and industry.[39] Benin's health minister, Colonel Andre Atchade, publicly denounced the plan and was dismissed from his post shortly thereafter.[40] Both arrangements were aborted once they became public knowledge. The BBC reported in 1988 that the Soviet Union was also guilty of dumping waste in Africa, which it denied in part by framing the practice as a distinctly capitalist one.[41] Aleksey Litvinov, a Soviet radio commentator, replied, "We in the Soviet Union firmly support the struggle waged by the African people against ecological imperialism, and together with them come out against any burial of nuclear or other industrial waste in Africa."[42] In all, during the 1980s, over half the countries on the continent were solicited to receive toxic waste.[43]

The snowballing accounts of these shady dealings going public looked as if a dystopian collaboration had evolved between economically opposing worlds. The industrialized world could no longer handle the magnitude of its waste generation, and the developing world was so economically prostrate that it was willing to take on the waste, though it had little infrastructure to handle it. Italy presents perhaps the best example of the gap that had developed between the West's ability to consume and its ability to dispose. In 1988, the country could only handle about 20 percent of the toxic waste it generated annually.[44]

Facilitating these exchanges was the continued rhetoric disguising toxic waste as harmless, or sometimes even as a material that might benefit an underdeveloped or "wasted" continent. The 15,000 tons of incinerator ash from Philadelphia dumped in Guinea was labeled "raw material for bricks,"[45] while the PCB waste from Italy that ended up in a backyard in Koko, Nigeria, was a highly carcinogenic compound the Italian government insisted was just "drums of coal tars, paint waste and industrial solvents."[46] Within the United States and abroad, industrial wastes full of heavy metals could be, and often were, reclassified as "fertilizer" simply by crossing state or national lines where regulations were looser.[47] Another popular euphemism for toxic waste when it came into ports was "construction materials."[48] The contrivance that harmful products were harmless potential resources had significant implications for just how these materials would "transform" the new environments in which they ultimately resided. This terminological disguise determined how the waste would be treated, and whether it would be dumped near unwitting populations, leaching into groundwater or wreaking other environmental and health hazards. Waste traders employed terminological transformations to obscure the biological transformations these highly toxic substances could effect, exploiting waste's liminality as a means to disguise it.[49]

While some Africans were complicit in this trade, members of the African press as well as a number of key politicians came out vociferously and publicly against hazardous waste dumping. Kenya's *Daily Nation*, for example, labeled the waste traders "western merchants of death."[50] The Organization of African Unity (OAU) was the first international political body to cooperatively seek to ban waste dumping, which it did in 1988, led by Nigerian president Ibrahim Babangida. Just days after he had been pushing the issue, though, the Koko dump in Nigeria was discovered. Babangida rushed to save face by arresting fifteen people, including several Italian nationals, and threatened any future suspect attempting to arrange a dumping scheme with execution by firing squad.[51] The hazardous waste was promptly sent back to Italy.

While the OAU ban was politically significant, it could not enforce a ban on the waste trade. The Basel Convention in 1989 became the most effective international attempt to ban transboundary trade of toxic wastes. Some critics, though, point out that it did not ban the trade so much as regulate it and exclude nuclear waste. The main result of the convention was that it forced all waste exporters to accurately label their product, get prior consent from the receiving country and the shipping companies, and to insure their cargo in case of ecological disaster. The convention also introduced the legally hazy notion that waste could only be shipped to places where it would be handled in "environmentally sound" ways.[52] In theory, the convention's labeling requirement would get rid of much of the deception surrounding these shipments, but in failing to regulate the trade in "recyclables," the convention left room for continued manipulation of terminology. International laws regarding the exchange of waste concentrated on regulating the journey rather than on its generation or what it would ultimately become where it ended up.

For most international policymakers, the waste trade is typically
characterized as a "transboundary" (or trade) issue, in that the locus
of the 'problem' is the actual movement of the wastes across borders:
the Basel Convention is on the of the few international environmental agreements that does not set targets to reduce the pollutant being
regulated.[53]

Thus, laws regulating transnational waste trading differ from most other international environmental laws, which highlights its ambiguity as an issue of
regulating commerce or regulating environments. Legislating waste trading
does not force industrialized countries to be custodians of their own waste, or
encourage them to produce less waste.[54]

Vastly different national regulations and capability to control the health of
the national environment leads to a *realpolitik* that diverges significantly from
the intentions of any international law. "As with the international politics of
poverty," Prins writes, "in the international politics of the environment there
may be a large gap between the words and actions of governments, international agencies and non-state actors."[55] Part of this gap stems from the fact
that with issues of poverty and environmental degradation, when it comes to
remuneration, it is hard to definitively pinpoint the cause of, say, air pollution
or lack of access to clean water. Particularly with transnational issues, cause
and origin become obscured in the wake of "multiple, tiny actions" that lead to
compounded and complex changes.[56] Prins cites the case of a pollution accident high on the Rhine River in 1986. Because the event was highly publicized,
it allowed Swiss and German companies to surreptitiously discharge their own
waste into the river as the toxic sludge passed downstream.[57] The lack of trans-
parent culpability leaves room for the transformation of objects as well as the
rhetorical obfuscation of problems. In the *realpolitik* of international environments, as demonstrated by the Rhine River and Somalia, companies and governments capitalize on chaotic political or environmental situations to disguise
their transgressions.

Perennially defined as chaotic in the international media, Africa has functioned as a vacuum for global irresponsibility. Yet, the arrival of waste on African
shores and its often-convoluted journey getting there marks the beginning of
its transformation, not the end. From there, waste potentially causes public
health problems, pollutes landscapes, bolsters economies, becomes alternative
energy, or is gleaned for its valuable reuseable elements.[58] On a larger scale,
toxic waste transforms into distrust of governments and contentious transnational political problems, and, as Lincoln would point out, attributes to the general pathology of being a "global remnant."

True to Desilvey's idea that waste is ever changing in both its form and how we perceive it, just twenty years past the high-water mark in 1988, the arrival of the West's (nonhazardous) waste in Africa may now, on occasion, be a less macabre omen. A 2008 project in Ghana shows that some places in Africa may now be clamoring for municipal waste from North America not as a backdoor deal but as an open economic endeavor. Because of its recent and ongoing power crisis, Ghana began negotiating with the Canadian government to receive its waste to use for energy generation. The project will cost Ghana about $250 million and is intended to provide the city of Kumasi fifty megawatts of energy annually for the next fifteen years. Without enough waste to fuel the project themselves, Ghana needs trash from abroad.[59] The site would also reportedly double as a tourist attraction due to its novelty as the first of its kind in West Africa. Although projects like the one in Ghana appear to indicate more local control over waste transformation, there remains an inevitable reckoning with "away" and with the question of which populations and environments will end up doing this reckoning.

Used Clothing

While toxic waste is clearly an example of potentially catastrophic transformation of goods disposed across the globe from their point of origin, the used-clothing market presents an example of waste trading where there is perhaps more room for cultural interpretation and adaptation. It would come as a surprise to most people that the cast-off clothes they donate to their local Goodwill are more often than not sold wholesale to Africa, ending up in small market stalls across the continent. Furthermore, most people would not readily identify used clothing as an example of "waste"; it is considered an act of charity to re-route something to a thrift store that would otherwise have been thrown away. Yet, since trade in used clothing exemplifies the general principle of exporting goods abroad that have no domestic value, it is apt to observe its physical and cultural transformations in Africa.

The Salvation Armies and Goodwill stores of America at one time were able to sell all their clothing in stores domestically but in the last twenty years supply has grown so dramatically that merely a fraction of used clothes remain in the United States.[60] The expansion of the market overseas has been extremely successful. While American consumers have more than they need, retailers in African nations welcome additional stock to meet local demand. The clothes recycling industry has been consistently successful in the last quarter century while there has been a long string of trade deficits for new merchandise and a collapse in the American textile business. From 1990 to 2003, the United States exported nearly 7 billion pounds of used clothing and textiles, and the country has more than 40 percent of the world market share in used clothing.[61] In 2001, the used clothing market between America and Africa yielded $61.7 million in sales.[62] Clearly, the West's "waste" in this regard can be translated into "wealth" in Africa. But, is there a cost associated with this trade?

The first question usually asked of the used clothing export industry is whether the flood of goods into Africa damages local textile markets and consequently agricultural production. With limited domestic manufacturing in Africa, there is little doubt that the trade in used goods has some effect. However, this does not answer the larger question of whether or not the industry's existence is economically detrimental for Africans. Used clothing is in fact one of the top ten exports to Africa from the United States, and to Tanzania it is the single largest.[63] Some economists see the used clothing industry in Africa as a potential example of a "global industry for the little guy," because it exhibits "perfect competition" once these items arrive in local markets.[64] Each individual seller can pick out his or her own goods and cultivate a customer base accordingly. Others scholars, critiquing Africa's growing dependence on foreign goods as an undeniable cause of its underdevelopment, argue that local textile manufacturing is an essential prerequisite for development.[65] In fact, states economist Garth Frazer, "with 95-percent confidence...no country has achieved per capita national income of 11,000 USD without having a clothing industry that employs at least 1 percent of its work force."[66] The individualized and customized nature of the used-clothing industry seems easy to overstate since the used-clothing market is not ruled by demand so much as the potluck of supply. The African market may be sophisticated, but it is still based on what has been discarded not just once but twice in the United States. When clothes do not sell at Goodwill or Salvation Army, they are then sold to companies such as Trans America Trading Company, where the clothes are sorted based on different markets such as the rare high-end vintage items, used clothing, cleaning rags.[67] Tattered T-shirts and other cotton goods get turned into "shoddy," which sells for 1 to 2 cents a pound and ends up in anything from car doors, mattresses, cushions, and insulation to caskets.[68] The remaining used-clothing items that are still in relatively good shape are then packaged into 500- to 1000-pound bales, placed into shipping containers, most of it heading to sub-Saharan Africa.

Once used clothing arrives in Africa, it becomes part of an already existing and fairly vibrant "used culture."[69] Journalist George Packer describes his conversation with local journalist Michael Wakabi on the nature and extent of Kampala, Uganda's, used culture:

The cars are used—they arrive from Japan with broken power windows and air-conditioners, so Ugandan drivers bake in the sun. Used furniture from Europe lines the streets in Kampala. The Ugandan Army occupies part of neighboring Congo with used tanks and aircraft from Ukraine. And the traditional Ugandan dress made from local cotton, called gomesi, is as rare as the mountain gorilla. To dress African, Ugandans have to have money.[70]

While examples abound of this conundrum in globalized economies, it has become much cheaper for Africans to wear clothing from halfway across the world than to buy cloth made domestically. The ubiquity of used clothing, however, does not mean it is accepted unequivocally. In fact, tracking the trade allows us to see how the meanings associated with these goods changes according to context. In some cases, for instance, the clothing is met with suspicion and rumor. Packer reports that in Somalia used clothing is called *huudhaydh*—as in "who died?" while in Togo it is called "dead white man's clothing," and in Sierra Leone, it is called "junks." These names capture the confusion of African buyers as to why these still perfectly wearable clothes would be discarded by their original owners. Packer recalls a Kenyan clothing seller who told him that, until very recently, many Kenyans assumed that not only was the clothing associated with dead people, but it had been removed from the bodies of the deceased and was therefore prone to carry skin diseases.[71]

There is no shortage of complex cultural values that have accompanied the ascendance of used clothing, particularly as pieces are altered, adorned, or transformed. In Zambia the word for used clothing is the Bembe word *Salula*, which means "to rummage through a pile," reflecting the fact that used clothing in Zambia offers customers the ability to choose.[72] The name also suggests that the journey itself and the manner in which the clothes arrive are part of their aesthetic appeal. Clothing with more wrinkles is actually preferred: "secondhand clothing displayed with folds and wrinkles straight from the bale is considered to be fresh from the source" and as a result, more genuine and real.[73] In my own research in Dar es Salaam, Tanzania, I found that the opening up of the domestic market to used goods from abroad in 1985 was a great relief for many poor people. Ali Hassan Mwinyi's presidency during this period became known by the term *Ruksa*, meaning "anything goes," because of his liberalization of the market. With a government that had previously tightly regulated all incoming commodities, the emergence of cast-off clothing and sewing machines, buses, cars, and tractors on the market allowed people to make a living in ways they had never been able to afford before. The culture of used goods diversified people's survival strategies in the city. Selling used clothing quickly became a new way to earn a living.

Cultural interpretations of these garments runs the gamut, from "newer" and more "alive" than local cloth to "tired" and "dead" in its association as something discarded.[74] As an industry, used clothing has variously been seen as enervating or resuscitating to economies. Fearful of its effect on local markets and the ascendance of Western wear over African clothing styles Nigeria beginning in the late 1970s banned the import of used clothing, or "cloth dumping" as they referred to it.[75] In the face of much debate, Nigeria as recently as November of 2010 lifted the ban on used clothing because many felt the ban had merely promoted corruption and smuggling.[76] Others fear that the competition from foreign textile firms will destroy Nigeria's textile industry.[77] While used clothing and toxic waste have very little in common materially, environmentally, or culturally, I argue they are theoretically bound by a journey that begins with being discarded. Considering the permutations of the West's worn-out T-shirts in Africa suggests that the act of "decay" over space and time can, in fact, represent a resurrection of sorts.

Food Dumping

The exportation of food to Africa both as a commodity on the open market and as aid has garnered debate similar to that surrounding the used-clothing industry. Both industries potentially stall out Africa's ability to become agriculturally self-sufficient and expand its industrial production. "Food dumping," as it is derisively called, takes many forms, and like waste dumping, impacts communities and environments in unintended and unpredicted ways. In general, food dumping occurs when foreign agricultural goods erode local markets by introducing comparable goods at much cheaper prices. These commodities are priced so cheaply (or handed out for free through aid arrangements) because they are being off-loaded from their own domestic markets and often priced based on what it would otherwise cost to dispose of them. In *The Wheat Trap*, published in 1985, Gunilla Andrae and Bjorn Beckman look at the effect of the "entrenchment of wheat bread" due to large scale importation of wheat had on the economy and consumption patterns in Nigeria. They argue that much of the food shortages Nigeria faced in the 1980s were caused by food importation rather than actual shortages. In fact, development scholar Calestous Juma claims that while Africa was food independent in the 1960s, by 1980 only 20 percent of the continent's cereals were produced domestically.[78] Since the 1960s, Africa's share of world agricultural exports has shrunk from 8 percent to 2 percent, and the sub-Saharan region has shifted from being a net food exporter to a net food importer.[79]

In Nigeria the ascendance of wheat during the 1970s and 1980s meant that bread—practically nonexistent in the country two decades before—quickly became a cheap and easy staple that families used to replace more nutritional cereals. Ninety-five percent of these wheat imports originated in the United States when the Nigerian government regulated its cheap price. Foreign consultants then suggested that Nigeria grow their own wheat to minimize its dependence on foreign food commodities. This led to massive government support of wheat-growing schemes; yet, foreign firms were employed to implement irrigation systems and to sell processing equipment to African growers. Foreign companies also typically owned the subsidiaries where the flour was milled. By January 1987, with the intent of supporting the domestic production of cereal crops, Nigerian president Ibrahim Babangida banned wheat imports. According to the United States Department of Agriculture, though, up to 300,000 tonnes of wheat were smuggled across the border from neighboring West African countries.[80] This large-scale shift in cereal demand and production in Nigeria transformed agriculture, health, food cultures, and markets in countless ways. The story of wheat's ascendance in Nigeria impels observers to reconsider the definition of "waste trading" since it suggests that we consider something that is nutritive and essentially unused as waste that brings with it myriad unintended consequences. And yet, these West African markets were established explicitly as a way to dispose of excess wheat in the United States.

In perhaps a more alarming example of food dumping, *Der Spiegel* published an article in 2007 chronicling the ongoing "chicken war" in Cameroon.[81] Since Europeans eat chicken breasts almost exclusively, the remaining chicken parts are considered waste and exported to West Africa at "dumping prices." This led to the near-collapse of the Cameroonian chicken industry, since a kilo of chicken legs from Europe sold for 800 West African francs, or €1.20, whereas domestic chickens sold live and unplucked cost twice the price.[82] The chicken-leg industry in West Africa dates back to the 1995 signing of the Marrakech Agreement establishing the World Trade Organization and the consequent lowering of tariff protections for small African farmers and raising of subsidies for European farmers. According to *Der Speigel*, one factor that made imported chicken legs cheap was that they were priced, not based on production costs in Europe, but on "the costs of disposal when [they] cannot be sold. In most cases, the producer has already earned his profit with the sale of the breast fillets, so that the rest of the bird can be sold at a price sufficient to cover costs."[83] Far more than just an economic debate, this "chicken war" was a political awakening for many Cameroonian farmers. Bernard Njonga, the appointed leader of the farmers' association, took on the cause of ending the dumping of chicken legs by going up against the country's major importers. Taking matters into their own hands, Njonga and the farmers had 200 chicken legs inspected, revealing that 83.5 percent of the imported meat was unfit for human consumption.[84] Their protests were publicized across the country and eventually caused the import business to collapse.

Ghana is facing similar problems with subsidized European poultry taking over domestic markets. In the early 1990s, poultry farmers still produced about 95 percent of the chickens sold on the Ghanaian market whereas by 2001 they only held an 11 percent market share.[85] In total, Ghana was importing almost one-third of the European Union's frozen chickens shipped to Africa.[86] This transformation, from food to waste to food again, has much in common with the economics of the hazardous waste trade, where disposal costs are what motivates the reconfiguration of something being discarded into a potential resource. What food dumping demonstrates is the larger set of relationships the West cultivated with Africa in the postcolonial era to create a marketplace for its own excess while preserving domestic prices of goods, especially agricultural commodities. Furthermore, it challenges scholars to consider the internal consistency of how waste is defined. In the context of waste trading, is waste defined by being valueless at its point of departure or is its definition based on what it becomes in its new location? The example of food dumping asks environmental historians to look at how production in one part of the world can very inadvertently dictate the production of similar goods in different part of the world.

In his work on toxic waste and environmental justice, David Naguib Pellow writes that global environmental inequality is fostered through "discourses that produce and intensify social distance between rich and poor and North and the South," as well as global financial institutions that further "geographic inequalities."[87] Thus, discussions of waste trading often end up as bifurcated by the journey from North to South as the cargo itself. Since this chapter considers the transformations that toxic waste, used clothing, and food undergo as they cross geopolitical borders, examining the terminological shifts incurred during the journey is also warranted. Waste often leaves the developed world cast as a potential environmental problem tied to disposal costs, shining a light on excessive consumption or overproduction. Upon its arrival in the developing world, it is viewed as symptomatic of a poverty problem (or disguised as a poverty solution) tied to underdevelopment and poor governance.

This hemispheric split in environmental history goes back at least as far as the Stockholm Conference in 1972, the first major United Nations conference addressing international environmental problems. Delegates from the global South coined the term "the pollution of poverty," to address environmental issues that resulted from poverty, such as sanitation, overcrowded cities, and lack of environmental standards. The term also came to demonstrate the rhetorical rift between the hemispheres, with the North discussing the environmental crisis in terms of industrial pollution and climate change, and the South suggesting that the biggest threat to the environment stems from poverty and lack of development.[88] When the "pollution of poverty" was coined, however, it did not explicitly implicate the North in intensifying the poverty and pollution of the developing world, a point that was taken up by environmental justice activists, who currently present waste trading as one of the most alarming examples of this relationship.[89] The waste recovery trades in the North and South exist and thrive for very different reasons that embody this divide. Recovery in developing countries tends to be driven by markets and employs complex domestic systems of salvage and resale that are motivated by necessity and tend to expand rapidly with little or no government support.[90] Recovery in the industrialized world, on the other hand, is usually motivated either by environmental watchdog groups or by government regulatory agencies such as the Environmental Protection Agency.[91] The paradox of the theoretical isolation of "northern" and "southern" environmental issues is that at the root of these problems exists a global economy contingent on these two worlds becoming ever more interconnected. Over the past thirty years, the act of throwing something "away" has become both harder and easier.

By examining disparate examples of waste trading, my intention has not been to conflate the different cargoes that are traded. Toxic sludge and chicken legs implicate problems of different environmental scale and political magnitudes. Rather, by repurposing DeSilvey's idea of "observing decay" to the waste trade, my intention is to conflate the processes of transformation in order to learn something from categorically observing the shifting biological, cultural, and economic fates of objects from one context to another. This task is the purview of a transnational environmental history that seeks out these latitudinal journeys within a historical framework.[92] Furthermore, these exchanges both create and represent larger entrenched relationships between nations, as is eminently obvious in the case of the Somali pirates. The waste trade is transformative both at the level of the object and the ecosystem. The object is renamed or reimagined between the points of departure and arrival, its journey carves out new global relationships, and when waste arrives at its destination, it inevitably changes the nature of people's relationships with their environments.

NOTES

1. Jeffrey Gettleman, "Somali Pirates Tell Their Side: They Only Want Money," *New York Times*, September 30, 2008, A6.

2. Officially the Puntland State of Somalia, a region in the northeast of Somalia along the Indian Ocean.

3. Najad Abdullahi, "'Toxic Waste' behind Somali Piracy," Aljazeera Net News Africa, October. 11, 2008, accessed April 21 2009, http://english.aljazeera.net/news/africa/2008/10/2008109174223218644.html. It is worth noting that Jay Bahadur, in his book *The Pirates of Somalia: Inside Their Hidden World* (New York: Random House, 2011), suggests that while there has been overfishing and nuclear waste dumping off the coast of Somalia, it does not necessarily explain the rise of piracy. Bahadur sees piracy as more directly a consequence of Somalia becoming a failed state. He touches on the fact that the spokesmen for the pirates are savvy at portraying a particular narrative of victimization that capitalizes on the essential nature of the international exploitation that Somalia has faced in the past twenty years. It remains a complicated and interesting example of the geopolitical fallout (and local consequences) of waste dumping in transnational environments.

4. Abdullahi, "'Toxic Waste' behind Somali Piracy."

5. Daniel C. Etsy, "Economic Integration and the Environment," in *The Global Environment: Institutions, Law, And Policy*, 2d ed., ed. Regina S. Axelrod, David Leonard Downie, and Norman J. Vig (Washington, DC: CQ Press, 2004), 191.

6. Ibid.

7. Zsuzsa Gille, *From the Cult of Waste to the Trash Heap of History: The Politics of Waste in Socialist and Postsocialist Hungary* (Bloomington: Indiana University Press, 2007), 23.

8. Ibid.

n9. Richard C. Foltz, "Does Nature Have Historical Agency? World History, Environmental History, and How Historians Can Help Save the Planet," *History Teacher* 37, no. 1 (2003), 16.

10. Ibid.

11. Gille, *From the Cult of Waste*, 25.

12. Ibid.

13. Joel A. Tarr, *The Search for the Ultimate Sink: Urban Pollution in Historical Perspective* (Akron, OH: Akron University Press, 1996), 8.

14. David Rich Lewis, "Skull Valley Goshutes and the Politics of Nuclear Waste," in *Native Americans and the Environment: Perspectives on the Ecological Indian*, ed. Michael Eugene Harkin and David Rich Lewis (Lincoln: University of Nebraska Press, 2007).

15. Eileen Maura McGurty, "From NIMBY to Civil Rights: The Origins of the Environmental Justice Movement," *Environmental History* 2, no. 3 (July 1, 1997): 301–23.

16. Caitlin DeSilvey, "Observed Decay: Telling Stories with Mutable Things," *Journal of Material Culture* 11 (November 2006): 318–38.

17. Ibid., 325.

18. Quoted in Rebecca Solnit, *Savage Dreams: A Journey into the Landscape Wars of the American West* (Berkeley: University of California Press, 1999), 91.

19. DeSilvey, "Observed Decay," 325.

20. Ibid., 329.

21. Wole Soyinka, *The Open Sore of a Continent: A Personal Narrative of the Nigerian Crisis* (New York: Oxford University Press, 1997), 78.

22. "Let Them Eat Pollution" *The Economist*, February 8, 1992, 66.

23. Ibid.

24. Gwyn Prins, "Politics and the Environment," *International Affairs* 66, no. 4 (1990): 713.

25. Ibid.

26. The stewardship and reinvention of discarded objects, however, was not new to urban Africans. See John Iliffe, *The African Poor: A History* (Cambridge: Cambridge University Press, 1987), 175.

27. Sarah Lincoln. "Expensive Shit: Aesthetic Economies of Waste in Postcolonial Africa." (PhD diss., Duke University, 2008), 5. The term "excremental vision" was originally used by J. Middleton Murry in his biography of Jonathan Swift. See J. Middleton Murry. *Jonathan Swift: A Critical Biography* (London, 1954), 432–48. The term was later used by Warwick Anderson in his article "Excremental Colonialism: Public Health and the Poetics of Pollution," *Critical Inquiry* 21, no. 3 (spring 1995): 640–69; and Joshua Etsy in "Excremental Postcolonialism," *Contemporary Literature* 40, no 1 (spring 1999): 22–59.

28. Lincoln, "Expensive Shit," 4.

29. Quoted in Peter C. W. Gutkind, "Tradition, Migration, Urbanization, Modernity, and Unemployment in Africa: The Roots of Instability," *Canadian Journal of African Studies* 3, no. 2 (summer 1969): 345.

30. Ibid.

31. "How Well is Your Town Run?" BBC News website, last updated September 20, 2006, http://news.bbc.co.uk/2/hi/africa/5349562.stm.

32. "Is Africa Drowning in Rubbish?" BBC News website, last updated January 18, 2006, http://news.bbc.co.uk/2/hi/africa/4610222.stm.

33. Ibid.

34. Ibid.

35. Keletso Atkins, *The Moon is Dead—Give Us Our Money! The Cultural Origins of an African Work Ethic, Natal, 1843–1990* (Portsmouth, NH: Heinemann, 1991); Melissa Leach and Robin Mearns, *The Lie of the Land: Challenging Received Wisdom on the African Environment* (Portsmouth, NH: Heinemann, 1996); and Kate B. Showers, *Imperial Gullies: Soil Erosion and Conservation in Lesotho* (Athens: Ohio University Press, 2005).

36. Blaine Harden, "Outcry Grows in Africa over West's Waste-Dumping: Governments Decry Toxic Terrorism," *Washington Post*, June 22, 1988, A15.

37. Matthew Connelly, "Taking Off the Cold War Lens: Visions of North-South Conflict during the Algerian War for Independence," *American Historical Review* 105, no. 3 (June 1, 2000): 739–69.

38. TED Case Studies Benin Hazardous Waste, accessed April 16, 2009, http://www1.american.edu/TED/benin.htm.

39. Jim Vallette and Heather Spalding, eds., *The International Trade in Wastes: A Greenpeace Inventory.* 5th ed. (Washington, DC: Greenpeace U.S.A., 1990), 67.

40. Ibid.

41. See Zsuzsa Gille's first two chapters in *From the Cult of Waste to the Trash Heap of History: The Politics of Waste in Socialist and Postsocialist Hungary* (Bloomington: Indiana University Press, 2007) for discussion of socialist versus capitalist wasting and the conceptions each propagated about the other.

42. Valette and Spaulding, *International Trade in Wastes,* 68.

43. Jennifer Clapp, "The Toxic Waste Trade with Less-Industrialised Countries: Economic Linkages and Political Alliances," *Third World Quarterly* 15 (1994), 4.

44. Loren Jenkins, "After Dumping on Nigeria, Italy Takes It All Back," *Washington Post*, September 3, 1988, A38.

45. Polly Diven, "Our New Hazardous Export," *Christian Science Monitor*, October 27, 1988, Opinion, 11.

46. Jenkins, "After Dumping on Nigeria," A38.

47. Duff Wilson, "Fear in the Fields: How Hazardous Wastes Become Fertilizer; Lack of Fertilizer Regulation in U.S. Leaves Farmers, Consumers Guessing about Toxic Concentrations of Farms," *Seattle Times*, July 4, 1997, accessed April 29, 2009, http://community.seattletimes.nwsource.com/archive/?date=19970704&slug=2547909.

48. Elli Louka, *Overcoming National Barriers to International Waste Trade: A New Perspective on the Transnational Movements of Hazardous and Radioactive Wastes.* (Dordrecht: Graham & Trotman / M. Nijhoff, 1994), 103.

49. Jorge Enrique Hardou, Diana Mitlin, and David Satterthwaite, *Environmental Problems in Third World Cities* (London: Earthscan Publications, 1992), 69.

50. Blaine Harden, "Outcry Grows in Africa over West's Waste-Dumping: Governments Decry Toxic Terrorism," *Washington Post,* June 22, 1988, A15.

51. Ibid.

52. Katharina Kummer, "The International Regulation of Transboundary Traffic in Hazardous Wastes: The 1989 Basel Convention," *International and Comparative Law Quarterly* 41, no. 3 (July 1992): 530–62.

53. Kate O'Neill, *Waste Trading among Rich Nations: Building a New Theory of Environmental Regulation* (Cambridge, MA: MIT Press, 2000), 46.

54. Ibid.

55. Prins, "Politics and the Environment," 713.

56. Ibid, 715.

57. Ibid.

58. Two examples of resulting problems are Lydia Polgreen and Marlise Simons, "Global Sludge Ends in Tragedy For Ivory Coast," *New York Times*, October 2, 2006, A1, and American Chemical Society, "Recycling of E-Waste in China May Expose Mothers, Infants to High Dioxin Levels, *Science Daily,*

October 22, 2007, accessed September 10, 2011, http://www.sciencedaily.com/releases/2007/10/071022094520.htm.

59. Frank Mensah, "Ghana to Import Garbage...As Canadians Inspect Landfill Site," *Ghanaian Chronicle*, November 25, 2008, http://www.modernghana.com/newsthread1/192139/1/39362.

60. Pietra Rivoli, *The Travels of a T-Shirt in the Global Economy: An Economist Examines the Markets, Power, and Politics of World Trade* (Hoboken, NJ: John Wiley and Sons, 2005), 176.

61. Ibid.

62. George Packer, "How Susie Bayer's T-Shirt Ended Up on Yusuf Mama's Back," *New York Times*, March 31, 2002, section 6, 54.

63. Rivoli, "Travels of a T-Shirt," 184.

64. Ibid, 178.

65. Neil Reynolds "Goodwill May Be Stunting African Growth," *Globe and Mail* (Toronto), December. 24, 2008, B2.

66. Ibid.

67. Rivoli, "Travels of a T-Shirt," 180.

68. Ibid., 187.

69. Packer, "Susie Bayer's T-Shirt," 54.

70. Ibid.

71. Ibid., 54.

72. Karen Tranberg Hansen, *Saluala: The World of Secondhand Clothing and Zambia* (Chicago: University of Chicago Press, 2000), 1.

73. Ibid., 172.

74. Ibid.

75. Ademola Oyejide, A. Ogunkola, and A. Bankole, "Import Prohibition as a Trade Policy Instrument: The Nigerian Experience," World Trade Organization website, accessed September 16, 2011, http://www.wto.org/english/res_e/booksp_e/casestudies_e/case32_e.htm.

76. Felix Onuah, "Nigeria Scraps Ban on Textiles, Furniture Imports," *Reuters*, November 30, 2010, Reuters (online), accessed Dec 20, 2011, http://www.reuters.com/article/2010/11/30/nigeria-imports-idUSLDE6AT1RH20101130.

77. "Nigerian Textile Factories May Close after Import Ban Lifted." *Bloomberg News* website, December 1, 2010, accessed December 20, 2011, http://www.bloomberg.com/news/2010-12-01/nigerian-textile-factories-may-close-after-import-ban-lifted.html.

78. Calestous Juma, *The Gene Hunters: Biotechnology and the Scramble for Seeds* (London: Zed Press, 1989).

79. Pascal Zachary, "Cheap Chickens: Feeding Africa's Poor" *World Policy Journal* 21, no. 2 (summer 2004): 47–52, 48.

80. Kevin Kimmage, "From 'Wheat Trap' to Wheat Boom in Nigeria," *Africa: Journal of the International African Institute* 60 (1991): 471–501, 477.

81. Uwe Buse, "The Chicken War: In Cameroon, Globalization's Losers Fight Back and Win," *Der Spiegel Online*, September 19, 2007, accessed April 12, 2011, http://www.spiegel.de/international/world/0,1518,506742-2,00.html.

82. Ibid.

83. Ibid.

84. Ibid.

85. Linus Atarah, "Playing Chicken: Ghana vs. the IMF," *CorpWatch Online,* June 14, 2005, http://www.corpwatch.org/article.php?id=12394.

86. Suleiman Mustapha, "The Dying State of Ghana's Poultry," *The Statesman* (Ghana), online, January 1, 2008, accessed April 12, 2011, http://www.thestatesmanonline.com/pages/news_detail.php?newsid=5675&section=2.

87. David Naguib Pellow, *Resisting Global Toxics: Transnational Movements for Environmental Justice* (Cambridge, MA: MIT Press, 2007), 99.

88. Jennifer A. Elliott, *An Introduction to Sustainable Development* (London: Routledge, 1999), 32.

89. Patricia McCarney, "Four Approaches to the Environment of Cities," in *Perspectives on the City,* ed. Richard Stren and Judith Kjellberg Bell (Toronto: Centre for Urban and Community Studies, 1995).

90. Pieter van Beukering and Vinod K. Sharma, eds., *Wastepaper Trade and Recycling in India* (Jodhpur: Scientific Publishers, 1997), 2.

91. Ibid.

92. Good recent examples of this sort of spatial environmental history are Matthew W. Klingle, "Spaces of Consumption in Environmental History" *History and Theory* 42, no. 4 (December 1, 2003): 94–110; and Matthew Evenden, "Aluminum, Commodity Chains, and the Environmental History of the Second World War," *Environmental History* 16, no. 1 (Jan. 1, 2011): 69–93.

Afterword

International Systems and Their Discontents

J. R. McNeill

The preceding chapters testify to the awkward fit between the modern international system and effective measures to combat environmental problems. Environmental stability is a collective good. Individuals and nations can hope to benefit from it without paying for it if others will assume their share of the burden. Within towns and nations, overarching authorities can resolve the conundrum by setting rules. But in an international system of diffuse sovereignty, with dozens or hundreds of states and no real supranational authority, fewer rules are set, and fewer still are enforced. The record of ineffective attempts to address climate change over the past quarter century illustrates the problem.

That uninspiring record also results from the problem of mismatched time horizons between problems and policies. This issue exists within national and local contexts, not merely international ones. Few office holders wish to call for sacrifice now to avoid greater sacrifice decades from now. They would rather delay and hand off the problem to their successors. For those interested in staying in office, this is rational behavior.

These two problems are tightly linked. The unwillingness to tackle problems with long time horizons exists on the local level, but it is usually more acute on the national level, because the need for shared sacrifice in the interest of future generations is a harder sell to a more diverse population. Nations with a strong sense of solidarity, usually a result of ethnic and cultural homogeneity, may find it easier to achieve goals that involve sacrifice now for benefits later. Those that are sociallyfragmented find it harder. In general, the problem escalates with both the size and diversity of the population (as well as with the legitimacy of whatever authority is calling for sacrifice). It is easiest (not to say easy) within families. It is hardest on the global scale, because people care much more about their own children and grandchildren than about those of people on the other side of the earth.[1]

These two entwined problems often prevent the rulers of states from squarely addressing transnational environmental issues, and to make matters worse, states often create environmental problems by pursuing their routine priorities. For the past two centuries, the foremost goals of most states have been security and economic growth. So they have built military-industrial complexes and nuclear weapons, at the cost of untold pollution. They have sought to make themselves self-sufficient in cotton or rubber, even when it required thorough reorganization of regional ecologies. They have built military roads and railroads, inadvertently opening new regions and resources to exploitation. They have sought to collect taxes from poor farmers, inadvertently driving them up into mountain forests, where their quest for livelihoods destabilized upland ecosystems. They have tried to populate frontier regions with loyal subjects, regardless of the frontier lands' capacity to support denser populations. They have tried to industrialize overnight so as to become more formidable against their foes, unconcerned that this might require stripping their forests for charcoal fuel. Sometimes knowingly, often unwittingly, states in pursuit of their routine goals have been much more effective as agents of environmental tumult than as agents of environmental protection.

From the point of view of environmental stability, an essentially anarchic international system composed of numerous states may well seem the worst of all possible arrangements. That could be true, but it is worth pointing out that other forms of international society had fatal weaknesses too. For most of the last 5000 years, in those parts of the world where states existed, diffuse anarchic systems of a sort regarded as normal today alternated irregularly with sprawling multinational empires. In the four centuries prior to the period taken up in this book, such empires held sway in China, India, the Middle East, the Andes, and Mexico—indeed, in all the world's major centers of population and wealth except West and Central Europe. The Ming and Qing dynasties in China, the Mughals in India, the Ottomans in the Middle East, and the Incas in Peru and the Aztecs in Mexico (followed by the Spaniards) maintained their empires by acquiring and mobilizing resources along their frontiers and, at times, by exploiting internal regions. None practiced an ecologically sustainable existence. They lasted as long as they could find new resources to metabolize, and as long as they could innovate in response to the ecological disruptions they created.[2]

Moreover, these sprawling multinational empires proved helpless, or close to it, in the face of certain problems, just as the modern international system seems to be. Those in Eurasia struggled for millennia to make satisfactory arrangements with nomads, both those on their frontiers and those within their (always porous and usually vague) borders. The latter they routinely sought to settle, to convert into sedentary taxpayers and conscripts—indeed, this effort continues on the Tibetan plateau today. The former they tried to bribe, or crush, or keep at bay with walls stretching beyond the horizon. But no solution worked, and many a ruling house fell due to pressures exerted by nomads. The great empires also coexisted uneasily with commercial cities. On the one hand, such cities were sources of taxable wealth. On the other, they were, as one German physician put it in 1796, the "open graves of mankind," so disease-ridden that they killed off an emperor's subjects at alarming rates.[3] Moreover, they were nests of cosmopolitanism, of unorthodox ideas and beliefs that might call into question the prevailing religion and the ruler's divine sanction. By the nineteenth century, sprawling multinational empires ran into intractable difficulties with nationalism.

Any and all arrangements for international society are imperfect and ill designed for some of the problems they face. The modern international system, like those before it, evolved out of compromises and struggles to deal with issues of the moment. The current system was born in the 1940s, and insofar as it was consciously designed, was calibrated to wrestle with the risk of descent into prolonged economic depression and the danger of world war. That it should prove unwieldy in the face of global environmental problems should come as no surprise. It is, rather, the historical norm. That such problems are normal and to be expected does not diminish their seriousness.

Confronting Slavery, Piracy, and Disease

Serious problems require seriously historical thinking. It might be instructive to consider some more-or-less successful responses of international society to a handful of transnational problems in modern history. Slavery, piracy, and infectious disease still exist in the twenty-first century, but between 1700 and today they have been attacked by international alliances and confined to the margins of modern life—at least in comparison to their former pervasiveness.[4] In effect, three examples of what one might call a "global regime of suppression" emerged squarely, addressing phenomena that came to be regarded both as undesirable and as appropriate targets for public policy.[5] How did this happen? What conditions allowed it?

Slavery in one form or another existed since the dawn of civilization and probably before. It was an economically rational response to labor shortages and every large-scale society practiced it to some degree. Where labor was scant, slavery (or serfdom) was pervasive. Most major religions and legal systems recognized slavery, and many legitimated it. Of course, many slaves resisted their treatment and fled their bondage or organized rebellions. Some may have regarded the institution of slavery as illegitimate and immoral, although since so few slaves left records it is hard to know how widespread such views may have been. However, between 1780 and 1880 slavery lost its moral legitimacy in many societies and cultures. In the Atlantic world it was politically destroyed and legally abolished between 1780 (the beginning of the "gradual abolition" came in Pennsylvania) and 1888 (abolition in Brazil). By 1981 slavery was illegal in every country (Mauritania was the last to abolish it).

Given the persistence of slavery over the millennia, abolition was remarkable. In the Western world it depended on a crusading morality that extended as far back as the broadsides of Bartolomé de Las Casas in the 1540s, but that came to a head in the 1780s. That moral crusade was cosmopolitan and international in character, although its representatives worked within the political, religious, and legal contexts of their own lands. In Britain and the United States, the antislavery cause was strongly identified with evangelical Protestantism and with Quakerism. Abolition had to overcome entrenched resistance from powerful people who denied that slavery was immoral, and who forecast disaster were it to come to an end. In Haiti and the southern United States, it took war to bring it about. In much of Africa and parts of Asia, it took imperialism and the imposition of alien values to achieve abolition, although the cause had many supporters within these continents. In every case, it took many people working together across borders, intellectually, politically, and sometimes militarily, to create a new regime in which slavery lost its legitimacy and retreated to the dark corners of the world.

Piracy is probably even older than slavery.[6] It blossomed where seaborne trade flourished, especially in and around narrow waters such as the Straits of Malacca, the Red Sea, or Gibraltar. Piracy was, and is, a rational economic activity except where ruthlessly suppressed. Like slavery, it enjoyed a certain legitimacy over the millennia, which extended to state support in many cases (e.g., the famous Barbary pirates). States and merchants objected when pirates attacked their subjects and ships, yet often engaged in piracy with respect to rivals. Curiously, the early eighteenth-century Caribbean variant of piracy enjoys not only popular interest, but also a retrospective legitimacy and admiration from scholars who regard pirate communities as examples of egalitarian worker democracy in action or free-market entrepreneurialism at its purest.[7]

Whether or not pirates deserve admiration as paragons of socialism or capitalism, states in a position to benefit from seaborne trade have routinely sought to suppress them. The Roman Empire invested heavily in pirate suppression in the eastern Mediterranean in the first century B.C.E.

According to Strabo, the Roman campaign led by Pompey in 67 B.C.E. destroyed some 1300 pirate ships in three months. To achieve this end, the Roman Republic had to grant Pompey special powers giving him full freedom of action throughout Mediterranean waters—a special legal and political proviso (the *Lex Gabinia*) created specifically to address piracy. Pompey also had to engage in coalition-building diplomacy to get local rulers to support his efforts and deny succor to pirates.[8] When Caribbean piracy reached a threshold in the early eighteenth century, Great Britain led a determined response, ca. 1715–1730, that mimicked Pompey's. A new legal regime made it much easier to try and hang pirates (and suspected pirates), and ad hoc antipirate diplomacy made it far harder for pirates to find shelter in French, Spanish, or Dutch territories.[9] When Great Britain sought to suppress piracy in the South China Sea and the Malay waters, ca. 1815–1860, tactical alliances with local rulers again proved essential, as did a casual approach to legal niceties.[10]

In these three cases of piracy suppression in the Mediterranean, Caribbean, and South China Sea, states found they had to secure one another's cooperation, and they either had to change the law to make the punishment of pirates easier or disregard the law when it proved convenient to do so. They had to engage in moral crusades, or propaganda campaigns, vilifying piracy and pirates, trying to convince as many people as possible that pirates were not plucky Robin Hoods giving the rich and powerful their just desserts, but rather menaces to the welfare of all. (It is unclear whether Pompey did this or simply relied on superior force to secure the cooperation he needed). Moreover, in each case a local hegemon with naval power (Rome or Britain) had to organize and lead the campaign. No new transnational institutions were created to combat piracy. Today, in contrast, the United Nations has created an antipiracy bureaucracy, and private firms have sprung up to sell protection against pirates off the Somali coast and in the Straits of Malacca.

In some important ways, the history of pirate suppression provides a sobering example of successful action in the face of a transnational issue. First, to achieve success, states had to grant themselves extra powers, which in the case of the *Lex Gabinia* and Pompey helped to undermine the Roman Republic and usher in dictatorship. Second, concerted action required a hegemon with coercive powers it was prepared to use. This seems an unlikely condition with respect to today's transnational environmental problems, as the plausible hegemons of the twenty-first century are, at present, among the least concerned about environmental issues such as climate change, and are in any case extremely unlikely to conclude that coercive force is an appropriate tool in this context. In short, successful piracy suppression rested on political circumstances not easily imaginable today and came at a cost not easily contemplated today.

A more cheerful example lies in the history of disease control. In some respects disease provides a closer analogue to current transnational environmental problems than does either slavery or piracy. Like greenhouse gas emissions (GHGs) or chloroflourocarbons (CFCs), pathogens may originate in a specific place but pose threats to people far away from the site of the original emission, albeit threats of differing magnitudes. For most of the last 5000 years, people had to accept disease as a routine part of life and reason for death. While sufferers employed healers and doctors, rarely did medicine succeed against such lethal infections as smallpox, measles, influenza, bubonic plague, or falciparum malaria. Most people understood disease to be part of the natural order and an indication of divine judgment. For believers, divine judgments are necessarily just and moral. Indeed, one may say in this sense that disease, like slavery and piracy in some contexts, enjoyed a form of legitimacy: it was normal, natural, and represented divine will. No one wished to be ill, just as no one wished to be enslaved. But that many people should fall ill, and many should die from disease, seemed (in most, if not all, cultures), until recently, legitimate and in any case inevitable.

Nonetheless, just as people employed doctors to combat illness, states adopted measures to try to limit infection. Most such measures were religious, propitiation of the gods through prayer or sacrifice. The first practical measure taken by states was quarantine, imposed ad hoc and unilaterally by cities and states hoping to avoid the spread of infections. The first clear instances of quarantine come in the late fourteenth century in Mediterranean ports fearful of plague. Indeed, according to one interpretation, the rise of early modern states had much to do with efforts at disease control.[11]

When exactly states began to cooperate in disease control is uncertain, but from the late eighteenth century, the Russian and Ottoman empires began to collaborate to restrict movement around the Black Sea in hopes of checking the spread of disease. They did so even though in most other respects they were enemies and rivals, and indeed were often at war.[12] On the whole, however, international cooperation in disease control remained the exception not the rule until the twentieth century. Different nations pursued different policies with respect to smallpox vaccination and quarantines, for example, and the inconsistencies reduced the overall effectiveness of all efforts, especially when and where movement among nations was commonplace. Even the cholera

epidemics of the nineteenth century, which in retrospect cried out for concerted action, did not prompt any significant cooperation. Perhaps the rise of
nationalism retarded any tendency toward medical internationalism.

By the end of the nineteenth century, however, medical congresses and
the like had built up networks of physicians and health professionals which
eventually acted as a lobby for international cooperation. International (at first
only European) sanitary conferences began in 1851 and occurred more often
as the century drew to a close. The intellectual shifts in the direction of the
germ theory of disease, which suggested that more diseases were transmissible than the result of imbalances in bodily humors or the exhalations of local
miasmata and filth, provided further reasons for international collaboration on
health issues. Plague outbreaks in South Asia in the 1890s and in Manchuria
in 1911–1912 helped inspire a measure of cooperation among Japan, China,
and some of the European empires. But it was not until the great typhus outbreaks in East and Central Europe following World War I that international
disease control genuinely took root. The intellectual and political climate had
shifted somewhat in favor of internationalism by 1919, bring forth new institutions such as the League of Nations, which included a health organization. The
US-based Rockefeller Foundation also made international health, and cooperation among nations on health issues, one of its priorities.[13]

The 1920s ushered in a new era of international cooperation in disease
control. The logic and practical rewards of the harmonization of standards and
procedures with respect to controlling lice, for example, became obvious: if
one country invests heavily in lice control but its neighbor does not, then the
investment is undermined by immigrant lice; but if all countries invest in lice
control, their investments are likely to pay off in the elimination of typhus.
Once the medical establishment accepted the notion that most diseases were
transmissible and researchers could identify the means of transmission in
dozens of instances, then the momentum for international cooperation gathered. Of course, lawmakers and bureaucracies had to be convinced, which took
time. But by the end of the 1920s the momentum toward cooperation on health
issues had yielded international agreements aimed at plant and animal diseases, and had even overcome the political objections to admitting Germany,
reviled for its role in provoking World War I, into the comity of nations.[14]

While the Great Depression and World War II chipped away at the achievements of the 1920s in the arena of international disease control, due both to
budget constraints and rampant nationalism, the climate immediately after the
war once again favored greater cooperation. The World Health Organization,
launched in 1948, served as the chief institutional home. It organized campaigns against malaria that were successful in some lands (thanks in part to the

use of DDT, as David Kinkela notes in chapter 6) but not in others. The WHO's greatest triumph to date is the eradication of smallpox, perhaps humankind's greatest nemesis in recent millennia, achieved at last in 1979. This success required decades of patient collaboration involving Cold War rivals. In 1958 the Soviets first suggested the WHO undertake smallpox eradication, and the Americans embraced the cause in 1965, paradoxically cooperating with the USSR in a project marketed to Congress and the public as a means to check the spread of communism. The WHO also played a role in the elimination of rinderpest, the greatest nemesis of cattle in recent history, achieved in 2011. If it did nothing else, the WHO did wonders for human health, wealth, and happiness in vanquishing smallpox and rinderpest.[15]

The very real successes in disease suppression required no moral crusade. Viruses and plasmodia had no supporters, unlike slavery and piracy. But disease suppression did require the erosion of the "legitimacy" of disease in the sense that people and institutions had to abandon fatalistic attitudes about it. They had to start seeking and accepting rational explanations for things instead of magical and mystical ones, a process Max Weber called "disenchantment" of the world and identified as one of the hallmarks of modernity. Disease suppression also resembled the suppression of slavery and of piracy in the sense that states had to assert new powers for themselves and devise new laws, in this case the right to make vaccination regimes mandatory. (Perhaps they did not need to do so, because for many infections vaccinating 70 percent to 80 percent of a population is just as good as vaccinating 100 percent of it, but in point of historical fact, mandatory vaccination was frequently adopted.)[16] Nations had to pass new laws empowering themselves to attack disease, just as in the past they had to change laws to ban slavery or to attack (and condemn) pirates. But perhaps the most effective instrument in the quest to constrain infectious disease was the founding of new institutions devised specifically for the task. First the League of Nations Health Organization and then, much more successfully, the WHO smoothed the exchange of information, the coordination of campaigns, the ratcheting down of geopolitical rivalries in the interest of disease suppression.

Confronting Climate Change

To address modern transnational environmental problems effectively seems likely to require new institutions and legal regimes. Those in existence since 1945, insofar as they were designed with conscious aims, were intended to cope with different sets of issues and show scant signs of evolving in directions that would make them capable of meeting current challenges. The spotty record of international efforts to deal with the environmental issues highlighted in the book makes that clear, as does the dismal record on climate change. At the same time, however, part II of this book shows that the circulation of knowledge and ideas regarding environmental issues is but little impeded by the clumsy architecture of international politics. At the turn of the last century, modern communications (the telegraph) and an old institution (the Jesuit order) sufficed to make great advances in protecting shipping from tropical cyclones, as Gregory Cushman demonstrates in chapter 7. At the same time, farmers and agricultural officials interested in pest control found it rewarding to exchange information (and species) regardless of borders and other constraints, as James McWilliams's chapter (8) makes clear for the American case. While states often do their best to inhibit the free flow of information, ideas, and scientific exchange on select subjects, in practice they regularly fail in this effort; even when they succeed temporarily, their actions leave plenty of room for the transmission of ideas. And transmission of ideas is the first step toward achieving any global regime of suppression.

The first step in achieving the suppression of slavery, piracy, and disease was the circulation of information and ideas that changed people's minds about the legitimacy and morality, the necessity and normality, of these phenomena. In the cases of slavery and piracy, that involved something of a moral crusade; in the case of disease, it required something of a scientific revolution and the "disenchantment" of the world. In the case of current environmental problems, climate change at least, it might require all of the above. States will have to agree, as they did before, to surrender a small sliver of their sovereignty in the interest of the greater good. And they will have to tackle powerful interest groups within their own societies, as many had to do in abolishing slavery. But at least the circulation of ideas and knowledge is not likely to stand in the way.

The second step toward achieving regimes of global suppression was even easier than the first. It was the recognition of the inadequacy of national and bilateral frameworks as the basis for action. This was acutely obvious in the case of piracy, nearly so in the case of slavery, and least so in the case of disease until the scientific sea change of the late nineteenth century brought almost all educated people into agreement about the transmissibility of infectious disease. Once that had occurred, by 1910 or so, the ground was prepared for international cooperation in disease control.

The intellectual armature needed to address most transnational environmental problems is already at hand. One simply has to revise accounting procedures. These procedures, as the academic subdiscipline of ecological economics points out, take no notice of "externalities" such as pollution. If the world adopted an accounting in which the true cost of emitting greenhouse gases somehow had to be paid, then GHG emissions would likely be a tiny fraction of what they now are. Much the same would be true of every form of pollution. There is no obstacle to the spread of this intellectual position. Even orthodox economics recognizes its truth in the abstract. The obstacles are more moral and political than intellectual: they lie in getting people and institutions to recognize in practice what they easily admit in principle. This is the third step in achieving a global suppression regime.

Achieving this agreement was in some respects easier generations ago than it has since become. In the heyday of imperialism, say 1890 to 1960, any global regime required only a few adherents because most of the world had no political freedom. If the political elites in a dozen world capitals could agree on something, it was as if everyone on earth agreed. Most of those capitals were in Europe or North America, so the cultural distance among them was modest, making agreement likelier. This, of course, did not prevent world wars and ideological struggles associated with fascism and communism. But it did permit the emergence and elaboration of the ambitions, programs, and institutions of disease suppression.

This third step, the establishment of new moral norms and appropriate political architecture, is by far the hardest part. It is disconcerting to note that in all three cases discussed here, the building of consensus around a new morality followed in the wake of disturbing events. In the 1780s the Atlantic slave trade reached its apex in quantitative terms. The bloody uprising in Saint-Domingue in the 1790s, the largest slave rebellion in world history, cost many tens of thousands of lives and concentrated minds around the issue of slavery like nothing else. The Roman suppression of piracy in the Mediterranean followed hard on the heels of a golden age for pirates, according to ancient authors, and the same was true of the effort led by Britain in 1715–1730. The rise of national disease-control efforts came in the train of bubonic plague in Mediterranean cities, and collaborative international disease control emerged (weakly) only after the cholera pandemics of the nineteenth century and (more strongly) after the influenza pandemic of 1918–1919 that killed tens of millions around the world. It is reasonable to suppose these events helped to provoke the new morality, norms, politics, laws, and in some cases, institutions, that soon consigned slavery and piracy to marginality, and reduced the sway of infectious disease. Following this logic, some ecological catastrophe may be required to concentrate minds on transnational environmental issues, and recent history suggests even something as dire as the Chernobyl radiation disaster is not enough.

Making the hardest part harder still, at present the policy of continued use of fossil fuels enjoys widespread and potent political support. By 1700, piracy had lost almost all of whatever public constituency it ever enjoyed. Slavery in Europe and America, as of 1800 or 1850, had lost many of its powerful supporters; the economic clout of its remaining proponents was quickly being overshadowed by new money. Infectious disease never had much political backing. The situation with respect to fossil fuels today is fundamentally different. National governments in oil- and coal-producing countries have a calculated interest in prolonging the current energy regime. Private interests in the form of energy companies have a vast stake in continuing the status quo, even if some of them may at the same time be preparing themselves for what will come next. So making the transition away from fossil fuels to prevent unwelcome climate change faces a more concerted and skillful political resistance than did the programs to suppress piracy, slavery, and infectious disease.

More heartening, in all three cases, something that had been entrenched for millennia came to be seen as immoral and worth abolishing. People, cultures, religions, ideologies, and institutions had a long time to accustom themselves to slavery, piracy, and disease. Indeed, all of these are so old that they co-evolved with cultures and adjusted to one another so as to become mutually compatible. Raising moral revolts was no easy business, even if in retrospect it seems only natural that legions would flock to the banners of antislavery or antipiracy campaigns.

Serious transnational environmental problems are comparatively new. Acquiescence to their existence seems deep already, but it cannot be as embedded as acquiescence once was to slavery and disease. So perhaps it will be easier to provoke the moral shifts that make pollution and rapid climate change seem unjustifiable and worth fighting against with all available weaponry.

No one can know what the future will bring in these respects. To my way of thinking, it is unlikely that efforts to check greenhouse gas emissions will meet with much success. Indeed, it is far likelier that our species will double down on its gambles with the biosphere by trying geoengineering, a term that refers to proposals to counteract the effects of higher greenhouse gas concentrations by, for example, splattering the stratosphere with tiny sulfate aerosols that reflect sunlight back into space. Or, to take an example on which experiments have already begun in the world's oceans, to encourage the growth of carbon-absorbing phytoplankton by seeding the sea with iron filings, a process called ocean fertilization or iron fertilization.[17] All geoengineering proposals bring potentially worrisome side effects. None can address the full range of menacing environmental issues. Their mere existence as ideas probably lowers the odds of serious reductions in greenhouse gas emissions through the operation of what is sometimes called "moral hazard," the principle by which people with flood insurance are thereby encouraged to build homes on floodplains. But geoengineering has the great appeal that it does not require significant sacrifice now to avoid greater sacrifice later; it does not require some to bear a cost that will confer benefits upon others; it does not require a successful moral crusade and the implementation of new norms, institutions, and legal regimes. It does require faith that the cure will not be worse than the disease, which perhaps amounts to a "reenchantment" of the world.

NOTES

1. A reflection on this theme appears in Adam Smith, *The Theory of Moral Sentiments* (London: A. Millar, 1759), III.i.46

2. This theme is crisply explained for the Roman Empire in Sander van der Leeuw and Bert De Vries, "Empire: The Romans in the Mediterranean," in *Mappae Mundi: Humans and their Habitats in a Long-term Socio-ecological Perspective*, ed. B. De Vries and J. Goudsblom (Amsterdam: University of Amsterdam Press, 2002), 209–56. See also Mark Elvin, "Three Thousand Years of Unsustainable Development: China's Environment from Archaic Times to the Present," *East Asian History* 6 (1993): 7–46.

3. Christoph Wilhelm Hufeland, *Makrobiotik* (Frankfurt, 1796), 131, cited in Joachim Radkau, *Nature and Power: A Global History of the Environment* (New York: Cambridge University Press, 2008), 144.

4. Readers may object that in the age of AIDS and persistent malaria infectious disease is not, as I claim, at the margins of modern life. However, in comparison to its position and role in human affairs over the past 5,000 years, it most certainly is. Its rollback is the primary reason people today live, on average, more than twice as long as people did 200, or 2000, years ago. I readily admit that this happy arrangement is provisional and could be undone through the emergence of fleets of new pathogens or the widespread breakdown of public health regimes. The same is true with respect to slavery and piracy: they are not fully extinct, nor are they likely ever to be, and in the right circumstances could make comebacks.

5. This concept is offered under the influence of political science. See Ethan A. Nadelmann, "Global Prohibition Regimes: The Evolution of Norms in International Society," *International Organization* 44 (1990): 479–526.

6. I will ignore its terrestrial counterpart, caravan raiding and highway robbery, which has a messier history.

7. Marcus Rediker, *Villains of All Nations: Atlantic Pirates in the Golden Age* (Boston: Beacon Press, 2004); Peter T. Leeson, *The Invisible Hook: The Hidden Economics of Pirates* (Princeton: Princeton University Press, 2009).

8. In addition to Strabo and Plutarch, see Manuel Tröster, "Roman Hegemony and Non-State Violence: A Fresh Look at Pompey's Campaign against the Pirates," *Greece and Rome* 56 (2009): 14–33; Philip de Souza, *Piracy in the Graeco-Roman World* (Cambridge: Cambridge University Press, 2002).

9. Peter T. Leeson, "Rationality, Pirates, and the Law: A Retrospective," *American University Law Review* 59 (2010): 1219–29.

10. Henry Keppel, *Voyage of H.M.S. Dido to Borneo for the Suppression of Piracy with Extracts from the Journal of James Brooke, Esq.* (London: Chapman & Hall, 1847), 303–14.

11. Mark Harrison, *Disease and the Modern World: 1500 to the Present Day* (Cambridge: Polity Press, 2004), 27–50.

12. Andrew Robarts, "A Plague on Both Houses? Population Movements and the Spread of Disease across the Ottoman-Russian Black Sea Frontier, 1768–1830s," PhD diss., Georgetown University, 2011.

13. D. P. Fidler, "The Globalization of Public Health: The First 100 Years of International Health Diplomacy," *Bulletin of the World Health Organization* 79 (2001): 842–9; A. M. Stern and H. Markel, "International Efforts to Control Infectious Diseases, 1851 to Present," *Journal of the American Medical Association* 292 (2004): 1474–9; John Farley, *To Cast Out Disease: A History of the International Health Division of the Rockefeller Foundation, 1913–1951* (New York: Oxford University Press, 2004).

14. Seth Rotramel, "International Health, European Reconciliation, and German Foreign Policy, 1918–1927," PhD diss., Georgetown University, 2011; Norman Howard-Jones, *International Health between the Two World Wars* (Geneva: World Health Organization, 1978).

15. Erez Manela, "Smallpox Eradication and the Rise of Global Governance" in Niall Ferguson, et al., eds., *The Shock of the Global: The 1970s in Perspective* (Cambridge, MA: Harvard University Press, 2010), 251–62; Bob Reinhardt, "The Global Great Society and the US Commitment to Smallpox Eradication," *Endeavour* 34 (2010): 164–72; M. C. Horzinek, "Rinderpest: The Second Viral Disease Eradicated," *Veterinary Microbiology* 149 (2011): 295–7.

16. Whether or not vaccinating 70 percent to 80 percent of a population will suffice to suppress an infection depends on the velocity of infection and the duration of the vaccine's effectiveness. It is often possible to achieve high rates of vaccination through exhortation and incentives.

17. P. W. Boyd et al., "Mesoscale Iron Enrichment Experiments, 1995–2003," *Science* 315 (2007): 612–7.

Index